The
HAMPTONS
Book
A Complete Guide

Hook Windmill

THE
HAMPTONS
BOOK
A Complete Guide

With Special Sections On
The North Fork and Shelter Island

FOURTH EDITION

Suzi Forbes Chase

Berkshire House Publishers
Lee, Massachusetts

The Hamptons Book: A Complete Guide
Copyright © 1994, 1997, 1999, 2001 by Berkshire House Publishers
Cover and interior photographs © 1994, 1997, 1998, 2001 by credited sources

Library of Congress Cataloging-in-Publication Data

Chase, Suzi Forbes.

The Hamptons book: a complete guide: with special sections on the North Fork and Shelter Island / Suzi Forbes Chase. — 4th ed.
     p. cm — (Great destination series)
Includes bibliographical references and indexes.
ISBN 1-58157-021-X
     1. Hamptons (N.Y.)—Guidebooks. 2. North Fork (N.Y. : Peninsula)—Guidebooks. 3. Shelter Island (N.Y. : Town)—Guidebooks. I. Title. II. Series.
F127.S9 C48 2001
917.47'21—dc21   00-05879

ISBN 1-58157-021-X
ISSN 1056-7968 (series)

Editor: Constance Lee Oxley. Managing Editor: Philip Rich. Text design and typography: Dianne Pinkowitz. Cover design and typography: Jane McWhorter. Index: Diane Brenner. Maps: Matt Paul/Yankee Doodles.

Berkshire House books are available at substantial discounts for bulk purchases by corporations and other organizations for promotions and premiums. Special personalized editions can also be produced in large quantities. For more information, contact:

Berkshire House Publishers
480 Pleasant St., Suite 5; Lee, Massachusetts 01238
800-321-8526
E-mail: info@berkshirehouse.com
Web site: www.berkshirehouse.com

Manufactured in the United States of America
First printing 2001
10 9 8 7 6 5 4 3 2 1

No complimentary meals or lodgings were accepted by the author and reviewers in gathering information for this work.

Berkshire House Publishers'
Great Destinations™ travel guidebook series

Right on the money.

— THE NEW YORK TIMES

Smart, literate, well-reported, and incredibly comprehensive.

— MID-ATLANTIC COUNTRY

. . . a crisp and critical approach, for travelers who want to live like locals.

— USA TODAY

Great Destinations™ guidebooks are known for their comprehensive, critical coverage of regions of extraordinary cultural interest and natural beauty. The authors in this series are professional travel writers who have lived for many years in the regions they describe. Each title in this series is continuously updated with each printing, in order to insure accurate and timely information. All of the books contain over 100 photographs and maps.

Neither the publisher, the authors, the reviewers, nor other contributors accept complimentary lodgings, meals, or any other consideration (such as advertising) while gathering information for any book in this series.

Current titles available:
The Adirondack Book
The Berkshire Book
The Charleston, Savannah & Coastal Islands Book
The Chesapeake Bay Book
The Coast of Maine Book
The Finger Lakes Book
The Hamptons Book
The Monterey Bay, Big Sur & Gold Coast Wine Country Book
The Nantucket Book
The Newport & Narragansett Bay Book
The Napa & Sonoma Book
The Santa Fe & Taos Book
The Sarasota, Sanibel Island & Naples Book
The Texas Hill Country Book
Wineries of the Eastern States

If you are traveling to, moving to, residing in, or just interested in any (or all!) of these enchanting regions, a **Great Destinations™** guidebook is a superior companion. Honest and painstakingly critical, full of information only a local can provide, **Great Destinations™** guidebooks give you all the practical knowledge you need to enjoy the best of each region. Why not own them all?

To my mother,
who first encouraged my sense of curiosity,
taught me the joy of discovery,
and who suggested my first trip to one of
"the last great places" — the Hamptons

Contents

CHAPTER EIGHT
Practical Matters
INFORMATION
223

CHAPTER NINE
From Vines to Wines
NORTH FORK
239

CHAPTER TEN
A Charming Green-Clad Island
SHELTER ISLAND
295

Acknowledgments

Writing this book was a privilege and a joy, but I couldn't have done it without some expert help.

In a guidebook, a photograph is worth a hundred words. If the photographs in this book allow people to visualize the Hamptons, it's because of the fine photographers who contributed their images. I especially want to thank Morgan McGivern, Tulla Booth, Laurin Copen, and Jason Green. Their excellent skills have given this book its spirit, style, and tone.

I also wish to thank several people who read portions of my original manuscript in 1994 for historical accuracy. Robert Keene, former town historian for the Town of Southampton, not only had an eagle eye for spelling, but also always had dependable answers when I frequently called him with questions.

Carleton Kelsey, the Director of the Amagansett Free Library, unselfishly shared his vast wealth of historical knowledge with me on numerous occasions. His expertise goes far beyond Amagansett. He has such a firm grasp of local history that each time I spoke with him, I came away richer.

Dorothy Ingersoll Zaykowski, former historian at the John Jermain Library in Sag Harbor, was kind enough to make several suggestions about Sag Harbor that improved my manuscript, but her help didn't end there. She continued to verify my facts and called several weeks after we had completed our discussion, saying, "I've been researching this issue and believe if you stated it this way, it would more clearly reflect what actually happened." Thank you.

Most of all, I wish to express my deep thanks to wonderful, marvelous Dorothy King, Librarian of the Long Island Collection at the East Hampton Library. I feel as though I lived at the library while I was conducting my research. As I got to the writing stage, I called her over and over again with obscure questions. She always knew exactly where to find the answers and often supplied me with additional information that helped fill out the book. Her wealth of knowledge was invaluable. Thank you, thank you, Dorothy.

Thanks also go to Marina Van, Director of the East Hampton Chamber of Commerce, and to Millie Fellingham, Director of the Southampton Chamber of Commerce, for their help. With their fingers on the pulse of the business community, they are always quick to tell me about new businesses or changes in existing ones.

My profound thanks also goes to the staff of Berkshire House Publishers: Jean Rousseau, publisher, who agreed to publish this book in the first place and to underwriting these updates (we all know how rapidly things change in the Hamptons) and for his constant support; Philip Rich, Editorial Director, who handled all of the details from photo selection and map designations to indexing and ushering the book through production — always with supreme diplomacy and humor; Constance Oxley, my fabulous editor, who pored through my manuscript and expertly suggested editorial corrections; Carol Bosco Baumann, who is one of the most enthusiastic and professional promotion and marketing representatives I've encountered in publishing; and special thanks to unsung hero Mary Osak, who patiently answered my questions, relayed my messages, and listened to me.

Finally, thanks go to my husband Dustin, who accompanied me to restaurants, and who spent many nights on his own while I slaved over the manuscript for this book. His encouragement and patience sustained me. It takes courage to agree to the expenditures necessary to put together a book of this nature, and I appreciate his belief in me.

I hope I have done justice to this "last great place." Each of us has our own favorite shop, restaurant, beach, and memory. There was so much more I would have liked to include, but space simply didn't permit it. If your favorite spot isn't here, it was just a judgment call. In the Hamptons, where the scene changes so rapidly, I will certainly do another revision before long.

Introduction

I'll never forget my first visit to the Hamptons. It was in 1972, and I was living in Seattle. I was on my first trip alone to New York City, and as much as I loved the city, I wanted to see the Hamptons. So I called for the train schedule. If I caught an early morning train (around 7am), I could be in East Hampton by 10am. That would give me time to see the village, spend time on the beach, and catch the afternoon train back.

Only it didn't work out that way. I fell in love with this idyllic place. It was one of those clear, blue-sky days, with the temperature hovering in the mid-70s. Luckily, I had packed a few essentials in my beach bag, so my first stop was The Maidstone Arms. What luck! One room had just been vacated. As the clerk took me up the back stairs, he explained that Joanne Woodward and her daughter Nell had checked out early that morning. The room was very modest (The Maidstone has since gone through two renovations), with camp-style, iron beds, and I believe the bath was down the hall. I couldn't have cared less.

I freely admit that I am a beach zealot. If the sun is shining, I can't resist. So, without further ado, I walked to the most spectacular beach that I had ever seen. I had lived in Hawaii, but nothing prepared me for the miles and miles of clean, broad, sparkling white sand, fringed by sea grass-covered dunes that I found in the Hamptons. I was hooked.

From that day on, I have returned to the Hamptons at every possible opportunity. While living in Seattle, it was generally once a year, but when I moved to New York City in 1979, I started spending summers here. At first, I stayed in different inns, motels, or bed-and-breakfasts every weekend (they were pretty funky then). Then I started renting houses or cabins for the summer, although I also frequently came in the spring, fall, and winter.

With the first hint of warm weather in the spring, I'd drive my 1966 MGB from Manhattan to the Hamptons to feast my eyes on all of the budding trees. I came in the fall to take home pumpkins and gourds, and I came in the winter to sit at Main Beach to hear the waves crash and to assure myself that it was all still here. Even after marrying in 1987 and moving to the Berkshires, I dragged my husband to the Hamptons three or four times a year.

I love the Hamptons when there's snow on the ground, and the bluebird sky beams down. I love to see the first buds of spring burst into flower against the tapestry of the evergreen trees. I love to see the osprey return in the spring and to see their babies begin to fly, to observe the cranes and egrets on the marshy bays as they fish for dinner, and to watch the way anything planted in the garden blossoms forth. I love the kaleidoscope of autumn's oranges and reds, and I love the beach — that glorious, ever-changing, constant expanse of white sand. I love early morning walks when the ocean spray lifts to meet the fog. The memories that I cherish most are here. There's a peace and a tranquility, but it's also rejuvenating, relaxing, inspirational, and exhilarating, all at the same time.

Frankly, writing a guidebook about the Hamptons has presented a conflict for me. The public's opinion of the Hamptons is that it's the playground of the rich, so why would the rest of us want to come? Part of me says it's better to allow that belief to remain, because the roads and the beaches are too congested in the summer as it is. On the other hand, if more people learn the secret joys of a walk through Morton National Wildlife Refuge in the spring or a canoe trip on Georgica Pond, then perhaps more visitors will appreciate the precious resource that we have and will help with its preservation.

Using this book as an outline, I encourage you to make your own discoveries, to delve into and savor the Hamptons' rich history, to reflect on the paintings inspired by our scenery, to admire the picturesque windmills and the traditional and futuristic houses — to canoe on the ponds, fish in the ocean, trek across the nature trails, and soak up the sun on the beaches — with a spirit of new discovery. Stop to smell the fresh salt air, to watch the magnificent osprey in their nests, and to feel the sand sift through your toes. Then you'll reach beneath the surface and touch the spirit of the Hamptons.

Suzi Forbes Chase
Long Island

THE WAY THIS BOOK WORKS

The *Hamptons Book* is divided into ten chapters. Entries in each of these chapters, except those in the Lodging, Restaurant, and Shopping chapters and those chapters about the North Fork and Shelter Island, are divided into Southampton Town and East Hampton Town. Under each of the towns, entries are further broken down by individual village in alphabetical order. In the Lodging, Restaurant, and Shopping chapters, the entries are broken down by villlage only.

Most entries include specific information about address, telephone number, hours of operation, and owners or managers to ease your quest for a reservation or information. Although we checked all of the information as close to publication as possible, it's best to verify hours and prices, as changes inevitably occur.

PRICES

You will note that specific prices are not listed, since they are likely to fluctuate. Instead, we have coded them within various ranges. Lodging price codes are based on the average between the highest and lowest rate per room, double occupancy. If a continental or full breakfast is included, it will be noted under "Special Features." In general, these rates exclude local taxes and any service charges that may be added to your bill.

Dining price codes indicate the average cost of an individual meal, including appetizer, entrÈe, and dessert, but excluding cocktails, wine, tax, or tip. Similarly, rather than indicating the exact hours that each restaurant is open, we have specified which meals are served.

Price Codes

	Lodging	**Dining**
Inexpensive	Up to $100	Up to $25
Moderate	$100 to $150	$25 to $35
Expensive	$150 to $200	$35 to $50
Very Expensive	$200 or more	$50 or more

Credit Cards

The credit cards accepted at restaurants and lodging establishments are coded as follows:

AE	American Express	DC	Diner's Club
CB	Carte Blanche	MC	MasterCard
D	Discover	V	Visa

AREA CODES

The area code for the East End of Long Island is 631. All telephone numbers are within that area code, unless otherwise noted.

TOWNS IN THE HAMPTONS

On Eastern Long Island, town government is the predominant local lawmaker and enforcement agency, but within each town, individual, incorporated villages are also self-governing. The incorporated villages generally have legal and enforcement influence within their boundaries, including maintaining their own police force, but smaller hamlets depend on the town for these services. Most villages have a village hall where local business is conducted. Beach permits for village beaches, for example, are issued by the village, while permits for the town beaches are issued at the town office.

There are two towns in the Hamptons. Southampton Town takes in the villages of (traveling from west to east) Eastport, Remsenburg, Speonk, West

Hampton Dunes, Westhampton, Westhampton Beach, Quogue, East Quogue, Hampton Bays, Southampton, Water Mill, Sag Harbor (although a portion of Sag Harbor is also in the Town of East Hampton), Sagaponack, and Bridgehampton. East Hampton Town is composed of Wainscott, East Hampton, Amagansett, Springs, and Montauk.

The
HAMPTONS
Book
A Complete Guide

CHAPTER ONE
The Land & Its Peoples
HISTORY

The history of the Hamptons is laced with adventure, intrigue, and wisdom — a romantic tale of daring and enterprise and of evolution. It's a region shaped by New England principles of hard work and thrift, stirred by strong religious convictions.

The Hamptons possess an unparalleled natural beauty — poets often rhapsodize about it, and artists spend lifetimes trying to capture it on canvas. The majestic Atlantic Ocean lies at its front door, while varied bays lie behind it. In between, the lakes and ponds are separated by hills and marshes — all interspersed with nature preserves, wildlife and bird sanctuaries, and hiking and nature trails.

Morgan McGivern

The Montauk Point Lighthouse is one of New York State's most popular attractions, with over 100,000 visitors a year.

NATURAL HISTORY

Long Island was formed some 15,000 years ago. It was shaped by the slow, relentless movement of ice and debris during the last Ice Age — the forward thrust of massive boulders, soil, and accumulated debris formed valleys and crevices as they were pushed along in front of the ice, and as the ice receded and melted, it left deposits of rocks and dirt in its wake.

The resulting pile left on the South Fork of Suffolk County is known as the Ronkonkoma Moraine. It is submerged beyond Montauk Point, but surfaces again to form Block Island, Martha's Vineyard, and Nantucket. The moraine also disappears beneath the sandy surface of Napeague, indicating that Montauk itself may, at one time, have been an island also. Even today, as the cliffs at Montauk Point continue their evolution through erosion, the residue is deposited at Napeague, creating an ever wider landmass. Probably about 4,000 years ago, after the ice receded and the soil began to nurture plant and animal life, the first humans arrived.

SOCIAL HISTORY

When the first English settlers landed on the shores of Long Island, they were greeted by tribes of peaceful Indians who were adept at farming and fishing. It is believed that these residents were descendants of tribes who had migrated to these shores after years of nomadic wandering, first across the Bering Strait, then east across North America, and eventually south to Long Island. The accounts of the earliest explorers indicate that the hills of Eastern Long Island were well populated. ". . . it was full of hilles, covered with trees, well peopled, for we sawe fires all along the coaste," recorded Giovanni da Verrazano, as he sailed along the south shore of Long Island in 1524.

Unlike the native inhabitants, who were content to live within nature's protective cloak, the colonists viewed the bounty of natural resources as a challenge placed there for them to tame, control, and use. In the years to come, these settlers cut down trees for their homes and mills; created thriving fishing and whaling industries; and harnessed wind and water to grind corn and wheat and to saw wood.

EARLY TRADERS

In 1633, only thirteen years after the landing at Plymouth Bay and only three years after the settlement of Boston, John Winthrop, governor of the Massachusetts Bay Colony, sent a ship to the Connecticut coast on an exploratory expedition. Much to his surprise, the captain returned and reported "having made a further discovery of that called Long Island." This discovery was particularly interesting because he brought back "wampampeag, both white and blue, it being made by the Indians there."

Whereas Indians elsewhere made pottery, blankets, or beaded headdresses, the early residents of Long Island made wampum, which was highly prized. They searched through piles of clam, whelk, and other shells on the beach, selecting those of the right size and color and then bore a hole through the small, highly polished beads for stringing; a pointed wooden stick was used for this painstaking, skilled work. Those who bored the holes rapidly without breaking the shell were considered true artisans. When the English arrived, they introduced these artisans to the mux, or awl, a sharply pointed metal instrument that made the job much easier. Individual beads were strung on sinew and hung around the neck or woven into a belt for transporting.

Wampum was the chief means of trade among the early colonists. They exchanged furs, coats, tools, and other implements with the natives for wampum, which the settlers then used to barter and buy goods among themselves. The value of wampum was as closely regulated by the colonists as United States currency is today.

Christopher R. Vagts described the importance of wampum in *Suffolk, A Pictorial History* (1983):

> *The fur trade went something like this: A European trader brought cheap woven trade cloth (duffel) to coastal Indians on Long Island. The cheap cloth was traded for wampum at a good rate of exchange. The wampum was taken to inland Indians where it was highly valued. Lengths of beads were exchanged for beaver and other furs. The furs were shipped to Europe where they commanded high prices. Thus, at each step of this trade, enormous profits were possible. Long Island — the wampum "mine" — was of critical importance!*

ENGLISH SETTLERS & SETTLEMENTS

One can only imagine the excitement generated in Massachusetts by the news of the wampum trade on Long Island. In order to get there before the Dutch, who had established a settlement at New York in 1625, Governor Winthrop encouraged Massachusetts residents to move to Long Island; several families from Lynn accepted the invitation. When the intrepid band of colonists landed at Conscience Point on Peconic Bay in 1640, they established the first English settlement in New York State, a village named Southampton in honor of the Earl of Southampton. These early colonists had received a land grant from James Farrett, the representative of the Earl of Stirling. Respectful of the Indians' claim to the land, the colonists also purchased the land from them.

The native residents were very helpful to the newcomers, sharing their agricultural and cooking techniques; teaching them to fertilize corn by placing a tiny, oily fish, the menhaden, in each seed hole; showing them how to use the bone and oil of beached whales; pointing out where to harvest an abundance of shellfish and demonstrating how to make *samp*, a porridge that became a staple on colonial tables. In exchange, the English provided the Indians with protection against other marauding tribes, particularly the Pequots and Narragansetts of Connecticut.

Although there appear to have been few conflicts between the new English settlers and the native inhabitants, life apparently did hold a few aggravations. Edward Johnson, an early settler, wrote in 1640, "There are many Indians on the greatest part of this Island who at first settling of the English there did much to annoy their Cattel with the multitude of Doggs they kept, which ordinarily are young wolves brought up tame, continuing of a very ravening nature."

Of much more serious consequences was the scalping of Phebe Halsey, one of the earliest settlers of Southampton. It was proven that those who broke into her home were from one of the Connecticut tribes intent on starting trouble

The East End's first settlers were New Englanders from Lynn, Massachusetts. They founded the village of Southampton in June, 1640.

Suzi Forbes Chase

between the Long Island natives and the English. They were captured quickly and sent back to Connecticut, where they were executed.

The indigenous tribes who resided on the South Fork when the English arrived were the Montaukets, who lived in Montauk and had an influence that extended throughout much of Eastern Long Island, and the Shinnecocks, who lived in Southampton. With no immunity from English diseases, however, the Shinnecock population decreased rapidly until, in 1686, there were only 152 survivors living in Southampton. Today, however, the Shinnecocks count approximately 400 tribal members residing on their reservation in Southampton.

Although early colonial life must have been difficult, settlers on Eastern Long Island were spared many of the tribulations encountered in other areas. The flat, treeless land with its rich soil was easy to till and produced bountiful crops; the sea yielded an abundance of seafood; and the freedom from attack encouraged the growth of stable, prosperous communities within a relatively short time.

The settlers from Lynn were New Englanders through and through. They built their houses and villages to reflect the styles of their northern neighbors, and their religion was strict Calvinist. Rev. Abraham Pierson was ordained minister of the Southampton Colony in 1640.

In his book, *The Early History of Southampton, L.I.* (1887), George Rogers Howell gives the following account of East End life:

An interesting question is that of the food and appliances of the table of the colonists of the Puritan period. They raised on the farm Indian corn, wheat (both winter and summer varieties), oats, barley, beans, and peas, but no potatoes. . . . The waters abounded in fish, clams, and oysters, though the shellfish seem to have been used but sparingly. Cows, oxen, goats, and sheep were raised in considerable numbers, both for home consumption and for export. At a later period, many horses were shipped to the West Indies. Tea and coffee were unknown.

Wine, cider, beer, homebrewed ale, milk, and water were the only drinks used by the settlers upon the table. (Tea arrived in England about 1657.)

Heavy farm work was done by oxen. The only vehicle in use for a long time was the two-wheeled oxcart. Men and women traveled on horseback, and when the horse was wanting, on one occasion at least, a bovine was pressed into service.

In Suffolk County, the Governor authorized in 1692 two fairs to be held, one at Southampton. These fairs were as in old England — an occasion for everybody to offer for sale whatever he wished to dispose of for money or by way of exchange. These fairs were frequented by peddlers on whom the ladies depended for articles of finery and light silk goods.

Although the settlers from Lynn are credited with establishing the first English colony in New York State, an English family was already in residence nearby when they arrived. In 1635, Lieutenant Lion Gardiner and his wife Mary sailed from London to the mouth of the Connecticut River. Mr. Gardiner was a military engineer who had been commissioned by Lords Say and Brook to build a fort in Connecticut where the town of Saybrook is now located. Upon completing his task in 1639, he received an entire 3,500-acre island located between the North and South Forks of eastern Long Island as a land grant. He also prudently purchased it from the native Indians and then changed its name from the Isle of Wight to Gardiner's Island. His daughter, Elizabeth, was the first English child born in New York State.

Lion Gardiner was both a diplomat and a statesman, and his influence extended throughout Eastern Long Island and into Connecticut. He learned the Montauk language and befriended Chief Wyandanch, *sachem* (leader) of the Montauks, who he had met at Saybrook — a friendship that proved to be mutually beneficial. At one point, Gardiner played an instrumental role in securing the release of the Chief's daughter, Heather Flower, after she was kidnapped by the Pequots on her wedding day. In appreciation, Wyandanch gave Gardiner a large tract of land in what is now Smithtown.

Lion Gardiner and his descendants, the "lords of the manor," created a self-sufficient agrarian economy on Gardiner's Island. They grew and raised their own food, as well as that needed for barter, and they exercised total manorial control of their island from 1639 until 1788, when it was annexed to East Hampton. Today, the island still is managed by the Gardiner family — the only known English land grant in America to remain in the possession of the original family.

At the suggestion of Governor Winthrop, Lion Gardiner sponsored a young man in the new colony of East Hampton by the name of Thomas James. Arriving in 1650, Mr. James became the first pastor in East Hampton, where he soon established himself as a highly influential cleric and businessman. It is noteworthy that the first settlers here were staunch Puritans who were so fiercely independent from the British crown that it would be 200 years before any Episcopal church (which was closely affiliated with the Church of

England) was established. On the other hand, even though they strongly advocated total separation of church and state, the clergy were hired by the town fathers, paid out of the town coffers, and furnished with a house and pastureland at town expense.

In matters other than religious, the spread of ideas and commercial activity expanded rapidly throughout the East End. Word quickly reached Connecticut and Massachusetts that Long Island offered a mild growing climate with temperate winters and cool summers, as well as rich soil that yielded abundant crops; that congenial settlers had formed agreeable communities; and, best of all, that the native Indians were accommodating. By 1649, the census lists forty-five heads of households in Southampton. Other settlements were soon established: East Hampton was settled in 1648; Wainscott in 1652; Springs in 1652; Bridgehampton in 1656; the village of Sagaponack in 1656; and Amagansett in 1680.

By 1644, the first crude post windmills were constructed to grind corn and

The Gardiner Windmill was built in 1771 and was in operation until the hurricane of 1938 incapacitated it. It was fully restored in 1999 and now sits on James Lane.

Morgan McGivern

wheat, saw wood, and perform other tasks. These first windmills were built on tall platforms supported by wooden frames. The structures were turned to catch the wind by means of long posts reaching to the ground. There are no remaining windmills of this type today, but the Hamptons can still claim the largest collection of windmills without posts in the United States.

By the late 1600s, technology had advanced beyond the early post windmills, and mills were built with the machinery housed in a stationary octagonal tower capped by a revolving hood that held the sails and turned to allow the sails to catch the wind. Several of these so-called smock windmills, built in the early eighteenth century, remain and are open for public viewing in Hamptons' villages.

The Dominy family of East Hampton built some of the finest windmills. They also were renowned for their finely handcrafted furniture, especially their extraordinary tall-case ("grandfather") clocks. In all, Nathaniel Dominy IV built six wind-powered gristmills and three wind-powered sawmills. The Hook Windmill in East Hampton is the finest example of his workmanship. Among the laborsaving devices in the Hook Windmill are a sack hoist, a grain elevator, a screener to clean the grain, and bolters to sift the flour and cornmeal.

The first gristmill in Water Mill was built in 1644 to provide the town of Southampton with grain. The town supplied the millstone and built the required dam. Edward Howell built the mill, which he powered by a huge waterwheel that depended on the ponds flowing into Mecox Bay. If there was an insufficient flow of water from the ponds to the bay, town law decreed that ". . . when the miller calleth, on three days warneing," the men of the village must gather to enlarge the water's passage into the bay.

This first gristmill in Water Mill's history has retained its usefulness and dignity over the years. As the needs of Southampton changed, however, so did the mill. It has been used as a place to spin yarn, to weave cloth, and to manufacture paper; as a place for ice storage; a post office; an ice-cream factory; and a tearoom. Today, the fully restored and functioning mill is known as the Water Mill Museum, and corn, ground into cornmeal, can be purchased here.

As early as 1656, the English settlers worried about Dutch expansion into their territory. In addition, they had learned of Dutch attempts to turn the neighboring Indians against them. They were, therefore, granted protection by their Connecticut neighbors to the north. Even when the Dutch surrendered New York to the English in 1664, the independent East Enders resisted association with the rest of Long Island. As far as they were concerned, they were New Englanders, and their loyalties remained with Connecticut.

This attitude created considerable anxiety in New York. Lord Cornbury wrote in 1803 that "the people of the East End of Long Island are not very willing to be persuaded to believe that they belong to this province. They are full of New England principles. They choose rather to trade with the people of Boston, Connecticut, and Rhode Island than with the people of New York."

Architecture, as well as politics in the early villages, followed New England examples. Wooden saltbox houses had steeply slanted roofs and were faced with shingles that were allowed to weather naturally. The houses were lined up on both sides of a grassy main road with dirt wagon tracks in the center; cows, pigs, sheep, and geese were allowed to graze on the grass. Eventually, villages required the residents whose homes bordered the road to build fences to contain their livestock. Most villages also set aside a common pasture for both cattle and sheep. The sheep pasture in East Hampton is still a public greensward — located opposite the post office.

By 1661, settlers had adopted the practice of collecting their cattle into one large herd and driving them to the hills of Montauk for summer fattening, along with sheep and horses. It's said that cattle joined these great drives from as far away as Patchogue. A description of the scene along the dusty Montauk route to pasture, traveling on what later became Montauk Highway, is contained in Madeline Lee's book, *Miss Amelia's Amagansett* (1976).

The high point of village life came twice a year when Main Street became the scene of immense cattle drives. Cattle and sheep raising was an important industry on Long Island from the seventeenth century through the nineteenth century, and the principal grazing grounds were . . . Montauk. 1,200 to 1,500 head of cattle were driven "on" to the pastures at Montauk in the spring and "off" again in the fall. From miles around, they would be funneled through the Amagansett Street, which was at that time 150 feet wide (and still is) to accommodate these herds.

These great cattle drives continued until the 1920s. Second House, one of three houses where the cattle and sheep tenders lived during those languid summer months, now houses a fascinating museum; Third House serves as the headquarters of Suffolk County's Theodore Roosevelt County Park.

The sight of ships rounding Montauk Point would not have surprised the Montauk cattle tenders, but one ship that must have aroused suspicion was an unwelcome visitor to Gardiner's Island in 1699. Pirates often plied the waters off the Long Island shore and are known to have landed at Montauk several times. In 1699, Captain William Kidd, a respected New York captain who had been hired by the British to detain French vessels and confiscate their cargo during a French/British war, ran afoul of his sponsors. They declared him to be a pirate.

One of the ships that Kidd waylaid was a French pirate ship loaded with bounty. Kidd was on his way to deliver the spoils to his sponsors but, under the circumstances, rightly feared for his life. He stopped at Gardiner's Island and persuaded John Lyon Gardiner, the third lord of the manor, to give him food and drink. Gardiner complied and also agreed to allow Kidd to bury his treasure on Gardiner's Island. Kidd then sailed on to Boston, where he had been assured of safety. Nevertheless, he was arrested. Gardiner was summoned to Boston to deliver the treasure and did so, but Kidd subsequently was taken to England and executed in spite of the treasure's return. Although the Gardiner family retains an ancient receipt for the bounty, a legend persists that a vast stash remains buried on Gardiner's Island, waiting to be unearthed by some future treasure seeker.

REVOLUTIONARIES

Fierce loyalty to New England principles of independence from the British prevailed on Long Island's East End at the onset of the American Revolution. Citizens were outraged at the heavy taxes imposed by England and by the events in Boston. In 1775, every eligible citizen of East Hampton signed a document that read, in part:

. . . shocked by the bloody scene now going on in Massachusetts Bay, do in the most solemn manner, resolve never to become enslaved and do associate under all the ties of religion, honor, and love to our country, to adopt whatever may be recommended by the Continental Congress.

In 1775, Sag Harbor resident John Hulburt organized a company of minutemen. One of their first acts was to march to Montauk Point, as they had learned about a possible British invasion. On arrival, they discovered three British man-of-war ships and nine transports — all of which were preparing to land. Determined to protect their land and grazing cattle, Hulburt ordered his men to march down a hill in sight of the British ships. At the bottom, where they were hidden from view, they turned their jackets inside out and then paraded back up the hill — thereby fooling the British into thinking that there were twice as many troops. The British decided not to land.

Later Hulburt's men marched to Ticonderoga, taking with them a flag designed with thirteen stars on a blue field and thirteen alternating red and white stripes. It is believed that this flag was the model that Betsy Ross used to create her flag.

When General Washington was defeated in the Battle of Long Island in August 1776, all of Long Island fell under British rule, and those who had signed patriotic documents had reason to fear for their personal safety and possessions. Many families fled to Connecticut and lived there for the seven years of British occupation. Those who remained were required to sign an oath of allegiance to England, which they reluctantly did, knowing that a signature on a piece of paper could not eradicate what they felt in their hearts.

Henry P. Hedges addressed the Sag Harbor Historical Society in 1896 and attempted to describe the troublesome times:

> *The history of that seven years' suffering will never be told. Philosophy has no adequate remedy for silent, unknown, unpitied suffering . . . . Left to the tender mercies of the foe; plundered by countryman and stranger of their property and ripened harvest; robbed of the stores which they reaped and garnered; slandered by suspicious brethren; taunted and scoffed at by the mercenary victors; they never wavered. Their hearts were in their country's cause; and in the memorable language of their great compatriot, "sink or swim, live or die, survive or perish," they were true to their country. Unterrified, unalterable, devoted Americans.*

Although the ramifications of war affected those living on the East End, the only military action that actually took place occurred in Sag Harbor and made Colonel Return Jonathan Meigs a hero.

The British had established a naval blockade and stationed a garrison there to prevent supplies from leaving Sag Harbor to aid American troops across Long Island Sound in Connecticut. On the night of May 23, 1777, Meigs sailed with his men across the sound from Connecticut to the North Fork of Long Island. They carried their boats over a narrow neck of land to Orient Harbor, and then, hugging the coastline between Shelter Island and the North Fork, they eventually crossed Shelter Island Sound, arriving near Noyack about midnight. After hiding their boats, the men marched to Sag Harbor, killed six sailors, captured the British commander along with ninety of his troops, set fire to twelve British brigs and sloops, and appropriated the needed supplies. Returning with their prisoners and the goods, Colonel Meigs miraculously accomplished his mission in twenty-five hours — and with no loss of American lives.

Every year the East Hampton Historical Society holds a Militia Weekend to acquaint adults and children with the customs, crafts, and foods of East Hampton's early settlers.

Morgan McGivern

In 1783, at the end of the British occupation, most home owners returned to their villages. Reconstruction was a slow, difficult process, however. Ground that had not been plowed had grown hard and unyielding. Family homes and possessions had been destroyed. Nevertheless, residents were much more concerned with the future than with the past.

Dr. Samuel Buell became the third pastor of the Presbyterian church in East Hampton in 1746 (his ordination was presided over by the renowned cleric Jonathan Edwards). He took an active but conciliatory role in the British occupation of the East End during the Revolution, and he made a lasting contribution by starting the first secondary school.

Although elementary schools had been organized shortly after East End villages were settled, Clinton Academy in East Hampton, which was established in 1784, was the first secondary school. One interesting facet of this academy is that although colleges, such as Harvard and Yale, were open only to men, Clinton Academy was always coeducational. In addition to the classics, such practical subjects as accounting, navigation, and surveying were taught. For almost 100 years, students from faraway places and nearby homes received their education there. Many graduates went on to Harvard, Yale, and Princeton. Finally, in 1881, its school days came to an end. It subsequently became the site of town meetings, plays, and dances, and eventually, it housed the *East Hampton Star* newspaper and the library. This impressive building still stands on Main Street, where it is now a museum devoted to local history.

WHALING, SHIPPING, MANUFACTURING

Long before the arrival of the English, whaling was an important activity for the Indians. When, during the winter months, the ocean tempests tossed a whale on the shore, they raced to the beach to carve up the giant mammal. The English were quick to learn the many uses for whale carcasses, and they soon joined forces with the Indians on these great whaling expeditions. By agreement, the settlers reserved the fins and tail for the native residents, as these parts were cherished for religious ceremonies. The rest of the whale, however, was tryed-out (boiled) or boned and used for a variety of purposes.

By the 1660s, the colonists, not content to wait for whales to float onto their beaches, established whaling companies with ships that sailed the ocean coast, searching for whales. By 1687, the fleet had grown to seven ships. Following these earliest whaling trips, the whales were brought to East End beaches where their blubber was boiled in giant black kettles called *try pots* to render the oil that was so highly valued for lamp fuel. Later, self-contained *try works* were constructed on the ships themselves. From the beginning, the colonists recognized the expertise of the native Indians and hired them as hands on the whaling vessels.

Designed by Minard Lafever in 1845 for whaler Benjamin Huntting, this noble Greek Revival mansion now serves as the Sag Harbor Whaling and Historical Museum. One enters the museum through the jaws of a right whale.

Morgan McGivern

Sag Harbor, established in 1730, soon became an influential whaling and shipping port. The first wharf was built in 1753, and construction on the grand Long Wharf began in 1771. Although the American Revolution interrupted the growth of Sag Harbor and the whaling industry for some ten years, in 1785, a Sag Harbor whaler returned from a voyage to Brazil with a load of 360 barrels of oil, and in 1789, Sag Harbor became the first port of entry in New York State.

Additions to Long Wharf in 1808 and 1821 increased its length to 1,000 feet, and Sag Harbor was poised on the brink of history. This bawdy, raucous seaport was the antithesis of the more elegant villages to the south. As the ports of call of Sag Harbor sailing ships became more diverse, so did the variety of men who returned to the home port.

James Fenimore Cooper came to Sag Harbor in 1818 and stayed on to purchase and outfit a whaling vessel. Later, he wrote the whaling adventure, *The Sea Lions* (1849), in which he describes Sag Harbor's attitude toward whalers:

> *There was scarcely an individual who followed this particular calling out of the port of Sag Harbor, whose general standing on board ship was not as well known to all the women and girls of the place, as it was to his shipmates . . . . His particular merit, whether with the oar, lance, or harpoon is bruited about, as well as the number of whales he may have succeeded in "making fast to."*

A red-light district sprang up in Sag Harbor, and taverns thrived; an anchored ship served as a jail for drunken sailors. A variety of new occupations kept Sag Harbor men employed in shipbuilding and manufacturing supplies for the whaling ships. By 1839, the whaling fleet had grown to thirty-one ships, making Sag Harbor the third largest whaling port in the world. Eighty businesses flourished there, including coopers, who made the barrels to store the whale oil, masons, boatbuilders, blacksmiths, and tool and rope manufacturers. The fleet had increased to sixty-three vessels by 1845, and the population had grown to approximately 4,000 residents. Sag Harbor became known the world over when a local whaler made the first voyage to the waters surrounding Japan.

In Herman Melville's *Moby-Dick* (1851), Queequeg comes to Sag Harbor to learn Christian ways:

> *But alas! the practices of whalemen soon convinced him that even Christians could be both miserable and wicked; infinitely more so than all his father's heathens. Arrived at last in old Sag Harbor, and seeing what the sailors did there, and then going on to Nantucket, and seeing how they spent their wages in that place also, poor Queequeg gave it up for lost. Thought he, it's a wicked world in all meridians. I'll die a pagan.*

People in nearby villages were fascinated by Sag Harbor and a bit envious as well. Business opportunities flourished in nearby communities. Shelter Island, for example, due to its abundance of white oak, became an impressive shipbuilding center. In some quarters, however, the village generated nothing but dismay. From his pulpit in East Hampton, Reverend Lyman Beecher railed against the Infidels, a Sag Harbor society organized specifically to attack the Christians.

On lower Main Street, which was filled with taverns, shops, and warehouses, the selling of rum was widespread. The downtown atmosphere was that of an energetic, irrepressible seaport. On upper Main Street, however, the fashionable homes of the shipowners stood in stark contrast. Cosmopolitan society held sophisticated balls and social gatherings; worshipers were welcomed at the elegant Whaler's Church, which was completed in 1844 and boasted a spectacular 185-foot steeple; and amusing vaudeville shows entertained citizens in the fine music hall.

In 1845, a devastating fire raged through Sag Harbor's downtown, destroying fifty-seven stores, shops, and warehouses, but merchants quickly rebuilt. The village's most productive year was 1847 when thirty-two vessels hauled in 3,919 barrels of sperm oil, 63,712 barrels of right whale oil, and 605,340 pounds of whalebone.

Then it was over. Petroleum products and gas lighting replaced whale oil. In 1849, only two whaling ships left the harbor. The discovery of gold in California in that same year created a mass exodus. The last-recorded voyage of a Sag Harbor whaler was in 1871. By 1913, this village, which once had been designated New York State's first port of entry, was decommissioned.

BAYMEN, TRAWLERS, BOOTLEGGERS

O ther industries replaced whaling on the East End. Fishing continued to yield a profit. Menhaden, the fish long used by the native Indians for fertilizer, was processed in large plants along Gardiner's Bay. At first, the catches were hauled in from the ocean, but by the 1890s, the shoreline of the bay was thick with ships using purse seines to gather the schools of fish. It was estimated that at one point over 230 sailing ships and twenty steam vessels were engaged in the trade. Eventually the last of these died out in the 1960s.

But the East Enders continued to gather other varieties of fish, as well. A local Water Mill resident recalls his youth with a fishing crew:

> When I was a kid, every so far along there were fishing crews on the ocean, and they had wood shanties on the beach with tar paper roofs . . . . A load of fish was a lot of fun. Men hung onto the net, while others crawled in to get the fish out of the net and throw them on the beach. We would load the fish onto handbarrows and carry them to the road . . . . We'd bring the fish home to pack them in wood boxes and ice them down. The trucks would come right to the house to pick up the fish and cart it to Fulton Street in New York. We always put a fish box out as a sign for the truck driver to stop, while another crew member tied a rag to a telephone pole to signal the driver.

Fishing and shellfishing remain important industries on the East End today, although local baymen are finding it more and more difficult to prosper. Delectable tiny bay scallops, cherrystone and littleneck clams, lobsters, mussels, and oysters are gathered seasonally for markets locally and in New York. Commercial and sportsfishing off Montauk Point yield striped bass, sturgeon, swordfish, white marlin, tuna, bluefish, and shark.

From 1920 to 1933, liquor was prohibited throughout the United States, and enterprising East Enders found a new profit center. Sag Harbor, along with North Haven and Noyack, became part of the infamous "Rum Row" that attracted bootleg boats from Europe. By 1927, however, bootleg distilleries in the United States were producing such high-quality products that illegal imports were no longer necessary, and the boat traffic dried up once more. During its heyday, however, the East End of Long Island was called the *wettest place in the country* — a bootlegger's paradise.

TRAVELERS & VISITORS

Passable roads were slow in reaching the Hamptons. Montauk Highway was paved to Amagansett in 1908, but not beyond to Montauk until 1921. Furthermore, the crude paths laid out in the area's earliest days to reach ports in the Northwest, North Sea, and Fireplace, where passengers and goods were ferried to Gardiner's Island, were the only access to these areas for many years. Eventually, several of them were used by scheduled horseback riders who delivered messages and mail to the isolated villages.

In 1772, a stagecoach route was established from the Fulton Ferry in Brooklyn to Sag Harbor; from Sag Harbor travelers could take a boat to Connecticut or even to Boston. The stagecoach brought passengers who needed places to eat and stay, and soon inns were situated along the route. The trip from Brooklyn to Sag Harbor took three days. Travelers stopped on the first night at Samuel Nichols' inn on the Hempstead Plains. On the second night, they rested at Benjamin Haven's inn in St. George's Manor, and on the final night, they dined, supped, and slept at Duke Fordham's in Sag Harbor. This popular inn also housed James Fenimore Cooper while he wrote his novel *Precaution* (1820), and it inspired this classic poem by an unknown author:

> *Long ago at the end of the route*
> *The stage pulled up, the folks stepped out.*
> *They all passed under the tavern door,*
> *The Youth and his bride and the gray three-score,*
> *Their eyes so weary with dust and gleam,*
> *Three days gone by like an empty dream,*
> *Soft may they slumber and trouble no more*
> *For their dusty journey, its jolt and roar*
> *Has come to an end at Fordham's door.*

Even after the arrival of the stagecoach, distant Montauk had no official mail delivery. This oversight was remedied by the tall, colorful Native American, Stephen (Pharaoh) Talkhouse, who charged $.25 to carry a letter from Montauk to the stage in East Hampton, stepping forth in the giant stride that allowed him to complete the round-trip, thirty-five-mile journey in one day.

With the advent of the railroad, branch lines fanned out across the United States, and eventually, the Long Island Rail Road was established. The main line along the North Fork to Greenport was completed in 1844. Then the South

Fork was added — first to Westhampton Beach, Bridgehampton, and Sag Harbor in 1870 and then to East Hampton, Amagansett, and Montauk in 1895. Before the easternmost extension, travelers would reach East Hampton and Amagansett by taking a stagecoach from the train station in Bridgehampton or Sag Harbor, or from the New York steamer pier in Sag Harbor. With the arrival of the railroad, the Hamptons began to change from a strictly rural and agricultural area to one that attracted leisure travelers.

All these new visitors needed places to stay, and village residents complied by opening their homes. By the 1850s, it was reported that all rooms in East Hampton were fully booked at $7 a night. Southampton soon built hotels to accommodate its many guests, notably the Canoe Place Inn and the grand Irving House, with its Terry Tavern annex. Due to the more remote location of East Hampton, however, boardinghouses remained the predominant accommodation there. It was reported that in 1895, when the railroad was completed to East Hampton, more than 800 summer visitors arrived to enjoy the balmy sea breezes and the beaches.

Carriages and buckboards parade at Mulford Farm in East Hampton.

Morgan McGivern

Julia Gardiner Tyler added a touch of glamour to the Hamptons in the mid-1800s. In 1844, at the age of 24, this beautiful, impetuous Gardiner married the tenth president of the United States, 54-year-old John Tyler. She brought the same style and elegance to East Hampton, where they summered, as she did to the White House. The vivacious heiress, who shared Tyler's life for eighteen years and bore him seven children, never forgot her heritage and ancestry, reveling in her jewels, fine clothes, and exquisite manners. The house they occupied on Main Street is still standing, although it is privately owned.

As the summer season attracted more and more industrialists, doctors, lawyers, and wealthy tycoons, the building boom that they created continued. Soon elegant mansions lined the beachfront from Westhampton Beach to Montauk.

THE HAMPTONS ATTRACTS ARTISTS

Lured by the rural quality of East Hampton, artists from New York began arriving in the 1870s. They were delighted with the bucolic charm, the seascape vistas, and the opportunity to congregate, to paint, and to live more economically than they could in New York City. Most of these artists were members of the Tile Club, an artist's organization founded to "preserve good fellowship and good talk." They gathered in Greenwich Village on long winter evenings to paint on eight-inch square Spanish tiles. Among the members of this group were Augustus Saint-Gaudens, Stanford White, Winslow Homer, William Merritt Chase, Thomas Moran, and Childe Hassam.

The Tilers at first stayed in East Hampton at the old house called Rowdy Hall, which was across the street from Clinton Academy, where they took their classes. Rowdy Hall was later moved to Egypt Lane, where it remains today. At one point, it was the childhood summer home of Jacqueline Bouvier Kennedy, who was born at Southampton Hospital.

William Oliver Stevens described the artists' visits in his book *Discovering Long Island* (1939):

> *The Tile Club made East Hampton their headquarters lured by the Lombardy poplars lined up like a regiment on each side of the street . . . .*
>
> *Naturally they sketched here with great zeal, not only along the street but also on the beach. The musicians (honorary members) loafed about and posed for their friends as quaint natives and old salts, whenever such figures were needed . . . .*
>
> *It was probably through these members of the Tile Club and their articles in* Scribner's Monthly *that word spread abroad regarding the artistic attractions of East Hampton, for within five years of their first visit, the village was being written up as the "American Barbizon." Thomas Moran (known for his paintings of the national parks) made his home here, and summer art classes flourished, especially large groups from the Art Student's League of New York. This all ended, however, when a Tile Club member, William Merritt Chase began his art school in Southampton in 1891, and suddenly everyone flocked there . . . .*

Nevertheless, another wave of artists arrived in East Hampton to capture this spectacular landscape in 1945. When the abstract expressionist Jackson Pollock and his wife, Lee Krasner, established their home and studio on a site overlooking Accabonac Harbor in Springs in 1945, other contemporary artists soon followed. Robert Motherwell, Willem de Kooning, Fairfield Porter, Alfonso Ossorio, and others enlivened the artistic scene. In the 1950s, New

York's Museum of Modern Art held summer classes at Ashawagh Hall in Springs and that firmly established the area's arts-oriented reputation. The Pollock-Krasner home is now an artistic study center and is open to the public.

FARMING TAKES ON NEW IDENTITIES

In the 1920s, small farms that grew a variety of crops gave way to large farms concentrating on single crops. The Hamptons' temperate climate, offering a growing season that begins in early April and lasts until mid-November, makes the area ideal for potato farming, and potatoes are now the predominant local crop. Each June, fields of white potato blossoms stretch down the neat rows, announcing the anticipated arrival of a new crop in the fall.

Another crop still closely associated with Long Island gained nationwide popularity in the 1930s. White Pekin (Peking) ducks, which have more succulent meat than domestic ducks, were imported from China to Long Island in the 1870s. Gradually, the famed Long Island Duckling became a necessary item on fancy menus across the United States. In 1939, there were ninety duck farms in Quogue alone, and in 1969, Suffolk County was raising fully sixty percent of the nation's ducks.

The ducks gained fame off the table as well, however. In *Discovering Long Island* (1939), Stevens says, "Its plumage is such a pure white that at a distance one of these duck farms looks like a field where patches of March snow have not yet melted. But he is something of a whited sepulcher, for all his angelic plumage. Each little White Pekin is a most active fertilizer factory, and when the wind is right, not all the perfumes of Araby could sweeten this little land of duck farms." Since that time, due to increasing land values, environmental concerns, and objections to the smell, the number of duck farms have been on the decline. Today about fifteen percent of the nation's ducks are raised on Long Island. Yet, across the country, restaurant menus proudly continue to offer "Long Island duckling," a name that's become synonymous with tender, flavorful duckling.

Although potatoes remain the principal crop of the Hamptons, the burgeoning winery business is once again changing the face of farming. In 1979, following extensive research by Alex and Louisa Hargrave, the first vineyards were planted on the North Fork. Their research paid off, and as the wines gained popularity, other growers were attracted to the area. Today, more and more land on the North Fork, in particular, is being cultivated into vineyards, and there are currently twenty-seven wineries on Long Island's East End.

MONTAUK'S SPECIAL PLACE IN HISTORY

Unlike the other Hampton villages, Montauk has both an older and yet a younger history. It boasts the oldest cattle ranch in the United States.

A Bonaker

The history of the tiny village of Springs is one of the most interesting in the Hamptons, although, to the uninitiated, the hamlet may appear to be no more than a cluster of nondescript buildings randomly placed at the junction of Springs Fireplace Road and Old Stone Highway. It's the heart of Bonakerland, an area that claims, among other things, a language all its own.

The Nature Conservancy, in the *South Fork Shelter Island Preserve Guide* (1990), defines a Bonaker as ". . . someone who descended from either the Bennett, King, Lester, or 'Green River' Miller families who lived in the area around the Springs and Three Mile Harbor. The Indian name Accabonac, however, means 'place where groundnuts are gathered.' This refers to a tuberous plant that once grew around the harbor, supplementing shellfish as the Indian's main source of protein."

Jason Epstein and Elizabeth Barlow in their excellent book, *East Hampton, A History & Guide* (1985), say, "'Bonaker,' the term often used to describe any East Hampton settler, originally meant a person who lived on Accabonac Harbor, particularly the baymen who made their living from the fish and shellfish in the harbor. When it first gained currency, 'Bonaker' was a derisive epithet akin to 'hick,' 'hayseed,' or more appropriately, 'lazy clamdigger.' Subsequently, it has become a chauvinistic badge."

It is unclear exactly how the longtime residents of Springs obtained their distinctive language, but recent scholarly studies indicate that it may be due to their relative isolation. This rural area of farmers, baymen, and fishermen seems to retain vowel pronunciations that hark back to the time of Shakespeare. Perhaps such pronunciations as "git" for "get," "yit" for "yet," "turrble" for "terrible," and "awchit" for "orchard" are simply the result of having so little contact with the rest of the population, they seldom heard the subtle changes. Local historian Stephen Taylor wrote in the chapter "Playing Hide and Seek with History," which was included in the pamphlet, *Springs — A Celebration:* "For three centuries, the residents of the Springs . . . continue to speak the dialect that their forebears brought from post-Elizabethan England . . . . Above all else, history is change: freeze the world in place and there's no history. The Springs appears to want no part of it. It's as if the Springs engages history in a subtle game of hide-and-seek."

Change has occurred in Springs, however. Beginning in the 1950s, Springs was discovered by developers, and forested acres gave way to housing. Taylor concluded his paper by writing, "Where tradition was once the real architect of most of the structures in the Springs, the designers of these newer ones are 'creative' and 'imaginative.' Clusters of older Springs houses become de facto historic districts, enclaves of times past . . . . . (but) what might seem like a desecration of history isn't anything of the sort; it *is* history — history catching up with the Springs at last."

The first of these new residents were artists (illustrators, writers, designers) who were looking for a peaceful, quiet hideaway. They were soon joined by painters, sculptors, and artists of considerable acclaim. Springs is now recognized as a secluded community of artists who live side by side with the descendants of the original Bonakers.

Today the term Bonaker is often used with pride, in recognition of a people who cling fast to old traditions. In fact, the East Hampton High School sports teams proudly call themselves the Bonakers, symbolizing a team that never gives up.

Deep Hollow Ranch was built in 1658 and claims to be the birthplace of the American cowboy. A descendant of those early summer grazing pastures, it includes Third House, where the early cattle tenders lived.

In an article in *Scribner's Monthly* in 1879 titled "The Tile Club at Play," Montauk was described as follows:

> . . . *our tourists came out upon a scene of freshness and uncontaminated splendor, such as they had no idea existed a hundred miles from New York. The woods rolled gloriously over the hills, wild as those around the Scotch lakes; noble amphitheaters of tree-tufted mountains, raked by roaring winds, caught the changing light from a cloud-swept heaven; all was pure nature fresh from creation.*

Walt Whitman, who was raised on Long Island, cherished Montauk's isolation. In celebration of its wild abandon, he wrote his acclaimed poem "Montauk Point" (1849).

Until 1879, Montauk languished peacefully with fishing and cattle ranching being virtually its only occupations. In that year, however, land developer Arthur Benson purchased much of Montauk for $151,000. Shortly thereafter he formed the Montauk Association and engaged the renowned architectural firm of McKim, Mead, and White and the landscape architect Frederick Law Olmsted. Benson invited several of his friends to join him in building houses on a bluff overlooking the ocean. McKim, Mead, and White built seven spectacular shingle-style houses with wraparound porches, gabled roofs, cupolas, and bay windows. Olmsted created roadways and gardens that enveloped the houses, as well as a clubhouse, laundry, and stables. The houses remain today and comprise a very private, exclusive compound.

In 1895, Austin Corbin, president of the Long Island Rail Road, extended the South Fork of his line to Montauk and laid plans to develop Fort Pond Bay as a transatlantic port of entry to New York City. It was a good idea — one that would have shortened the journey from Europe by at least a day and would have avoided the congestion of New York harbor. Due to his untimely death in a carriage accident in 1896, however, his dream was never realized.

In 1898, Teddy Roosevelt and 30,000 of his Rough Riders, fresh from the Spanish-American War, spent several months recuperating at Third House. A general breakdown of medical and sanitary conditions had left some of the men with yellow fever, malaria, or typhoid. Numerous casualties were taken ashore on litters and were detained at Montauk until the danger of contagion was past.

Another dreamer, in 1926, ventured to Montauk with a plan. Carl G. Fisher had developed Miami Beach and the Indianapolis Speedway. He reasoned that just as visitors flocked to Miami in the winter, they would flock to Montauk in the summer. He and his investors bought 10,000 acres, which included nine miles of waterfront. High on Fort Hill, he built Montauk Manor, a luxury hotel, and on Montauk's town square, he built a seven-story office building. A golf

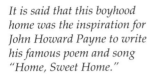

It is said that this boyhood home was the inspiration for John Howard Payne to write his famous poem and song "Home, Sweet Home."

Morgan McGivern

course, polo grounds, yacht club, and a pier followed. He filled his office building with salesmen, poised to find buyers to fulfill his grand scheme, but it was not to be. The stock market crash of 1929, a decline in the Florida real estate market, a hurricane in Florida, and the Great Depression conspired to bring an end to the "Miami of the North."

RECENT HISTORY

The Great Hurricane of 1938 devastated the East End. The glorious steeple on the Whaler's Church in Sag Harbor came crashing to the ground, as did that of the Methodist Church. Trees were uprooted; roofs and porches blew away. The turbulent sea cut a new inlet into the barrier reef, separating the ocean from Moriches Bay at Westhampton Beach. Another more recent storm in 1992 destroyed parts of Dune Road and washed away many houses, creating a new island. Yet, despite such devastation, the natural beauty of the Hamptons prevails.

And so history moves on — never ending, always evolving. After all, tomorrow's history is today's news event. The history of the Hamptons is as entwined with the baymen's efforts to eke out a living, The Nature Conservancy's land preservation efforts, and the Peconic Land Trust's attempts to preserve farmland, as it is with the glittering social scene and the sprawling estates. The latter lasts for two months each summer, but the former is the true heart of the Hamptons.

CHAPTER TWO
The Journey & The Visit
TRANSPORTATION

Before the first settlers arrived, the Indians of eastern Long Island frequently crossed the great body of water now known as Long Island Sound. The sixteen miles of water between Long Island and the Connecticut/Rhode Island shore offered a more hospitable and a considerably shorter route than by traveling overland. In canoes they carved from trees that covered the hillsides, they traveled back and forth to hunt, fish, trade, and barter with other tribes.

Morgan McGivern

When it snows, creative modes of transportation must be used.

It was natural, then, for the settlers to follow the Native Americans' example. They first arrived on Long Island via Connecticut, and transportation and communication were, at first, developed solely with Connecticut rather than with the western part of Long Island, which was settled by the Dutch rather than the English.

This strong link to New England created East End towns that looked and felt like New England towns. The English created common greens for grazing community cattle, built New England saltbox cottages, and constructed a planned, strictly regulated community where only those settlers who possessed skills needed by the town were invited to live.

Eastern Long Island became more and more English because overland communication was infrequent and slow. Western Long Island, on the other hand, developed strong loyalties and ties to the Dutch, who occupied New York City. As might be imagined, loyalty to New England caused East Enders considerable discomfort during the American Revolution.

Pony express mail routes were established in the early 1700s, but more sophisticated communication links waited until the first stagecoach route was initiated in 1772. This route from New York to the South Fork would serve as the only overland transportation link for almost 100 years. In 1844, the Long Island Rail Road built a rail line from New York to Greenport on the North Fork. Finally, in 1870, the line was extended along the South Fork to Bridgehampton and Sag Harbor. It wasn't until 1895 that it reached East Hampton and Montauk.

The access provided by the railroad forever changed the face of Eastern Long Island. At first, rail service provided a valuable transportation link for farmers, who could ship their produce by train to lucrative markets in New York, but as more and more people traveled to the East End, the permanent and summer populations mushroomed. Slowly, an economy that once had depended on the sea and the land evolved into one that supported a tourist and weekend population. Old main streets of dirt, sand, crushed shells, and rock were joined in a paved road of stone and tar called Montauk Highway, which reached Amagansett in 1908; it was extended to Montauk in 1921.

In 1912, horse and buggies, automobiles, and bicycles were all typical forms of transportation in East Hampton.

C. Frank Dayton Collection, East Hampton Library Historical Collection

Transportation continues to play an important role in the life of the Hamptons. As road space becomes more and more scarce, alternatives to traveling by car are devised. Several excellent bus companies now relieve the congestion on the highways and augment the mass transportation services provided by the Long Island Rail Road. In addition, a number of airports offer charter services and landing space for small aircraft.

Today, there are several options for getting to and from the Hamptons and also for traveling around while here. Just remember, any travel difficulties will fade into dim memories once you arrive.

GETTING TO THE HAMPTONS

BY CAR

L et's go to the Hamptons! Get the kids, pack the car, and, inevitably, the question is, "What route do we take?" No matter how the conversation starts, if the destination is the Hamptons (a distance of about 100 miles from Manhattan), the quest for the illusive back roads that avoid the congested, bumper-to-bumper traffic on Montauk Highway becomes the hot topic.

A book titled *Jody's Shortcuts* lists a few secret back roads, and a librarian in East Hampton claims that the easiest way to reach the Hamptons is to "just turn right." There are old favorites that, if you are a true believer in back roads, will get you around all of the Montauk crawl. Those in the know, however, say you won't save time, just aggravation; and, generally, these roads are considerably out of the way, unless your destination happens to be the villages along the north shore of the South Fork — Noyack, Sag Harbor, or Springs, for instance.

Turtles are cautioned to stay within the 35 mph speed limit in East Hampton.

Suzi Forbes Chase

Personally, I think it's a shame to bypass the villages because they're all so charming. I want to see what new shops have opened and what they have to offer; how the restaurants are doing; and what has happened since last week. One way to avoid the traffic is to leave for the Hamptons by 12 noon on Friday and return at dawn on Monday, although at times I have started for the Hamptons at dawn on Saturday and returned at 4pm on Sunday, with no significant traffic problems.

With agreeable road conditions, the trip from New York City to Southampton should be an easy two-hour drive. As Timothy McDarrah said, however, in

Dan's Papers, "One thing about roads: If you build them, cars will come. One thing about roads to the Hamptons: There are no shortcuts."

From New York City, most people head straight out on the Long Island Expressway (Interstate 495). I must admit my preference, however, is the Northern State Parkway because generally it has fewer cars, and trucks are prohibited on all New York State parkways. Nevertheless, when the Northern State Parkway ends at the Sagtikos Parkway, the Long Island Expressway cannot be avoided. Most drivers leave the Expressway at Exit 70 in Manorville to take Route 111 on its straight diagonal course to Route 27, the Sunrise Highway. If your destination is Westhampton Beach, Hampton Bays, or another town west of these villages, you probably won't find many traffic problems at all.

If, however, you run into congestion as Route 27 narrows to two lanes on the outskirts of Southampton, you might find it easier to turn south onto Tuckahoe Road, which runs alongside the Southampton Campus of Long Island University, and head for Route 27A, Montauk Highway. Turn left there and continue through the village of Southampton on that route, which is called Hill Street within the village.

One difficulty with traveling by car from Southampton to Montauk is that all of the roads are two lane; a tractor or a truck can slow traffic to a crawl for miles. Many residents prefer it that way, hoping to discourage further development. After all, the farmers were here first. Others join in a frustrated howl.

An alternative, of course, is to let someone else do the driving. We'll get to the train, bus, plane, and boat options in the following pages, but it's not that unusual to see limousines and chauffeured town cars stuck in the same traffic jams as everyone else, while their passengers work diligently on a laptop computer or relax with a good book. If this is a driving option that appeals to you, here are several suggestions. Otherwise, pack a selection of cassette tapes or CDs and endure the inevitable snags.

Archer Town Car	800-273-1505
(town cars only)	
Classic Limousines	631-567-5100
(outside NY state 800-666-4949;	
www.classictrans.com)	
Colonial Limousine	631-728-0063
East Hampton Limousine	631-324-5466
Hampton Hills Limousine Ltd.	631-653-7820;
	800-795-6801
Hampton Jitney (limousines)	631-287-4000
Southampton Limousine, Ltd.	631-287-0001

For information about rental cars and taxis, see the section Getting Around Once You're Here (page 33).

BY BUS

Not long ago the only method of travel to the Hamptons was by car, train, or private plane, but Hampton Jitney changed that.

HAMPTON JITNEY
631-283-4600 (Long Island); 800-936-0440 (New York metro area only); 800-254-8639 (outside New York metro and Long Island).
Mailing Address: The Omni, County Rd. 39A, Southampton, NY 11968.
Price: Southampton–Montauk $24 one-way, $43 round-trip; seniors and children $20 one-way, $39 round-trip; lower midweek rates to Westhampton Beach; pets $10 (in carriers only); bicycles $10.
Credit Cards: AE, MC, V.
Schedules: (summer hours) 7am–11:30pm from New York City; 4:30am–10:30pm from the Hamptons (varies by day of week).
Reservations: Strongly recommended.

Hampton Jitney began service in 1974, and now has a large fleet of buses that ply the highways between New York City and the Hamptons many times a day. In addition to regular departure points, they have four pickup spots along Lexington Ave. in Manhattan, from 86th St. to 40th St. Also, they will drop off passengers at points on the Upper East Side on Third Ave., as well as on the Upper West Side on selected trips. In general, the trip takes 2 hours from Manhattan to Southampton. There's an airport connection also, with pickup and drop-off service to several metropolitan airports. Package service and limousines can also be arranged. Hampton Jitney buses are modern, comfortable touring buses, with air-conditioning, wide seats, plenty of legroom, large windows, and rest rooms. An attendant on each bus serves coffee, juice, or water with a muffin, peanuts, or chips, depending on the time of day; newspapers are provided as well. Since the schedule does change according to requirements, it is prudent to call ahead. Reservations are often filled far in advance, especially on holiday weekends, so make yours early.

Hampton Jitney offers an alternative to automobile travel to the Hamptons.

Courtesy Hampton Jitney

Suffolk Transit (631-852-5200; www.sct-bus.org) is discussed in more detail under the section about travel within the Hamptons (see page 34). When traveling to the South or North Forks from points within Suffolk County, however, this local bus company is certainly an option. It serves the county from Massapequa to Montauk or Orient Point, with regular service daily, except Sun.

BY TRAIN

LONG ISLAND RAIL ROAD
718-217-5477 (New York);
 516-822-5477 (Nassau County);
 631-231-5477 (Suffolk County);
 718-558-8070 (parlor car reservations).
Price: Peak hours $15.25 one-way, $30.50
 round-trip; off-peak hours $10.25 one-
 way, $20.50 round-trip; $17.50
additional for parlor car service; no
charge for pets but must be in an
approved AKC carrier; $5 permit
required for bicycles, but permit takes
about 2 weeks to obtain.
Schedule: 7:49am–10:36pm leaving New
 York City; 5:35am–12:52am leaving
 Montauk.

The Long Island Railroad has an excellent reputation for dependability, and for many, it's the only way to travel to the Hamptons. Now that Pennsylvania Station in Manhattan has been renovated, Manhattan departures and arrivals are much more pleasant than in the past. Clean, modern cars equipped with rest rooms, are now augmented by "The Sunrise Fleet" of special parlor cars, available on selected weekend trips to the Hamptons. These are carpeted cars with comfortable seats; an attendant serves light snacks and beverages, ranging from beer, wine, and mixed drinks to soda and bottled water; a special parlor car reservation is required. The trip takes about 2 hours from New York City to Westhampton Beach and 3.75 hours to Montauk, with about eight trains a day on summer weekends. For those traveling to the North Fork, three or four trains leave and arrive daily at Riverhead during the week, but only two trains on the weekends. No reservations are taken on the Long Island Rail Road (except for the parlor cars). For fare and schedule information, consult local newspapers or call ahead.

The Long Island Railroad has put new, sleek double-decker trains on the Hamptons and North Fork routes.

Suzi Forbes Chase

Amtrak (800-523-8720) travels from Pennsylvania Station (NYC) to New London, CT, where **Cross Sound Ferries** (860-443-5281) provide transportation to Orient Point on the North Fork. (See ferry information below.) Pets are not allowed on Amtrak. Bicycles are permitted, as long as the train has a baggage car or a bicycle rack. If the bicycle is to be transported in the baggage car, it must be in a box, which can be purchased at Pennsylvania Station for $5. The train station in New London is an easy walk from the ferry terminal.

BY FERRY

Ferry service to Long Island is a pleasant option, especially if traveling from New England.

BRIDGEPORT & PORT JEFFERSON STEAMBOAT COMPANY
631-473-0286.
Price: $36 car and driver; $10 each additional passenger; pets must be on leash; bicycles $1.

Credit Cards: D, MC, V.
Schedule: 6:30am–9:30pm in summer from Bridgeport; 6am–9pm in summer from Port Jefferson; shorter hours rest of year.
Reservations: Required for cars.

This ferry operates about 10 trips daily in summer for passengers and cars between Bridgeport, CT, and Port Jefferson on Long Island's North Fork, with fewer trips the rest of the year. The drive from Port Jefferson to Southampton takes about 1 hour. These are large ferries, with snack bar service, a lounge where drinks are served, rest rooms, and plenty of deck space to relax in the sun during the 90-minute trip. Pets are allowed on deck, and bicycles are welcomed. A reservation is necessary for cars, especially during the summer months; cars are taken on a standby basis, if you forget to call. It's advisable to go upstairs shortly after you get on the ferry to purchase the ticket from the purser, as standing in line can take awhile. Tickets are collected when you reach the other side.

CROSS SOUND FERRY
860-443-5281.
Price: Car ferries: $34 one-way car and driver; $10 additional adult; $4.75 children 2–11; no charge children under 2; no charge for pets but must be leashed; bicycles $2. Sea Jet:

adults, $15.50; children 2–11, $7.50; children under 2, free.
Credit Cards: D, MC, V.
Schedule: 7am–9pm from New London; 7am–9pm from Orient.
Reservations: Required for cars.

Cross Sound Ferry travels between New London, CT, and Orient Point on the North Fork. It is the most direct route from Boston, Cape Cod, Rhode Island, and points east. There are about 15 trips daily in the summer, but the ferry does run year-round. These are large ferries. The biggest are able to accommodate up to 16 motor coaches. Car reservations are absolutely necessary to avoid a pro-

MILEAGE AND TRAVELING TIMES

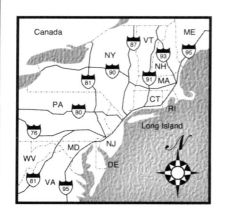

Location From Manhattan:	Mileage	Traveling Time
Westhampton Beach	83 mi	1 1/2 hrs
Southampton	96 mi	2 hrs
East Hampton	106 mi	2 1/2 hrs
Sag Harbor	105 mi	2 1/2 hrs
Montauk	123 mi	3 hrs
Greenport	102 mi	2 1/2 hrs

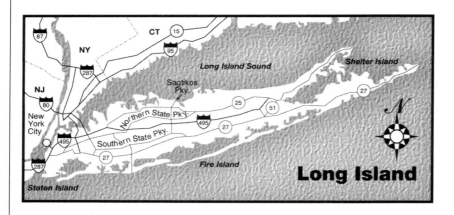

Location	Mileage	Traveling Time
Boston to Greenport (via Cross Sound Ferry from New London, CT to Orient Point)	141 mi to New London Ferry Crossing	3 hrs 1 hr 20 mins
Orient Point to Greenport (North Ferry)	10 mi	15 mins
North Ferry, Shelter Is., and South Ferry		1 hr

longed wait for space. The trip takes about 90 minutes, and there are outdoor and indoor spaces for relaxation, as well as rest rooms and snack bars. On the largest boats, there are full-service lounges with drinks, televisions, and a jukebox, as well as a video game room. Pets are allowed on deck. If you decide not to take the car, a high-speed boat (Sea Jet) has been added to the fleet; this makes 6 trips daily each way, and the crossing is only 40 minutes.

NORTH FERRY
631-749-0139.
Price: $7 one-way car and driver, $8 same day round-trip; $1 each additional passenger; $3 one-way, $4 round-trip bicycles.
Schedule: 5:40am–11:45pm from Shelter Island; 6am–12 midnight from Greenport. Extra summer trips.
Credit Cards: None.
Reservations: None.

SOUTH FERRY
631-749-1200.
Price: $7 one-way car and driver, $8 same day round-trip; $1 each passenger; $2 one-way, $3 round-trip bicycles.
Schedule: 6:05am–1:50am from North Haven; 6am–1:45am from Shelter Island.
Credit Cards: None.
Reservations: None.

The North Ferry from Greenport to Shelter Island crosses in about 10 minutes.

Suzi Forbes Chase

Those traveling from New England to the Hamptons generally drive from Orient Point to Greenport and then travel across Shelter Island, taking the North Ferry from Greenport and South Ferry from Shelter Island to North Haven, just north of Sag Harbor. These ferries that putt back and forth are efficient throwbacks to an earlier age. There are no amenities here, just a drive- or walk-on, open-decked ferry that shuttles back and forth between the island and the North and South Forks. Both ferries operate year-round, but the schedule is more frequent in the summer than the rest of the year.

BY AIR

The nearest airport providing scheduled service by major airlines is **Long Island/Islip MacArthur Airport** in Ronkonkoma. For recorded information about all airlines, call 631-467-3210. The following airlines, with their direct reservation numbers, serve MacArthur Airport.

American Eagle	800-433-7300
Atlantic Southeast Airlines	
(The Delta Connection)	800-282-3424
Comair (The Delta Connection)	800-354-9822
Continental Express	800-523-3273
Delta Express	800-325-5205
Northwest Air-link	800-225-2525
Southwest Airlines	800-435-9792
Spirit Airlines	800-772-7111
U.S. Airways Express	800-428-4322

Several other airlines offer charter services to Montauk Airport, East Hampton Airport, and Suffolk County Airport (Francis S. Gabreski Airport) in Westhampton Beach. For information about prices and availability, contact: *Action Airlines Charter* (800-243-8623); *Air East Airways* (800-597-0866); *Aviation Resources* (631-537-3737); *Eastway Aviation* (516-737-9911); *Executive Airlines* (631-537-1010); *Executive Fliteways Inc.* (516-588-5454); *New England Airlines* (800-243-2460); *Shoreline Aviation* (800-468-8639); and *Summit Aviation* (516-756-2545; 800-255-4625); or contact *Sound Aircraft* (800-443-0031 outside 631 or 516 area codes only; 631-537-2202 locally for information about the airlines that they represent). They offer charter flights between East Hampton, New York's La Guardia Airport, and New York's 23rd St. Seaport, as well as charter service throughout the east. They have some planes that can land either on land or water. Should you and your friends want to fly directly to your hunting preserve on an isolated island with no airport, these folks can help.

If you own your own plane and wish to wing it, the following airports offer landing and tie-down services, and all can accommodate small jets. Then, just like local luminaries, you can be a true jet-setter.

East Hampton Airport	631-537-1130
Montauk Airport	631-668-3738
Suffolk County Airport-Francis S. Gabreski	
(in Westhampton Beach)	631-852-8095

GETTING TO AND FROM AIRPORTS

Classic Airport Share-Ride (631-567-5100; 800-666-4949 outside New York State only; www.classictrans.com) Provides door-to-door transportation from Long Island airports to anywhere on Long Island. Their courtesy 24-hour telephones are located at LaGuardia, Kennedy, and Islip airports, and one of their vans will be there to pick you up within 15 minutes. They're friendly, courteous, and helpful.

Hampton Coach (631-728-0050; 631-728-0500) Operates Lincoln town cars for 1–6 passengers and passenger vans that accommodate 10–14, from all major New York City airports, including Islip and Newark.

Winston Transportation (888-444-4425; 800-424-7767) Provides door-to-door transportation between your home and Islip, LaGuardia, Kennedy, and Newark airports. Rides are shared so they take longer than direct service, but the price is lower. The company is efficient and reliable.

GUIDED TOURS

There are several guided tours to the Hamptons from New York. The Long Island Rail Road offers tours from Pennsylvania Station (NYC), and bus companies also offer convenient ways to see the area without the trauma of fighting traffic. Travel agents are the best source of information for these tours, and some include overnight accommodations along with the ride.

In Bridgehampton, a road race was first run in 1915 with new cars. Today, the race is recreated with antique cars.

Morgan McGivern

CAMELOT STAR
860-345-8591.
Departure: Tour leaves from Haddam, CT.
Mailing Address: 1 Marine Pk.,
Haddam, CT 06438.
Season: Mid-June–Labor Day operating

Tues., Thurs., Sun.; Labor Day–mid-
Sept. operating Sun. only.
Reservations: Not required.
Rates: Adults $22.50; children under 12
years, $10; those under 5, free.
Credit Cards: AE, D, MC, V.

The *Camelot Star* is a 560-passenger cruise ship from Haddam, CT, that operates excursion trips to Sag Harbor during the summer. The 3-hour cruise
leaves Haddam at 9am and arrives in Sag Harbor at 12 noon; there are 3 hours
on shore for possible shopping, sight-seeing, or lunch in a restaurant prior to
the 3pm return to Haddam. The ship is air-conditioned and heated, and there's
also an outside observation deck. Bicycles are welcome at no charge.

LONG ISLAND RAIL ROAD
718-558-7498.
Departure: Tours leave from
Pennsylvania Station (NYC),
Brooklyn, Jamaica, and Mineola.
Mailing Address: Sales & Promotions
Dept. #1424, Jamaica, NY 11435.

Season: Mem. Day-early Nov.
Rates: Hamptons tour (includes lunch):
adults $58; children $46. Montauk
tour (no lunch included): adults $40;
children $30.
Credit Cards: AE, D, MC, V.

The Long Island Rail Road organizes a series of delightful tours each summer,
including two to the Hamptons. They are offered about six times annually
from July–Nov. One trip goes to Southampton, where you can visit museums or
shop in the classy boutiques, eat lunch, and then go on to East Hampton, where
there's time for more shopping before you catch the train back to Manhattan.
The other goes directly to Montauk, where you have time to shop and to eat
lunch on your own before boarding a bus out to the Montauk Lighthouse for a
tour of this historic landmark. Then it's back on the train in Montauk for the
return trip to New York. Reservations are absolutely necessary.

SPECIALTY TOURS

Several specialty tours are also available to the Hamptons. For bicycling and
hiking tours, see the section "Bicycling" in Chapter Seven, *Recreation*, or
contact **Brooks Country Cycling Tours** (212-874-5151; www.brookscountry
cycling.com).

For organized tours *from* the Hamptons, the **Hampton Jitney** (631-283-4600)
offers a variety of tours, including theater, museum, and shopping trips to New
York City, as well as trips to Florida and to the Foxwoods Casino in Connecticut.

GETTING AROUND ONCE YOU'RE HERE

Getting here isn't nearly as much fun as getting around once you arrive. If you prefer to drive someone else's car instead of your own, here are several car rental options. Please be sure to call in advance to reserve. Or for short-term transportation, the following taxis are reliable and often will deliver packages and make deliveries. Village location doesn't mean that a taxi is restricted to that village.

CAR RENTALS

All County Rent-A-Car (631-324-1018; Georgica Getty Station, Toilsome Ln. and Montauk Hwy., just outside East Hampton) Rents used cars (some of them great old classics) that may be used for driving in Suffolk County only. Rentals are by the week.

Avis Rent A Car (National Reservation Number 800-331-1212; 631-283-9111; 59 Maple Ave., Southampton, NY 11968) Open May–mid-Sept. only.

Enterprise Rent-A-Car (631-283-0055; Omni, 395 County Rd. 39A, Southampton, NY 11968) Next door to Hampton Jitney, take the Jitney to Southampton. Open Mon.–Sat.; or East Hampton Airport (631-537-4800).

Hertz (National Reservation Number 800-654-3131; 631-537-8119; Montauk Hwy., Bridgehampton, NY 11932); or East Hampton Airport (631-537-3987).

Pam Rent-A-Car (631-727-7020; 150 North Main St., East Hampton, NY 11937).

Rent A Wreck (631-728-153; 18A Ponquogue Ave., Hampton Bays, NY 11946).

TAXIS

AMAGANSETT

Amagansett Taxi (631-267-2006)

EAST HAMPTON

East Hampton Taxi (631-324-9696)

HAMPTON BAYS

Colonial Taxi (631-589-7878)
Hampton Coach (631-728-0050; 631-728-0500)

MONTAUK

Celtic Cab (631-668-4747)
Pink Tuna Taxi (631-668-3838).

SAG HARBOR

Sag Harbor Car Service (631-725-9000)

SOUTHAMPTON

Atlantic Taxi (631-283-1900)
Lindy's Taxi (631-283-0242)

WESTHAMPTON BEACH

Westhampton Beach Taxi & Limo (631-288-3252)

PUBLIC BUSES

Suffolk Transit (631-852-5200; www.sct-bus.org) Mon.–Sat. $1.50, with additional charge of $.25 for each transfer; seniors and handicapped riders $.50. Operates buses that crisscross the Hamptons, from Montauk to Westhampton and beyond, including the North Fork as far as the Orient Point Ferry. For some reason, the information numbers are always busy, and they're only in operation Mon.–Fri. 8am–4:30pm. The best bet is to pick up the schedule and fare information from local chamber of commerce offices. The schedules are well prepared, with maps that clearly show the routes, the transfer points, and just about anything you need to know. Suffolk Transit will stop anywhere along the route if you flag them down. In general, the buses travel each way about every 2 hours. You must tell the driver when you get on if you want a transfer. **Please note:** Exact fare is required, as the drivers do not carry change.

CHAPTER THREE
Hospitality Hamptons' Style
LODGING

Hampton residents have been taking in boarders for more than 200 years. In her book, *Up and Down Main Street, an Informal History of East Hampton and Its Old Houses* (1968), Jeannette Edwards Rattray states that the Huntting Inn (then the Huntting home) accommodated boarders as early as Revolutionary times. It's still an inn on Main Street in East Hampton. It is said that in the eighteenth century, the 1770 House (also still an inn on East

Morgan McGivern

The Hedges Inn originally was home to one of the founding families of East Hampton. It's now an inn and a restaurant.

Hampton's Main Street) was open on Saturday nights to God-fearing church-goers who came from other villages to attend East Hampton's churches. Rowdy Hall was housing guests when the artists of the Tile Club first discovered the Hamptons in the late 1800s. (This was later moved to Egypt Lane in East Hampton, where it is a private home.) W. L. Osborn and his wife ran a boardinghouse as early as 1858 in "their big house on the little hill overlooking Town Pond." The Sea Spray Inn in East Hampton was legendary (gone now), as was the Irving House in Southampton (also gone).

Duke Fordham's inn on Sag Harbor's main street was certainly in business before the stagecoach route from the Fulton Ferry in Brooklyn to Sag Harbor was established in 1772; it was chosen as the final stop on the three-day stage-coach trip. In 1877, Addison Youngs opened the American Hotel in Sag Harbor. This hotel was one of the most modern hotels on Long Island, with steam heat, electric lights, and indoor bathrooms. (It's still an inn and restaurant.) Sag Harbor's Sea View Hotel was built in 1891 and stood on a hill overlooking Noyack Bay; it was famous for attracting celebrities, such as Enrico Caruso. Later called Hill Top Acres, it burned to the ground in 1970.

Ye Olde Canoe Place Inn was built on the small isthmus where native inhabitants carried their canoes from the Great Peconic Bay to the Shinnecock Bay. First constructed in 1750 as a small house, it later became a stagecoach stop. Over the years, it was owned by the Buchmüller family, who had previously owned the Waldorf-Astoria Hotel, and by Julius Keller, owner of Maxim's restaurant in Manhattan. The inn was destroyed by fire on July 4, 1921, but was rebuilt to follow the lines of the original. The new structure included thirty-four bedrooms, four banquet rooms, twenty baths, and a gigantic kitchen. It became a favorite watering hole during the Roaring Twenties, and its Saturday night dances attracted hundreds. Among its famous guests were Governor Al Smith, who made it his summer headquarters for some thirty years, Franklin Roosevelt, John L. Sullivan, Helen Hayes, Albert Einstein, and Cary Grant. The inn is still in operation as a nightclub and restaurant.

Of the old-time inns, the American Hotel in Sag Harbor, The Huntting Inn, 1770 House, The Hedges Inn, and The Maidstone Arms in East Hampton, are still welcoming guests, but most of the others have long since burned or been demolished. The Irving Hotel in Southampton, for example, survived until the 1970s, only to be demolished. The Irving Annex across the street, however, survives as the main house of the Village Latch Inn.

Innkeeping continues to be a Hampton tradition today, much as it was some 200 years ago, but with modern comforts. Today's inns often include cable television, VCRs, telephones with voice mail and dataports, air-conditioning, fluffy down pillows and comforters, and chocolates on your pillow. Private baths may include a collection of amenities, from special soaps and shampoos to thick towels and warm robes.

High season in the Hamptons runs from the July 4th weekend through Labor Day. Almost all bed-and-breakfast establishments, inns, and motels, however, open earlier and close later in the season, and more and more are remaining open year-round. When possible, dates of operation are indicated, but since they may vary from year to year, it is best to call first. Also in high season, inns and motels often require two- and three-night minimum stays on weekends and four-night stays on holidays.

Bed-and-breakfast establishments are as varied as their owners. Some are elegant and classy, while others are whimsical and humorous, with all the variations in between. Some are decorated with such élan that they belong in *Architectural Digest*; others offer a homey combination of handmade quilts and pillows. Some pride themselves on the complete breakfasts they serve; others lay out a buffet of fruits and breads. The one common thread, however, is that each owner of a bed-and-breakfast has invested a bit of himself or herself in their establishment; staying in one is often a very personal experience.

Hamptons' inns and bed-and-breakfasts have a limited number of rooms, and it is necessary to reserve the finest rooms well in advance. Therefore, it is advisable to make reservations as soon as you know your plans. A deposit generally will be required, and strict cancellation policies are followed. Be sure that you understand the policy and abide by it; otherwise, you may lose your deposit.

Children under the age of 12 and pets are often discouraged in bed-and-breakfasts in the Hamptons. Most have strictly enforced no-smoking policies within the house, but some do allow smoking on porches or on the grounds. In-room telephones are often available in bed-and-breakfasts now, and a surprising number of inns are offering color televisions with cable hookups, and even VCRs. Although most inns now provide air-conditioning, it had been assumed for some time that the balmy ocean breezes make it unnecessary; generally, that is true.

This chapter offers a guide to places to stay from Montauk to Eastport. Please consult Chapter Nine, *North Fork* and Chapter Ten, *Shelter Island* for places to stay in those locations.

In the block of information printed with each lodging description, you will see a price code rather than specific prices. This code is based on the average between the highest and lowest rates per room, double occupancy. If a continental or full breakfast is included, it will be noted in the information block under "Special Features." The rates indicated throughout this book are subject to change, so to be safe, confirm prices when you call for reservations. These rates generally exclude local taxes and any service charges that may be added to the bill. The price codes are as follows:

Price Codes

Inexpensive	Up to $100	Expensive	$150–$200
Moderate	$100–$150	Very Expensive	$200 and up

The credit cards that are accepted by each establishment are identified by the following abbreviations.

Credit Cards

AE	American Express	DC	Diner's Club
CB	Carte Blanche	MC	MasterCard
D	Discover	V	Visa

The East Hampton and Southampton Chambers of Commerce operate an excellent accommodation referral service. Each publishes a free book that lists its members, including those who offer lodging. They also have information and telephone numbers of homes, inns, hotels, and motels that have current vacancies.

East Hampton Chamber of Commerce (631-324-0362; www.easthampton chamber.com; 79A Main St., East Hampton, NY 11937)

Southampton Chamber of Commerce (631-283-0402; www.southampton chamer.com; 76 Main St., Southampton, NY 11968)

BED-AND-BREAKFASTS, INNS, RESORTS

AMAGANSETT

The Gansett Green Manor is a lovely collection of cottages — each with its own kitchen and patio.

Morgan McGivern

THE GANSETT GREEN MANOR
631-267-3133.
www.gansettgreenmanor.com.
273 Main St., Amagansett.
Mailing Address: PO Box 799,
　Amagansett, NY 11930.
Innkeeper: Gary Kalfin.
Open: Year-round.

Price: Moderate–Very Expensive.
Credit Cards: AE, MC, V.
Special Features: Spacious landscaped
　grounds; smoking permitted in
　rooms; kitchens; cable TV; children
　welcome; pets with prior permission.
Directions: On Montauk Hwy. (Rte. 27)
　in village.

The Gansett Green, a fixture of Amagansett life since 1915, is in tip-top shape. What was once a ramshackle collection of cottages has been transformed into a delightful haven. Each weathered shingle cottage now has crisp white trim, an individual garden or patio, and wainscotted interior walls; the decor is inspired. The Hidden Garden suite is furnished with rare, blackwood Chinese pieces, imported from China by Gary, and has a walled garden with a fishpond. Several of the cottages, including the Hampton Classic Horse Room, have furniture that is hand-painted by artist David Tabor. All fourteen units have kitchens, private baths, new flagstone terraces, antiques, and so much more. The two-acre parcel that once was overgrown with weeds and brush held many surprises; Gary found an old tandem wooden sled and beside the big barn, a covered wagon. All such discoveries remain, as well as the fountains and meandering pathways that lead to fanciful lawn sculptures.

THE HERMITAGE
631-267-6151; fax: 631-267-1071.
www.duneresorts.com.
2148 Montauk Hwy., Amagansett.
Mailing Address: PO Box 1127,
Amagansett, NY 11930.
Manager: Yasmin Malliet, Dune Resorts.
Open: Mid-Mar.–New Years.
Price: Moderate–Very Expensive.

Credit Cards: MC, V.
Special Features: On ocean; kitchens; pool;
tennis courts; private sundecks; 7 landscaped acres; cable TV/VCR; smoking
permitted in rooms; air-conditioning;
telephones; children welcome;
no pets.
Directions: On Montauk Hwy. (Rte. 27),
5 miles east of Amagansett.

Located on the expansive sandy beach of Napeague, midway between Amagansett village and Montauk, these ultramodern, bleached wood, two-story buildings rise from the surrounding dunes. Each of the fifty-six units has two bedrooms, two baths, living room, full kitchen, dining room, and deck for private sunbathing. The decor is the typical Hampton motif of pale woods and pastel fabrics. Views from the ocean side rooms are spectacular. The seven acres of landscaped grounds include two tennis courts and a pool with a lifeguard in attendance. This is a great place for children.

MILL-GARTH COUNTRY INN
631-267-3757.
23 Windmill Ln., Amagansett.
Mailing Address: PO Box 700,
Amagansett, NY 11930.
Innkeeper: Tommie Alegre.
Open: Year-round.
Price: Expensive–Very Expensive.

Credit Cards: MC, V.
Special Features: Wheelchair access;
nonsmoking inn; 2 landscaped acres;
some units with kitchens; continental
breakfast; children under 12 free; no pets.
Directions: From Montauk Hwy. (Rte. 27),
turn onto Windmill Ln. at Miss Amelia's
Cottage. Inn is on left in .25 mile.

The Mill-Garth has a certain lived-in comfort to it. The collection of cottages on two acres (it always seems larger than that) enfolds private little bowers, as well as open spaces, which are popular for weddings and receptions. The pretty tile-floored, lattice-enclosed arbor is filled with white wicker and is the preferred place for breakfast and afternoon tea. Accommodations are widely varied and include five cottages, four suites, and three studio apartments. The decor is eclectic, not elegant, but yet spiced with some nice old pieces. You'll love the tiny duplex windmill that has a desk and a telephone for guests to use. The Dairy Cottage is light and airy, with a black-and-white tile floor in the kitchen. The English Ivy Cottage has ivy stenciling across the door frames and the ceiling moldings. A private flagstone patio with wicker furniture makes this pretty cottage a particular favorite. The continental breakfast includes homemade muffins and coffee cake.

**OCEAN COLONY BEACH AND
    TENNIS CLUB**
631-267-3130; fax: 631-267-1032.
www.duneresorts.com.
2004 Montauk Hwy., Amagansett.

Mailing address: PO Box 7050, Amagansett,
NY 11930.
Manager: Virginia Reynolds, Dune Resorts.
Open: Apr.–Oct.
Price: Moderate–Very Expensive.

Credit Cards: D, MC, V.
Special Features: On ocean; heated pool; tennis courts; kitchens; air-conditioning; smoking permitted in rooms; telephones with voice mail; cable TV; game room; children welcome; no pets.
Directions: Located on Montauk Hwy. (Rte. 27), 4 miles east of Amagansett.

The Ocean Colony Beach and Tennis Club is a sixty-nine-unit, weathered gray, three-level resort built in 1983. It is located on an eight-acre site with 400 feet of private oceanfront. Units range in size from studios to three-bedroom units; all contain a living area, sleeping area, kitchenette, and private deck or terrace. Some have ocean views, and all have handsome furnishings. Unit 16-21 is a well-designed, three-bedroom unit with a powder room on the first level, and a full bath upstairs, but no ocean view. The cottage (Room 511) has a very private site on the ocean with walls of windows and wraparound decks for direct views of the crashing waves. There are two bedrooms, bath, and superb kitchen. The grounds include a pool, two tennis courts, and a clubhouse/game room with Ping-Pong.

SEA CREST ON THE OCEAN
631-267-3159; 800-SEA DAYS; fax: 631-267-6840.
www.duneresorts.com.
2166 Montauk Hwy. at Navajo Ln., Amagansett.
Mailing Address: PO Box 7053, Amagansett, NY 11930.
Manager: Richard Sackmann, Dune Resorts.
Open: Year-round.
Price: Inexpensive–Very Expensive.

Credit Cards: D, MC, V.
Special Features: On ocean; pool; tennis courts; kitchenettes; playground; basketball; racquetball; volleyball; handball; shuffleboard; cable TV/ VCR; telephones with voice mail; air-conditioning; smoking permitted in rooms; outdoor grille; children welcome; no pets.
Directions: Located on Montauk Hwy. (Rte. 27), 5 miles east of Amagansett.

Sea Crest on the Ocean is a co-op, set on over nine acres, with 150 yards of unspoiled beach. The gray-shingled resort contains seventy-four units, ranging from studios to two-bedroom units. Facilities in buildings named Rapallo, Saint-Tropez, and San Remo have views of the ocean, while those in the other buildings have views of the pool or partial views of the ocean. All, however, have pleasing, well-designed living and sleeping areas, kitchenettes, and private decks or terraces; larger accommodations have two levels with two decks. All units received new kitchens, carpeting, and wallpaper in 2000, but the furniture will vary with the tastes of the co-op owner. The grounds are very well maintained and include abundant flower beds, a heated pool, two tennis courts, and an elevated boardwalk over the dunes to the beach; a variety of activities are also held on the grounds.

BRIDGEHAMPTON

BRIDGEHAMPTON INN
631-537-3660; fax: 631-537-3589.
2266 Montauk Hwy., Bridgehampton.

Mailing Address: PO Box 1342, Bridgehampton, NY 11932.

Elegant and dignified, the Bridgehampton Inn offers a convenient location plus European sophistication.

Morgan McGivern

Owners/Innkeepers: Anna and Detlef Pump.
Open: Year-round.
Price: Moderate–Very Expensive.
Credit Cards: AE, MC, V.
Special Features: Nonsmoking inn; full breakfast; gardens; telephones; cable TV; air-conditioning; children welcome; no pets.
Directions: On Main St. (Rte. 27), just west of village.

This venerable, old colonial home is one of the most handsome in town. Circled by a white picket fence, the white-shingled structure was totally restored in 1993. The decor has a restrained elegance that's punctuated by clever artwork and extravagant floral displays in the common rooms. There's a welcoming fireplace in the living room, with French doors leading to several brick terraces and expansive gardens beyond. The decor in the four guest rooms and two suites is sophisticated, with beige carpeting, handcrafted four-poster beds, antique dressers and tables, and well-designed marble and tile baths that feature unique European fixtures, including mansion-sized showers with a showerhead in the middle of the ceiling rather than on the wall. My favorite is Room 7, which has red-striped twill fabric on a Victorian settee and a polished antique chest with brass pulls; a Victorian table holds the TV. Room 6, a suite, is furnished with a spectacular eight-piece antique Biedermeier suite. The owners also own the popular Loaves and Fishes catering company, so breakfasts are divine. A full breakfast that includes Swedish pancakes with fresh blueberry sauce, ham and eggs, and homemade pastries is included in the price of the room.

THE ENCLAVE INN
631-537-0197; 877-998-0800;
   fax: 631-537-5436.
www.enclaveinn.com.
E-mail: hello@enclaveinn.com.

2668 Montauk Hwy., Bridgehampton.
Mailing Address: PO Box 623,
   Bridgehampton, NY 11932.
Owner/Innkeeper: Michael Wudyka.
Open: Year-round.

Price: Inexpensive– Expensive.
Credit Cards: AE, MC, V.
Special Features: Nonsmoking inn;
 muffins and coffee in morning; garden;
 pool; telephones; refrigerators; cable
TV/VCR; air-conditioning; business
center with fax and copier; children
welcome; no pets.
Directions: On Rte. 27, about 1 mile east of
 center of village.

It may look like a motel from the street, and in fact, that's how it began its days, but then Alexis Stewart (daughter of Martha) purchased it in 1993 and transformed it into a chic, little St. Bart's-style retreat. And then it closed for several years. Reopened in 2000, the ten smallish rooms are as stylish as ever with their brightly colored tile floors, skylights, and in-room sinks surrounded by steel countertops. Each private bath is tiny but beautifully tiled and impeccably clean. And how often do you find a room for $89 (during the week off-season) — and even less if you stay several nights — anywhere in the Hamptons? Located on two acres, there's a beautiful side yard for relaxed reading and a swimming pool in back. Check it out!

EAST HAMPTON

BED AND BREAKFAST ON COVE HOLLOW
631-324-7730.
145 Cove Hollow Rd., East Hampton.
Mailing Address: PO Box 2234, East
 Hampton, NY 11937.
Innkeeper: Ann Colonomos.
Open: May–Oct.
Price: Moderate–Very Expensive.
Credit Cards: AE.
Special Features: Nonsmoking B&B; pool;
 lovely flower gardens; continental
 breakfast; bicycles; outdoor shower;
 hammock; not appropriate for children;
 small dogs acceptable.
Directions: From Montauk Hwy. (Rte. 27),
 turn south onto Cove Hollow Rd. (Cafe
 Max on right and Red Horse Market
 across street). Inn is on right, behind
 Cafe Max.

This charming, shingled cottage offers a terrific bed-and-breakfast option. It's used exclusively by guests, and the owner lives in a separate cottage behind. There's an attractive living room with natural wood floors and a full kitchen. All four rooms are bright and cheerful and include painted white wood floors, covered by a rag or a sisal rug, with oak dressers and wicker beds, dressed in sunwashed fabrics. Two rooms have private baths, and the other two rooms share a bath. In the back, a pool is surrounded by a brick terrace and enclosed by a fence, and there are brick pathways through the garden. Breakfast, which is laid out on the kitchen counter each morning, consists of fresh muffins, croissants, fruit, juice, granola, cereals, coffee or tea. I love to take my breakfast outside to the tables on the lawn behind the house and watch the bees flit from flower to flower in the abundant border flower beds. This is also the perfect spot to relax with a glass of wine after a hot day on the beach. Note: During the summer, Ann rents the house by the week only.

CENTENNIAL HOUSE
631-324-9414; fax: 631-324-0493.
www.centhouse.com.
E-mail: centhouse@ hamptons.com.

East Hampton's elegant Centennial House offers gracious accommodations featuring Oriental rugs and antiques, plus a secluded landscaped garden with a pool.

Morgan McGivern

13 Woods Ln., East Hampton, NY 11937.
Innkeepers: David A. Oxford and Harry Chancey, Jr.
Manager: Sue Maynard.
Open: Year-round.
Price: Expensive–Very Expensive.
Credit Cards: MC, V.

Special Features: Nonsmoking inn; pool; lovely landscaped grounds and gardens; full breakfast; telephones with voice mail; TV/VCR; air-conditioning; not appropriate for children; pets with prior permission.
Directions: On Rte. 27, just before traffic light at Town Pond.

When the innkeepers were restoring this gracious old East Hampton house in 1988, they found a board with the year "1876" carved into it, inspiring the inn's name. From the broad porch overlooking Woods Ln. (Rte. 27) to the handsome gray-shingled exterior with its white trim, it is obvious that this was the residence of prosperous owners. Today, the inn is reminiscent of an English country home. Oriental rugs decorate polished pine floors, and antique chairs are upholstered in English floral-glazed chintz. There are European oil paintings on the walls, a grand piano, and a fireplace. The stunning dining room has floor-to-ceiling bookshelves in a corner and an elegant, antique breakfront, holding heavy silver serving pieces. Breakfast is eaten on gilt-edged china on a magnificent mahogany table, lighted by a brass chandelier. The meal includes fruit, juice, bacon, eggs, pancakes, French toast, or some other special treat. The Bay Room has an antique, tobacco four-poster bed, wide-plank pine floors, Spy prints, a fireplace, and a large bath with a former pulpit that has been turned into a sink. My favorite room is the green-and-burgundy Lincoln Room, which has an ornate armoire and matching Victorian bed, similar to the one in which Abraham Lincoln died; its bath has a marble sink with brass legs. The grounds are as lovely as the house. There are spacious lawns, a profusion of flowers in season, and a pool tucked away in a secret spot in the back. A three-bedroom cottage offers an ideal accommodation for families; a barn is outfitted with fitness equipment.

EAST HAMPTON HOUSE

631-324-4300; 800-698-9283;
fax: 631-329-3743.
www.duneresorts.com.
226 Pantigo Rd., East Hampton, NY
11937.
Manager: Jo Anne Koehler, Dune Resorts.
Open: Year-round.
Price: Inexpensive–Very Expensive.
Credit Cards: AE, D, MC, V.
Special Features: Pool; tennis courts; telephones with voice mail; cable TV/VCR; air-conditioning; smoking permitted in rooms; children under 2 discouraged in summer; no pets.
Direction: On Rte. 27, 1 mile east of East Hampton.

From the street, this appears to be merely an attractive, well-maintained motel, but in reality, the white brick two-story buildings envelop five parklike acres of flower beds and manicured lawns that include a pool, tennis courts, and a children's play area. This is a co-op, so the decor of the units may vary, but each is superbly maintained and attractively furnished. There are two sizes of rooms: studios and two-room suites, and each of the fifty-six units has either a private sundeck or a patio. In summer, a light continental breakfast is available, which may be taken to the room. Although the beach is about a mile away, the pool and the lovely landscaping make this one of the most popular motels in the Hamptons.

The cottages at East Hampton Point are joined by brick walkways and profuse flower beds.

Suzi Forbes Chase

EAST HAMPTON POINT

631-324-9191; fax: 631-324-3751.
www.easthamptonpoint.com.
295 Three Mile Harbor Rd., East Hampton.
Mailing Address: PO Box 847, East Hampton, NY 11937.
Manager: Dominique Cummings.
Open: Year-round.
Price: Expensive–Very Expensive.
Credit Cards: AE, D, MC, V.
Special Features: Pool; tennis court; fitness center; saunas; masseur on call; continental breakfast in summer; telephones with voice mail; air-conditioning; smoking permitted in rooms; cable TV; 5.5 wooded acres; van service, including airport pickup; fine restaurant and marina on premises; children and pets welcome.
Directions: Turn left off Main St. at windmill. When road forks, turn left again onto Three Mile Harbor Rd. Cottages are on left in 4 miles.

It's hard not to fall in love with these jewel box cottages. Each has a modern kitchen with a refrigerator and a Jenn-Aire stove, Mexican tile floors, bleached pine cabinets, tile baths, and private brick patios or wooden decks. Some of the thirteen cottages have duplex bedrooms and skylights. There are both one- and two-bedroom units, and all but one of the baths has a Jacuzzi. Cottage 2 is absolutely stunning: the main floor has a terrific kitchen, large deck, and tiled powder room; upstairs, there's a bedroom and a bathroom that boasts a glass ceiling, Mexican tile floor, large Jacuzzi, and a room-sized glass shower. As one might imagine, this cottage is especially popular with honeymooners. The cottages are connected by brick pathways and are bordered by abundant flower beds, all in a very private, wooded setting. In the midst, there's a small chapel that's been converted into a fitness center, complete with TV. Although the popular East Hampton Point restaurant is on adjacent property, it's well removed from the cottages, as is the pool. There's a marina down on the harbor and a ship's store where guests can purchase breakfast in the morning and snacks all day.

THE HEDGES INN

631-324-7100; fax: 631-324-5816.
74 James Ln., East Hampton, NY 11937.
Innkeeper: Linda Calder.
Open: Year-round.
Price: Moderate–Very Expensive.
Credit Cards: AE, DC, MC, V.
Special Features: Smoking outside only; continental breakfast; air-conditioning; telephones with voice mail; cable TV; restaurant (James Lane Cafe) on premises; children welcome; no pets.
Directions: When entering town from west, drive straight ahead at traffic light instead of turning left. Inn is straight ahead.

The Hedges Inn is one of the oldest and most historic inns on the East End. The Hedges family, one of the founding families of East Hampton, began taking in boarders as early as 1870; it is believed that parts of the house date from the mid-1700s, and legend has it that the famous underground wine cellar was once part of the Underground Railroad. The main house became an acclaimed inn in 1935, when Mrs. Harry Hamlin restored it and put her own cook and butler in charge. It achieved widespread acclaim in the 1950s, when it became home to a restaurant owned by famed chef and restaurateur, Henri Soulé. Today, The Hedges Inn has been fully restored and all eleven rooms have private baths. Room 1, for example, has creamy beige walls with white wainscotting, turquoise carpeting, a taupe-colored sofa, and an iron canopy bed. The baths are done in sparkling white tile, with black marble counters. A continental breakfast, consisting of fruit, juice, and muffins or croissants is served in the pretty, airy breakfast room. A side terrace serves as an auxiliary breakfast room in the summer, but it's also a refined place to sip a glass of wine in the afternoon. The beautiful restaurant, the James Lane Cafe, is open year-round.

THE HUNTTING INN

631-324-0410; fax: 631-324-6122.
94 Main St., East Hampton, NY 11937.
Innkeeper: Linda Calder.
Open: Year-round.
Price: Moderate–Very Expensive.
Credit Cards: AE, DC, MC, V.

Special Features: Smoking outside only; continental breakfast; air-conditioning; telephones; cable TV; fine restaurant (The Palm) on premises; children welcome; no pets. Directions: On Rte. 27 at Huntting Ln.

This old inn, dating from the Revolutionary War, has been a prominent fixture on East Hampton's Main St. since 1699, when it was built as a home for Reverend Nathaniel Huntting, the second minister of East Hampton. Over the years, it has grown as it took in more and more boarders, which accounts for the narrow hallways with their quirky twists and turns. The Hampton Jitney stops directly in front of the inn, making it a most convenient place to stay. The tiny lobby of the Huntting bustles at night when it serves as the greeting place for diners at The Palm restaurant, which is located on the main floor. Off the bar, however, there are several parlors where guests can spend quiet time in the afternoon, viewing the gardens. The nineteen guest rooms vary in size and are often funky, although each has a smattering of antiques and a private bath (often very tiny). Room 105 has an iron and brass bed, and Room 102 is a suite that is decorated in peach and white colors. The side flower garden is a riot of color from spring to fall.

Morgan McGivern

There are private spots for relaxation in the formal gardens of The J. Harper Poor Cottage. Inside, the decor was inspired by William Morris.

THE J. HARPER POOR COTTAGE
631-324-4081; fax: 631-329-5931.
www.jharperpoor.com.
E-mail: info@jharperpoor. com.
181 Main St., East Hampton, NY 11937.
Innkeepers: Gary and Rita Reiswig.
Open: Year-round.
Price: Very Expensive.
Credit Cards: AE, DC, MC, V.

Special Features: Smoking outside only; full breakfast; afternoon refreshments; air-conditioning; cable TV/VCR; telephones with voice mail; video library; masseur available; room safe; pool; sauna; hot tub; exercise room; children welcome; no pets. Directions: On Rte. 27 in center of village.

For many years, this distinctive, buff-colored stucco mansion was the home of the owners of 1770 House and served as an adjunct to the rooms in their inn. In 1996, however, the handsome house was transformed by Gary and Rita Reiswig, formerly the owners of The Maidstone Arms, into the Hamptons' premier bed-and-breakfast. Every detail of the major restoration has been executed to perfection. The original structure dates to the 1650s, although the house has been expanded and embellished significantly over the years. In the early 1900s, Mr. Poor created its current appearance, and the Reiswigs have restored it to that period. In the sunken living room, there are bay windows, a carved plaster ceiling, and a massive tile-fronted fireplace. An oak library table graces the library, which has a wall of books. In keeping with the age of the house, the elegant furnishings are all in an Arts and Crafts style. The guest rooms, which have beamed ceilings, are very large, with roomy closets and equally spacious tiled baths; most have fireplaces. My favorite is Room 13, which has an iron bed, a wood-burning fireplace, hand-hewn beamed ceilings, paneled walls, and a private balcony, overlooking Main St. All the rooms have William Morris-style fabrics and wallpapers imported from England, Ralph Lauren bed dressings, and fluffy Frette bathrobes. A spa level was added in 2000 and contains a pool, sauna, hot tub, exercise equipment, and showers. Breakfast is served in the informal lounge, which has wicker chairs, a plumped sofa in front of a woodstove, a bright blue rug on the wood floor, and a beamed ceiling. The full breakfast may include an omelette or pancakes, accompanied by freshly baked breads, fruit, and juice. In the afternoon, wines and hors d'oeuvres are set out in the informal lounge.

Lysander House, a Victorian farmhouse on Main Street, was built in 1885. It is decorated with interesting folk art pieces.

Morgan McGivern

LYSANDER HOUSE
631-329-9025.
132 Main St., East Hampton, NY 11937.
Innkeepers: Larry and Leslie Tell Hillel.
Open: Year-round.
Price: Expensive–Very Expensive.
Credit Cards: None.

Special Features: Smoking outside only; wraparound porch; 2 grassy acres; full breakfast; afternoon refreshments; air-conditioning; children over 14 welcome; no pets.
Directions: On Rte. 27 in center of village.

L arry and Leslie Hillel traveled the globe before settling in East Hampton and opening their bed-and-breakfast. Their 1885 Victorian farmhouse inn, situated on two grassy acres, is charmingly filled with art that they collected along the way. In the parlor, masks from Mexico and Japan march across the walls, and there's an engaging New England village folk art scene painted on a wooden plank by Neil Connell that hangs over the fireplace. All of the floors are painted, and there is wonderful, antique furniture, mixed with painted chests and tables. In the dining/living room, which is a cheery yellow with white trim and white shutters on the windows, there's a Japanese step tansu, a clever device that at one time served both as a stairway and as a storage space; it has drawers under each of the stairs. The three guest rooms are light and bright and also cleverly decorated. Each has a private tiled bath. Liza's Suite, which is the largest, has a pink sitting room and a bedroom with an iron headboard, pine bookcase, and pine dresser; there's a contemporary watercolor in the bedroom, while a folk art painting graces the sitting room. The bath has wainscotted walls, a pedestal sink, and a tiled shower. Alexander's Master Bedroom, which is painted a sunny yellow, includes an iron and brass bed, a pine wardrobe, and a wonderful folk art painting by Neil Connell over the bed. All of the rooms have custom-made mattresses imported from Sweden, so you're assured of a comfy, sweet-dream night. Breakfast is a gourmet treat that includes freshly baked breads, muffins, or scones and a hot entrée, such as a frittata or oatmeal-yogurt pancakes. You'll depart this delightful inn with a bag of freshly baked cookies.

A boardinghouse or inn has welcomed guests to the site of the current Maidstone Arms since 1750.

Morgan McGivern

THE MAIDSTONE ARMS
631-324-5006; fax: 631-324-5037.
www.maidstonearms.com.
207 Main St., East Hampton, NY 11937.
Owner: Coke Anne Saunders.

Managing Director: William S. Valentine.
Open: Year-round.
Price: Expensive–Very Expensive.
Credit Cards: AE, MC, V.
Special Features: Limited wheelchair

access; smoking in lounge only; overlooks Town Pond; continental breakfast; maid service; telephones with voice mail; cable TV; fireplaces in

cottages; fine restaurant on premises. Directions: On Rte. 27 across from Town Pond.

There's been an inn on this site, looking much as the present Maidstone Arms does today, since 1750. In 1992, this grand dame of East Hampton inns was purchased by Coke Anne Saunders, an architect, at which time it was fully restored. Located on a knoll across from Town Pond, the inn is a classic beauty, with a white-shingled exterior with blue shutters and a Greek Revival doorway. The clubby Water Room, just off the lobby, has a woodstove, antique love seats, plaid-upholstered chairs, and walls decorated with hunting and fishing prints and antique fishing gear. This is the perfect place to sip a hot mulled wine in the winter, while watching children ice skate on Town Pond. It's also a pleasant place to begin the day while reading your complimentary copy of the *New York Times*. There are sixteen guest rooms and three cottages, all with private baths; some have fancifully painted furniture, and others have antiques. The duplex cottage suite has a beige carpet, white walls, a walnut sleigh bed, and a fireplace with a tile front. Room 14 has a verdigris iron bed and French doors leading to a private, glassed-in porch with wicker furniture.

MILL HOUSE INN

631-324-9766; fax 631-324-9793.
www.millhouseinn.com.
E-mail: innkeeper@ millhouseinn.com.
31 North Main St., East Hampton, NY 11937.
Innkeepers: Gary and Sylvia Muller.
Open: Year-round.
Price: Very Expensive.

Credit Cards: MC, V.
Special Features: Nonsmoking inn; full breakfast; telephones with voice mail; cable TV/VCR; children welcome; no pets.
Directions: From Main St., turn left at fork just before Hook Windmill. Inn is on left, across from windmill.

The charming Mill House Inn enjoys a convenient, in-town location and a lovely view of the historic Hook Windmill. Now under the guidance of Gary and Sylvia Muller, the inn has been decorated in the Arts and Crafts style. There are hand-hewn beams in the living room and the breakfast room; the living room has a fireplace with a white mantel, mellow leather sofas and chairs, and a pine cupboard; the breakfast room has soothing sage green walls, mission-style chairs, and a needlepoint rug. Each of the eight rooms has a private bath — four of them have whirlpool tubs — and six of the rooms have working fireplaces. Hampton Breezes, for example, has a cherry, Shaker-style, hand-crafted sleigh bed and a bentwood chair upholstered in leather. There's a fireplace, and the large tiled bath has a whirlpool tub. The Garden Room has tranquil blue walls and blue-and-green decor. The mahogany furniture is elegant, and the tiled bath has a whirlpool tub. Although some of the baths are small, they are being upgraded with tile as rapidly as possible. Gary is a chef, so breakfasts here are quite exceptional. You can choose from ten different egg dishes, as well as pancakes or brioche French toast. Or you might have fresh fruit or Irish oatmeal with dried cranberries, blueberries, and strawberries. We love to follow a day at the beach with some quiet time on the screened-in porch or in the beautifully landscaped back yard, sipping a refreshing lemonade.

THE PINK HOUSE
631-324-3400; fax: 631-324-5254.
www.thepinkhouse.com.
26 James Ln., East Hampton, NY 11937.
Manager: Mercedes Dekkers.
Open: Year-round.
Price: Expensive–Very Expensive.

Credit Cards: AE, MC, V.
Special Features: Nonsmoking B&B;
  pool; full breakfast; air-conditioning;
  telephones with voice mail, cable TV;
  children over 5 welcome; no pets.
Directions: James Ln. parallels Main St.
  on opposite side of Town Pond.

This lovely, pink Victorian house, in a central in-town location, feels secluded and private. Perhaps it's the tall hedges that enclose it or that it's located next door to St. Luke's Rectory, but loud noises seldom seem to disturb the quiet. The broad porch, with its wicker furniture, is an inviting place to relax and admire the flower gardens. Inside, the living and dining rooms, which are low-key and traditional in decor, are spiced with interesting sculptures and paintings. Do take note of the lively watercolors painted by Walter Steinhilber, the former owner's grandfather — all colorful images of his journeys around the world. Also, note the lamp in the living room that was made from a street lamp rescued from Brooklyn's old Myrtle Avenue El as it was being demolished. A bountiful breakfast of Belgian waffles, banana-walnut pancakes, or frittatas, along with homemade granola, yogurt, fresh fruit, and juice, is served on the back porch in summer or in the formal dining room in winter. All five guest rooms are stunning, and they all have private baths. The Garden Room has a four-poster bed, a marvelous marble bath, and a private garden with a brick courtyard. The Elk Room on the top floor, however, is the most remarkable. It has beamed ceilings, a bed with a beautiful, red floral tapestry on the wall above, and a striking marble bath with a whirlpool tub and a dramatic view of St. Luke's church (and yes, there is an elk head on the wall). The pool in the back is a very private retreat, with comfortable lounges for sunning and tables for reading.

1770 HOUSE
631-324-1770.
www.1770house.com.
143 Main St., East Hampton, NY 11937.
Innkeepers: Wendy and Burton Van
  Deusen.
Open: Year-round.

Price: Moderate–Expensive.
Credit Cards: AE, MC, V.
Special Features: Nonsmoking inn; full
  breakfast; air-conditioning; telephones
  with voice mail; working fireplaces; no
  children under 12; no pets.
Directions: On Rte. 27 in center of village.

Although 1770 House has been graciously welcoming guests for over 200 years, it doesn't look its age thanks to the loving care of its current owners. Located in the heart of the original village, over the years it's served as a general

This elegant hand-carved bar graces the library/lounge of 1770 House, which also includes a handsome corner shell cabinet, beamed ceilings, and a fireplace in a paneled wall.

Morgan McGivern

store, a dining hall for Clinton Academy, a private home, and a public inn. When Sid and Mim Perle purchased the inn in 1977, they began a restoration that transformed the tired house into a fine country inn. Now run by their daughter and her husband, you'll find lovely antiques, oil paintings, and polished furniture throughout. All of the guest rooms have private baths. Room 2 is a large room with a paneled wall, canopied bed, and fireplace; Room 10 is even larger, with a fireplace, dressing room, and private entrance. The library, with another paneled wall, fireplace, and carved shell corner cupboard, is a cozy nook where one can contemplate dinner plans while sipping an aperitif. Breakfast may include fresh juice, challah French toast served with raspberry-melba sauce, or another of Wendy's creative dishes. Do go into the office before you leave to see the remnants of the East Hampton Post Office that Sid salvaged. The old brass window cages, glass headers, carved walnut front panels, and even the old mailboxes are all here.

SNUG COUNTRY COTTAGE
631-324-4920; fax: 631-324-5189.
156 Montauk Hwy., East Hampton.
Mailing Address: PO Box 606, East
    Hampton, NY 11937.
Innkeepers: J. Gerald Groppe and
    Robert L. Schider.
Open: Year-round.
Price: Expensive.

Credit Cards: AE, MC, V.
Special Features: Smoking permitted in
    common rooms only; full breakfast;
    air-conditioning; telephones; cable
    TV/VCR; pool; children welcome;
    no pets.
Directions: On Rte. 27, 1 mile west of
    traffic light at Town Pond.

Tucked away behind a high hedge, this little jewel box is a hidden secret. You will enter a tiled foyer that leads to a gracious living room with a handsome fireplace. The open kitchen, where a full breakfast of perhaps French toast or pancakes is prepared, is light and bright. Behind the house, there are colorful perennial gardens that surround a glistening pool. The three guest rooms are small but beautifully decorated in white wicker, and all have private baths that are fully tiled.

EASTPORT

A VICTORIAN ON THE BAY
631-325-1000; 888-449-0620;
  fax: 631-325-9659.
www.victorianonthebay.com.
E-mail: rbarone@hamptons.com.
57 South Bay Ave., Eastport, NY 11941.
Innkeepers: Rosemary and Fred Barone.
Open: Year-round.
Price: Moderate–Very Expensive.
Credit Cards: AE, MC, V.
Special Features: Nonsmoking B&B;
  water views; air-conditioning; cable
TV/VCR; telephones with dataports;
balconies; fireplaces; marina nearby;
exercise room; children over 12
welcome; no pets.
Directions: From Sunrise Hwy. (Rte.
27), take exit 61 onto Eastport Manor
Rd. (Rte. 55). Follow to end at Rte.
27A (Montauk Hwy.). Turn left (east)
onto Montauk Hwy. and drive .7
mile to South Bay Ave. Turn right
and follow almost to end to #57. B&B
is on right.

I'll never forget my amazement when I stumbled across this beautiful new (in 1998) Victorian B&B. It's located down a quiet seaside road in an unchic-Hampton town (but definitely in Southampton township). There are water views galore and a fine restaurant just down the street at water's edge. Rosemary and Fred Barone found this fabulous three-and-one-half-acre property and built their dream B&B to enhance it. You drive up a circular driveway and immediately want to linger on the broad, wraparound front porch. Tarry not, as what lies beyond is even better. A handsome living room, with fireplace, is decorated in soft yellows. There's a piano available for tickling the ivorys should you be so talented and shelves of books and videos for borrowing. The guest rooms, which are located on the second floor, all have distant water views and baths with whirlpool tubs. The Master Suite has a four-poster feather bed and a porch from which to enjoy the water view. Breakfasts are divine. You might indulge in challah French toast, plus Rosemary's Victorian Sweet Secret — shhhhh, we won't tell.

MONTAUK

GURNEY'S INN RESORT & SPA
631-668-2345; fax: 631-668-3576.
www.gurneysweb.com.
290 Old Montauk Hwy., Montauk, NY
  11954.
General Manager: Paul Monte.
Open: Year-round.
Price: Moderate–Very Expensive.
Credit Cards: AE, D, DC, MC, V.
Special Features: Spectacular ocean views;
  beach access; 10 landscaped acres; health
and beauty spa; indoor-heated seawater
pool; MAP only, breakfast and dinner
vouchers issued; 2 restaurants on
premises; air-conditioning; smoking
permitted in rooms; telephones with
voice mail; cable TV; conference
facilities; children welcome; no pets.
Directions: Located on Old Montauk
Hwy., about 10 miles east of Amagansett
and 2.5 miles west of Montauk.

Gurney's was the first spa on the East Coast, and it's been sitting on its bluff, overlooking the Atlantic Ocean, for more than seventy years. Taking advantage of its natural access to saltwater, this is the only spa on the North American continent to use marinotherapeutic treatments — the therapeutic use of seawater and seaweed. In addition to the spa treatments, there are numerous health and fitness activities, such as aerobic beach walks, tai chi, yoga, and a full range of exercise equipment, including a cardiovascular fitness circuit. The Sea Grill, an elegant restaurant serving three meals a day (including a slimming spa menu), has panoramic views of the ocean below. Caffe Monte offers a more casual dining experience, and it's open for breakfast, lunch, and dinner. Nightly entertainment includes tarot card readings, bridge, bingo, and karaoke. Because of its range of activities and size, Gurney's is popular for conventions and tour groups. Gurney's 109 guest rooms are eclectic in style, reflecting the varied tastes of the individual time-share co-op owners. Rooms in the Foredeck and Forward Watch buildings have private decks and unobstructed ocean views. Several beachside cottages have fireplaces, and one has a Jacuzzi. The most private cottage, Skipper's Cottage, sits on a bluff overlooking the ocean.

Montauk Manor was built in 1927 by Carl Fisher, the developer of Miami Beach, as part of his grand plan to turn Montauk into the Miami of the North.

Morgan McGivern

MONTAUK MANOR
631-668-4400; fax: 631-668-3535.
www.montaukmanor.com.
236 Edgemere St., Montauk.
Mailing Address: RD #2, Box 226C,
   Montauk, NY 11954.
Manager: Janice Nessel.
Open: Year-round.
Price: Inexpensive–Very Expensive.
Credit Cards: AE, D, MC, V.
Special Features: Wheelchair access;
   designated nonsmoking rooms;
   indoor and outdoor pools; cable
TV/VCR; air-conditioning;
telephones with voice mail; kitchens;
doorman; maid service; health club
with Jacuzzi and saunas; conference
facilities; seasonal van service; 3
tennis courts; exercise room; indoor
squash court; restaurant on premises:
B, L, D in summer; BR Sat., Sun., L
Sat., Sun., D Fri.–Sun. rest of year.
Directions: From Main St., travel north
   on Edgemere St. and follow signs to
   resort. Resort is up hill on right.

Montauk Manor was built by Carl Fisher, the developer of Miami Beach, in 1927 as part of his grand plan to turn Montauk into the Miami of the North. It's an imposing building that resembles a feudal English Tudor castle, and it sits high on Montauk's highest hill — it's on the National Register of Historic Places. It boasts spectacular views of the harbor, where Fisher planned to build grand docks for the ocean liners that were to depart and arrive from Europe. None of that came to pass, however, and for years the hotel sat idle. In 1987, it was converted to 140 co-op apartments (seventy are rented on a transient basis) that range in size from studios to three-bedroom units. Half of the units have balconies, and most have views. The lobby, soaring three stories high, has multiple massive fireplaces along its tiled corridor. The rooms are well designed and tasteful, each with a modern kitchen and tile bath. If you are lucky enough to rent unit 135, you'll find the arched fireplace that once graced the dining room, a sofa bed in the living room, a loft bedroom, and an arched doorway framing French doors to a mammoth terrace; mirrored walls in the dining and living rooms expand the space.

**MONTAUK YACHT CLUB RESORT
& MARINA**
631-668-3100; fax: 631-668-3303.
www.montaukyachtclub.com.
32 Star Island Rd., Montauk.
Mailing Address: PO Box 5048,
  Montauk, NY 11954.
Manager: Phillipe Fontanelli.
Open: Apr.–Nov.
Price: Moderate–Very Expensive.
Credit Cards: AE, DC, MC, V.
Special Features: Wheelchair access;
  designated nonsmoking rooms;
waterfront; outdoor and indoor
pools; tennis courts; resident pro;
health club; marina; 2 restaurants on
premises; lounge; cable TV; air-
conditioning; telephones with voice
mail and dataports; conference
facilities; children welcome; no pets.
Directions: Travel east on Montauk
Hwy., continuing through Montauk.
Turn left onto West Lake Dr. Travel
1.8 miles and turn right onto Star
Island Causeway. Yacht Club is on
right in about 1/4 mile.

The Montauk Yacht Club Resort & Marina underwent a multimillion dollar renovation in 1998 that transformed it from a struggling bank-owned property to the luxury resort that it used to be. This one-stop retreat offers complete lodging, restaurant, and recreational facilities for the entire family. Each of the 107 guest rooms has been attractively upgraded with light colors against a background of beige and white. They are equipped with contemporary furniture. Some of the rooms have water views, and all feature telephones with voice mail and dataports, hair dryers, and coffeemakers. The rooms in the former Florenz Ziegfield estate, located a short drive away at the end of the street, have individual charm. Built in the 1920s, the twenty-three "villas" have interesting little alcoves with pretty patios, and some feature fireplaces. The Lighthouse Grill is a fine restaurant offering dining with views of the bay and entertainment on weekends. Breezes Café, which is open for breakfast and lunch only, has a casual, comfortable ambience.

PERI'S BED & BREAKFAST
631-668-1394; fax: 631-668-6096.
www.perisb-bmontauk.com.
206 Essex St., Montauk, NY 11954.
Owner: Peri Aronian.
Open: Year-round.

Price: Inexpensive–Very Expensive.
Credit Cards: MC (3% surcharge), V.
Special Features: Nonsmoking B&B; full
breakfast; afternoon wine and hors d'oeuvres; gardens; children welcome during
week; children over 12 only on weekends.

You understand that a creative talent with an artist's eye is at home at Peri's the minute you walk in the door. Peri Aronian used to be a New York fashion designer. Now she has transformed this beautiful Carl Fisher Tudor house of stucco and half-timbers into a fabulous B&B that's full of elegant furnishings laced with playful whimsy. The living room, for example, has a gorgeous, carved, wooden fireplace mantel and polished oak floors topped with an Oriental rug. The three bedrooms transport their occupants to Peri's favorite travel destinations. Marais, which inspires dreams of Paris, has lime green walls, oak floors, a beautiful French marble-topped dresser, and a French bed; there's also a lovely black-and-white tile bath and a little private balcony with a spiral stairway that leads to a terrace and the gardens. Peri's home had at one time been owned by Henri Soulé, the famed proprietor of New York's Le Pavillion restaurant. One imagines gracious dinner parties in the huge billiard room, which has French doors leading to a flagstone patio. Peri recreates that same Hamptons' weekend gustatorial experience with her gourmet breakfasts (served either in the burgundy red dining room or out on the terrace at the splendid, long refectory table) and afternoon get-togethers for wine and hors d'oeuvres. For utter relaxation, however, guests may partake of a soothing massage or facial al fresco or in the privacy of the quiet treatment room, or they can romp in the yard with Cyrus, her Rhodesian ridgeback, a huge, gentle, friendly dog.

THE SURF CLUB
631-668-3800; 800-LASTWAVE;
fax: 631-668-9296.
www.duneresorts.com.
Surfside Ave. and South Essex St.,
Montauk.
Mailing Address: PO Box 1174, Montauk,
NY 11954.
Manager: Maria Del Vecchio, Dune Resorts.
Open: Mid-Apr.–mid-Nov.

Price: Inexpensive–Very Expensive.
Credit Cards: None.
Special Features: Limited wheelchair access;
on ocean; smoking permitted in rooms;
air-conditioning; telephones with voice
mail; cable TV; tennis courts; pool;
kitchens; daily maid service; steam baths;
workout room; children welcome; no pets.
Directions: From Montauk's Main St., turn
south onto Essex St. Resort is at end.

This luxurious, gray-shingled, oceanfront resort, with its 500 feet of private beach, is the classiest resort in Montauk. It has ninety-two one- and two-bedroom units, each with a modern kitchen, living and dining area, and private terrace for sunbathing; the units in the oceanfront buildings have spectacular views. The resort is located on eight acres that include a pool with brick terraces and wraparound wooden decks, two tennis courts, and landscaped grounds. Most of the units feature a second-story bedroom with a color television in both the living room and bedroom. The decor in the units is attractive and contemporary.

QUOGUE

THE INN AT QUOGUE
631-653-6560; fax: 631-653-8026.
www.innatquogue.com.
E-mail: inn@quogue.com.
47-52 Quogue St., Quogue.
Mailing Address: PO Box 521, Quogue,
　NY 11959.
Manager: Elizabeth Murray.
Open: Year-round.
Price: Moderate–Very Expensive.
Credit Cards: AE, MC, V.
Special Features: Limited wheelchair
　access; smoking permitted in guest
rooms; 5 landscaped acres;
continental breakfast in summer;
pool; spa offering facials, massages,
manicures, body wraps; some units
with kitchens; fine restaurant on
premises; bicycles and beach passes
available; children and pets welcome
in "cottages," but not in main houses.
Directions: From Sunrise Hwy. (Rte.
27), travel south at exit 63 (Rte. 31) to
Montauk Hwy. (Rte. 27A), then east
to Quogue St. Turn right on Quogue
St. Inn is on right in 1/2 mile.

Quogue is known as the "quiet Hampton," and it's so quiet that many don't consider it a Hampton at all. It's a jewel of a village, composed mostly of gracious old homes on lovely, wide, tree-lined streets. Ideal for walks and bicycling excursions, the streets are wide and flat; there's a bicycle path along Dune Rd. to the beach. The main building of The Inn at Quogue dates from the early 1800s, but following the multimillion-dollar renovation that began in 1999 and continued through 2000, you'd be hard pressed to find anything old about it. All seventy rooms have been renovated and are now bright and beautiful. Even the former motel rooms have tile baths, pedestal sinks, wainscotted walls, and handsome linens on the beds. My favorite rooms are still those in the main house; they have interesting little nooks and crannies. Room 14 has been decorated in a subdued Ralph Lauren-style and has antique painted chests and tables, fireplace, and bath with wainscotted walls and whirlpool tub. I also love the one-bedroom cottage, which has a small kitchen, blue-and-white furniture, and private garden in back. There is a nice pool, and guests may use the Quogue village beach and a nearby tennis club. The inn has an attractive restaurant and an inviting bar with a fireplace, where a pianist often performs on weekends. This inn has long been one of my favorites. Hurray for the renovation! It can now be heartily recommended again as an ideal place to truly "get away."

SAG HARBOR

AMERICAN HOTEL
631-725-3535; fax: 631-725-3573.
www.theamericanhotel.com.
25 Main St., Sag Harbor.
Mailing Address: PO Box 1349, Sag
　Harbor, NY 11963.
nnkeeper: Ted Conklin.
Open: Year-round.
Price: Moderate–Very Expensive.
Credit Cards: AE, CB, D, DC, MC, V.
Special Features: Smoking permitted;
　continental breakfast; whirlpool tubs;
　Itelephones; fine restaurant on
　premises; children welcome, but
　rooms accommodate 2 people only;
　no pets.
Directions: On Main St. in center of
　village.

The American Hotel in Sag Harbor has been welcoming guests since 1877.

Morgan McGivern

The American Hotel, that great, early-Victorian brick edifice on Sag Harbor's Main St., dates back to 1845 when Nathan Tinker, a cabinetmaker, built it to house his cabinet shop. As an adjunct to the shops on the ground floor, he built apartments above. In 1877, the building was converted to a hotel by Addison Youngs, and with the addition of steam heat, baths, and electric lights, it became one of the most modern hotels on Long Island. Owned by Ted Conklin for almost thirty years, this gem of a hotel retains all of the charm of a fine Victorian inn. The tiny parlor has games of backgammon and checkers awaiting players, and the glass-topped reservation counter displays a selection of fine cigars. The restaurant, considered by many to be the best classical restaurant in the Hamptons is contained in four main-floor rooms. There are eight spacious and highly distinctive guest rooms in the hotel — all have tall ceilings and are decorated with Victorian and art deco antiques that exude a faded men's club gentility. There are overstuffed chairs, massive dressers with ornate mirrors, worn antique Oriental rugs, mahogany sleigh beds, carved, Victorian walnut headboards, and brass beds. There's also an antique Victorian table set with cordials, liquors, and crystal glasses, and accent pieces might include an old manual typewriter or radio. All of the baths are private, and each has a tile floor, a Jacuzzi for two, and an impressive array of soaps, shampoos, and lotions.

LIGHTHOUSE ON THE BAY
631-725-7112; fax: 631-725-7112.
Mashomack Dr., Sag Harbor, NY 11963.
Innkeepers: Regina and Stephen Humanitzki.
Open: Year-round.
Price: Expensive–Very Expensive.
Credit Cards: None.
Special Features: Nonsmoking inn; full breakfast; water and marsh views; private beach reached by boardwalk; spacious decks; air-conditioning; robes in rooms; complimentary beach towels and chairs; children over 8 welcome; no pets.
Directions: Provided when reservations made.

If you are seeking a wonderfully romantic night in a magical setting, I can't imagine a better place than Lighthouse on the Bay. The panoramic views are positively breathtaking from the living room, dining area, and wraparound decks, as well as from the guest rooms. On one early summer afternoon, I was able to spy on a pair of swans sitting on their nests in their close-up marshy habitat. The house was built by Regina and Stephen Humanitzki in 1997 to resemble a lighthouse (or, more accurately, two lighthouses joined together). "When we bought this property, we had fallen in love with the land and intended renovating a house on the property, but we decided instead to tear it down and start over." The result is a contemporary house sheathed in natural shingles and on a stone foundation, with flagstone floors, walls of floor-to-ceiling windows, and expansive decks. The Tower Suite, on the second floor, is the premier guest haven. This six-sided room has a fabulous view from the bedroom, but the clincher is the observation room reached via a spiral stairway that has a 360-degree water view. There are comfortable sofas up here as well as a TV. The Queen Room, on the first floor, has a pine sleigh bed. My favorite bedroom, however, is the Round Room; it has a round tower of clerestory windows, an expansive view, private deck (also with a view), and a wonderful tile bath with a Jacuzzi enclosed in a mahogany cabinet and a granite surround, and the iron canopy bed is draped in gauzy fabric. Regina, who loves to cook, serves a full breakfast that might include fresh fruit, home-baked muffins or bread, and maybe a cheese soufflé or her special French toast.

SOUTHAMPTON

EVERGREEN ON PINE
631-283-0564.
www.evergreenonpine.com
89 Pine St., Southampton, NY 11968.
Innkeepers: JoAnn and Peter Rogoski.
Open: Year-round.
Price: Expensive–Very Expensive.
Credit Cards: D, DC, MC, V.

Special Features: Smoking outside only; continental breakfast; children over 12 welcome; no pets.
Directions: From Main St., travel east on Meeting House Ln. B&B is on corner of Meeting House Ln. and Pine St.

Were I to come to the Hamptons on business, I would choose to stay at Evergreen On Pine. Not only would I have an attractive room with my own bath, but also I would have my own telephone, complete with a dataport and modem so I could connect my PC. Best of all, I could step right outside my door and walk to the fantastic shops on Main St. and Job's Ln. or to a sophisticated restaurant. This glistening white house is entered from the sidewalk through an arched privet hedge. Flowers spill from borders along the walkway leading to the broad porch, which has wicker chairs and tables. Inside this center-hall colonial, there are oak floors and a fireplace in the dining/living area. The five bedrooms, each with its own private bath (two are in hallways), are nicely decorated. One has a brass bed, another has a canopy bed, and a third has a mahogany four-poster bed. Elegant, white metal furniture with umbrellas

Evergreen On Pine in Southampton is filled with lovely antiques. Breakfast is served in this elegant dining room.

Morgan McGivern

are placed on a brick side terrace, a sought after spot for breakfast and for afternoon relaxation.

THE IVY
631-283-3233; fax: 631-283-3793.
www.theivy.com.
244 North Main St., Southampton, NY 11968.
Innkeepers: Melody Kniley and Phil Tierney.
Open: Year-round.
Price: Expensive–Very Expensive.

Credit Cards: AE, MC, V.
Special Features: On almost 1 acre; pool; gardens; full breakfast; smoking outside only; children over 12 welcome; no pets.
Directions: From County Rd. 59/Rte. 27 traveling east, turn right at traffic light onto North Main St. B&B is seventh house on left.

The Ivy has a wonderfully romantic story to tell. Thirty years ago Melody Kniley was dating Phil Tierney when he was sent to Vietnam, and his letters were still neatly bundled in a box when they were reacquainted at their thirtieth high school reunion. Although he had just moved to Arizona and Melody lived in New York, neither of them wanted to be GU (geographically undesirable) to one another. So, Melody gave up her career in the fashion industry, and Phil sold his home in Arizona. They bought a pretty shingled house on a street not far from Southampton's train station and wove their lives together. As Melody said, "We often sit out on the terrace, [which is covered by a latticed arbor, trailing wisteria and clematis] with a cup of coffee in the morning, admiring the flowers and trees in the garden, and laugh out loud at how lucky we are." But so are guests at this very special B&B. You will enter a spacious, brick-floored living room with butter yellow barnwood walls and white trim. A pretty fireplace is flanked by sofas dressed with yellow floral Ralph Lauren fabric. There's a huge pine breakfront in the living room and another in the dining room, which has raspberry red walls. The five guest rooms, which all have private baths, are charming. Room 3 has yellow walls, a four-poster rice bed, and a terrific tiled bath with a skylight. In Room 2, which has a cathedral ceiling, black-and-white toile fabric is combined with a dramatic striped fabric on the polished steel canopy bed, and a tiled bath has exposed beams. The gardens and lawn are spacious and very private, and in a raised secluded spot, there's a pool, with a brick apron hidden behind a latticework fence, reached by climbing several grass-clad stone stairs.

MAINSTAY INN
631-283-4375; fax: 631-287-6240.
www.hamptons.com/mainstay.
E-mail: elizmain@hamptons.com.
579 Hill St., Southampton, NY 11968.
Innkeeper: Elizabeth Main.
Open: Year-round.
Price: Moderate–Very Expensive.

Credit Cards: AE, MC, V.
Special Features: Smoking outside only; continental breakfast; pool; gardens; behaved children welcome; no pets.
Directions: Located about 1 mile west of Southampton on Rte. 27A (Old Montauk Hwy.) and Hill St.

Elizabeth Main is always doing something new and wonderful to her inn. This 1870s colonial had good "bones" to begin with, with a weathered shingle exterior and white trim. The building began life as a country store. The whimsy of the decor is evident as you enter the foyer, which is sponge-painted in a spring green. The adjacent parlor has dried flowers over the door, a bead board ceiling, and a fireplace. In the kitchen, which is open to guests, a marvelous mural of English climbing roses covers a wall, while in the country dining room, there are sponge-painted ochre walls fancifully painted with grapes, apples, and pears. This room also has wainscotted walls and a great, old woodstove. A country pine cupboard displays a collection of colorful pottery made by Elizabeth that is used for the breakfast meal. Each of the guest rooms is furnished with either an iron or a country pine bed, and all are for sale. Of the eight rooms, five have private baths, and three share a bath. Room 5 has a fireplace and a wall of books, while Room 6 has painted hydrangeas climbing the walls in such profusion that the iron and brass bed seems to be in a garden. Room 8 is the newest room; it is a two-room suite and has a bath with wainscotted walls and a slanted ceiling. In the gardens, iron and wicker furniture provide additional retreats for private breakfasts or afternoon refreshments. There's a secluded pool in the back.

1708 HOUSE
631-287-1708; fax: 631-287-3583.
www.1708house.com.
126 Main St., Southampton, NY 11968.
Innkeepers: Skip and Lorraine Ralph.
Managers: Peter Rever and Bernadette Meade.
Open: Year-round.
Price: Very Expensive.

Credit Cards: AE, MC, V.
Special Features: Smoking outside only; wine cellar; on 1 acre; continental breakfast; beach passes provided; children over 12 welcome in main house, under 12 in cottages only; no pets.
Directions: On Main St., just beyond Saks Fifth Avenue.

In the heart of Southampton, next door to Saks Fifth Avenue, parts of the 1708 House date to 1648.

Morgan McGivern

I love to see an old building brought back to life. Skeptics had advocated tearing the old house down, but fortunately, Skip and Lorraine Ralph had a better idea. They transformed it into Southampton's finest bed-and-breakfast. From top to bottom, this inn shines. The house dates to 1648, one of the oldest in Southampton, and remarkably, it has only been in three families during that time. In the parlor, there are polished pine floors, exposed hand-hewn oak beams, and a wood-manteled fireplace. The elegant antique tables and chairs were supplied from the couple's antique shop around the corner and are for sale. An adjoining parlor, with tables that are used for card games in the evening and for breakfast in the morning, has a fireplace and the original paneled walls. Downstairs, there's a brick room where wine and cheese are served as classical music plays in the background. Each of the nine guest rooms and three cottages is spacious and luxurious. The South Wing is on two levels and has a huge private deck. Suite 2 has fabulous antique beds, an armoire, bead board walls, and pine floor. There are two two-bedroom cottages, each with an eat-in kitchen, and there's a cabana cottage in the back. Gracious flower gardens surround spacious lawns. For breakfast, guests enjoy fresh fruit, juice, croissants, bagels, and perhaps quiche.

SOUTHAMPTON COUNTRY HOUSE
631-283-7338.
485 North Main St., Southampton, NY 11968.
Innkeeper: Colleen D'Italia.
Open: May–Aug.: daily; Sept., Oct.: weekends; call for availability rest of year.
Price: Expensive–Very Expensive.

Credit Cards: None.
Special Features: Smoking outside only; full breakfast; pool; air-conditioning; children over 12 welcome; no pets.
Directions: From Rte. 27/County Rd. 39 traveling east, turn north onto North Main St. at traffic light. B&B is on left in .75 mile, just past horse farm.

I t's as if Martha, Ralph, and Laura came to play. From the wraparound porch, you can sit in the pretty wicker chairs or laze away in the hammock, while gazing out at pastures of grazing horses, enclosed by neat, white fences. This country-style, classic Hamptons shingled "cottage" has all the appealing aspects you generally find in larger B&Bs. You enter a beautiful family room/open kitchen with a pretty window seat dressed in a red-and-white checked cushion and with a huge brick fireplace. There's a wonderful collection of flag-related items — birdhouses, painted wooden flags, and more. Beyond, a pool with a brick surround beckons. The King Room has a blue-and-white quilt and is decorated with white wicker; its beautiful black-and-white tile bath has a black marble counter. An entire apartment is the perfect Hamptons' hideaway for a family or two couples traveling together. It has a living room, two bedrooms, kitchen, and full-tiled bath. Colleen serves a full country breakfast that might include French toast, pancakes, or an egg dish.

SOUTHAMPTON INN
631-283-6500; 800-832-6500;
  fax: 631-283-6559.
www.southamptoninn.com.
91 Hill St., Southampton, NY 11968.
General Manager: Barry M. Shatoff.
Open: Year-round.
Price: Moderate–Very Expensive.
Credit Cards: AE, D, DC, MC, V.
Special Features: Designated nonsmoking rooms; continental breakfast (full breakfast available at addl. charge); air-conditioning; telephones with voice mail and dataports; cable TV; refrigerators; conference facilities; café serving breakfast and lunch; tennis; croquet; pool; game room with pool table and children's play area; seasonal shuttle to beach; children and pets welcome.
Directions: From Main St., turn west onto Job's Ln. Drive through traffic light, street becomes Hill St. Turn right at first intersection. Hotel is on left.

If you are coming to the Hamptons for a meeting, this would be a terrific spot. Following a total renovation, the Southampton Inn (really a ninety-room hotel) is looking better than ever. One enters an elegant lobby and reception area. Beyond, there's a spacious Great Room with a domed ceiling, gas fireplace, and shelves of books for borrowing. It's decorated with classy beige carpeting, sofas, and chairs. French doors open to reveal a grand deck offering views of the abundant flower gardens and lawns. The generous guest rooms have all been updated as well, and the baths are sparkling with black-and-white tile floors and pedestal sinks. Room 18 was designed by Paloma Picasso; it has beige walls, a pine armoire, and terrific artwork on the walls and bedcoverings. The lower level of the hotel contains extensive meeting facilities, as well as a café.

WESTHAMPTON

WESTHAMPTON COUNTRY MANOR
631-288-9000; fax: 631-288-3292.
www.hamptonsbb.com.
E-mail: innkeepers@ hamptonsbb.com.
28 Jagger Ln., Westhampton, NY 11977.
Innkeepers: Susan and Bill Dalton.
Open: Year-round.
Price: Inexpensive–Very Expensive.
Credit Cards: AE, MC, V.
Special Features: Smoking outside only; on 2.5 acres; full breakfast; afternoon cordials; pool; business amenities; telephones with answering machines; children over 14 welcome; no pets.

Westhampton Country Manor, which is located on a quiet country road, has a pool and spacious guest rooms.

Suzi Forbes Chase

Directions: Located bet. Westhampton Beach and Remsenburg. From Montauk Hwy. (Rte. 27A), travel south on Tanners Neck Rd. to South Country Rd. Turn right. Inn is on corner of South Country Rd. and Jagger Ln.

When Bill and Susan Dalton decided to "retire," they began their search for an ideal bed-and-breakfast. They found a beauty in this historic 1865 house. Originally a stagecoach stop, then a doctor's home and office, and eventually a boardinghouse, today the old house serves a much more sophisticated clientele. There's just about any amenity a business traveler might want, including a PC, fax machine, on-line connection, laser printer, copier, and desk. The location is as quiet as country can get and well off the beaten track. This buff-colored colonial with front dormers sits on two and one-half acres that include a cottage near the road and a picturesque green barn. A swimming pool is surrounded by a picket fence, and a Har-tru tennis court is nearby. The house itself is spacious and welcoming; there is a generous living room with a handsome fireplace and a concert grand piano. Cordials and stemmed crystal glasses sit on a silver tray, waiting for guests to imbibe. To the side, a screened-in porch, filled with wicker furniture and an abundance of plants, beckons guests in the summer. The dining room, with its stained glass lamp and huge round table, is where the gourmet breakfast is served, except in summer when it's frequently served on the patio. Beside the dining room, a comfortable and homey room has been set aside for TV watching and games. There are five guest rooms in the main house, and all have lovely, fully tiled private baths. You will find iron beds, a room with a spool bed, and pretty quilts covering them. In addition, there's a wonderful, shingled Guest House that will accommodate up to six people. It has three spacious bedrooms, one bath, and a living room with a fireplace. An attached charming Honeymoon Suite has a private entrance, abedroom with a king-sized bed, a fireplace, and a bath with whirlpool tub.

OTHER ACCOMMODATIONS

There are so many inns, B&Bs, cabins, motels, and resorts in the Hamptons that it was impossible to describe them all. The codes, following the accepted credit cards for each listing, indicate whether it is a bed-and-breakfast (B), a series of cabins (C), a motel (M), or a full-service resort (R).

AMAGANSETT

White Sands Motel On The Ocean (631-267-3350; 28 Shore Rd., PO Box 747, Amagansett, NY 11930) Owners: Bernhard Kiembock and Sara Menboza; Price: Moderate–Very Expensive; Open: Mid-Apr.–mid-Oct.; 20 units; on ocean; private location; spotlessly maintained; outdoor grill area; family operated; children welcome; no pets; *highly recommended*; MC, V; (M).

EAST HAMPTON

Eastern Star (800-445-5942; www.easternstarcruises.com; E-mail: info@eastern starcruises.com; Gardiner's Marina, Three Mile Harbor, East Hampton, NY 11937) This sleek 85-foot yacht operates as a cruising country inn in the Hamptons during the summer months. It can accommodate up to 12 passengers, who might book a stateroom for a cruise to coastal Connecticut towns, or if the ship is scheduled to remain in port, they can simply book a stateroom and stay overnight. Either way, they'll be royally treated to gourmet meals, prepared by a chef who graduated from the French Culinary Institute, and can lounge in an elegant salon of mahogany, brass, and even a fireplace; (B).

HAMPTON BAYS

Bowen's By The Bays (631-728-1158; 177 West Montauk Hwy., Hampton Bays, NY 11946) Owners/Managers: Kevin and Eileen Bowen; Price: Inexpensive–Very Expensive; Open: Apr.–Oct.; 16 units (8 motel rooms; cottages with 1–2 bedrooms); on 3.5 acres; pool; lighted tennis court; playground; kitchens; cable TV; air-conditioning; shuffleboard; AE, D, MC, V; (C) (M).

The Hampton Maid (631-728-4166; 295 Montauk Hwy., PO Box 713, Hampton Bays, NY 11946) Managers: Marion and John Poulakis; Price: Inexpensive–Moderate; Open: May–Oct.; 30 units; pool; antique shop; cable TV; air-conditioning; telephones; restaurant (breakfast only); AE, MC, V; (M).

MONTAUK

Lenhart Cottages (631-668-2356; www.montauklife.com; 421 Old Montauk Hwy., Montauk, NY 11954) Manager: Charles Pilch; Price: Moderate–Very Expensive; Open: Year-round; 12 individual cottages, ranging from studios to two-bedroom units; shingled exterior; ocean view; log-burning fireplaces; kitchens; pool; cable TV; air-conditioning; highly recommended; MC, V; (C).

Snug Harbor Motel and Marina (631-668-2860; fax: 631-668-9068; www. peconic.net/snugharbor; 156 West Lake Dr., Montauk, NY 11954) Manager: Cynthia Brauch; Price: Inexpensive–Expensive; Open: Mar.–Thanksgiving; 34 units, ranging from studios to one-bedroom apartments; on lake; some kitchens; pool; marina; playground; bicycles; outdoor grill area; waterskiing; telephones; cable TV; air-conditioning; AE, MC, V; (M).

SAG HARBOR

Sag Harbor Inn (631-725-2949; fax: 631-725-5009; West Water St., PO Box 2661, Sag Harbor, NY 11963) Manager: Diane Weber; Price: Moderate–Very Expensive; Open: Year-round; 42 units in a hotel-style building, most with balconies or patios and some overlooking the bay and furnished with repro-duction eighteenth-century pine beds; telephones; nonsmoking; continental breakfast; pool; air-conditioning; children welcome; no pets; AE, MC, V; (M).

SOUTHAMPTON

The Atlantic (631-287-0908; 877-UTOPIA8; www.utopiainns.com; 1655 County Rd. 39, Southampton, NY 11968) Manager: Remco Loevendie; Price: Moderate–Expensive; Open: Year-round; Following a total renovation of a formerly tired motel, this 62-unit (plus 5 suites) inn can now be *highly recom-mended*. There are new tile baths, iron beds, fine linens, and plenty of space. Each unit has a mini bar, hair dryer, iron and ironing board, and much more. On 5 acres of landscaped grounds, there are a pool and gazebo, 2 Har-tru tennis courts, and hammocks; AE, MC, V; (M).

WAINSCOTT

Cozy Cabins (631-537-1160; Montauk Hwy., PO Box 848, Wainscott, NY 11975) Owner: Dennis Lazicki; Price: Inexpensive–Moderate; Open: Mid-Apr.–mid-Nov.; 22 cabins, ranging from studios to one-bedroom units; some fireplaces; kitchens; hot tub; shuffleboard; outdoor grill; *excellent value*; MC, V; (C).

WATER MILL

The Inn at Box Farm (631-726-9507; fax: 631-726-5074; www.boxfarm.com; 78 Mecox Rd., Water Mill, NY 11976) Owner: Michael Barrett; Price: Very Expensive; Open: Year-round; Although the common rooms of this historic B&B are utterly charming, with their wide-plank pine floors and beautiful fireplaces, the baths still need some attention (several are not en suite), and the property borders Montauk Hwy., so the front rooms are noisy. Two of the rooms, however, have fireplaces, and the grounds are spacious; MC, V; (B).

CHAPTER FOUR
From the Bounty of the Land
RESTAURANTS & FOOD PURVEYORS

When the renowned Manhattan restaurateur, Henri Soulé, opened his summer restaurant in the village of East Hampton in 1954, he launched a trend. Lured by the abundance of farm fresh vegetables and fruit, fish from local waters, and duck from nearby duck farms, he created a respect and appreciation for local cuisine that has increased every year. Not only did he attract gourmet diners who couldn't abide a summer away from the elegant cuisine that he had made famous at Le Pavillion, but he also attracted other fine chefs to the Hamptons. Pierre Franey, his executive chef in New York, came to the Hamptons. Craig Claiborne, food editor for the *New York Times*, and chef and author Michael Field soon came as well. Soulé had struck a nerve. Where fish houses on the docks had once prevailed, appreciation for the finer nuances of food preparation was gaining ground.

Morgan McGivern

Fresh produce, freshly baked breads, entrées, desserts, and friendly service are among the specialties at the Barefoot Contessa.

Today, Henri Soulé would be proud of Hamptons' chefs and the cuisine they are creating; the dishes are inventive, well presented, and, in general, prepared in healthful ways. Butter and cream-based sauces have been replaced by those made of vegetable reductions. Fresh local seafood and produce, the pride of the Hamptons, are used cleverly and well.

Henri Soulé's original restaurant is now The James Lane Cafe at The Hedges Inn, and it's still noted for its cuisine. The Maidstone Arms, located down the street, is also still recognized for its terrific food. In addition, a remnant from the old East End whaling days, the venerable 1846 American Hotel in Sag Harbor, is known nationally for its food and wine.

Italian restaurants seem to be the most popular today with French restaurants coming in a distant second. Naturally, fine seafood restaurants are also in abundance, and American cuisine, served in bistro settings, is also popular. Fish houses on the docks of Montauk allow diners to watch as the catch of the day is transferred from boat to dock to table, and the spectacular sunsets from East Hampton Point are renowned. The decor of choice, however, seems to be a blend of Santa Fe, California, and Italy, with spare furnishings, tile floors, and whitewashed walls that blend together to create a distinctive Hamptons' chic.

This chapter is not intended to be a critical review of all of the restaurants in the Hamptons. If a restaurant does not meet the criteria that would allow its recommendation, it has not been included. Furthermore, there are so many fine restaurants in the Hamptons that space precludes including every single one. Instead, I have incorporated only those that I believe are the very best. I welcome your comments, however.

When deciding which restaurants to include, I consider the same criteria as I use for the *ZagatSurvey* — food, decor, and service. The excellence of the food and the expertise of the chef in preparing and presenting the food are certainly key factors. But the overall comfort level and inviting appeal of a restaurant are equally important, as are the service and attitude of the staff. Especially in better restaurants, it is imperative that the staff know which ingredients are used in a dish and understand its preparation. It is also important — especially on Long Island's East End where wine has assumed such a prominent role — to have knowledgeable staff who can make specific wine recommendations and who appreciate the pairing of wines with specific appetizers, entrées, and desserts.

A concerted effort has also been made to include the best cafés and budget-priced restaurants. It is my intention to profile the restaurants that offer the best dining experiences in the Hamptons in a broad range of price categories.

As much information as possible about each restaurant has been included. Rather than indicating the exact hours that each restaurant is open, I have specified the meals that are served. In the block of information included with each description, abbreviations are used for any accepted credit cards. In addition, price codes, rather than specific prices, are indicated. These codes are based on the average cost of a meal for one person, including appetizer, entrée, and dessert, but not cocktails, wine, tax, or tip. Many Hamptons' restaurants offer prix fixe menus at exceptionally low prices off-season. This is a great way to eat out without breaking the bank. Be aware that days and hours of operation change with the season. It's always best to call ahead.

The restaurants are listed alphabetically according to the village where they are located. If you are not sure in which town a restaurant is located, please refer to the index in the back of the book. Restaurants on the North Fork and on Shelter Island are included in those specific chapters.

Serving Codes

B	Breakfast	HT	High Tea
BR	Brunch	D	Dinner
L	Lunch	LN	Late Night

Credit Cards

AE	American Express	DC	Diner's Club
CB	Carte Blanche	MC	MasterCard
D	Discover	V	Visa

Price Codes

Inexpensive	Up to $25	Expensive	$35–$50
Moderate	$25–$35	Very Expensive	$50 or more

RESTAURANTS

Strange to see how a good dinner and feasting reconciles everybody.

Samuel Pepys, *Diary*, November 9, 1660

AMAGANSETT

ESTIA
631-267-6320.
177 Main St., Amagansett.
Mailing Address: PO Box 4126,
 Amagansett, NY 11930.
Owner/Chef: Colin Ambrose.
Cuisine: American.

Serving: B, L, D.
Open: Year-round: B, L daily; June–Aug.:
 D daily; Sept.–May: D Thurs.–Sun.
Price: Inexpensive– Moderate; prix fixe
 offered.
Credit Cards: MC, V.
Directions: On Rte. 27 in center of village.

Alec Baldwin says this original Amagansett down-home, all-American place is his favorite restaurant. The rest of us also love its straightforward, honest food — and now there are two. Estia's Little Kitchen (631-725-1045; 1615 Sag Harbor Tpke., Sag Harbor, NY 11963; open daily B, L; D Wed.–Sun. in summer) is in a tiny building on the turnpike connecting Sag Harbor to Bridgehampton. For breakfast, there are lots of omelettes prepared as you like them and "tortilla starts," such as a breakfast burrito or a white vegetable quesadilla. Naturally, you can also get bagels, muffins, or freshly made oatmeal. Dinner features owner/chef Colin Ambrose's appetizers of Turtle Rolls (it's a secret), as well as fresh, homemade pasta dishes that include a longtime favorite called Sophia's Choice (a Mediterranean-style dish with tomato sauce, olives, and feta). The wine list includes about thirty selections. The ambiance is that of a 1950s

American diner with booths upholstered in watermelon-colored vinyl, pine tables, knotty pine walls, paper place mats, and stools at the long counter.

George Polychronopoulos has been creating some of the Hampton's finest cuisine for 25 years.

Morgan McGivern

GORDON'S
631-267-3010.
231 Main St., Amagansett.
Mailing Address: PO Box 91, Amagansett, NY 11930.
Owner/Chef: George Polychronopoulos.
Cuisine: Continental.
Serving: L, D.
Open: Mar.–Jan.: D Tues.–Sun.in summer; fewer days rest of year; L Tues.–Fri. except closed for L Mem. Day–Labor Day; closed Feb.;
Price: Expensive–Very Expensive; prix fixe offered.
Credit Cards: AE, DC, MC, V.
Special Features: Wheelchair access.
Directions: On Rte. 27.

Gordon's is one of the most personal, hands-on restaurants in the Hamptons. Locals, who have been coming here for years, know it's also one of the best, but it's not on the trendsetter's prowl. It's the creation and passion of owner/chef George Polychronopoulos who has been doing what he does so well for more than twenty-five years. As George said, "We're not trendy. I just want to prepare good food that people will enjoy." Listen to the nightly specials and follow the advice of the knowledgeable waiters, who still wear tuxedos, just as they did in the 1960s. Fishermen, baymen, and farmers deliver their best to the kitchen door everyday. One night in the early fall, we had a dish of Peconic bay scallops that were absolutely ambrosial — fresh, tender, and lightly broiled with butter and lemon. That's the key to George's success. He understands and appreciates the ingredients that he uses and doesn't try to alter them with elaborate sauces or seasonings. George's wine list is one of the largest and most impressive in the Hamptons. He has more than 230 selections and a 4,000+ bottle cellar. It includes local wines, as well as rare imported vintages, and they're surprisingly well priced.

OBSTER ROLL RESTAURANT
7-3740.
.lobsterroll.com.
Montauk Hwy., Amagansett.
ng Address: PO Box 1320,
nagansett, NY 11930.
ner/Manager: Andrea Terry.
sine: Seafood.
ving: L, D.

Open: Mem. Day–mid-Sept.: daily;
weekends only Apr.–Mem. Day & mid-
Sept.–mid-Oct.; closed rest of year.
Price: Inexpensive–Expensive.
Credit Cards: MC, V.
Special Features: Wheelchair access;
outdoor dining; family oriented.
Directions: Located on Rte. 27, about 4
miles east of Amagansett.

veryone knows it as "Lunch" because of the huge, red neon sign on the
roof. Don't be fooled, they also serve dinner. There are no pretensions here.
's a roadside fish shack with paper place mats on picnic tables, butter in foil,
nd good, fresh fish at realistic prices; most of the fish is caught locally. Fish
ind chips and the tender, juicy puffers (blowfish) are prepared in a finger
lickin' good tempura batter, and the creamy tartar sauce is so good, we wish it
was served in larger cups. A specialty of the house is, of course, the lobster
roll, but there's a lot more on the menu, too, including seafood platters, fresh
flounder in season, and tuna burgers. The wine and beer list is limited.
Desserts include pies made by Briermere Farms in Riverhead. The fresh fruit
cream pies, such as peach with blueberries, are fabulous! This is a great place
to bring the kids, as plate sharing is approved, and toys are provided.

PACIFIC EAST
631-267-7770.
415 Main St., Amagansett.
Mailing Address: PO Box 854,
Amagansett, NY 11930.
Owners: Michael Castino and Aram
Sabat.
Manager: Sean Powers.
Chef: Michael Castino.
Cuisine: Asian Seafood.
Serving: D.

Open: In summer: daily; fewer days rest
of year.
Price: Expensive–Very Expensive; prix
fixe offered.
Credit Cards: AE, MC, V.
Special Features: Wheelchair access; brick
courtyard; sushi bar.
Directions: From center of Amagansett,
proceed east on Montauk Hwy. (Rte.
27). Restaurant is on left in about 1/2
mile.

ichael Castino has been fascinated with Asian cuisine since he was a
child, so it's not surprising that Pacific East, which opened in Amagansett
in 1997, should fuse Asian and American cuisine in a new and trendy way. So,
although you could feast at the sushi bar, you might start a meal in the crisp
white rooms with a lobster and shiitake pancake in champagne kim-chi cream
or with a cool shrimp spring roll. Fish is king here, so although you could order
hicken, pork chops, or roast duck, you may want to try a whole ginger-stuffed
llowtail snapper tempura with green curry, rice noodles, and sizzling Hong
ng dipping sauce. There's a spacious bar at the entrance and a brick court-
facing the street. Snowy white linen tablecloths are set with cobalt blue
holding an orchid stem or a sprig of flowers. This is a terrific addition to
mptons' restaurant scene.

BRIDGEHAMPTON

BOBBY VAN'S
631-537-0590.
2393 Main St., Bridgehampton.
Mailing Address: PO Box 3055,
 Bridgehampton, NY 11932.
Manager: James Phair.
Chef: Joel A. Reiss.
Cuisine: American Steak House.
Serving: D daily, L Mon.–Fri., BR Sat., Sun.

Open: Daily.
Price: Moderate–Very Expensive; prix
 fixe offered Sept.–June.
Credit Cards: AE, MC, V.
Special Features: Wheelchair access;
 smoking at bar only.
Directions: On Montauk Hwy. (Rte. 27)
 in center of village.

The venerable old name lingers on, but except for the old original bar and its collection of celebrity photographs, this is a shiny new version. The dark room with its quiet, seductive corners has been replaced with closely packed tables, divided occasionally by floor-to-ceiling potted palms. There are ceiling fans, bistro chairs, and absolutely first-rate steaks. Crowds pack the place, even in the winter. The piano has been moved to the window, and there's a pianist throughout dinner. It's a thoroughly 1990s place cloaked in 1960s nostalgia. In the summer, the French doors open directly onto the sidewalk. The menu includes a good selection of seafood and pastas, but unless you're a vegetarian, don't pass up one of Bobby Van's tender, succulent steaks, accompanied by a side of creamed spinach.

Wainscotted walls and a fabulous tin ceiling are handsome backdrops for the terrific American-French cuisine at Henry's.

Morgan McGivern

HENRY'S
631-537-5665.
2495 Main St., Bridgehampton.
Owner: Frank Gemino.
Chef: Paul Del Favero.
Cuisine: American-inspired French
 cuisine.
Serving: D, BR (Sun. only).
Open: In summer: daily; fewer days

rest of year.
Mailing Address: PO Box 766,
 Bridgehampton, NY 11932.
Price: Expensive–Very Expensive.
Credit Cards: AE, MC, V.
Special Features: Wheelchair access.
Directions: On Montauk Hwy. (Rte. 27)
 in center of Bridgehampton at
 monument.

The light and bright interior of this pretty building is a real beauty. It has a spectacular 1902 pressed tin ceiling and pressed tin-boxed beams. The walls are sponged a sun-splashed yellow, and the banquettes are gaily covered in bright Provençal fabric. A mahogany bar is separated from the dining tables by a frosted glass divider. The owner, Frank Gemino, had been a part-owner of the restaurant that formerly occupied this space, the Bridgehampton Cafe. Paul Del Favero, formerly the acclaimed chef at Nick & Toni's, is presiding over the kitchen. Among his signature dishes are an appetizer of gâteau of jumbo lump crabmeat with fresh horseradish and cilantro-mint vinaigrette and an entrée of porcini-crusted tuna with wild mushrooms and sautéed spinach. A favorite dessert is the lemon tarte with a sugar cookie crust and a caramel cage.

95 SCHOOL STREET
631-537-5555.
95 School St., Bridgehampton.
Mailing Address: PO Box 423,
    Bridgehampton, NY 11932.
Owner: Stuart Kriesler.
Executive Chef: Andrew Engle.
Cuisine: Long Island Regional.
Serving: D, BR (Sun. only).

Open: May–Sept.: daily; closed several
    days rest of year.
Price: Moderate–Very Expensive; prix
    fixe offered.
Credit Cards: AE, DC, MC, V.
Special Features: Limited wheelchair
    access.
Directions: From Main St., turn onto
    School St. at Community Center.

The spare, white setting, the selection of newspapers and magazines to read while waiting, and the fact that it buys its chickens from the local Iacono Farm and its duck from Crescent Farm in Aquebogue has endeared this restaurant to local diners. The servers are eager and friendly, and the background music includes such old classics as "Frankie and Johnnie." In addition, it serves terrific food. The trinette loaded with fresh lobster meat, corn, saffron, and basil puree is original and satisfying. The luscious dessert cobblers vary with the season. In early Sept., I had a peach cobbler, served with a scoop of gelato and garnished with blueberries and raspberries. The wine list contains one of the best selections of Long Island wines in the Hamptons, although there are excellent California, Italian, and French selections as well. This is a good place to try some delightful East End wines, served with excellent local cuisine.

WORLD PIE
631-537-7999.
2402 Main St., Bridgehampton.
Mailing Address: PO Box 1012,
    Bridgehampton, NY 11932.
Owners: Michael Mannino and Ralph
    Pagano.
Chef: Ed Hannibal.

Cuisine: Global Italian.
Serving: L, D, BR (Sat., Sun.)
Open: Year-round: daily.
Price: Moderate.
Credit Cards: AE, MC, V.
Special Features: Outdoor dining; bocci
    court; jazz at brunch.
Directions: On Main St. near Corwith Ave.

When Bridgehampton's popular eatery Karen Lee's, which had occupied this spot for many years, closed in 1999, Michael Mannino and Ralph Pagano seized the opportunity. Michael has been in the restaurant business for many years (his family own the O'Mally restaurants), and Ralph had been the chef at Bobby Van's, so the team are definitely not neophytes. And their Global Italian menu is unique and ambitious. Not only do they feature wood-oven pizzas, pastas, entrée salads, and panini sandwiches, but also a range of veal and chicken dishes, and there might be an Asian spin on dishes every once in a while. There's an outside patio for summer dining and a bocci court to while away a pleasant evening.

EAST HAMPTON

BLUE PARROT BAR & GRILL
631-324-3609.
33A Main St., East Hampton, NY 11937.
Owners: Lee Bieler and Roland Eisenberg.
Manager: Roland Eisenberg.
Chef: Rafael Godoy.
Cuisine: Southern California/Mexican.
Serving: L, D, LN.
Open: Apr.–Dec.: in summer: daily; fewer days rest of season.
Price: Inexpensive–Moderate.
Credit Cards: AE, MC, V.
Special Features: Limited wheelchair access; smoking on patio only; covered patio.
Directions: From Main St., walk down little mews to restaurant, next to Park Pl. parking lot.

Tucked away in a little courtyard between Main St. and the Park Pl. parking lot, this little bar/restaurant serves up hefty margaritas that are so potent, you may begin talking to the stuffed parrot. The decor is funky and original and very casual — the perfect place to go before a movie. The floor is painted blue, and antlers and old movie posters hang on the walls. There are colorful serapes at the windows, and strings of lighted chili peppers hang from the tiled bar. They modestly claim, "This is the best Mexican food this side of Baja." — and they may be right! The nachos grande are enormous with plenty of cheese, black beans, sour cream, guacamole, salsa, and jalapeño peppers. The Mexican lasagna, which uses tortillas in place of pasta is great. Desserts include a homemade flan and a real key lime pie. There's also a late-night (after 11pm) menu that features South of the Border tortilla wrap sandwiches and Southwestern sushi. (Honest!!)

BOSTWICK'S SEAFOOD GRILL AND OYSTER BAR
631-324-1111.
39 Gann Rd., East Hampton, NY 11937.
Owners: Kevin Boles and Chris Eggert.
Chef: Chris Eggert.
Cuisine: Seafood.
Serving: D.
Open: In summer: daily; fewer days rest of season; closed Columbus Day–Mem. Day.
Price: Moderate; prix fixe offered.
Credit Cards: MC, V.
Special Features: Water and sunset views; boat moorage.
Directions: From Main St., turn left just before Hook Windmill onto North Main St. After 2 street lights, road will fork. Take left fork onto Three Mile Harbor Rd. Gann Rd. is on left in about 5 miles. Drive to end of road and turn right into marina parking lot. Restaurant is straight ahead.

Located at Harbor Marina, Bostwick's has been an East Hampton fixture for many years, although not always in this location. Fortunately, this is the best. Occupying the second floor of a marina office, there are glorious views of the harbor and evening sunsets. The large enclosed porch, with its crisp blue-and-white colors is where everyone wants to sit, but there is also an indoor dining room. Start with the raw bar sampler of oysters, clams, and shrimp served with a zippy cocktail sauce, then move on to the broiled local flounder or the catch of the day. Gentle prices and a casual dress code make this an exceptionally popular spot.

CAFE MAX
631-324-2004.
85 Montauk Hwy., East Hampton, NY 11937.
Owners/Managers: Max and Nancy Weintraub.
Chef: Max Weintraub.
Cuisine: American/Continental.
Serving: D, BR (Sun. off-season only).
Open: Apr.–Feb.; daily in summer except Tues.; fewer days rest of year; BR Sun. Oct.–May; closed Mar.
Price: Moderate–Expensive; prix fixe offered.
Credit Cards: MC, V.
Special Features: Limited wheelchair access; award-winning wine list.
Directions: On Rte. 27 at Cove Hollow Rd.

The greeting and the decor at Cafe Max are warm and inviting. There are rough-sawn cedar walls, a cathedral ceiling, natural oak floors, and paisley drapes that give the space a country feeling. Old photographs of Nancy's family line the walls of the bar. We love the food at Cafe Max. The crab cake appetizers are light and fluffy and the perfectly roasted free-range chicken is seasoned with rosemary and herbs. The wine list contains 102 selections — it's been winning *Wine Spectator* awards since 1995. Most of the wines are from California, although there are several Long Island choices — and a nice range is available by the glass every night.

DELLA FEMINA
631-329-6666; fax: 631-329-3547.
99 North Main St., East Hampton.
Mailing Address: PO Box 4215, East Hampton, NY 11937.
Owners: Jerry Della Femina and Judy Licht.
Manager: Walter Strubel.
Chef: James Carpenter.
Cuisine: Globally influenced, seasonal American cuisine.
Serving: D.
Open: In summer: daily; rest of year: Wed. (or Thurs.)–Sun.
Price: Expensive–Very Expensive; prix fixe offered.
Credit Cards: AE, MC, V.
Special Features: Wheelchair access; fireplace.
Directions: From Main St., continue past traffic light and turn left at fork before windmill. Drive past windmill (on right) and under railroad trestle. Restaurant is on left at first traffic signal.

When Jerry Della Femina opened this restaurant in 1991, it was an immediate hit. Unlike East Hampton Point, which he also owns, Della Femina provides a private, but still celebratory atmosphere. This restaurant works well. A profusion of colorful flowers spill from the window boxes in the summer. The bar is light and airy, and it's fun to join the game of seeing how many of the caricatures of local luminaries you can identify. There's abundant space between tables in the quiet, elegant dining room, which is decorated mostly in subdued, earthy beiges and whites. The food is first-class. One night, for an appetizer, we had a grilled Hudson River Valley foie gras with a blackberry "Johnny cake" and Sag Pond verjus and maple sauce; it was excellent. Montauk striped bass comes with truffled veal reduction, smashed purple potatoes, roasted French chanterelles and pearl onions. The wine list is extensive. Definitely save room for the decadent, warm Valrhona chocolate cake, an unmolded ramekin of chocolate with a mound of espresso gelato and chocolate sauce on the side. The desserts, just as the entrées, are not served, but presented. In this case, the cake is dusted with confectioners' sugar, and the plate is decorated with the sauces. It's worth every calorie.

The outside deck at East Hampton Point is a popular spot for afternoon lunch.

Suzi Forbes Chase

EAST HAMPTON POINT
631-329-2800.
www.easthamptonpoint.com.
295 Three Mile Harbor Rd., East Hampton, NY 11937.
Managers: B. J. Calloway and Caroline Scarpinato.
Chef: Matthew Ross.
Cuisine: American.
Serving: L, D, BR (Sun. only).
Open: Apr.–Sept.: July–Labor Day: L, D daily, BR Sun.; fewer days rest of year.

Price: Expensive–Very Expensive; prix fixe offered.
Credit Cards: AE, MC, V.
Special Features: Wheelchair access; smoking on outside deck and in bar only; waterfront views; outside dining; boat dock.
Directions: From Main St., turn left just before Hook Windmill onto North Main St. After 2 street lights, road will fork. Take left fork onto Three Mile Harbor Rd. Driveway to restaurant is on left in about 4 miles.

Were someone unfortunate enough to have time for only one restaurant dinner while in the Hamptons, I would recommend East Hampton Point. The food and service are excellent, and the sunset view is stunning.

Brilliant pink, orange, and red streak across the sky and reflect in the calm waters of Three Mile Harbor, where the slap of sailboat rigging against masts provides soothing background music. Happy memories invariably result. The tiered dining room provides a watery view from every seat by the use of cleverly placed mirrors, and the crisp, marine blue-and-white decor is so subtle that it offers no distractions. Even so, the spacious deck is the place to be on a clear, warm night. The entrées are straightforward and expertly prepared. Juicy chicken comes with a Vidalia onion crust and is served with roasted garlic mashed potatoes and a lemon-rosemary sauce. A portion of the deck is dedicated to casual dining and cocktails; a lighter menu is available. Sailors arrive in their yachts from nearby estates with their weekend guests in tow for the generous buffet brunch on Sun. Even the bar has a special attraction; a polished mahogany 5.5-liter sloop is suspended from the ceiling where it divides the bar from the restaurant.

The Farmhouse burst on the dining scene in 1996. There are six distinctive dining rooms and a pretty garden in back.

Morgan McGivern

THE FARMHOUSE
631-324-8585.
341 Montauk Hwy., East Hampton, NY 11937.
Owners: Fred and Susan Lieberman.
Manager: Michael Gluchman.
Chef: Frederick Keiffer.
Cuisine: American Bistro.
Serving: D.
Open: Year-round: daily.

Price: Moderate–Very Expensive; prix fixe offered.
Credit Cards: AE, MC, V.
Special Features: Wheelchair access; outdoor dining; fireplaces; happy hour Thurs.
Directions: From center of East Hampton, travel east on Montauk Hwy. (Rte. 27) for 1 mile. Restaurant is on left.

This is one of the most famous (or infamous) drinking and eating establishments on the East End. It boasts the oldest bar (ca. 1926-après Prohibition) in the Hamptons, and at one time it was the place to be seen. On one sad night in 1956, this is where Jackson Pollock had been drinking just before he raced to his death on the road to his home in Springs. (Beware of the Pollock-sized, 8-

ounce martinis served today.) Just like a cat with seven lives, this drinking hole has been through a number of deaths and rebirths of its own. Now, it appears there's a winning team in charge who have dedicated themselves to creating a fine restaurant. For one thing, the seven dining rooms have been decorated in a subdued Ralph Lauren style. They have wide-plank pine floors (original), beige burlap café curtains on the windows, and bunches of dried flowers hanging on the walls and from the hand-hewn exposed beams. There are fireplaces in several dining rooms, and Mason jars hold fresh flowers. Two flagstone-floored garden rooms are wonderful summer venues. The cuisine is first-rate. Entrées include horseradish-crusted salmon with beet risotto and chive butter sauce and the grilled bistro steak comes with Farmhouse pommes frites and bordelaise sauce. For dessert, try the flourless chocolate cake fondant with white chocolate bavarian cream and raspberry puree.

GEORGICA GRILL
631-329-9821.
47 Montauk Hwy., East Hampton, NY 11937.
Owner/Chef: Michael Cinanni.
Cuisine: Eclectic.
Serving: D.
Open: Year-round: Wed.–Mon.; closed Tues. (perhaps closed addl. days off-season).
Price: Moderate; ask about frequent diner card.
Credit Cards: AE, MC, V.
Special Features: Courtyard dining.
Directions: On Rte. 27 about 2 miles west of center of village.

A former roadside bar was turned into an excellent, casual, affordable restaurant in 2000. Michael Cinanni (formerly at 75 Main) has given this space a new lease on life by jazzing up the pillars near the copper-topped bar with mosaic tiles and painting it a mild beige with white accents. The food is a combination of seafood/American/Southwestern. You might have potato and Dijon-crusted salmon, Southwestern lime chicken, or even a grilled tuna sandwich — all at very moderate prices for this pricey Hamptons' locale. A courtyard in back is a welcome addition.

JAMES LANE CAFE at THE HEDGES INN
631-324-7100.
74 James Ln., East Hampton, NY 11937.
Chef: Ron Reid.
Cuisine: Continental/Mediterranean.
Serving: D.
Open: Year-round.
Price: Moderate–Very Expensive.
Credit Cards: AE, MC, V.
Special Features: Wheelchair access; patio dining.
Directions: At traffic light on Rte. 27, before turning left toward village, restaurant is straight ahead.

The James Lane Cafe at The Hedges Inn has one of the most attractive dining rooms in the Hamptons. There are polished pine floors, a fireplace, and French doors leading to an enclosed flagstone-floored garden room. This is definitely the preferred place to eat on balmy summer evenings when the perfume from the flowers, spilling from the planters, and the sounds of chirping birds through the open windows heighten the sense of romance. Although under the same management as The Palm restaurant at the Huntting Inn, the cuisine here is more delicate and refined than the heavy steaks for which its sister property is known. You might have plank-roasted salmon crusted with horseradish or a grilled veal chop that's been marinated in garlic and fresh rosemary. There's a moderate-sized, reasonably priced wine list. The desserts are good, but not adventurous and include crème brûlée, tiramisù, and mascarpone cheesecake in a chocolate-walnut graham cracker crust.

THE LAUNDRY
631-324-3199.
31 Race Ln., East Hampton, NY 11937.
Owner: Stuart Kreisler.
General Manager: Bill Bonbrest.
Executive Chef: Andrew Engle.
Cuisine: American/Mediterranean.
Serving: D.
Open: Year-round: daily.
Price: Moderate–Very Expensive; prix fixe offered.

Credit Cards: AE, CB, DC, MC, V.
Special Features: Wheelchair access; fireplace; award-winning wine list; Artist's & Writer's courtyard bar; reservations not accepted.
Directions: From Main St., turn onto Newtown Ln., then turn left onto Railroad Ave. Turn left again at light onto Race Ln., just past train station. Restaurant is on right in middle of block.

This casual, comfortable, jeans-OK place just keeps on serving good food. As one waiter said, "Some places you put down the dish and run before they throw it at you. Here, you wait to hear the raves." The building was once the East Hampton Steam Laundry, and the extractor still sits in the courtyard next to the bocci court. A gorgeous bouquet of fresh flowers on the bar sets the mood. The walls are brick and rough-sawn cedar. There are vaulted ceilings and a free-standing brick fireplace in a sunken conversation pit with black vinyl banquettes. A hip, older crowd has made this their own; celebrities gravitate to the raised portion behind the fireplace wall where they can dine without being noticed; and children congregate in the fireplace pit early in the evening to draw and talk among themselves. Later at night, the conversation pit is a relaxed place to sit while waiting for a table, which is generally necessary as no reservations are accepted. For entrées, the sautéed dayboat cod, which is served with sweet corn, cherry tomatoes, and lemon confit, is firm but juicy, and the chicken has a crispy, delicate skin and flavorful, moist meat. For dessert, a rustic apple galette with calvados crème fraîche is fabulous.

THE MAIDSTONE ARMS
631-324-5006; fax: 631-324-5037.
www.maidstonearms.com.
207 Main St., East Hampton, NY 11937.
Owner: Ms. Coke Anne Saunders Wilcox.
Managing Director/Chef: William S. Valentine.

Cuisine: New American.
Serving: B, L, D, BR (Sat., Sun.).
Open: Year-round: daily.
Price: Expensive–Very Expensive; prix fixe offered.
Credit Cards: AE, D, MC, V.
Special Features: Fireplace; outdoor

patio in summer; award-winning wine list.

Directions: Overlooks Town Pond on south end of Main St.

Although The Maidstone Arms is an inn as well as a restaurant, this is anything but a typical hotel dining room. The food is absolutely first-class. William S. Valentine is a fitting descendant of the Maidstone's previous culinary days of glory in the 1950s, when chef and cookbook author Michael Field presided here. For a trip to yesteryear, Hamptons' style, The Maidstone Arms can't be beat. The Water Room lounge is clubby and sophisticated; guests can enjoy a drink before the woodstove while waiting for their table, and the patio in the back is a refreshing summertime oasis. There are two distinctly different dining rooms. The Boat Room is informal and cozy with polished pine floors, a massive fireplace, and upholstered armchairs for seating. A multitude of boat paintings and prints line the walls. The main dining room has blue plaid carpet, blue walls, and a fireplace; blue-and-white porcelain plates and floral prints decorate the walls. The setting is elegant and comfortable, without being stuffy. Chef Valentine, who formerly brightened the restaurant scene in Los Angeles, has created a menu that reflects creativity and imagination. Try his roast lacquered duck with coconut-almond rice and shiitake mushroom jus. The wine list is remarkable for its depth and breadth, as well as for its bargains. An excellent selection of white and red Long Island wines are particularly praiseworthy. Breakfast and lunch are popular here, too.

MICHAEL'S AT MAIDSTONE PARK

631-324-0725.
28 Maidstone Park Rd., East Hampton, NY 11937.
Manager: Tim Myers.
Chefs: Tommy Jacobs and Sean Rafferty.
Cuisine: American.
Serving: D.
Open: Year-round: daily.
Price: Inexpensive–Moderate; prix fixe offered.

Credit Cards: AE, MC, V.
Special Features: Wheelchair access; non-smoking section.
Directions: From Main St., turn left just before Hook Windmill onto North Main St. Drive through 2 traffic lights and take left fork onto Three Mile Harbor Rd. Follow road for 5 miles to Flaggy Hole Rd. Turn left onto Flaggy Hole and left again onto Maidstone Park Rd. Restaurant is on left.

Because this is an out-of-the-way restaurant in a residential neighborhood, it's important to lure customers beyond the village limits. Tim Myers does this by offering special prices year-round. For example, every night there's a $16.95 early-bird special from 4:30pm–6pm, and on Sun.–Thurs., there's an $18.95 prix fixe all night; on Fri., Sat., prix fixe dinners, including soup or salad, entrée, and dessert are offered for $22.95. Consequently, this is a very popular restaurant, especially with local, year-round residents. Few tourists even stumble across it. But now you know! Be forewarned. You must make reservations. The decor is old-fashioned and romantic; soft candles glow against the knotty pine walls; church pews are used as seats in one of the rooms. Seniors love this place, both for the value and for the food. It's a chalkboard menu, but most of the items do not change. Michael's serves good, substantial, all-American, home-style food. The duck is crisp skinned, and the steak is large. The wine list is OK. Desserts are limited, but good.

One of the most popular restaurants in the Hamptons, Nick & Toni's offers a casual setting and a convivial atmosphere.

Morgan McGivern

NICK & TONI'S
631-324-3550.
136 North Main St., East Hampton, NY
   11937.
Owners: Jeff Salaway and Toni Ross.
Manager: Bonnie Munshin.
Chef: Joseph Realmuto.
Cuisine: Italian/Mediterranean.
Serving: D, BR (Sun. only).
Open: In summer: D daily; fewer days
rest of year; BR every Sun.
Price: Moderate–Very Expensive; prix
   fixe offered at times.
Credit Cards: AE, MC, V.
Special Features: Wheelchair access;
   tables on outdoor covered porch.
Directions: From Main St., turn left just
   before Hook Windmill. Restaurant is
   on right, .1/8 mile beyond second
   traffic light.

There's something so comfortable about Nick & Toni's that one visit is never enough. Casual attire is fine; babies are welcome; seniors love it; this is family. What puts it at the top of the class? Everything just clicks: the food is often sensational; the help is knowledgeable, professional, and friendly; the setting is crisp and airy; the wine list is well chosen — and there are no pretensions, and no apologies are needed. It's the kind of place where celebrities eat frequently, because they know they're among friends, and no one will bother them. Background music leans to progressive and vocal jazz. Hot, thickly sliced Tuscan bread comes to the table in a wooden trough to be dipped in zippy Monini olive oil; the combination is so terrific, it's devoured in a flash. No one should miss the zucchini chips; these little round morsels of paper-thin zucchini are dipped in a chickpea flour batter and deep-fried. A 620° wood-burning oven prepares meat with crackly crisp skin and tender, juicy meat. The wine list is well chosen and includes Italian, French, and American wines, with some North Fork selections. Desserts include a pecan shortbread sundae with malted milk ball sauce that is absolutely fabulous.

The Palm at Huntting Inn, a branch of The Palm in Manhattan, is noted for its thick, juicy steaks and enormous helpings.

Morgan McGivern

THE PALM AT HUNTTING INN

631-324-0411.
www.thepalm.com.
94 Main St., East Hampton, NY 11937.
Manager: Tomas Romano.
Chef: Simone Collado.
Cuisine: American.
Serving: D.

Open: In summer: daily; in winter: may
  close 1–2 nights midweek.
Price: Expensive–Very Expensive.
Credit Cards: AE, DC, MC, V.
Special Features: Guest rooms on premise.
Directions: On Montauk Hwy. (Rte. 27) in
  center of village.

A visit to The Palm is like a trip to New York City, with none of the aggravation. This East End brother of the famous Manhattan steak house, which has been in the same family for three generations, has established itself as a Hamptons' fixture. It's the same formula as the original, but there are no sawdust floors here. The predominance of dark wood, booths, pressed tin ceiling, oak mirrors, and Victorian light fixtures is reminiscent of a pub of yesteryear. The enclosed porch, which is also used for dining, is bright and airy. The food is the same as you'll find at the original. Steaks are thick and cut from the finest meat. Portions are huge, but split plates are an alternative. The lobster is so large that it spills over the edge of its platter. Take-home portions are so huge, they are returned to the table in shopping bags. No vegetables come with the entrées, but the Palm is noted for its creamed spinach. We generally order a combination plate of cottage fries and deep-fried onions; the fries are crisp, and the onions are sliver thin. The high-priced wine list is well chosen and features California and Long Island wines, with a smattering of imported selections.

PECONIC COAST

631-324-6772.
103 Montauk Hwy., East Hampton, NY
  11937.
Owners/Managers: Dennis MacNeil
  and Dede McCann.
Chef: Dennis MacNeil.

Cuisine: Mediterranean-influenced
  American.
Serving: D.
Open: Year-round: daily.
Price: Inexpensive–Expensive.
Credit Cards: AE, MC, V.
Special Features: Patio dining in

summer; reservations not accepted; smoking in bar only; fireplace.

Directions: On Montauk Hwy. about 1.5 miles west of East Hampton.

This bright Hamptons' restaurant comes with excellent credentials. Both Dede and Dennis were at The Laundry for many years, so their own unique approach to Hamptons' dining has evolved naturally. The restaurant is located in a building surrounded with windows and featuring soaring ceilings, giving the tiered dining room a bright and open feel. A lounge with leather chairs offers a relaxing spot to wait for tables. Entrées include a fabulous just-caught striped bass that is served on a bed of zucchini gratin. The wine list is broad and very well priced, and there are some excellent selections by the glass. Desserts are good, too. One fall night we had a wonderful apple and blueberry crisp served with vanilla ice cream.

Morgan McGivern

Riccardo's Seafood House overlooks Maidstone Marina, where evening often rewards diners with spectacular sunsets.

RICCARDO'S SEAFOOD HOUSE
631-324-0000; fax: 631-324-7369.
313 Three Mile Harbor Rd., East Hampton, NY 11937.
Owner/Chef: Riccardo Traslavinia,
Cuisine: Seafood with South American flair.
Serving: D, BR (Sat., Sun. only).
Open: In summer: daily; fewer days rest of season; closed Nov.–Apr.

Price: Expensive; prix fixe offered.
Credit Cards: MC, V.
Special Features: View of marina; boat dock.
Directions: From Main St., turn left just before Hook Windmill onto North Main St. After 2 street lights, road will fork. Take left fork onto Three Mile Harbor Rd. Restaurant is on left in about 4 miles.

Riccardo Traslavinia has been chef at 95 School St. and The Laundry. Now he's got a place all his own, and it's a beauty. Overlooking Maidstone Marina, which borders on Three Mile Harbor, a covered porch is enhanced by green tables and chairs, and there's also a bar and an inside dining room. Local art (for sale) lines the walls. The menu is a reflection of the chef's Latin heritage (he's from Santiago, Chile). For appetizers, you could choose ceviche (mixed seafood marinated in lime juice) or chicharrón de calamares (lime-mustard battered calamari). Entrées range from fish dishes wrapped in a banana leaf or a cornhusk to Argentinean rib eye steak. There's live Latin music at brunch on Sun.

SANTA FE JUNCTION
631-324-8700.
www.santafejunction.net.
8 Fresno Pl., East Hampton, NY 11937.
Owners: Chris Eggert and Kevin Boles.
Manager: Lisa Narizzaro.
Chef: Moises Goodey.
Cuisine: Southwestern.
Serving: D.
Open: Year-round: daily.

Price: Moderate–Expensive.
Credit Cards: MC, V.
Special Features: Wheelchair access; reservations not accepted.
Directions: From Main St., turn onto Newtown Ln., then turn left onto Railroad Ave. Drive past train station and straight ahead at traffic light. Turn left at Fresno Pl. Restaurant is on left.

Santa Fe Junction, located on an illusive side street running between Gingerbread Ln. and Railroad Ave., is definitely worth the effort to find. Opened in November 1994, it has been earning justifiable high praise for its food, decor, and service ever since. Santa Fe Junction features inventive, Southwestern cuisine. The setting is casual and comfortable with rough-sawn, cedar-planked walls, green vinyl banquettes, maroon tablecloths, and cactus centerpieces. A geometric, Native American frieze circles the room, while Western paintings and a deer skull with antlers decorate the walls. Skylights in the raftered ceiling allow light to stream in during the day. The cuisine is inspired. The Blooming Onion appetizer, for example, is as pretty as it is delectable and is a marvelous shared dish. All of the grilled items are cooked over mesquite, and they include smoked St. Louis ribs with a thick and tangy barbecue sauce and sea bass crusted with sweet potatoes and served on a bed of spinach. For dessert, the banana taco, a grilled banana rolled in a cinnamon crêpe and served with pecans and vanilla ice cream, topped with caramel sauce, is a house favorite.

TSUNAMI
631-329-6000; fax: 631-329-9638.
www.nvbar.com.
44 Three Mile Harbor Rd., East Hampton, NY 11937.
Manager: Frank Cilione.

Chef: John O'Connell.
Cuisine: Asian/Fusian.
Serving: D, LN.
Open: In summer: Thurs.–Tues.; closed Wed.; fewer days rest of year.

Part restaurant, but mostly classy dance club, this place is glitzy and great. The small dining room's walls, ceiling, and bar are slathered in shiny coppery paint, and Oriental rugs lay on otherwise bare floors. A brick fireplace offers a cozy touch. There's the requisite raised VIP booth, but otherwise tiny tables line the walls and sit before ingenious, round cushioned benches. To emphasize the Pan Asian menu, waitresses are dressed in charming Chinese dresses. You may have a "small plate" of spring rolls that include tasso ham,

Price: Very Expensive; $24.95 prix fixe.
Credit Cards: AE, MC, V.
Special Features: Dance club on
  premise; outdoor bar.
Directions: From Main St., turn left just

before Hook Windmill onto North
Main St. After 2 street lights, road will
fork. Take left fork onto Three Mile
Harbor Rd. Driveway to restaurant is
on right in about 1/4mile.

goat cheese, and broccoli rabe or a salmon roll with avocado and scallions. The entrées of sha shang duck with scallion pancake or the miso and sake marinated Chilean sea bass are terrific. Save room for dessert. The coconut crème brûlée with candied ginger and berries is lush.

TURTLE CROSSING
631-324-7166; fax: 631-324-7253.
221 Pantigo Rd., East Hampton, NY 11937.
Owner/Manager: Nancy Singer.
Owner/Chef: Stanley Singer.
Cuisine: Southwestern/BBQ.
Serving: L, D.

Open: Year-round.
Price: Inexpensive–Moderate.
Credit Cards: AE, MC, V.
Special Features: Outside dining; takeout.
Directions: On Montauk Hwy. (Rte. 27),
  1.5 miles east of village.

T he heady aroma wafting from the hardwood smoker in the kitchen will draw you in, but the juicy, smoky, tender ribs and chicken with their tasty barbecue sauces will keep you coming back. The *New York Times* has called this the best BBQ on Long Island, and this is President Clinton's favorite local stop. Stanley Singer grew up in Oklahoma City, where BBQ is king. After a stint in Paris at La Varenne, he and his wife Nancy opened this welcome addition to the Hamptons' dining scene. The front room of the restaurant is mostly for takeout, and there's a steady stream of people throughout the day. A small, adjacent dining room has a vinyl floor and Naugahyde booths along a wall that has been painted with a huge mural of rodeo riders. Typical Southwestern cow skulls gaze down on the room. You can choose from spit-roasted platters of chicken or smoked BBQ platters of ribs, chicken, brisket, pork, or duck, or a combination of several. With that order, you'll get corn bread and an order of "fixins," which change nightly and might include black beans, rice, or other side dishes. You can also order a quesadilla or a wrap. There's a full bar and a selection of Mexican beers, tequila, and frozen drinks. The children's menu includes a peanut butter and jelly sandwich and chicken fingers.

EASTPORT

TRUMPETS ON THE BAY
631-325-2900.
www.trumpetsonthebay.com.
58 South Bay Ave., Eastport.
Mailing Address: PO Box 505, Eastport,
  NY 11941.
Owner: Helen Fehr.

Cuisine: Continental.
Serving: L, D, BR (Sun. only).
Open: Year-round.
Price: Expensive.
Credit Cards: AE, MC, V.
Special Features: Waterside views; fire-
  place; outside deck.

Directions: From Sunrise Hwy. (Rte. 27), take exit 61 and follow service road to Eastport exit. Turn right (south) onto Eastport Manor Rd. Take road to end. Turn left (east) onto Montauk Hwy. and drive 0.7 mile to South Bay Ave. Turn right (south) and continue to #58, at end on left.

If you're thinking along romantic lines, steer out to this protected point on Moriches Bay, almost on the Brookhaven line. You'll find waterside tables (especially in the back dining room or on the deck) that are seductively lighted by candles, sentimental background music, and inventive cuisine. What more can you ask for? Even the service is informed and attentive without being overbearing. I had a wonderful entrée one night of macadamia nut-crusted Chilean sea bass in a light and refreshing mango beurre blanc, sided with a pineapple compote and julienne vegetables. There's a nice wine list, although I would love to see more local wines included.

EAST QUOGUE

NEW MOON BAR & GRILL
631-653-4042.
524 Montauk Hwy., East Quogue.
Mailing Address: PO Box 3028, East Quogue, NY 11942.
Owners: Ron and Shana Campsey.
Chef: Robert Larkin.
Cuisine: Mexican.
Serving: D, L, BR.
Open: D Wed.–Sun., L Sat., BR Sun.
Price: Inexpensive.
Credit Cards: AE, D, MC, V.
Special Features: Outdoor patio.
Directions: On Montauk Hwy. (Rte. 27) in center of village.

Calling all cowpokes! If you've got a hankerin' for good ol' finger lickin' barbecued beef or chicken, a sizzlin' plate of chicken fajitas, or maybe some spicy blackened catfish, head on down to the New Moon. You'll recognize this institution (it's been around since 1977) by the wooden cactus cutouts flanking the building and the flower-filled window boxes. Inside, you'll sit on church pews while you sip your frozen margarita or piña colada. And you won't leave until you've had one of Shana's "handmade" desserts, such as the luscious banana cream pie, rice pudding, or ice-cream float. Mmmmmm, who can resist?

STONE CREEK INN
631-653-6770.
405 Montauk Hwy., East Quogue.
Mailing Address: PO Box 1751, East Quogue, NY 11942.
Owner/Manager: Elaine DiGiacomo.
Owner/Chef: Christian Mir.
Cuisine: French/Mediterranean.
Serving: D.
Open: Mar.–Dec.: in summer: daily; fewer days rest of year.
Price: Expensive–Very Expensive; prix fixe offered.
Credit Cards: AE, DC, MC, V.
Special Features: Wheelchair access; fireplaces in dining room and bar.
Directions: On Rte. 27, .5 mile east of village.

This welcome addition to the Hamptons' dining scene opened in 1996 in the white-shingled building that used to be the Ambassador Inn. Following a thorough face-lift, the space has now been voted the prettiest restaurant in the

The Stone Creek Inn, with its elegant dining rooms enhanced by fireplaces, offers an award-winning French-Mediterranean menu.

Suzi Forbes Chase

Hamptons by readers of *Dan's Papers*. In the bar, the 1930s carved mahogany back bar is enhanced by a tile floor and a pretty mantel over the fireplace. The two dining rooms have oak floors and tall mullioned windows. Massive palm trees reach toward the tray ceilings, rustling gently in the breeze from the ceiling fans and giving the restaurant a romantic, tropical air. Clever bark vases hold fresh flowers, and lovely Bernardaud china graces the tables. The young chef/manager, a husband and wife team, met while both were working at Tavern on the Green in New York City. Christian was raised in France, and his dishes exhibit a strong French influence. He uses local, seasonal ingredients, thus the menu changes frequently. In the fall, an entrée of crispy salmon was moist and pink inside and was served with whipped potatoes, baby carrots, and several poached oysters on the side. The excellent wine list leans heavily toward French wines. Do not miss the scrumptious desserts: I love the stack of dark and white chocolate mousse layered with phyllo and topped with candied orange peel — all accented by dark and white chocolate sauce and garnished with a sugar-coated strawberry and a white chocolate cigarette.

HAMPTON BAYS

BISTRO 26
631-723-2626.
26 Montauk Hwy., Hampton Bays, NY
  11946.
Owner: Scott Collins.
Chef: George Torres.
Cuisine: French Bistro.
Serving: D.

Open: In summer: Wed.–Mon.; fewer
  days rest of year.
Price: Moderate; prix fixe offered.
Credit Cards: AE, MC, V.
Special Features: Pianist/singer some
  nights in summer.
Directions: On Montauk Hwy. (Rte.
  27A) in center of village.

This friendly, casual street-sider opened in 1998. It has mellow wood floors, French bistro chairs, and a comfortable ambience. The rosemary chicken is roasted and served with garlic mashed potatoes and sautéed spinach. The modest prices (especially the three-course $25 prix fixe) keep the place packed. It's a great addition to the village.

INDIAN COVE
631-728-5366.
252 Montauk Hwy., Hampton Bays, NY 11946.
Owner/Chef: Bernard Miny.
Cuisine: French/fresh local seafood.
Serving: D, BR (Sun. only).
Open: In summer: daily; fewer days rest of season; closed Jan.–Mar.
Price: Inexpensive; $22.75 prix fixe always.
Credit Cards: AE, MC, V.
Special Features: Water views: no reservations accepted.
Directions: From Montauk Hwy., turn south onto Canoe Place Rd. Immediately turn left at restaurant sign and follow signs to restaurant.

Located on a high point of land at the southern end of the Shinnecock Canal, diners at Indian Cove get a front row seat for viewing all the passing yachts. The building is composed of a natural rough cedar exterior with a dining room on the main floor and an indoor/outdoor bar upstairs. Both levels are wrapped with windows or decks. Bernard Miny grew up in Lyon, France, and learned many of his techniques from such luminaries as Paul Bocuse. His prix fixe concept is a fabulous bargain. For $22.75, you can get a choice of appetizers (such as lobster bisque velouté or Caesar salad), an entrée (try the horseradish-crusted salmon with mustard-dill hollandaise), and dessert (perhaps carrot cake or chocolate crème caramel). In each category, there are other dishes with supplemental prices, should you wish to splurge — and there's a wonderful wine list, too!

WHITE WATER GRILL
631-728-7373.
7 North Rd., Hampton Bays, NY 11946.
Owner: James Carroll.
Manager: Peter Mendelsohn.
Chef: Ken Pulomena.
Cuisine: Seafood.
Serving: L, D.
Open: July 4–Labor Day: daily; rest of
season: Thurs.–Sun.; closed Nov.–Apr.
Price: Moderate.
Credit Cards: AE, MC, V.
Special Features: Waterside dining; live music Thurs.–Sun.
Directions: From Montauk Hwy. (Rte. 27A), turn north onto North Rd. Restaurant is down flight of stairs at water's edge.

The setting is ideal. Diners sit at waterside tables right on the Shinnecock Canal where they can watch the procession of boats and yachts parade past. A hot spot with hip dot.coms, the lively outside bar features a band Thurs.–Sun. nights. The pretty inside dining room features crisp navy blue-and-white decor and marine scenes on the walls. The menu is mostly composed of seafood. You can get lobster, sole, crab cakes, and oysters, as well as the house cioppino.

MONTAUK

DAVE'S GRILL
631-668-9190.
www.davesgrill.com.
468 Flamingo Rd., Montauk.
Mailing Address: PO Box 1491, Montauk,
NY 11954.
Owners/Managers: David and Julie
Marcley.
Chef: David Marcley.
Cuisine: American/Seafood.
Serving: D.
Open: July–Labor Day: daily; May, June,
Sept., Oct.: fewer days; closed
Nov.–Apr.
Price: Moderate–Very Expensive; prix fixe
offered.
Credit Cards: AE, D, DC, MC, V.
Special Features: Outdoor patio in
summer; live entertainment.
Directions: From center of village, take
Edgemere St. north until it becomes
Flamingo Ave. Continue on Flamingo
Ave. Restaurant is on right along docks.

David Marcley, a chef, met Julie Goldstone, a singer, and eventually they fell in love, bought a dockside diner that served breakfast to fishermen all night, and got married in Barbados. As Dave's Grill gained popularity, they started serving dinner instead of breakfast. Now all remnants of the diner have vanished. The restaurant has an interior of dark wood and brass; a pretty patio overlooks the harbor for summer dining. Dave selects the fish right off the boats, and the nightly specials reflect his choices. There may be flash-fried Montauk flounder fillet with an onion and potato crust or Dave's cioppino, a combination of fish, lobster, scallops, clams, shrimp, mussels, and calamari. There's an excellent wine list that includes Long Island whites and reds, as well as wines from California, France, Spain, and Italy. Some nights (generally Fri.) guests gather to listen to jazz, with Julie at the microphone.

GOSMAN'S DOCK
631-668-5330.
West Lake Dr., Montauk.
Mailing Address: PO Box 627, Montauk,
NY 11954.
Owner/Manager: Roberta Gosman.
Chef: Sam Joyce.
Cuisine: Seafood.
Serving: L, D.
Open: Mem. Day–Labor Day: daily;
fewer days rest of season; closed
mid-Oct.–mid-Apr.
Price: Inexpensive–Moderate.
Credit Cards: AE, MC, V.
Special Features: Wheelchair access;
outside dining in summer; fish market;
clam bar.
Directions: From center of village, take
Edgemere St. north until it becomes
Flamingo Ave. Continue on Flamingo
Ave. to West Lake Dr. and follow to
end.

Gosman's is the ultimate fish house — casual and noted for its good fresh fish. There's a view from the dining room of the fishing fleet entering the harbor, but because of Gosman's volume, this is not the sort of place that encourages dawdling over coffee. The decor is of the dark, lacquered table, Windsor chair, and paper place mat variety. Nevertheless, the seafood is fresh off the boat. The lobster is always a good choice, and the mahimahi, which is in a delicate herb crust made of Oriental tempura flakes with ginger and cilantro, is crunchy but moist — a very nice dish. Gosman's is a popular meal stop for families and bus tours. A clam bar next door offers a quick lunch, and the seafood market (also next door) is impressive for the variety and volume of seafood available.

HARVEST ON FORT POND
631-668-5574.
11 South Emery St., Montauk.
Mailing Address: PO Box 473, Montauk,
 NY 11954.
Owner: John Erb.
Chef: John Weston.
Cuisine: Northern Italian.
Serving: D.
Open: In summer: daily; fewer days rest
 of season; closed Jan.–mid-Mar.

Price: Very Expensive.
Credit Cards: AE, D, DC, MC, V.
Special Features: Beautiful water view;
 boat dock; pretty side garden with
 benches.
Directions: From Main St. (Rte. 27)
 traveling east, turn left at tower onto
 Edgemere St. Turn left again at first
 street onto South Euclid St. Drive 2
 blocks to South Emery St. and turn
 right. Restaurant is on left.

The beautiful garden with its brick pathways and garden benches announce that this is an owner who deeply cares about his customers and his business. I can't imagine a lovelier place to enjoy an after-dinner drink on a warm summer evening. But the inside is equally pleasant. There are wide-plank pine floors and walls of soft, muted earth tones mixed with white. The wraparound, enclosed porch offers fabulous views of the pond (you have the impression of being suspended over it). This is one of the finest places to eat in Montauk. You might start with the grilled asparagus with fresh mozzarella and onion-parsley sauce, then move on to the roast pork with hazelnut crust and Grand Marnier sauce. No matter what you choose, you won't be disappointed. And you'll have a selection of great wines to go with it!

OYSTER POND
631-668-4200.
4 South Elmwood Ave., Montauk.
Mailing Address: PO Box 1900, Montauk,
 NY 11954.
Owner/Chef: Lonny Lewis.
Cuisine: Contemporary American.
Serving: D, L (off-season only), LN.

Open: Year-round.
Price: Expensive; prix fixe offered.
Credit Cards: AE, MC, V.
Special Features: Jazz Fri. nights.
Directions: From Montauk Hwy.
 (Main St.) traveling east, turn right
 onto Elmwood Ave. Restaurant is
 on right.

Located in the heart of Montauk village, Oyster Pond just keeps getting prettier. It has a beige shingle exterior with a green-and-white striped awning and window boxes spilling over with colorful flowers in the summer. You will enter through a brick-floored bar and then proceed to the crisp and smart dining room. You might start the meal with a sampling from the raw bar and then have the oven-roasted Atlantic salmon that's been wrapped (along with red peppers, fennel, and onions) in Chinese cabbage or try the grilled fillet of ostrich.

QUOGUE

RESTAURANT IN THE INN AT QUOGUE
631-653-6800.
www.innatquogue.com.
52 Quogue St. (in The Inn at Quogue),
    Quogue.
Mailing Address: PO Box 521, Quogue,
    NY 11959.
Manager: Donna McBride.
Chef: Jeff Trujillo.
Cuisine: American Country.

Serving: D, BR (Sun. only).
Open: In summer: D daily; may be closed
    several days rest of year.
Price: Expensive–Very Expensive.
Credit Cards: AE, D, DC, MC, V.
Special Features: Working fireplaces;
    outside terrace.
Directions: From Montauk Hwy., follow
    Quogue St. for .5 mile to The Inn at
    Quogue, located in center of village at
    Jessup Ave.

The beautiful Restaurant in The Inn at Quogue recently experienced yet another change. Under new management, it's been redecorated in Ralph Lauren style with green-and-white striped ticking covering the chairs, wide-plank pine floors, and white wainscotted walls. Fireplaces in the main dining room, as well as in the bar, offer cuddly warmth on spritely nights. The menu features such classics as grilled pork paillarde with a tart cherry sauce and sautéed chicken breast with whole grain mustard sauce — all fare that's appropriate for an upscale county inn — but with a new millenium appeal.

SAGAPONACK

Alison By The Beach is a little Hampton bistro located on Montauk Highway.

Morgan McGivern

ALISON BY THE BEACH
631-537-7100.
3593 Montauk Hwy., Sagaponack, NY
    11962.
Owner: Alison Becker Hurt.
Chef: Robert Gurvich.

Cuisine: Country French.
Serving: BR/L (Sun. only, Labor
    Day–Mem. Day), D.
Open: Year-round: in summer: daily;
    fewer days rest of year.
Price: Expensive–Very Expensive.

Credit Cards: AE, D, DC, MC, V.
Special Features: Wheelchair access; outside dining; fireplace.

Directions: On Rte. 27 at Town Line Rd., 2 miles east of Bridgehampton.

Alison on Dominick St. in Manhattan is a favorite with New York City diners — now there's also a beachhead on the East End. Well, perhaps, not actually a beachhead, as that is a bit misleading. The restaurant is actually on Montauk Hwy. and is surrounded by potato fields; the nearest beach is about a mile away. Nevertheless, this lovely little French bistro is a welcome addition to the Hamptons' dining scene. There are three dining rooms, including the barroom. In the winter, the most romantic tables are by the fireplace near the bar. In the summer, tables are set up on the patio. The food is excellent. A goat cheese and potato terrine, served with a roasted beet salad and walnut oil, is one of my favorite summer appetizers. For an entrée, the fillet of sautéed striped bass, served with a crispy potato roof is light and satisfying. Desserts include such marvelous confections as a warm chocolate and hazelnut soufflé, served with burnt caramel ice cream and chocolate sauce.

SAG HARBOR

AMERICAN HOTEL
631-725-3535.
25 Main St., Sag Harbor.
Mailing Address: PO Box 1349, Sag Harbor, NY 11963.
Owner: Ted Conklin.
Chef: Peter Dunlop.
Cuisine: French/American.
Serving: L, D.
Open: Year-round: D daily; L weekends only off-season.
Price: Moderate–Very Expensive; prix fixe offered.
Credit Cards: AE, CB, D, DC, MC, V.
Special Features: Exceptional wine list; fireplace; singer/pianist on weekends; guest rooms; bar; covered porch.
Directions: On Main St. in center of village.

It was almost thirty-five years ago when Ted Conklin purchased this 1846 hotel, one of the few remnants of Sag Harbor's glorious whaling days. The charming, Victorian rooms have such a European ambience that you feel as if you're eating in a French country inn. The rooms are formal and romantic and range from the dark, convivial bar with its fireplace to the skylighted atrium with its brick wall. Classical music plays gently in the background. An international crowd chatters away in a variety of languages, and the dress is partly New York chic and partly Hamptons' casual. The American Hotel has consistently won *Wine Spectator* Grand Awards for its legendary forty-six-page wine list, which includes a 1929 Château Margaux for $1,000 and a 1975 Château Latour for $450; it also offers a broad range of California and Long Island wines at lower prices. There are few half-bottles, but wines available by the glass are as well selected as those by the bottle.

Over the years, the menu has slowly evolved away from strictly classical French dishes to some French, some American, and even some spa entrées.

Dinner might start with a fresh sautéed foie gras laced with Sauterne, and entrées include a pecan-crusted, baked chicken breast and a filet mignon with a sauce mignonette. There's a lovely selection of after-dinner Sauternes and Ports. Upstairs, there are eight remarkable guest rooms that are filled with antique furniture and Oriental rugs and have fantastic bathrooms with whirlpools. (see Chapter Three, *Lodging*).

THE BEACON
631-725-7088.
8 West Water St., Sag Harbor, NY
    11963.
Owners: David Loewenberg and Kirk
    Basnight.
Manager: David Loewenberg.
Chef: Sam McLelland.
Cuisine: French-inspired American.
Serving: D.

Open: In summer: Thurs.–Mon.; fewer
    nights rest of season; closed Oct.–Apr.
Price: Moderate–Expensive.
Credit Cards: AE, MC, V.
Special Features: Fabulous waterside set-
    ting and view; reservations not
    accepted.
Directions: Turn off Main St. onto Water
    St. Restaurant is on right in about 1
    block, near Bridge St.

Although it's tiny, this new venture by the experienced team of David Loewenberg and Kirk Basnight (also the owners of red bar brasserie in Southampton) packs a big wallop. For one thing, the restaurant is located on the second floor of a building that offers stunning views of the harbor, especially at sunset. A light and breezy menu has been created to match the casual bistro setting. There's soy-glazed salmon with sesame-cucumber slaw on potato and rock shrimp hash that's positively yummy. Desserts should not be missed, especially the toasted almond crème brûlée napoleon (a luscious confection if there ever was one) and the warm crêpe soufflé filled with orange pastry cream.

B. SMITH'S
631-725-5858.
Long Wharf Promenade at Bay St., Sag
    Harbor.
Mailing Address: PO Box 600, Sag
    Harbor, NY 11963.
Owners: Barbara Smith and Dan Gasby.
Manager: Christine Buechting.
Chef: John Poon.
Cuisine: International/Eclectic.
Serving: L, D.

Open: May–Sept.: daily; shorter hours rest
    of season; closed Nov.–Apr.
Price: Moderate–Very Expensive.
Credit Cards: AE, MC, V.
Special Features: Wheelchair access:
    waterfront dining on spacious decks;
    bar/lounge area.
Directions: Traveling north on Main St.,
    cross over Rte. 114 (Bay St.) and con-
    tinue down Long Wharf. Restaurant is
    on right.

B. Smith's has been a popular Manhattan theater-area restaurant for some time. Now Ms. Smith has joined the Hamptons' scene as well. The location has long been one of the premier sites in the Hamptons, as it overlooks the harbor and marina where huge sailboats and cruisers sit at anchor. B. Smith's strikes just the right note, as the owners have thoughtfully allowed the view and the food to take front seat. Creamy yellow walls are accented with white, marine blue-and-white striped banquettes line the wall, huge blue pots hold palm trees, and ceiling fans whir silently overhead. A multitude of French doors open the interior dining room to the outside. B. Smith is noted for its hickory ribs, which are served with corn, onion crisps, and "moppin'" sauce. You can also get fresh fish, roast chicken, and some lovely pastas. An excellent wine list that includes some local East End wines is available.

This local favorite features luscious Italian cuisine enhanced by lacy curtains on the windows and raffia-wrapped wine bottles hanging from the ceiling.

Morgan McGivern

IL CAPUCCINO RISTORANTE
631-725-2747.
30 Madison St., Sag Harbor.
Mailing Address: PO Box 1438, Sag Harbor, NY 11963.
Owner: Achille Tagliasacchi.
Manager/Chef: Jim Renner.
Cuisine: Northern Italian.

Serving: D.
Open: Year-round: daily, except major holidays.
Price: Moderate–Expensive.
Credit Cards: AE, MC, V.
Directions: From Main St., bear left at monument onto Madison St. Restaurant is on right.

This rambling, old, red, wood building has three dining rooms, with tables and chairs tucked into various nooks and crannies. It's a restaurant of red-checked tablecloths, brown-painted floor, and bentwood chairs. Decorations include original oil paintings by owner Achille Tagliasacchi, raffia-wrapped Chianti bottles hanging from the ceiling and walls, and lace curtains. A tumbling-down storefront next door was torn down and replaced with a new, similar building in 1995; this expanded the seating for summer dinners and for private parties. This is a homey Italian restaurant that could just as easily be located on a street in Naples. Everyone loves the hot, knotted, homemade dinner rolls, topped with garlic and parsley and dredged with melted butter. It is customary to sop up every drop of the potent garlicky butter from the bottom of the paper-lined basket. For entrées, there are chicken, fish, and pasta winners. Tortelloni al pistacchio is an excellent pasta stuffed with ricotta and served in an Alfredo sauce with Parmesan cheese.

PARADISE CAFE
631-725-6080.
126 Main St., Sag Harbor.
Mailing Address: PO Box 779, Sag
 Harbor, NY 11963.
Owner: Hal Zwick.
Chef: Stephen Putnam.
Cuisine: New American.

Serving: B, BR, L, D.
Open: Year-round: daily.
Price: Expensive.
Credit Cards: AE, MC, V.
Special Features: Located within a book-
 store; outside deck.
Directions: On Main St. in center of vil-
 lage.

Hal Zwick has taken the Barnes & Noble concept of café/bookstore a step further — and we love it! This terrific restaurant is located on the main floor of the Sag Harbor Book Hampton. Black-and-white tile floors, wainscot walls, and reed chairs give it a pseudo-French café atmosphere, and there's a little deck in back for outside dining. Chef Stephen Putnam (who formerly worked in New York and Connecticut) has won many awards. For dinner, try his nori-wrapped salmon with a wasabi-red onion purée and crispy shiitake mushrooms. (You see, this is serious food.) But if it's morning and you're in the mood for a great place to read the morning paper, you just might slip in for a stack of challah French toast or a bowl of Irish oatmeal with brown sugar and cinnamon.

PHAO
631-725-0055.
62 Main St., Sag Harbor.
Mailing Address: PO Box 3138, Sag
 Harbor, NY 11963.
Owner: Jeff Resnick.
Manager: Seth Kelley.
Chef: Narong Phutthasangkharat.

Cuisine: Asian Bistro with Thai and
 French influences.
Serving: D.
Open: Year-round: in summer: daily; call
 for days rest of year.
Price: Expensive.
Credit Cards: AE, MC, V.
Directions: On Main St. in center of village.

Newly opened in 2000, this French/Thai Asian bistro has gone off the charts in popularity. The setting combines brick walls, tall ceilings, and spare decor, spiced by banquettes in watermelon-colored Ultrasuede. We love the gai pad, a luscious combination of sautéed chicken with sliced cashews, onions, scallions, celery, and mushrooms.

SEN
631-725-1774.
23 Main St., Sag Harbor.
Mailing Address: PO Box 3138, Sag
 Harbor, NY 11963.
Owner: Jeff Resnick.
Manager: Seth Kelley.
Chef: Shigeki Tanaka.
Cuisine: Japanese.

Serving: D.
Open: Year-round: daily; closed Tues.
 in summer: call for days rest of year.
Price: Expensive–Very Expensive.
Credit Cards: AE, MC, V.
Special Features: No reservations
 accepted.
Directions: On Main St. in center of
 village.

Spare and lean, this Japanese standout has pale green sponged walls, oak floors, and a sushi bar. Other than white sconces, the walls are unadorned. But folks don't come for the decor, they come for the super fresh sushi and other gourmet Japanese delights. You might try the chilean sea bass moromiso, which comes with baby arugula and sun-dried tomatoes or one of the teriyki or tempura dishes. Or, you might choose from one of the extensive hand-rolled sushi or sashimi plates. There's a select list of wines, Japanese beers, and sake to accompany the meal.

Morgan McGivern

Comfortable and very pretty, this Italian Sag Harbor Main Streeter has oak floors and oil paintings on the walls.

SERAFINA
631-725-0101.
29 Main St., Sag Harbor.
Mailing Address: PO Box 3292, Sag
  Harbor, NY 11963.
Owner/Manager: Lynn Cardile.
Owner/Chef: Frank Caniglia.
Cuisine: Italian.

Serving: D.
Open: In summer: Wed.–Mon.; closed
  Tues.; rest of season: Thurs.–Mon.;
  closed Jan.–mid-Feb.
Price: Moderate–Expensive.
Credit Cards: AE, D, MC, V.
Special Features: Unique ladies room.
Directions: On Main St. in center of village.

Serafina (the restaurant is named for Lynn's great-grandmother) is one of the prettiest restaurants around. There are oak floors, tapestry draperies at the windows, fringed tapestry shades on the lamps, and elegant paintings on the walls. And although it may seem peculiar to rhapsodize about a restaurant ladies room, this one is pretty terrific. It's a two-level room decorated with teddy bears, dolls, plants, and a Gothic-backed chair. Friendly, obviously happily employed staff are able to describe the ingredients and preparations of dishes with knowledge and enthusiasm. For entrées, there are numerous pastas and veal dishes, such as veal Bettina, a dish of sautéed veal with wild mushroom-saffron demi-glaze. The dessert list is long and varied. You might have a toasted almond-amaretto cream cake or end the meal in a traditional Italian manner with biscotti and espresso.

SOUTHAMPTON

AMAZONIA
631-283-9113.
450 County Rd. 39, Southampton, NY
 11968.
Owner/Chef: João Garcia.
Cuisine: Brazilian.
Serving: D.

Open: Year-round.
Price: Inexpensive.
Credit Cards: MC, V.
Special Features: Fireplace; bossa nova
 nights.
Directions: On County Rd. 39 beside
 Southampton Motel.

It takes a leap of faith to open a little restaurant that's beside an old, decrepit, closed motel that's barely visible from the road. But with assurances that the motel would soon undergo a pretty face-lift, João Garcia opened his authentic Brazilian churrascaría in 1999. That he has succeeded so admirably even though the motel is still boarded up, speaks volumes about his cooking. You can get feijoada, the Brazilian national dish, which includes black beans with beef, pork, sausage, and ribs and rodizio, a selection of skewered beef, pork, poultry, and sausage. Best of all, the prices are so low you wonder how he can do it — and the wine list has some lovely selections from Chile, Portugal, and Argentina — none of which top $22.

Sophisticated and stylish, basilico has made its mark on Southampton.

Morgan McGivern

basilico
631-283-7987.
E-mail: basilico@prodigy.net.
10 Windmill Ln., Southampton, NY
 11968.
Owner: Philipp Manser.
Manager: Gayle Donahue.
Chef: John Wayne Viosie.
Cuisine: Italian.

Serving: L, D.
Open: Year-round: D daily; L Sat., Sun.
 and occasionally addl. days.
Price: Moderate–Very Expensive; prix
 fixe offered.
Credit Cards: AE, D, MC, V.
Special Features: Wheelchair access.
Directions: On corner of Windmill and
 Job's Lns.

This restaurant has that fresh, airy feeling of Santa Fe, but the food is strictly Northern Italian. Stucco walls, tiled floors, high ceilings, and unusual, hanging, beaded lamp shades create a casual, but upscale atmosphere. The menu offers a good selection of antipasti, pastas, and several interesting pizzas. But this is a much more serious restaurant than those dishes suggest. For example, imagine a chicken breast marinated in lemon and fresh herb oil, then grilled and charred on the outside, but tender and juicy on the inside. The wine list is almost exclusively Italian, with only one Long Island Merlot and four California whites, but the Italian wines are well selected, if pricey. All desserts are made on the premises and include a tiramisù, chocolate-raspberry cheesecake, and crème brûlée.

THE COAST GRILL
631-283-2277; fax: 631-287-4496.
1109 Noyack Rd., Southampton, NY 11968.
Owner/Manager: Joseph Luppi.
Chef: Brian Finnegan.
Cuisine: American Contemporary/Seafood.
Serving: D.
Open: YMid-June–mid-Sept.: daily; rest of year: Fri.–Sun.

Price: Expensive.
Credit Cards: AE, MC, V.
Special Features: Wheelchair access; on the water.
Directions: From Montauk Hwy., drive north on North Sea Rd. to intersection with Noyack Rd. Restaurant is 2 miles east on Noyack Rd. in Peconic Marina.

The Coast Grill serves absolutely fresh fish prepared in a simple, straightforward manner. Before opening this restaurant, owner Joseph Luppi served as cooking assistant to the *New York Times* food editor, Craig Claiborne, and to the late chef and columnist Pierre Franey, so he learned from the best. The menu is not extensive, but diners can depend on expert attention to the preparation of each dish. An entrée of seared salmon is served with a horseradish and watercress vinaigrette. Every night the list of specials features the daily catch, which might include Peconic bay scallops, wild striped bass, or soft-shell crabs. As one might expect, the wine list offers excellent accompaniments to the menu, with about thirty white wines and about twenty-five red wines.

LE CHEF
631-283-8581.
75 Job's Ln., Southampton, NY 11968.
Owner/Chef: Frank Lenihan.
Manager: Shane Dyckman.
Cuisine: French.

Serving: L, D.
Open: Year-round: daily; closed Thanksgiving, Christmas.
Price: Inexpensive; prix fixe offered.
Credit Cards: AE, MC, V.
Special Features: Wheelchair access.

This pretty little restaurant with its tiny, up-front bar serves creative French fare, at very reasonable prices. The lovely restaurant attracts patrons who appreciate fine cuisine in a congenial setting at reasonable prices. The $20.95 prix fixe dinner is the best buy in the Hamptons (how do they do it?). You can choose from about fifteen soups or salads. The mild, curried carrot soup is delicious, and the biscuit-sized crab cakes are creamy and filled with chunks of flaky crab. Next you can choose from about fifteen entrées. The grilled fillet of salmon with a mustard-dill hollandaise is outstanding. Other entrées might include lobster, veal chop, or fresh sea bass. (Although there are supplemental charges for several, all entrées come with vegetables and potato or rice.) For dessert, the selection includes cappuccino mousse, cheesecake, crème caramel, and many more. Naturally, there's a fine wine list.

PLAZA CAFÉ
631-283-9323.
www.plazacafesouthampton.com.
61 Hill St., Southampton, NY 11968.
Owner/Chef: Douglas Gulija.
Cuisine: New American.
Serving: D.
Open: Year-round: in summer: daily; rest of year: Tues.–Sun.; closed Mon.

Price: Expensive.
Credit Cards: AE, DC, MC, V.
Special Features: Fireplace.
Directions: From Hill St., turn north by Southampton Inn. Restaurant is tucked into shopping plaza on right side of street behind 71 Hill St. Plaza.

Proponents of this New American restaurant rave about the caring service, the pretty setting, and the accomplished kitchen. Chef Doug Gulija, who was chef previously at Le Grand Vefour in Paris, has created a distinctive cuisine that somehow manages to be cutting edge without losing a certain comfort level. His signature dish of seafood "Shepherd's Pie" uses local lobster, shrimp, shiitake mushrooms, and corn in a chive-potato crust, which leaves diners begging for more. It's all served in a soothing setting that combines a cathedral-ceilinged room with gold-sponged walls, gray carpet, and a fireplace.

Casual but gracious, the red/bar brasserie attracts a chic following.

Suzi Forbes Chase

red/bar brasserie
631-283-0704.
210 Hampton Rd., Southampton, NY 11968.
Owners: Kirk Basnight and David Loewenberg.
Chef: Erik Nodeland.
Cuisine: French-inspired American Brasserie.

Serving: D.
Open: Year-round: Wed.–Mon.
Price: Expensive.
Credit Cards: AE, MC, V.
Directions: From Main St., drive east on Hampton Rd. Restaurant is on right in about 1 mile.

Romantic and casual, red/bar has become a favorite Southampton destination since its opening in 1998. The setting is crisp, airy, and elegant, highlighted by the walls of windows on three sides that permeate the room with light in daytime and act as reflectors for the candles that light the tables at night. The food is consistently good. One of the most popular dishes is the pan-roasted poussin with black olive mashed potatoes and provençal vegetables. The amaretto cheesecake with raspberry compote is wonderful.

SANT AMBROEUS
631-283-1233.
30 Main St., Southampton, NY 11968.
Chef: Mario Daniele.
Cuisine: Italian Ristorante/Pasticcerìa.
Serving: L, D.
Open: Apr.–Dec.: in summer: daily;
fewer days rest of season.
Price: Moderate–Very Expensive.
Credit Cards: AE, MC, V.
Special Features: Wheelchair access; espresso bar; pasticcerìa.
Directions: On Main St. in center of village.

Similar to its sisters in Milan and New York, this authentic Italian confetterìa has glass cases in the front where the most remarkable cakes and pastry confections are displayed. Sant Ambroeus has such a Milanese flavor that you feel as if you should speak Italian. The tempting selections in the front include gelati and Italian cakes, pastries, cookies, and chocolates. Midway into the restaurant, there's an espresso bar, and behind the bar is a small, white linen tablecloth restaurant. Watermelon-colored Ultrasuede banquettes and bentwood chairs offer sophisticated backdrops for the wonderful meat dishes, risottos, pastas, and salads. There are about fifteen selections of both red and white Italian wines to accompany the meal.

SAVANNA'S
631-283-0202.
268 Elm St., Southampton, NY 11968.
Manager: Roberto Polesello.
Chefs: Javier Sanchez and Barry Gladman.
Cuisine: Contemporary American.
Serving: D, BR/L (Sat., Sun. only).
Open: In summer: daily; fewer days rest of season; closed Oct.–Apr.
Price: Moderate–Very Expensive; prix fix offered.
Credit Cards: AE, D, DC, MC, V.
Special Features: Wheelchair access; outdoor dining pavilion; fireplace.
Directions: From traffic light in center of village, travel east on Hampton Rd. Turn left onto Elm St. and follow to end. Restaurant is on right before train station.

Slick and trim, Savanna's is also beautiful. In this transformation of Southampton's old village hall (and later a funky bar/restaurant), the formerly dark interior walls have been removed, and three exterior walls contain windows, so a light-filled space now reigns. At night, votive candles line the windowsills, creating a magical effect. There are columns inside the restaurant and a fireplace at one end. In the summer, an outdoor pavilion in back is a marvelous place to dine; a tentlike structure is supported by Grecian columns. The entrées are presented with flair: the Chilean sea bass is accompanied by haricot vert, roasted garlic, orzo, and fresh sun-dried tomato paste. The wine list is excellent, both in selections by the glass and range of wines by the bottle. There are Long Island wines, as well as California, Italian, and French, including a vintage Margaux. After dinner, while you are contemplating the dessert selections, coffee is served with little teasers of peanut brittle and cookies.

75 MAIN STREET
631-283-7575.
75 Main St., Southampton, NY 11968.
Owner: June Spira.
Chef: David Girard
Cuisine: Long Island Regional.
Serving: D, BR/L, LN.

Open: Year-round: daily.
Price: Moderate–Very Expensive.
Credit Cards: AE, MC, V.
Special Features: Wheelchair access; smoking in bar only.
Directions: On Main St. in center of village.

Attracting a young, upscale crowd, 75 Main is trendy and casual. It has oak floors, daffodil-colored sponged walls and wainscotting, and French doors across the front that open to the sidewalk. The bar area in the front is as large as the restaurant in the back. It's a popular place to see and to be seen. Furthermore, the food keeps getting better and better, and the wine list won a *Wine Spectator* award in 1996. The brick oven, behind a brightly tiled counter in the back, is responsible for several dishes, such as the roast organic chicken stuffed with spinach and arugula.

SOUTHAMPTON PUBLICK HOUSE
631-283-2800; fax: 631-283-2801.
www.publick.com.
40 Bowden Sq., Southampton, NY 11968.
Manager: Kevin Sullivan.
Chef: Donald Sullivan.
Cuisine: Contemporary American/Microbrewery.
Serving: L, BR, D.
Open: Year-round.

Price: Inexpensive–Expensive; early-bird Mon.–Fri.; prix fixe Thurs., Sun.
Credit Cards: AE, D, MC, V.
Special Features: Wheelchair access; porch dining; fireplaces; live music Fri., Sat.
Directions: From traffic light in center of village, travel north on North Sea Rd. to intersection with Bowden Sq. Restaurant is on right.

The enormous stainless steel vats behind their glass viewing windows dominate one end of the dining room but that just adds to the charm of this casual restaurant. There are brick walls, oak floors, stenciling on boxed beams, a tin ceiling and tin walls, and fireplaces in the dining room and tap-room. On the menu, you'll find herb-roasted salmon and ale-battered fish and chips. The most expensive item on the menu is the hefty, 20-ounce, Cajun-spiced rib eye steak at $20. There are eight microbrews on tap, and the wine list includes some local wines. On weekends, there's live entertainment. There's a wonderful, broad front porch that serves as an outside dining room almost year-round.

SPEONK

CANTUSA
631-325-9024.
www.cantusa.com.
190 Montauk Hwy., Speonk.
Mailing Address: PO Box 572, Speonk,
NY 11972.
Owners: Isabelle and Craig Cohen.
Cuisine: Eclectic.
Serving: D.

Open: In summer: Wed.–Mon.; closed
Tues; call for days rest of year.
Price: Moderate.
Credit Cards: AE, MC, V.
Special Features: Lounge with music and
dancing Fri., Sat.
Directions: On Rte. 27, 1/4 mile east of
Speonk and 2 miles west of
Westhampton.

L ocated in a rambling old roadhouse (it used to be the Millstone), Cantusa charms us with its stained glass windows, lace curtains, red velvet flocked loveseats at the entrance and the enthusiasm of its owners. Craig, who is from the U.S. met Isabelle, who hails from Canada, and the restaurant name is a contraction of the two countries. You might start with an appetizer of Champagne-battered lamb chop with vanilla-pepper cream or bass ale chili with veal, wheat berries, and crumbled blue cheese. For an entrée, you can't surpass the pan-bronzed veal chop with marinated figs and Stilton cheese in a roasted garlic Port wine demi-glace. There's a separate bar and beyond that, a cozy lounge where you can mellow out while listening to jazz or blues on the weekend, or you can dance cheek to cheek.

WAINSCOTT

SARACEN
631-537-6255.
108 Montauk Hwy., Wainscott, NY
11975.
Owners: Robert Silvestri and Michael
Tadross.
Chef: Franco Russo.
Cuisine: Coastal Italian.
Serving: D, BR (Sun. only).

Open: Year-round: in summer: daily;
fewer days rest of year.
Price: Expensive–Very Expensive.
Credit Cards: AE, DC, MC, V.
Special Features: Glass-enclosed porch
overlooking Georgica Pond;
Champagne brunch on Sun.
Directions: Located on Montauk Hwy.
(Rte. 27) at Wainscott Stone Hwy.

P ino Luongo's showstopper restaurant Sapore di Mare could be counted on for excellent cuisine, professional service, and a lovely setting adored by celebs and wanna-bes for almost fifteen years, but then he decided to sell. Now Saracen occupies this ample space — the East End creation of Robert Silvestri, a Manhattan restaurateur and his partner. The beautiful setting, on the banks of Georgica Pond, and the multilevel dining rooms that overlook the seductively peaceful view remain as romantic as ever. An evening dinner on the porch over-looking the pond, where exterior lighting casts a magical mood as it lights up the trees and the calm waters and as diners watch swans glide by, turns a dinner here into an unforgettable experience. And the food is good, too. You might start with a light pasta dish, then feast on Chilean sea bass with crispy leeks.

WATER MILL

MIRKO'S RESTAURANT
631-726-4444.
www.mirkosrestaurant.com.
Water Mill Sq., Montauk Hwy., Water Mill.
Mailing Address: PO Box 217, Water Mill,
NY 11976.
Manager: Eileen Zagar.
Chef: Mirko Zagar.
Cuisine: Continental.

Serving: D.
Open: In summer: Thurs.–Mon.; fewer
days rest of year.
Price: Expensive–Very Expensive.
Credit Cards: AE, MC, V.
Special Features: Wheelchair access;
outdoor patio; fireplace.
Directions: After turning into Water Mill
Sq., turn left. Restaurant is at end.

Mirko Zagar is Yugoslavian born, and his inventive cooking reflects an Eastern European influence as well as that of France. The restaurant is tucked away in the back of Water Mill Sq., definitely not a place you'd stumble onto by accident. Once there, however, you'll find a tranquil setting, far from the traffic noise of Montauk Hwy. You'll also find a husband and wife team who are absolutely dedicated to making your dining experience so memorable that you'll return again and again. Eileen will greet you at the door and see to your every dining need. Grilled shrimp and bacon is a wonderful appetizer — plump shrimp are wrapped in bacon, grilled, and served in a light lemon, pepper, and white wine sauce, laced with coarsely diced shallots. For entrées, the rack of lamb has a mustard seed crust. There's also a well chosen wine list. Among the desserts, I love the house specialty, "The Pear," which is as much a work of art as a sweet; a whole poached pear is balanced atop ice cream and drizzled with chocolate and raspberry sauces. Mirko and Eileen even grow their own herbs and vegetables behind the restaurant. Inside the dining room, the fireplace is welcoming on chilly nights, and the small details — golden yellow sponged walls, Pierre Deux fabrics, exquisite sconces with pretty shades, lace curtains, and wainscotted walls — conspire to transport us to Europe.

ROBERT'S
631-726-7171.
755 Montauk Hwy., Water Mill, NY 11976.
Owner/Manager: Robert Durkin.
Chef de Cuisine: Natalie Byrnes.
Cuisine: Italian Coastal.
Serving: D.

Open: In summer: nightly; in winter:
fewer days.
Price: Very Expensive.
Credit Cards: AE, MC, V.
Special Features: Wheelchair access;
working fireplace.
Directions: At traffic light in Water Mill.

Robert Durkin, the longtime owner of Karen Lee's in Bridgehampton, has moved down the highway to Water Mill and transformed his French/ American menu into a lively Coastal Italian bill of fare. Located in a charming pre-Revolutionary War building with low, beamed ceilings, wide-plank pine floors, and a fireplace (it housed Jenny's in 1998), the new place is intimate and utterly romantic. There's a preponderance of seafood on the menu. Among the favorites are the grilled salmon on warm white beans with roasted fresh morels. My favorite dessert is a fallen chocolate hazelnut soufflé cake, but the silky smooth panna cotta with biscotti and a glass of vin santo will fill you with reminiscences of your most memorable meal in the heart of Tuscany.

A new look and globally-inspired International cuisine transformed the former Station Bistro into this smart destination in Water Mill's former train station.

Morgan McGivern

STATION ROAD
631-726-3016.
50 Station Rd., Water Mill.
Mailing Address: PO Box 356, Water Mill, NY 11976.
Owner: Dean Golden.
Manager: Carol Covell.
Chefs: Tim Smith and Orlando Strauss.
Cuisine: Globally inspired International.
Serving: D.

Open: In summer: Wed.–Mon.; closed Tues.; in winter: fewer days.
Price: Expensive.
Credit Cards: MC, V.
Special Features: Wheelchair access; in 1903 train station; outdoor patio.
Directions: From Montauk Hwy., turn onto Station Rd. just east of Water Mill at traffic light. Restaurant is at end of road.

All aboard! The International Express is bound for taste sensations! Where once there was French Provincial fare and then Mediterranean, new owner Dean Golden is transporting us to far-flung destinations with a menu that combines local produce with Asian and South American spices. An appetizer of sesame-crusted lemongrass and scallion crab cakes flecked with ginger and an entrée of roasted North Fork Crescent duck with cherry-rice wine sauce and yucca-scallion cake are only two examples. The setting in Water Mill's charming 1903 brick railroad station (the train no longer stops here) is as delightful as ever. Light streams in the tall windows during the day, and a massive chandelier, hanging from the tall ceiling, takes over the job at night. Fresh flowers and candlelight make this a romantic retreat. There's a pretty brick courtyard, where drinks are served on hot summer days, and a covered porch for summer dining. The bar in an adjacent restored railroad club car is open on Fri. and Sat. nights; it has stunning stained glass windows and polished mahogany paneling.

WESTHAMPTON BEACH

MAISON ROUGE
631-288-3009.
10 Beach Rd., Westhampton Beach.
Mailing Address: 23 Sunset Ave.,
Westhampton Beach, NY
11978.
Owner/Chef: Ali Fathalla.
Cuisine: French Provincial.
Serving: D.

Open: In summer: daily; fewer days off-
season.
Price: Expensive.
Credit Cards: AE, D, MC, V.
Special Features: Fireplace; outside
courtyard.
Directions: From Main St., turn north
onto Beach St. Restaurant is on right
bet. Main and Church Sts.

This charming, red wooden building (which explains its Maison Rouge moniker) looks like an 1850s stagecoach stop, but it was once the game room of the Howell House, a hotel that was located on Main St. The charm of the exterior is carried through to the inside, with beamed ceilings, paneled walls, and cheery fireplace. Ali Fathalla, who has been the chef proprietaire of Le Bistro (formerly called Saffron) in Westhampton Beach for many years, took over this restaurant in 2000. He serves a French Provincial menu that includes Long Island duck à l'orange and roasted rack of lamb with fresh rosemary sauce.

Starr Boggs exceptional fare is enhanced by a setting of seagrass and sand dunes bordering the ocean.

Morgan McGivern

STARR BOGGS
631-288-5250; fax: 631-288-5050.
379 Dune Rd., Westhampton Beach, NY
11978.
Owner/Chef: Starr Boggs.
Manager: Lenny Reggio.
Cuisine: Continental.
Serving: D, (L in summer).
Open: In summer: daily; rest of season:
Thurs.–Sun.; closed Dec.–mid-May.

Price: Expensive–Very Expensive; prix
fixe offered.
Credit Cards: AE, CB, DC, MC, V.
Special Features: Oceanside dining with
view; live entertainment some nights.
Directions: From Main St., Westhampton
Beach, drive south on Jessup Ln. across
bridge to Dune Rd. Restaurant is in
Dune Deck Hotel, on left 1.2 miles.

Starr Boggs' setting in the Dune Deck Hotel is dramatic in its simplicity, highlighted by a mirrored wall that reflects the spectacular dunes and ocean outside. The story here is the food, however, not the setting. Chef Boggs is very particular about all of his raw ingredients. He does his own purchasing, often taking early morning trips to farm stands and fish markets to see what's best. He has his own label of wines, but also carries an excellent selection of Long Island, California, and French wines. For dinner one night I started with his Virginia crab cake (he hales from Virginia), which was light and moist. My entrée was an almond-crusted flounder with lemon butter and a glazed banana. All presentations are colorful and attractive, but this was exceptionally so. My dessert of fallen chocolate soufflé was fabulous — served on crème anglaise with fresh raspberries.

On Mon. nights things really swing — a distinct departure from the more sedate dining the rest of the week. Starr sets up a buffet lobster bake on the beach that includes a raw bar, plenty of salad and vegetables, and strawberry shortcake for dessert. A hot reggae band swings into action, and everyone heads for the dance floor.

TIERRA MAR

631-288-2700.
www.tierramar.com.
231 Dune Rd. (Westhampton Bath & Tennis Hotel), Westhampton Beach.
Mailing Address: PO Box 1648, Westhampton Beach, NY 11978.
Owner/Executive Chef: Todd Jacobs.
Cuisine: American with classical French overtones.
Serving: B, L, D.

Open: In summer: daily; fewer days rest of year.
Price: Expensive–Very Expensive.
Credit Cards: AE, D, MC, V.
Special Features: Fabulous ocean views; outdoor deck.
Directions: From Main St., Westhampton Beach, drive south on Jessup Ln. across bridge to Dune Rd. Turn left. Restaurant is in Westhampton Bath & Tennis Hotel on right.

The ocean side setting is spectacular, and even though the dining room is large, it is divided by wide floor-to-ceiling columns that are draped in a soft blue-and-white striped fabric, giving tables an intimacy. The ceiling is tented in the same fabric, and there's a magnificent crystal chandelier hanging in the center. Dramatic as the decor is, however, nothing can compare with the stunning view of the ocean from the floor-to-ceiling windows. In 2000, Todd Jacobs moved his Montauk Hwy. restaurant, Tierra Mar, to this location (where he had previously operated his summer only Atlantica). An entrée of pan-roasted free-range chicken with fresh rosemary was crispy on the outside and tender and succulent on the inside, just as it should be, while the grilled Shinnecock striped bass is served with carrot broth infused with ginger and lemongrass.

FOOD PURVEYORS

Social events, dinner parties, art gallery openings, fund-raising benefits, and al fresco picnics consistently give business to Hamptons' caterers, bakers, restaurant chefs, confectioners, delis, gourmet shops, and wineshops. Fish markets stock fish fresh from the morning catch, and farmers' markets sell produce straight from the field. Specialty food shops are filled with homemade jams, jellies, chutneys, and breads, as well as with the pungent smells of aging cheeses and freshly brewed coffee. Juice bars offer thick mixtures of fresh strawberries, bananas, lemons, and other fruits in season that are cool refreshers after a hot day at the beach. Coffee bars serve cappuccinos, espressos, lattés, and American coffees.

BAKERIES

SOUTHAMPTON

Tate's Bake Shop (631-283-9830; www.tatesbakeshop.com; 43 North Sea Rd., Southampton, NY 11968) Open daily 8am–6pm; in summer: weekends 8am–7pm. Kathleen King opened her shop at this location more than twenty years ago — eventually building a distribution network that supplied more than 300 upscale gourmet shops nationwide — so when she resigned following a dispute with out-of-state backers, you could hear the cry of dismay all the way to Manhattan. Now we're happy to report that Kathleen's back in business. The shop is now called Tate's after Kathleen's father, but the baked goods are as fabulous as ever, and once again you can buy those chocolate chip cookies, apple crumb pies, breads, and scones. Best of all, her baked goods are good for you. She uses all natural products with no preservatives and makes everything herself from scratch, just as our grandmothers used to do.

WAINSCOTT

Breadzilla (631-537-0955; 84 Northwest Rd., PO Box 384, Wainscott, NY 11975) Open year-round: Tues.–Sat. 8am–5:30pm, Sun. 8am–3pm. Nancy and Brad Thompson have filled their wonderful shop with home-baked breads, cakes, pies, cheesecakes, and individual desserts. The Parmesan bread is crusted with yummy cheese, and the chocolate mousse is divine.

WESTHAMPTON BEACH

Beach Bakery Cafe (631-288-6552; 112 Main St., Westhampton Beach, NY 11978) Open daily 7am–6pm; in summer: 7am–12 midnight. The wonderful aroma wafting from this little bakery is like a magnet, but so are the delicious goodies. Great breads, cookies, cakes, pies, and much more are made by Simon, the owner, and they are baked on the premises. In summer, he also makes a terrific pizza that he will deliver. Simon tripled the size of his bakery in 1998 to make room for little café tables and chairs, where you can munch a goodie or savor some ice cream.

Holey Moses Cheesecake (631-288-8088; Bldg. 115, Frances S. Gabreski Airport, Westhampton Beach, NY 11978) Open Mon.–Sat. 8:30am–5pm; closed Sun. Chris Weber's cheesecakes are sold in 300 restaurant and food outlets in an eight-state region. He'll take orders for a single cheesecake, or 1,000. His cheesecakes are so popular that restaurants proudly proclaim "cheesecakes from Holey Moses." His most popular flavors are pumpkin, Oreo cookie, lime, and original recipe.

CAFES & COFFEEHOUSES

A restaurant is listed here as a café if, in general, dinner is not served. In several of the following, dinner is served as well as breakfast and lunch, but if it is best known and loved as a breakfast and lunch spot, it has been placed in the café category.

AMAGANSETT

Hampton Chutney Co. (631-267-3131; Amagansett Sq., PO Box 273, Amagansett, NY 11930) Open in summer: 10am–7pm; fewer days and shorter hours rest of year. Gary and Isabel Mac Gurn have moved their terrific chutney company (try the cilantro or tomato) to Amagansett Sq., where diners can sit at picnic tables in the grassy square and eat the lovely dosas, which are light, thin, and crispy crêpes made with rice and lentils and filled with interesting ingredients, such as grilled chicken with goat cheese, spinach, and roasted tomato. They can also get a tall, refreshing lassi, a smoothie made with yogurt and fresh fruit.

BRIDGEHAMPTON

Bridgehampton Candy Kitchen (631-537-9885; Main St., PO Box 3011, Bridgehampton, NY 11932) Open in summer: daily 7am–10pm; in fall: daily 7am–8pm; in winter: daily 7am–7pm. The spot for breakfast or an afternoon ice-cream treat! This old-fashioned coffee shop and soda fountain has been in business since 1925. It's a legendary star hangout that looks much as it did when it opened. The food hasn't changed much either. Breakfast is of the bacon and eggs variety. In the afternoon and evening, there are hamburgers, clubs, and grilled cheese sandwiches. Milk shakes, ice-cream sodas, and egg creams are just as they should be. Sundaes have sauce dripping down the sides, with a mound of whipped cream, chocolate sprinkles, and a cherry. You can also get cherry and lemon Cokes. The ice cream is made on the premises in a wide variety of flavors. There's nothing fancy here, just old-fashioned, good food.

The Golden Pear Café (631-537-1100; 2426 Main St., Bridgehampton, NY 11932; 631-329-1600; 34 Newtown Ln., East Hampton, NY 11937; 631-283-8900; 97-99 Main St., Southampton, NY 11968; 631-288-3600; 103 Main St., Westhampton Beach, NY 11978) Open daily 7:30am–5:45pm. Owner Keith Davis's Golden Pear Cafés, now in four locations, offer both eat-in and takeout. Newspapers are on hand, and these bright, welcoming, convivial spots are great for breakfast, for lunch, or just relaxing with a friend over a cup of coffee. There's nothing fast-food about these restaurants; each has its own chef who prepares the menu items. There are fresh muffins and cookies hot from the oven, excellent salads, and a variety of hot dishes, such as pastas, chilies, chicken pot pies, and pies and cakes available whole or by the slice.

Starbucks (631-537-5851; 2478 Montauk Hwy., Bridgehampton, NY 11932) Open in summer: daily 6:30am–10pm; shorter hours rest of year. Finally, in 2000, a Starbucks opened in the Hamptons. Located in the fabulous old Bridgehampton Bank building, right at the monument in the center of the village, it's the classiest Starbucks we've seen. It's all done in gold, brick, and mocha colors, and there's a carpeted area with comfortable chairs and sofas. For a refreshing summer drink, try the fruit tiazzis.

EAST HAMPTON

Babette's (631-329-5377; 66 Newtown Ln., East Hampton, NY 11937) Open in summer: daily 8am–10pm; fewer days and shorter hours rest of year. Babette's has earned high esteem both with health-conscious celebrities and with non-vegetarians for its interesting and unusual vegetarian and organic dishes. Try the gift-wrapped burritos with grilled tofu, tempeh, tuna, chicken, or shrimp. Sip a smoothie at an outside table — you may be sitting next to Meg Ryan or Bernadette Peters.

Snowflake Cafe (631-329-7867; 277 Pantigo Rd., East Hampton, NY 11937) Open in summer: 8am–11pm; fewer days and shorter hours rest of year. Manager: Louise Weber. The Snowflake has been around as an old-fashioned drive-in for years, but new owner Hal Zwick completed a makeover in 2000 that brought the terrific old café into the twenty-first century. There's a courtyard for outside dining that's hidden behind a privet hedge and inside dining that's comfortable and contemporary. You can still get a hot fudge sundae, an ice-cream soda, or a super thick shake, but you can also get a smoothie, French toast made with challah, a lobster roll, and crispy fried chicken.

CIGAR & TOBACCO CAFES

Even as restaurants are banning smoke in their dining rooms, the popularity of cigars are on the increase. In the Hamptons, as in Manhattan, exclusive clubs where one may smoke cigars are rising from the smoke. Often these include special rooms, open to members only, that offer locked, individual humidors and comfortable lounges where cigar smoking is welcomed. There also may be a Scotch and cordial bar and live entertainment.

SAG HARBOR

The Cigar Bar (631-725-2575; 2 Main St., Sag Harbor, NY 11963) Open in summer: 12 noon–4am; slightly shorter hours rest of year. This elegant shop has a fine selection of thirty-forty imported cigars; pick your choice from those in a 12 x 10-foot walk-in humidor. You can also buy cigar accessories, including an elegant Spanish cedar humidor. There are overstuffed chairs, Oriental rugs on the floor, and a lounge with original art on the walls. At the little bar, you can select cognac, single malt Scotch, wine, espresso, or cappuccino for sipping. A pianist entertains on weekends.

EGGS & POULTRY

EAST HAMPTON

Iacono Farms (631-324-1107; 106 Long Ln., East Hampton, NY 11937) Open June–Sept.: Mon.–Sat. 8:30am–5pm, Sun. 10am–12:30pm; Oct.–May: closed Mon., Tues. The plump, juicy chickens that Salvadore and Eileen Iacono have been raising since 1948 are deservedly popular, as are their super fresh eggs. It's often advisable to order in advance on summer weekends, because they sell out early. And you'll also want to take home some of the breads and cookies made by their daughter. The Iaconos are some of the busiest and nicest folks around. No matter how many grouchy, impatient customers are lined up, there's always a pleasant word for each.

SOUTHAMPTON

North Sea Farms (631-283-0735; 1060 Noyac Rd., Southampton, NY 11968) Open year-round: daily 7:30am–6:30pm. Owner: Richie King. This terrific farm raises succulent, fat chickens that are prized for their tenderness, and many restaurateurs come here for their supply. But you don't have to go to a restaurant to sample them. You can pick up a fresh hen here for a tasty summer barbecue at home, and while you're at it, you might pick up some fresh eggs and organic produce.

FARMS & FARM STANDS

AMAGANSETT

Amagansett Farmers Market (631-267-3894; 367 Main St., Amagansett, NY 11930) Open July–Aug.: daily 7am–8pm; Mar.–July, Sept.–Thanksgiving:

*Vegetables and fruits grow in
abundance in the Hamptons.*

Tulla Booth

daily 8am–6pm, weekends 8am–7pm; closed Dec.–Mar. The steady expansion of this market over the years makes it popular on a variety of levels. It's the place to go, for example, on a sunny day for the newspaper, coffee, and sticky buns from the bakery. Patrons are encouraged to relax on the lawn or on benches down by the fishpond. The variety of fresh produce and fruit is staggering. In addition, the market includes a deli section with salads, pâtés, cheeses, and roast or fried chicken; a gourmet packaged goods grocery; and a cold section with sodas, egg creams, milk, eggs, and ice cream. Outside, there's a selection of plants for the garden. You can also buy prepared foods made right at the market: jellies, jams, preserves, pickles, barbecue sauce, chutneys, fresh peanut butter, catsup, syrups, sauces, and dried fruit — all carrying the Amagansett Farmers Market label.

BRIDGEHAMPTON

Hayground Market (631-537-1676; Montauk Hwy., PO Box 623, Bridgehampton, NY 11932) Open Apr.–Nov.: in summer: daily 7am–9pm; in fall: daily 7am–8pm; closed Nov.–Mar. You'll recognize the Hayground Market by the tall ear of corn at the edge of Montauk Hwy. or the big cauliflower on a farm wagon. You'll also notice piles of pumpkins attractively displayed in the fall and washtubs full of brilliantly hued zinnias earlier in the season, as well as bountiful displays of produce, fruits, and berries. The 200-acre home farm that supports this large market has been in the Reeve family for many generations, and the farm stand has been operating since the early 1950s.

EAST HAMPTON

Round Swamp Farm Country Market (631-324-4438; 184 Three Mile Harbor Rd., East Hampton, NY 11937) Open May–Nov.: Mon.–Sat. 8am–6pm, Sun.

8am–5pm; closed rest of year. Round Swamp Farm, "Farmers of Land and Sea," is supported by the twenty-acre Lester Farm that has been in the family for 250 years. Carolyn Lester Snyder started selling the family bounty when she was a child from a tiny, roadside stand built for her by her father. Now sixteen family members contribute goods to the market. Piles of tender, white corn are heaped on a farm wagon; tomatoes, potatoes, and onions fill the bins; and the chilled produce room is stocked with a variety of lettuces, peppers, herbs, fruit, and berries. Baked goods are a family specialty. Cookies, breads, muffins, chutneys, relishes, and cakes are snapped up by loyal customers. Homemade soups and a small selection of salads are also popular. An adjacent fish market supplies fresh fish daily and also has a refrigerated milk, egg, and cheese section. Freshly cut flowers are also available.

WATER MILL

The 77-acre Halsey Farm, which has been in the same family since 1644, supplies The Green Thumb market in Water Mill with its organic produce.

Morgan McGivern

The Green Thumb (631-726-1900; Montauk Hwy., Water Mill; mail: 132 Halsey Ln., Water Mill, NY 11976) Open May–Dec.: daily 8am–6pm; later in midsummer. The seventy-seven-acre Halsey Farm has been in the family since 1644 and is now in the capable hands of the eleventh generation. It's an award-winning, certified, fully organic farm. For dependable, high-quality produce, this farm stand can't be beat. The Halsey family grows over fifteen varieties of lettuce, twelve kinds of salad greens, nineteen different herbs, a colorful variety of sweet peppers, red and gold raspberries, beans, tomatoes, squash, pumpkins, flowers, and much, much more. At The Green Thumb, you can buy the tiny French green beans (haricots verts) and succulent, little yellow pear tomatoes, as well as other, more unusual varieties. In summer, there are pony rides for children.

FISH MARKETS

AMAGANSETT

Stuart's Fish Market (631-267-6700; 41 Oak Ln., PO Box 1859, Amagansett, NY 11930) Open year-round: daily 9:30am–6pm; longer summer hours. Stuart's Fish Market is definitely not on the beaten track. It's on a narrow, residential side street between East Hampton and Amagansett, not even close to any water. Nevertheless, the owners are fishermen who catch what they sell. They're in Montauk waters in summer, and off the Florida coast in winter. There's a good seafood selection, with fresh shellfish still in their watery tank. Several local specialties also are made by Stuart's — the clam chowder (both New England and Manhattan varieties) is thick with chunks of potatoes, carrots, celery, onions, bacon, and clams, and the New England clam chowder is made with real cream. On request, they'll order the best homemade clam pies that you'll ever have.

MONTAUK

Gosman's Fish Market (631-668-5645; 484 West Lake Dr., PO Box 2340, Montauk, NY 11954) Open Apr.–Nov.: daily 10am–5pm; closed rest of year. Gosman's Fish Market is located on the Montauk docks near their restaurant. The range of fish and shellfish is one of the largest on the East End. You'll find tanks of clams, oysters, and lobsters and cases of shrimp, salmon, bass, flounder, tuna, shark, and just about anything else — fresh from the fishing boats. Many locals consider this their favorite fish market.

WAINSCOTT

The Seafood Shop (631-537-0633; 356 Montauk Hwy., PO Box 246, Wainscott, NY 11975) Open year-round: daily 8am–8pm. The Seafood Shop carries a wide array of fresh fish and shellfish. In addition, it has a crew of fishmongers who will fillet a whole fish, cut custom-ordered fish steaks, or prepare just about any other special order that you may want. This fish market has been around a long time and has a loyal following of summer and year-round residents.

GOURMET FOOD SHOPS & MARKETS

In general, the following shops operate busy catering businesses as well as storefront shops, and they have many more recipes in their culinary repertoire than meet the eye. If planning a party or a catered dinner, be sure to discuss the event with the catering manager, who can plan a menu specifically for you.

BRIDGEHAMPTON

Razzano's (631-537-7288; Bridgehampton Commons, Bridgehampton; mail: c/o Bravo Foods, 35 Bethpage Rd., Hicksville, NY 11801) Open daily 9:30am–7:30pm; restaurant open 11:30am–8:30pm (later in summer). Vincent Razzano opened this terrific Italian market and café in 1994, and its popularity just keeps growing. Fresh pastas, homemade sauces, a full bakery with hearty Italian breads, crisp cookies, and a variety of cakes, plus a full line of takeout from lasagnas, meatballs, and rotisserie-baked chicken to olives, salads, and freshly made sausage are available. Imported bulk and grated cheeses, olive oils, vinegars, and freshly roasted coffee beans, as well as cappuccino, espresso, and latté are here. The adjoining restaurant serves pizza, pasta, and a variety of main-course dishes that include fish, veal, and chicken.

EAST HAMPTON

Barefoot Contessa (631-324-0240; 46 Newtown Ln., East Hampton, NY 11937) Open July 4–Labor Day: Sun.–Thurs 9am–5:30pm, Fri., Sat. 9am–6pm; fewer days rest of year. This is the Dean & Deluca of the Hamptons (actually Dean & Deluca occupied this building previously), and owner Ina Garten is one of the Hamptons' most popular caterers. The prepared foods available in her store, which used to be the East Hampton Post Office, are staggering. Near the entrance, there's a mouthwatering display of pies, cakes, and other desserts. Straight ahead are piles of fresh breads. Glass counters enclose salads, cheeses, and prepared foods. Along the walls, floor-to-ceiling wire racks hold gourmet bottled and packaged items, and refrigerated cases display ice creams and soft drinks. The big event every year, held on Martin Luther King's birthday (Jan. 15), is the annual sale when everything is reduced by one-third!

Dreesen's Excelsior Market (631-324-0465; www.dreesens.com; 33 Newtown Ln., East Hampton, NY 11937) Open year-round: Mon.–Thurs. 7am–5pm, Fri., Sat. 7am–5:30pm; closed Sun. In business since 1920, Dreesen's is the local breakfast and lunch stop for East Hampton merchants and clerks. Freshly made doughnuts, which you can watch being made in the window, are legendary. This is how doughnuts are supposed to taste — crispy on the outside and soft and airy inside. Owner Rudy DeSanti claims that they put all of the calories in the hole, so that you can eat as many as you like. You can also get deli sandwiches and salads, gourmet grocery items, and top-quality meats. Delivery service is available.

Jerry and David's Red Horse Market (631-329-6655; 74 Montauk Hwy., East Hampton, NY 11937) Open year-round: daily 6:30am–7pm. From the time Jerry Della Femina and his partners opened the Red Horse Market in the summer of 1993, it's attracted a devoted clientele who know they can purchase all of their cooking needs in this large, well-stocked market. There are sections of fresh produce that stretch the length of the building, a fresh meat market, and a separate fish and shellfish section. Breads and cookies come in a variety of sizes and flavors; the chocolate chip cookies are so popular that they sell out quickly. There are sections of fresh flowers, prepared salads, entrées, and cheeses. You can even buy the daily newspapers here.

Plain and Fancy (631-324-7853; 85 Springs Fireplace Rd., East Hampton, NY 11937) Open year-round: in summer: daily 8am–5pm; rest of year: daily 8am–4pm. Lines form around this shop on Sat. and Sun. mornings for Maria Bernier's fresh bagels, crullers, sticky buns, and scones. David Bernier's rosemary bread and entrées are equally popular. For example, the moist, tender chicken Francaise and the soft-shell crabs, dipped in milk and seasoned flour, grilled, and served on a French roll with fresh, homemade pesto sauce are marvelous. Quiches are thick and peasant-style and might include ham and Brie or asparagus with goat cheese. Individual fruit tarts feature in-season berries or fruit and have crumb toppings. Brownies range from a black, white, and raspberry (sensational) to lemon or coconut with raisins and pecans, as well as the traditional chocolate.

Villa Italian Specialties (631-324-5110; 7 Railroad Ave., East Hampton, NY 11937) Open year-round: Mon.–Sat. 8:30am–6:30pm, Sun. 9am–2:30pm. This wonderful Italian deli, owned by Saverio and Carmela Naclerio, has been in business for almost twenty years, so you know that it's doing something right. For fresh Parmesan Reggiano or Pecorino Romano, real prosciutto, fresh puttanesca sauce, fresh ravioli or tortellini, or entrées, such as eggplant Parmesan or chicken cacciatore, this is definitely the place to come.

QUOGUE

Quogue Country Market (631-653-4191; fax: 631-653-6226; Jessup Ave., PO Box 1419, Quogue, NY 11959) Open year-round: in summer: Mon.–Fri. 7am–8pm, Sat., Sun. 7am–10pm; in winter: daily 7am–6pm. This is a large, well-stocked market and deli that dates from the 1920s. In the fresh produce section, you can purchase farm fresh produce. There are over twenty kinds of prepared salads, a meat market (no packaged meats), a fresh fish counter, a large selection of gourmet canned and bottled food products, a fresh bakery with tiny little muffins (very popular), an ample cheese counter, and fresh coffee and cappuccino. An extensive catering menu ranges from baked lasagna to stuffed fresh flounder with herbed cream cheese. They also sell newspapers, greeting cards, small gift items, and more. Bob and Gary Curran, the owners, are friendly, helpful, and knowledgeable.

SAGAPONACK

Loaves and Fishes (631-537-0555; 50 Main St., PO Box 318, Sagaponack, NY 11962) Open Mem. Day–Labor Day: daily 9am–5:30pm; Easter–Mem. Day, Labor Day–Christmas: Fri.–Sun. 9am–5:30pm; closed Christmas–Easter. Anna

Pump has operated this respected catering and gourmet food shop for more than fifteen years. She's earned a deserved reputation for excellence. From her fork-tender beef filet to the chicken curry salad, from condiments, such as curried apricot mayonnaise or lemon curd to freshly baked breads and exotic soups — some of the best dinner parties are catered by Loaves and Fishes.

Sagaponack Main Store (631-537-6036; fax: 631-537-3696; 542 Sagg Main St., PO Box 151, Sagaponack, NY 11962) Open year-round: in summer: daily 7am–6pm; shorter hours rest of year. The Sagaponack Main Store is the heart and soul of the hamlet of Sagaponack. The store takes up one-half of an old, white clapboard building, with the local post office occupying the other half. Customers arrive for the mail, morning paper, and a cup of coffee in their own Sagaponack Main Store mug and sit on the steps to chat. Tom Wolfe, Kurt Vonnegut, George Plimpton, and other notables are as at home here as you and I. Bob and Rick Terando are the owners. You can get baked country hams with a honey-mustard glaze, roasted turkeys, pies, cakes, sandwiches, and lots more.

SAG HARBOR

Espresso (631-725-4433; 84 Division St., PO Box 44, Sag Harbor, NY 11963) Open daily 8am–9pm; longer hours in summer. Located off the beaten track in the village of Sag Harbor, Espresso is a great Italian deli/grocery that just keeps getting better. Luigi Tagliasacchi's hot focàccia bread, sprinkled with rosemary and garlic and splashed with olive oil, is heavenly. The market is run by Mr. Tagliasacchi and his wife Robin. The packaged Italian specialties include items that you don't often find at the finest Italian groceries in Manhattan. Prepared foods include salads, pastas (one special was spinach fettuccine with creamy Gorgonzola sauce), and a variety of entrées. Inventive breakfasts are served in the morning, and sandwiches are made-to-order at lunch.

SOUTHAMPTON

The Curious Cook (631-283-1701; 24 Jagger Ln., Southampton, NY 11968) Open year-round: daily 6am–8pm. Owner/Chef Larry Butler has built a solid reputation for his catering business and tiny café. In the morning, residents come here for the newspaper, a cup of coffee, and fresh, hot muffins. Among the items that he will happily cater are a variety of cakes and pies, herbed leg of lamb, grilled shrimp in garlic, and poached salmon with dill-cucumber sauce. He'll prepare a clambake for the beach.

Village Cheese & Gourmet Shop (631-283-6949; 11 Main St., Southampton, NY 11968) Open year-round: Mon.–Thurs. 7:30am–6pm, Fri., Sat. 7:30am–6:30pm, Sun. 7:30am–5pm. The first thing that you do upon entering Rosemary and Adam Batcheller's cheese shop is to take a number; you can't place your order without a number in hand. Much more than a cheese shop, this is the place to come for a newspaper, coffee, and a bagel first thing in the morning or for a terrific deli sandwich before heading for the beach. You will find prepared hot dishes, salads, cold drinks, pâtés, charcuterie items, and a good selection of cheeses.

WATER MILL

Citarella (631-726-3636; 760 Montauk Hwy. (Citarella Plaza), Water Mill; mail: 2135 Broadway, New York, NY 10023) Open in summer: daily 9am–7pm; call for hours rest of year. Owner Joe Gurrera has stocked his new Water Mill shop (opened in summer 2000) just like those in Manhattan with a fabulous array of gourmet items. There's a fresh fish and shellfish section that has ten kinds of oysters and a tank containing not only live lobsters, but also live Dungeness crab. The meat market has every imaginable cut of meat, and the cheese section is equally impressive. Of course, there's a bakery. The prepared food section includes salads, pasta dishes, vegetable napoleans, and prepared meats. Local farms supply the fresh produce. An inside stand-up café and outdoor summer dining on the patio complete the picture.

WESTHAMPTON BEACH

Sydney's "Taylor" Made Cuisine (631-288-4722; 194 Mill Rd., Westhampton Beach, NY 11978) Open year-round: daily 7am–6pm. After catering parties and events for several years, Erin Finley and David Blydenburgh built a brand new building and opened a classy, gourmet food store and deli. You will find a large selection of cheeses, salads, desserts, pâtés, and rotisserie-baked chickens and ducks. There are smoked fish, a full bakery selection, and bottled and packaged gourmet foods. In addition, a pretty brick court-yard contains tables for eating outside.

ICE-CREAM PARLORS

AMAGANSETT

The Ice Cream Clubs (631-267-3099; Main St., Amagansett, NY 11930; 631-668-3115; Main St., PO Box 2409, Montauk, NY 11954) Open in summer: daily 11am–12 midnight; shorter hours rest of season; closed Oct.–Apr. You can get hard ice cream, soft ice cream, candy, yogurt, milkshakes, and malts at these old-fashioned ice-cream parlors.

BRIDGEHAMPTON

Bridgehampton Ice Cream and Yogurt Company (631-537-0233; 2462 Main St., PO Box 1190, Bridgehampton, NY 11932) Open July 4–Labor Day:

Sun.–Thurs. 12 noon–11pm; Fri., Sat. 12 noon–2am; May, June, Sept., Oct.: fewer days and shorter hours; closed rest of year. Bridgehampton Ice Cream and Yogurt Company carries Steve's Ice Cream, Columbo Frozen Yogurt, and American Glacé.

EAST HAMPTON

Scoop du Jour (631-329-4883; 37 Main St., East Hampton, NY 11937) Open July 4–Labor Day; Sun.–Thurs. 12 noon–11pm; Fri., Sat. 12 noon–12 midnight; rest of season: weekends only; closed Thanksgiving–Mem. Day. Great ice cream, an old-fashioned soda fountain, and a location across the street from the East Hampton Cinema make this a very popular spot. They carry Steve's Ice Cream, T & W ice cream, and Columbo and American Glacé yogurt. This is also a coffee bar with espresso and cappuccino, ice-cream sundaes, sodas, and a comfortable atmosphere.

MONTAUK

Ben & Jerry's Ice Cream (631-668-9425; West Lake Dr., PO Box 257, Montauk, NY 11954) Open midsummer: Sun.–Thurs. 12 noon–11pm (later Fri., Sat.); shorter hours rest of season; closed Columbus Day–mid-May. Yes, you can get that creamy, rich Ben & Jerry's stuff right here in Montauk.

SOUTHAMPTON

The Fudge Co. (631-283-8108; 67 Main St.; 66 Job's Ln., Southampton, NY 11968) Open in summer: daily 11am–12 midnight; rest of year: Sat., Sun. 12 noon–5pm. From these two respected shops, Hugo and John Fudge sell Columbo Soft Yogurt, Cream-of-the-Hamptons' ice cream, and their luscious homemade candies.

Sip 'n Soda (631-283-9752; 40 Hampton Rd., Southampton, NY 11968) Open in summer: daily 7:30am–10pm; shorter hours rest of year. Terrific homemade ice cream is served here at a counter. It's good enough to stand in line for.

WINESHOPS

AMAGANSETT

Amagansett Wine & Spirits (631-267-3939; 203 Main St., PO Box 1060, Amagansett, NY 11930) Open Mon.–Thurs. 10am–8pm, Fri., Sat. 10am–10pm. Amagansett Wine & Spirits can rival the finest shops in Manhattan, both for the depth of its wine collection and for its prices. Owner Michael Cinque buys directly from France and has assembled one of the finest wine cellars on the East End. If you walk the cool basement recesses with him, you will see rare old Latours and Margaux. He sponsors sophisticated wine tastings in the Hamptons and New York City, as well as wine appreciation classes. He also carries one of the most complete selections of Long Island wines and a wide variety of affordable, drinkable, light wines. His prices are so popular that he makes two to three delivery trips to Manhattan each week to supply his regular customers.

BRIDGEHAMPTON

A jug of wine, a loaf of bread, and a puppy.

Morgan McGivern

DePetris Liquor Store (631-537-0287; 2489 Main St., PO Box 3036, Bridgehampton, NY 11932) Open Mon.–Thurs. 9am–8pm, Fri., Sat. 9am–9pm. A good selection of Long Island, California, and European wines is available at this well-stocked store. The Long Island wines, in particular, are well represented, with selections from most East End wineries.

EAST HAMPTON

Wines by Morrell (631-324-1230; 74 Montauk Hwy., East Hampton, NY 11937) Open year-round: in summer: Mon.–Thurs. 9am–8pm, Fri., Sat. 9am–10pm; shorter hours rest of year. Located in the Red Horse Market, this branch of the great Manhattan store offers an excellent selection of wines, especially those from Long Island wineries. Throughout the shop, you will find unusual and interesting wines that are not available elsewhere.

SAG HARBOR

Long Wharf Wines & Spirits (631-725-2400; 12 Bay St., PO Box 519, Sag Harbor, NY 11968) Open Mon.–Sat. 10:30am–8:30pm. This well-stocked wineshop is strong on Long Island and Californian wines. The owner, David Mangusso, will help with selections for a casual, drinking wine or to match courses for a dinner party. The shop holds frequent wine tastings.

SOUTHAMPTON

Herbert and Rist (631-283-2030; 63 Job's Ln., Southampton, NY 11968) Open Mon.–Thurs. 9am–8pm, Fri., Sat. 9am–9pm. This excellent wineshop carries a good selection of Long Island wines, as well as those from California and Europe. Whether you're looking for a cold bottle to go with a sandwich, while sitting on the banks of Agawam Pond or a case for a party, this is the place to find it.

WINERIES ON THE SOUTH FORK

Viticulture and wine production have become big business on Long Island's East End. One day it may rival some California areas in quality, if not in production levels. Because most wineries are located on the North Fork, Chapter Nine, *North Fork* contains extensive information about winemaking on the East End, wineries to tour, wine activities, and much more.

Wine production on the South Fork is more recent. Bridgehampton Winery, which is now defunct, began production in 1983, but they bought their grapes from other growers. Sagpond Vineyards planted the first vineyards intended for wine production on the South Fork in 1988. Their first bottling took place in 1993. It's always interesting to visit wineries during the harvest, when the overflowing trucks bring the tiny grapes to the winery for processing. The following wineries offer tours, samples, and sales rooms.

Channing Daughters Winery (631-537-7224; 1927 Scuttle Hole Rd., PO Box 2202, Bridgehampton, NY 11932) Open daily 11am–6pm. The phenomenal success of Long Island wines has given encouragement to new ventures. Channing Daughters is one of the newest. Walter and Molly Channing, who have four daughters, planted twenty-six acres of their rather remote property north of Bridgehampton in 1988 in a mixture of Chardonnay and Merlot. They produced their first commercial wine, a 1993 Merlot, in 1995 and a Chardonnay in 1996. Larry Perrine is the winemaker. For a light, refreshing, drinkable wine with no pretensions of grandeur, his Sauvignon

Blanc is fabulous! There's a pretty tasting room and a courtyard for outside sipping. Don't miss the interesting and unusual wooden sculptures!

Duck Walk Vineyards (631-726-7555; 162 Montauk Hwy., PO Box 962, Water Mill, NY 11976) Tasting and sales room open daily 11am–6pm. The former Southampton Winery was purchased in 1994 by Dr. Herodotos Damianos, who also owns Pindar Vineyards on the North Fork. The magnificent brick château, with its lush lawns and large terrace, was built in 1986, reputedly for $17 million. With the capability of producing 50,000 cases a year, the production had reached 30,000 by 2000. This stunning building is located on a slight hill overlooking the vineyards. It would be worth the trip to visit the vineyards and sample their steadily improving wines.

Sagpond Vineyards (631-537-5106; 139 Sagg Rd., Sagaponack, NY 11962) Tasting and sales room open daily 11am–6pm. Sagpond Vineyards was the first South Fork winery to produce estate-bottled wines. The first of its fifty-five acres of grapes was planted in 1988, with two-thirds in Chardonnay and one-third in Merlot. The first Chardonnays were produced in 1991. About 13,000 cases of wine were processed in 2000. (The Domaine Wölffer Chardonnay Reserve is a lovely accompaniment to fish; it is light, smooth, and complex.) The land and winery are owned by Christian Wölffer, who also owns Sagpond Farms, the horse farm next door. Roman Roth is the winemaker. A lovely winery building was completed in 1997. It is reminiscent of an Italian villa with ivy climbing the burnt umber stucco walls, fountain courtyards, and a covered patio overlooking the vineyards. It contains not only a tasting room, which overlooks the stainless steel vats, but also a wonderful museum of antique faïence wine jugs and painted wineglasses, as well as a very classy art gallery.

CHAPTER FIVE
Shop 'Til You Drop
SHOPPING

Shopping in the Hamptons can be as rewarding as shopping in Manhattan — and every bit as much fun. Many creative people have decided to live here, including a number of designers whose own workrooms are in the Hamptons, although they sell through larger retail outlets in New York City. As a result, you probably will pay less if you buy locally. And, in addition, some designers and entrepreneurs choose to offer

Morgan McGivern

During the summer, antique shows and sales take place frequently in the Hamptons. This one is at Mulford Farm in East Hampton.

their particular brand of artistry only in the Hamptons, priding themselves on bringing a unique flair and personality to their shops that can't be reproduced elsewhere. Manhattan shops have branches here, too. Whether choosing clothing or art, the Hamptons are a treasure trove.

The Hamptons offer another boon to treasure seekers. Yard and tag sales abound, and they're unlike those that you'll find anywhere else. Many people bring items from their New York City apartments to the Hamptons for their annual yard sale. You'll find everything from priceless antiques to lawn mowers; from china to tools; from artwork to games; and from designer clothes to books. Artists hold home-based sales, book dealers weed out extra stock, and home owners do their spring cleaning in the summer. People review local newspapers every Friday night, hit the sales on Saturday from 8am–12 noon, and then head for the beach.

In addition, transfer stations have an unofficial recycling center for furniture, rugs, and other large pieces. Especially at the end of the summer, you can find some real treasures discarded there.

There is only one true mall in the Hamptons, although there are numerous shopping plazas. The huge Tanger Factory Outlet Center in Riverhead certainly qualifies as a mall, and it has a wonderful array of merchandise at discount prices, but Riverhead is not in the Hamptons. Please consult Chapter Nine, *North Fork*, for details about Tanger.

Bridgehampton Commons, on the South Fork, deserves special mention. In addition to K-Mart, King Kullen, and Rite Aid Pharmacy, the Commons also contains the following shops: The Gap, The Gap Kids, Williams-Sonoma, Hallmark Shop, Speedo Authentic Fitness, Sunglass Hut, Banana Republic, Eddie Bauer, Athlete's Foot, Kay-Bee Toys, Wild Bird Crossing, Lisan & Co., Brennan's Bit and Bridle, Lechter's, Coconuts, Motherhood Maternity, Talbots, T. J. Maxx, Radio Shack, Razzanos, and Hampton Photo Arts, among others.

In this chapter, we have not tried to list every gallery, shop, and store. Instead, we have featured those that offer articles unique to the Hamptons. Although every attempt has been made to list the correct hours, they do change frequently. If in doubt, call.

ANTIQUE DEALERS & SHOPS

AMAGANSETT

Balassas House Antiques (631-267-3032; 208 Main St., PO Box 711, Amagansett, NY 11930) Open in summer: daily 10:30am–5pm; closed Tues., Wed. rest of year. Owners: George and Teda Balassas. From quirky pincushions to elegant, marble fireplace mantels, you'll find hundreds — probably thousands — of antiques and reproductions at Balassas. The rambling old house has room after cluttered room of both old and new, ranging from English tables to old tools, dishes, and mirrors, plus American and French furniture. When you've finished looking in the house, be sure to see the barn and the basement for even more finds.

BRIDGEHAMPTON

The American Wing (631-537-3319; Main St., PO Box 1131, Bridgehampton, NY 11932) Open in summer: daily 11am–5pm; fewer days rest of year. Mark Olives has assembled a wonderful collection of English and American furniture and decorative objects, as well as toys, wicker and rattan items, and architectural and garden accessories.

Devonshire (631-537-2661; Main St., PO Box 1860, Bridgehampton NY 11932); Devonshire (631-329-5392; 52 Newtown Ln., East Hampton, NY 11937) Open Mem. Day–Labor Day: daily 10am–5:30pm, Sun. 11am–5pm; Apr.–Mem. Day, Labor Day–Thanksgiving: closed Tues., Wed.; Thanksgiving–Apr.: closed. Devonshire carries an elegant selection of interesting antique garden furniture and accessories. They include pretty garden benches and tables, painted watering cans, birdhouses, hand-painted lamp shades, pillows

Morgan McGivern

*Devonshire has two shops that specialize in fine garden and interior furniture and accessories.
This bi-level store is in East Hampton.*

made of vintage fabrics, books, china, iron gates, and other original items, all beautifully displayed.

English Country Antiques (631-537-0606; Snake Hollow Rd., PO Box 1995, Bridgehampton, NY 11932); English Country Antiques (631-329-5773; 21 Newtown Ln., East Hampton, NY 11937) Open Mon.–Sat. 9am–5:30pm, Sun. 10:30am–5:30pm. Chris Mead has assembled an extensive collection in his warehouse-sized showroom that specializes in English (and some French) antiques and reproductions. Most of the armoires, china cabinets, beds, breakfronts, and tables are in pine. You'll also find birdcages, mirrors, lamps, chandeliers, candlesticks, weather vanes, whirligigs, and much more.

Gemini Antiques Ltd. (631-537-4565; www.julgert@geminiantiques.com; 2418 Montauk Hwy., PO Box 1752, Bridgehampton, NY 11932) Open in summer: Mon., Thurs. 11am–5pm, Fri., Sat. 11am–8pm, Sun. 10am–5pm; fewer days and shorter hours rest of year. This little shop holds an incredible collection of folk art — all part of the personal collection of Leon and Steven Weiss and all in impeccable condition. There are toys, doorstops, mechanical banks, weather vanes, and much more, all beautifully organized on two floors.

House of Charm Antiques (631-537-3335; 222.HouseOfCharmAntiques.com; 2411 Montauk Hwy., PO Box 2411, Bridgehampton, NY 11932) Open in summer: daily 11am–5pm; fewer days rest of year. I love to meander through the back yard that Rosemary Nelson has filled with interesting old garden antiques, but inside you'll find elegantly polished chests and tables, as well as china, silver, and statues. Don't miss the basement.

John Salibello Antiques (631-537-1484; Montauk Hwy., PO Box 98, Bridgehampton, NY 11932) Open in summer: Sat. 11am–5pm, Fri.–Mon. 11am–6pm rest of year or by appt. John Salibello is noted for his opulent and elegant furnishings. In this shop — the East End branch of his Manhattan store — he carries a vast array of antiques, from jewelry and cast-iron doorstops to gilt French side chairs.

Ruby Beets (631-537-2802; 1703 Montauk Hwy., Bridgehampton; mail: PO Box 596, Wainscott, NY 11975) Open in summer: daily 11am–5pm, Fri.–Sun. only rest of year. As though from a page of a Mary Emmerling book, this historic little 1790 house is crammed to the rafters with old painted furniture, baskets, pottery, enameled pitchers, weather vanes, and other funky country pieces. Outside, the lawn is cluttered with wood and iron chairs, garden urns and perhaps a clever garden bench with a picket fence back.

Simply French (631-537-7444; 2487 Main St., Bridgehampton; 631-283-5115; 18 Job's Ln., Southampton; mail: PO Box 9000, Bridgehampton, NY 11932) Open daily 10:30am–5:30pm. These marvelous shops specialize in fine French country items, especially those from Provence. There's eighteenth- and nineteenth-century country French furniture, including iron beds, French chandeliers, upholstered chairs, and painted chests, as well as soap from St. Rémy, colorful French fabrics and linens, an elegant two-toned cashmere throw, dolls, pottery and faïence, art, and more. If you're a Francophile as I am, you'll return again and again to these shops.

At Urban Archeology in Bridgehampton, you can purchase beautiful architectural elements from houses and buildings about to be demolished and use them in new or renovated structures.

Morgan McGivern

Urban Archeology (631-537-0124; 2231 Montauk Hwy., PO Box 191, Bridgehampton, NY 11932) Open Wed.–Mon. 10am–5:30pm. Owner: Gil Shapiro; Manager: Michael Scutellaro. Urban Archeology was born because the owners wanted to salvage great architectural elements from buildings about to be demolished. For antique columns, plumbing fixtures, fireplace mantels, letter boxes, lighting fixtures, and carousel horses, this is the place to come. The demand for the great old pieces has been so steady that the company now has its own line of reproductions: artisans in Spain make alabaster lamps; in Italy, they create iron pieces; and in Manhattan, they make a variety of objects in the lower recesses of the main store.

EAST HAMPTON

Architrove (631-329-2229; 74 Montauk Hwy., East Hampton, NY 11937) Open in summer: daily 10am–5pm; closed Tues., Wed. rest of year. Owner: Gary. Located in the Red Horse Market, Architrove carries a marvelous selection of elegant, antique marble- and wood-carved fireplace mantels, columns, top-quality furniture, crystal chandeliers, sinks, and even doorknobs and hinges. Everything is neatly arranged and very clean. You may run into Christy Brinkley here, just as I did recently.

The Grand Acquisitor (631-324-7272; 110 North Main St., East Hampton, NY 11937) Open in summer: Thurs.–Mon. 11am–5pm; fewer days rest of year. Owner: Maria O. Brennan. For elegant linen and lace tablecloths, sheets, coverlets, napkins, lacy pillowcases, and charming children's dresses, this marvelous store can't be beat. (This should be your first stop for an antique christening dress.) All the merchandise is neatly boxed and labeled, so items are easy to find even though the store inventories over 200,000 items. There are a few pieces of furniture, china, and silver, but Ms. Brennan is most noted for her linens and fabric conservation.

Victory Garden (631-324-7800; 63 Main St., East Hampton, NY 11937) Open in summer: daily 10am–6pm; Thurs.–Mon. rest of year. Owner: Paula Schulhof. If you have a secret garden that you've been wanting to embellish with cast-iron French furniture, the Victory Garden is just the place to look. This very elegant, French store also has French faïence, chandeliers, long baguette baskets, dining room furniture, needlepoint pillows, and so much more. The lovely aroma when you enter the shop is from the potpourri and rose balls.

SAG HARBOR

Fisher's Antiques (631-725-0006; Main St., PO Box 2100, Sag Harbor, NY 11963) Open year-round: daily 10am–6pm. Owners: Susan and Bob Fisher. This large shop features country pine antiques and reproductions, as well as iron beds and painted and distressed furniture, plus a vast selection of interesting and unusual home furnishings. You'll find 1940s flowered tablecloths and napkins, botanical prints, Soleido tablecloths and napkins, decorative pillows, and china. Pine furniture can be custom–ordered, and there's a restoration studio for repairs and custom finishes.

Madison Antiques (631-725-5940; 43 Madison St., PO Box 35, Sag Harbor, NY 11963) Open Fri., Sat. 11am–5pm; Sun., Mon. 11am–4pm. Owner: Richard DePierro. The interesting and unique garden furniture, fountains, mirrors, lighting fixtures, statuary, and beautiful American and Continental furniture and accessories make this shop worth a detour on any antiquers schedule. It's all lovingly displayed in a great old Sag Harbor house and garden.

Main Street Antiques (631-725-8656; Main St., Sag Harbor; mail: 55 Crescent St., Sag Harbor, NY 11963) Open Mar.–mid-Dec.: Thurs.–Sun. 9:30am–6pm or by appt.; closed rest of year. Owners: Claire and Herb Siegel. If you're looking for a painted wooden Indian lady, a great old flag, a model sailing ship or tug boat, old costume jewelry, or brass telescopes, this shop has a wonderful selection.

SOUTHAMPTON

Ann Madonia (631-283-1878; 631-741-1882; 36 Job's Ln., Southampton, NY 11968) Open in summer: daily 11am–5pm; Fri.–Sun. rest of year or by appt. Owner: Ann Madonia. This store sells some of the most elegant antiques in town, from fine English and French furniture to silver and other accessories — all on two floors in a spacious, refined setting. The enclosed garden in back displays select garden furniture. There's another location in Garden City, if you don't find what you want here.

Another Time Antiques (631-283-6542; 765 Hill St., Southampton, NY 11968) Open in summer: Fri.–Mon. 11am–5pm; shorter hours rest of year. Owners: Meredith and Thomas Joyce. The owners have filled their shop, as well as two adjacent buildings, to the rafters with dolls and toys, wicker chairs and desks, oak and mahogany tables, costume jewelry, collectible figurines and dishes, and much more. There are treasures to be found here.

Old Town Crossing (631-283-7740; 46 Main St., Southampton, NY 11968) Open year-round: Mon.–Fri. 10am–5pm, Sat. 10am–5:30pm, Sun. 12 noon–5pm. Don't let this diminutive shop on Main St. fool you. Although Judith Hadlock displays an impressive array of mirrors, lamps, silver, silk tassels, and elegant, small furniture pieces, the bulk of the inventory is located nearby in a 5,000-square-foot warehouse. Customers are welcome to poke around the collection of eighteenth-century English beds, tables, dressers, and more.

Second Chance (631-283-2988; 45 Main St., Southampton, NY 11968) Open Mon.–Sat. 10am–5pm, Sun. 11am–5pm. Sheila Guidera is a fussy buyer. She'll only purchase antiques that are in the very best condition for her shop, thereby assuring her customers of top-notch quality. Among her finds are such treasures as Mme. Alexander and Nancy Ann dolls, antique cutwork linens, vintage floral drapes, Fiesta Ware, chenille bedspreads, jewelry, and a large collection of exquisite sterling silver pieces: flatware, bowls, trays, napkin rings, and much more.

25 Hampton Road (631-287-3859; 25 Hampton Rd., Southampton, NY 11968)

Open daily 11am–5pm. Owners: Skip and Lorraine Ralph. With a collector's eye for fine antiques, Skip and Lorraine Ralph, who also own 1708 House, an inn just around the corner, have filled this shop with the very highest quality English, French, and American antiques and art. There are mahogany dining room tables and chairs, elegant walnut armoires, and beds with elaborately carved headboards and footboards. You can also see and purchase the antique pieces that are on display in the guest rooms and common areas of the inn.

WAINSCOTT

The finest Hampton homes are often outfitted with furnishings from Georgica Creek Antiques.

Morgan McGivern

Georgica Creek Antiques (631-537-0333; Montauk Hwy., PO Box 877, Wainscott, NY 11975) Open Mon.–Sat. 11am–5pm, Sun. 11am–4pm. Jean Sinenberg has collected a marvelous array of unusual and interesting antiques in her spacious white building. On a recent visit, I spotted a wonderful, carved French dresser, a cache of beautiful antique quilts in perfect condition, lamps, ornate silver candlesticks, a great crystal chandelier, and a set of beautiful gold-rimmed Limoges dishes. In back, there's a garden full of architectural elements, such as columns and pillars, as well as wicker and Victorian wire planters and garden furniture.

WATER MILL

Donna Parker Habitat (631-726-9311; 710 Montauk Hwy., PO Box 1071, Water Mill, NY 11976) Open in summer: 11am–5pm; fewer days rest of year. Donna Parker sells an array of important French and Italian furniture and decorative objects, such as a leafy iron table, or a crystal chandelier, or marble pedestals holding bronze busts or gilt mirrors, crystal lamps, and much more.

Water Mill Antiques (631-726-4647; 700 Montauk Hwy., PO Box 546, Water Mill, NY 11976) Open year-round: daily 11am–4pm. Owner: Richard DiPierro. This interesting farmhouse is stuffed with antique furniture, chandeliers, mirrors, rugs, and decorative objects, and the front yard is so full of antique planters, garden benches, birdcages, weather vanes, statuary, and garden furniture that you can hardly thread your way to the door. But along the way, you'll stumble across some wonderful bargains.

WESTHAMPTON BEACH

La De Da (631-288-5988; 8B Moniebogue Ln., Westhampton Beach, NY 11978) Open in summer: daily 11am–6pm; shorter hours rest of year. Located in a charming building with a garden in front, this shop offers such treasures as antique building pediments, picture frames, mirrors, unique birdhouses, objets d'art, and salt-and-pepper shakers from the 1950s.

The Mill at Westhampton (631-288-0206; 164 Montauk Hwy., Westhampton Beach, NY 11978); The Mill at Bridgehampton (631-537-5577; 2287 Montauk Hwy., Bridgehampton, NY 11932) Open year-round: daily 9:30am–6pm. Owner: Claudette Romano. The original shop in Westhampton Beach is located in a picturesque old mill, while the Bridgehampton shop is in a brand new building. Mill Antiques sells antiques and manufactures finely carved French country furnishings (antique replicas), such as armoires, tables, chairs, and sofas; some pieces are upholstered in elegant French tapestries. They also import intricate architectural ironwork gates, fences, and other pieces.

BOOKS, MAGAZINES, TAPES

EAST HAMPTON

The three extraordinary Book Hampton stores offer an extensive supply of reading material. Call this branch, the East Hampton store, for their schedule of author appearances.

Morgan McGivern

Book Hampton (631-324-4939; 20 Main St., East Hampton, NY 11937) Open in summer: weekends 9am–11:30pm, weekdays 9am–11pm; closes 8pm rest of year. Manager: Chris Avena. This is the Hamptons' all-purpose, everything-you-want bookstore. It has a wide selection in every category: best-sellers, paperbacks, local history, children's books, travel, cookbooks, videos, and tapes. Upstairs, local authors often give readings and sign books. Before the movies, after the movies, anytime — this is a great place to shop.

Glenn Horowitz-Bookseller (631-324-5511; 87 Newtown Ln., East Hampton, NY 11937) Open Apr.–Dec.: daily 10am–5pm; shorter hours rest of year. Specializing in fine old books and prints, this shop has an excellent selection. There are a number of books and photographs that relate to local history, as well as some rare, old, leather-bound and first-edition volumes. If what you're looking for isn't here, it may be at their New York branch, or they'll do a search for you.

Long Island Sound (631-324-2660; 34 Main St., East Hampton, NY 11937) Open in summer: daily 10am–10pm; 10am–7pm rest of year; **Long Island Sound** (631-283-6683; 76 Job's Ln., Southampton, NY 11968) Open in summer: daily 10am–9pm; shorter hours rest of year. Not only do these stores carry a full selection of tapes, CDs, and accessories, but they also sell tickets for local events.

MONTAUK

The Book Shoppe (631-668-4599; The Plaza, PO Box 750, Montauk, NY 11954) Open in summer: daily 9:30am–12 midnight; closed Tues. rest of year and shorter hours. Owner: Jeff Earns. This little bookstore may be small, but it's packed with great things. Not only can you purchase or order the latest books, but you can also buy cards and little gifts.

SAG HARBOR

Book Hampton (631-725-1114; 126 Main St., Sag Harbor, NY 11963) Open in summer: daily 8am–11pm, weekends longer hours; in winter: shorter hours. Manager: Frank Banfi. This great new Book Hampton, which opened in the spring of 2000, has two levels of bright, light space and a terrific assortment of books. In addition, there's a restaurant on the main floor where you can get breakfast, lunch, and dinner (see Chapter Four, *Restaurants & Food Purveyors*).

Canio's Books (631-725-4926; 290 Main St., Sag Harbor, NY 11963) Open Mar.–Dec.: daily 12 noon-6pm.; Jan.–Feb.: Fri.–Sun. only 12 noon-6pm. Owner: Canio Pavone. Canio is the literary community's friend. Not only is his shop a great place to find out-of-print books and new ones, but on many Saturdays at 6pm, there are book signings or poetry and book readings.

Ned Parkhouse (631-725-9830; 150 Main St., PO Box 1651, Sag Harbor, NY 11963) Open most of the time 11am–5pm. Owner: Ned Parkhouse. This tiny little shop has a wonderful selection of classical music and jazz, hard-to-find and antique CDs and records. You wouldn't believe what you can find here.

SOUTHAMPTON

Book Hampton (631-283-0270; 91 Main St., Southampton, NY 11968) Open most days in summer: daily 9am–9pm, weekends slightly longer hours; in winter: shorter hours. Manager: Jane Cochran. This branch of Book Hampton (all owned by Hamptons' impresario Hal Zwick) has the same extensive, all-encompassing selections as the other two. A great place to shop or browse.

Sam Goody (631-287-7119; 14 Main St., Southampton, NY 11968) Open Mon.–Wed. 10am–8pm, Thurs.–Sat. 10am–9pm, Sun. 11am–5pm. Music fans will find a prodigious selection of CDs, records, tapes, cassettes, videos, and other music-related items in this store. It's the place to pick up a Walkman and a few tapes before heading to the beach, as well as blank tapes or new headphones.

WESTHAMPTON BEACH

The Open Book (631-288-2120; 128A Main St., Westhampton Beach, NY 11978) Open Mem. Day–Labor Day: Mon.–Thurs. 10am–7pm, Fri.–Sun. 10am–10pm; daily 10am–5pm rest of year. Owner: Terry Lucas. The Open Book has a good selection of hardbound and softcover books and greeting cards and is especially strong in children's literature, including the classics.

CHILDREN'S SHOPS

CLOTHING

BRIDGEHAMPTON

C & W Mercantile (631-537-7914; Main St., PO Box 1275, Bridgehampton, NY 11932) Open in summer: daily 10am–6pm; in winter: shorter hours. Owner: Barbara Dutton. Frothy and feminine children's dresses share space in this adorable shop with table linens, gifts, candles, and elegant bed dressings. This shop rivals the finest that the tony Upper East Side has to offer.

Gap Kids and Baby Gap (631-537-2428; Bridgehampton Commons, Bridgehampton, NY 11932) Open year-round: Mon.–Sat. 10am–8pm, Sun. 10am–6pm. Great stylish play clothes that are comfortable and durable — from T-shirts to jeans. Also, check out the Baby Gap and Gap Kids discount shops in the Tanger Mall in Riverhead.

EAST HAMPTON

Bonne Nuit (631-324-7273; 55 Main St., East Hampton, NY 11937) Open daily 10am–6pm; in summer: daily 10am–11pm; Jan.–Mar.: possibly closea Tues., Wed. Owners/Managers: Ashlyn and Lorna Maloney. This fine lingerie shop carries the most beautiful, European children's clothing. Delicate, smocked dresses in Liberty of London fabrics and French sundresses, made of a Swiss cotton so fine that it feels like silk, are only a few of the offerings.

Calypso (631-324-8146; 17 Newtown Ln., East Hampton, NY 11937) Open in summer: daily 10am–8pm; in winter: shorter hours. If you've got a Caribbean kid with a yen for bright colors, bring her here. There are wonderful little girl dresses in bright colors, ornaments for the hair, splendid thongs with flowers over the toe, and lots more. Best of all, these goodies come in mommy sizes, too.

Punch offers adorable children's clothing in this shop in East Hampton, as well as in their Sag Harbor shop.

Morgan McGivern

Punch (631-329-3897; 55 Newtown Ln., East Hampton; 631-725-2741; Main St., Sag Harbor; mail: PO Box 1112, Sag Harbor, NY 11963) Open in summer: daily 9am–7pm; daily 9am–6pm rest of year; closed in Mar. These fine children's clothing shops have outfits for all ages starting with newborns. There are coats, bathing suits, knit sweaters, felt-appliquéd jackets, corduroy overalls, and lots more.

The Red Pony (631-329-6685; 74 Montauk Hwy., East Hampton, NY 11937) Open in summer: daily 10am–5pm; closed Tues., Wed. rest of year. Hampton moms need not traipse to Manhattan to elegantly outfit their children. Children's clothing made of the finest fabrics and in the latest designs can be purchased right here at home. Located in the Red Horse Market.

SOUTHAMPTON

Aunt Suzie's Clothes for Kids (631-287-4645; 20 Hampton Rd., Southampton, NY 11968) Open Mon.–Fri. 10am–5:30pm, Sat. 10am–6pm, Sun. 12 noon-5pm; Christmas to just before Easter: closed Sun. This large shop for kids has a wide selection of clothing in sizes ranging from newborn to preteen. For summers in the sun or back to school, this can't be beat. Toys, too.

Calypso (631-283-4321; 24 Job's Ln., Southampton, NY 11968) Open in summer: daily 10am–8pm; in winter: shorter hours. This branch of the East Hampton shop also carries terrific, brightly patterned children's clothing.

Laura Ashley (631-287-2104; 87 Main St., Southampton, NY 11968) Open daily 10am–5:30pm. Cute clothes for kids in the signature style and fabrics that the Laura Ashley lines are noted for. The shop also has children's bedding.

WESTHAMPTON BEACH

Shock Kids/Baby Shock (631-288-2522; 99 Main St., Westhampton Beach, NY 11978) Open year-round: in summer: daily 10am–9pm or later; shorter hours rest of year. Owner: Elyse Richman. Remember your lime green and shocking pink capri pants from the '60s? You can outfit your pint sized in '60s retro at this blast from the past shop. There are short leather skirts with cropped tops and handknit dresses and tops, as well as hats and so much more. Once your kid looks oh so cool, you can have a treat in the ice-cream parlor, where there's homemade ice creams, yogurts, and Italian ices. It's a great place for a party, too!

GAMES & TOYS

BRIDGEHAMPTON

Penny Whistle Toys (631-537-3875; Main St., PO Box 1180, Bridgehampton, NY 11932) Open daily 9am–6pm, weekends 9am–8pm. This child-friendly store, which also has two branches in Manhattan, has adorable and wonderful delights for young and old alike. It's filled with interesting and unique finds that spill out into the courtyard in summer.

EAST HAMPTON

Rumrunner Kid (631-329-5870; 41 Main St., East Hampton, NY 11937) Open in summer: daily 10am–8pm; in winter: daily 10am–6pm. You can spend hours in this great shop — a fantasyland of terrific kids' things brought to you by the same folks who own Rumrunner across the street. There are pretty

From pretty painted children's furniture to games, dolls, and even clothing, Rumrunner Kid excels.

Morgan McGivern

painted cribs and dressers, chenille-stuffed animals, lamps, and creative children's clothing and accessories.

Second Star to the Right (631-329-3750; 56 Newtown Ln., East Hampton, NY 11937) Open Mon.–Thurs. 10am–7pm, Fri., Sat. 10am–10pm. Marianne Kearns has stuffed her little shop with cute stuffed animals. They fill the display window and include giant teddy bears and tiny teddys, as well as little stuffed dogs, cats, bunnies, and more.

Village Toy Shop (Generations) (631-324-6455; 45 Main St., East Hampton, NY 11937) Open in summer: daily 10am–10pm; in winter: fewer days and shorter hours. The Wilsons have been feeding our nostalgia buds for many years, and we just can't get enough. This shop is for adults as much as for children. You'll find collectible tin soldiers, entire train sets, real wooden toys, and so much more. It's a throwback to the kind of store where our grandmothers bought toys for us — a must for those of us who want to buy toys for our children and grandchildren that can be handed down.

SOUTHAMPTON

Judith Anne's (631-283-4044; www.judithannes.com; 71 Job's Ln., Southampton, NY 11968) Open in summer: daily 9am–9pm; shorter hours rest of year. Located on tony Job's Ln., this cute shop has a great selection of toys, games, dolls, and even lots of ballet outfits for little girls.

Story Time (631-287-9035; 20 Hampton Rd., Southampton, NY 11968) Open Mon.–Sat. 10am–6pm, Sun. 1pm–5pm. This educational store offers books, games, and toys designed to help curious minds grow. There are also creative and interesting activities for children: on one day, children of reading age might participate in a class designed to teach character through literature; on another day, toddlers will meet with Ivy Geranium to listen to well-known children's stories.

MEN'S & WOMEN'S CLOTHING

BRIDGEHAMPTON

Brennan's Bit and Bridle, Inc. (631-537-0635; Bridgehampton Common, Plaza East, PO Box 1677, Bridgehampton, NY 11932) Open in summer: daily 10am–5pm; Thurs.–Sun. rest of year. This is the place to come for elegant riding apparel, including crops, boots, custom-ordered saddles, tack, blankets, and bridles. They also carry a good selection of horsey gift items.

tutto bene (631-537-3320) and tutto bene II (631-537-2224) both on Main St., PO Box 1156, Bridgehampton, NY 11932) Open Mon.–Sat. 10am–6pm, Sun. 11am–5pm; in winter: closed Wed. Joanne Kahn and Barbara Remia have filled the main store with shoes and accessories to go with the wonderful linen shirts and dresses for summer wear and the classy sweaters found in tutto bene II — some are imported from Italy, but they all have a classic, Italian chic style.

EAST HAMPTON

Ann Crabtree (631-329-6653; 20 Newtown Ln., East Hampton, NY 11937) Open in summer: daily 10am–6pm; fewer hours and days rest of year. Owner/Manager: Ann Crabtree. For stylish, classy sports clothes, Ann offers a great look — perky Moschino shorts, cropped tops in lime green and orange, and classic slacks and sweaters.

Betsey Johnson (631-329-5797; 54 Park Pl., East Hampton, NY 11937) Open in summer: Mon.–Thurs. 11am–8pm, Fri., Sat. 11am–9pm, Sun. 11am–7pm; in winter: shorter hours. Ever-popular designer Betsey Johnson has finally opened her own shop in the Hamptons — and it's retro '60s. She's designed a shop, located off the Park Pl. parking area, that's pink, pink, pink. It has a pink floor, pink ceilings, and pink walls, as well as painted iron furniture in hot pink — all accented with lime green. Her clothes are clingy, young, sexy, and just as hip now as they were in the '60s. She's even got some vintage frocks.

Biba (631-324-2300; 66 Newtown Ln., East Hampton, NY 11937); **Biba** (631-287-2300; 28 Job's Ln., Southampton, NY 11968) Open in summer: daily 10am–7pm; call for winter hours. Owner: Barbara Blatt. Mais Oui! A visit to the Hamptons wouldn't be complete without a stop at these Parisian outposts. These elegant shops carry only the finest imported French apparel — just the thing to wear to the most elegant Hamptons' events.

Billy Martin's (631-329-7676; 47 Newtown Ln., East Hampton, NY 11937) Open daily 10am–5:30pm; in winter: closed Tues. Part-owner Robert Curtis, Jr. has established a home on the range for this outpost of the shop by the same name in Manhattan. You can get denim jackets, jeans, and terrific cowboy boots, Stetson hats, and silver-buckled belts to wear when you ride the trails at Deep Hollow Ranch.

Blanc Bleu (631-329-2552; 53 Main St., PO Box 4165, East Hampton, NY 11937) Open in summer: weekdays 10am–7pm, weekends 10am–10pm; in winter: fewer days and shorter hours. As the name suggests, this very French shop (they also have branches in France) offers most things in either white or blue — but oh la la, what terrific clothes! All of the fabulous men's and women's casual wear is imported from France and has that distinctive French-chic flair.

Bonne Nuit (631-324-7273; 55 Main St., East Hampton, NY 11937) Open daily 10am–6pm; Jan.–Mar.: possibly closed Tues., Wed. Owners/Managers: Lorna and Ashlyn Maloney. Bonne Nuit, owned and operated by sisters, is also located in Manhattan. The stores carry fine lingerie, such as Pluto, chenille bed jackets, hair accessories, and pretty, painted ballet slippers.

Cashmere Hampton (631-324-5000; 85 Main St., East Hampton, NY 11937) Open in summer: daily 10am–6pm; closed Tues., Wed. rest of year. This upscale store sells chic merchandise that includes a wide variety of sweaters in various styles and colors, dresses, jackets, and skirts, all made of the softest and finest cashmere, plus silk shirts and skirts made of iridescent silk.

Cynthia Rowley (631-324-1722; 73 Main St., East Hampton, NY 11937) Open in summer: Sun.–Thurs. 10am–7pm, weekends longer hours; in winter: shorter hours. This exceptionally popular designer, who has shops in Manhattan as well, has filled her store with her simple, flirty, eminently wearable clothes.

Daryl Westfall (631-329-1664; 79 Main St., East Hampton, NY 11937) Open daily 10am–5pm. Daryl Westfall has personally designed many of the fabulous bags in her shop, and then she has supplemented with a few others. There are beach bags in creative, brilliantly colored fabrics, as well as embroidered, sequined, and beaded evening bags — also calfskin and canvas daytime bags. You'll also find other accessories such as scarfs, jewelry, and more. Daryl's designs are seen at all the best Hamptons' parties.

Eileen Fisher (631-324-4111; 26 Newtown Ln., East Hampton, NY 11937) Open in summer: daily 10am–6pm; Nov.–Apr.: closed Tues., Wed. Located in the quirky, old shingled building that was formerly the Odd Fellows Hall, Nancy Goell has assembled a fine collection of svelte women's clothing, mostly in basic black, white, or brown — all designed for comfort, as well as style.

Entre Nous (631-324-8636; 37 Newtown Ln., East Hampton, NY 11937) Open in summer: daily 10am–6pm; closed Tues., Wed. rest of year. Owners: Phyllis Baden and Priscilla Helman. This shop has very elegant European clothing — silk knit sweaters, wool gabardine slacks, exclusive suits, and cocktail dresses. All clothing is imported from France or Italy, and much of it is specially ordered for their customers.

Georgina Boutique (631-907-0670; 48 Main St., East Hampton, NY 11937) Open in summer: daily 10am–10pm; in winter: fewer days and shorter hours. Owner: Christina Makowski. This very upscale women's boutique, with branches in Manhasset and Hewlett Harbor, carries elegant designer evening wear, sports clothes, and daytime wear.

J. Roaman (631-329-0555; 48 Newtown Ln., East Hampton, NY 11937) Open daily 10am–6pm. Owner: Judy Roaman. Ms. Roaman sells both men's and women's DKNY clothing in her bright shop. You'll find classic jackets, skirts, and slacks for women and slacks, sweaters, and jackets for men.

Polo Country Store (631-324-1222; 33 Main St., East Hampton, NY 11937) Open in summer: Mon.–Thurs. 10am–9pm, Fri., Sat. 10am–10pm, Sun. 10am–7pm; 10am–6pm rest of year. In the trademark setting of wooden floors, old resort signs, and leather, Ralph Lauren has done it again. If you've been invited to a garden party and you want something smashing to wear, this is the place to come. Men buy white linen slacks and "the blazer," as well as jeans, sweaters, and all of the classically correct Ralph Lauren gear. Women love the long, white linen dusters and swingy flowered skirts. This is a full-service Lauren shop, so in addition to clothing, you can find bedding, furniture, and even little herb garden identification stakes.

Shoe-Inn (631-329-4500; 36 Main St., East Hampton, NY 11937) Open in summer: daily 10am–9pm; Shoe-Inn (631-288-0999; 123 Main St., Westhampton Beach, NY 11978) Open in summer: Sun.–Wed. 10am–6pm, Thurs. 10am–8pm, Fri., Sat. 10am–10pm. These stores are devoted to shoes designed by fashion designers. There are Anne Klein, Calvin Klein, and Ralph Lauren, among many others. The designers often make announced visits to the store to promote their shoes, which creates a bit of a ho-hum in the Hamptons, where celebrity sightings are commonplace.

Waves (631-329-0033; 25 Newtown Ln., East Hampton, NY 11937); Waves (631-537-7767; Main St., PO Box 1273, Bridgehampton, NY 11932) Open daily 9:30am–6:30pm; in winter: shorter hours. Owner: Linda Li. In summer, Waves has floral chintz shorts, French ballet slippers, and canvas espadrilles, along with Lucy Isaacs and Native American turquoise jewelry. In winter, there are chic chenille sweaters and scarves in gem tones, panne velvet dresses, and floral oilcloth umbrellas.

SOUTHAMPTON

Cose Belle (631-283-7564) 79 Job's Ln., Southampton, NY 11968) Open in summer: Mon.–Sat. 10am–6pm, Sun. 11am–5pm; spring and fall: weekends only; in winter: closed. Owner: Shannon McLean. This very classy branch of an upper East Side Manhattan shop has all Italian clothing in the classic lines and natural fibers for which the Italians are so well known. The wool crepe slacks and linen tunics are simple and very elegant.

Laura Ashley (631-287-2104; 87 Main St., Southampton, NY 11968) Open daily 10am–5:30pm. This combined clothing and decorator shop has pretty sundresses for women and children, as well as pleated lamp shades, sheets, and wallpaper.

Saks Fifth Avenue (631-283-3500; Main Store, 1 Hampton Rd., also Men's Store, 50 Main St., both in Southampton, NY 11968) Open Mon.–Thurs.

10am–6pm, Fri. 10am–7pm, Sat. 10am–9pm, Sun. 11am–6pm. A mini version of its big sister in Manhattan, you can outfit an entire family, from jewelry to shoes and from handbags to evening gowns.

Smythe Country Store (631-287-4565; 28 Job's Ln., Southampton, NY 11968) Open daily 10am–6pm. Danielle Smith has filled her elegant shop with some of the greatest sports and day wear we've ever seen. The slim and short, periwinkle blue coat looks terrific with classic suede slacks, and for a casual summer beach party, I love the calf-length drawstring pants in lime-and-pink polished chintz.

Steven Stolman (631-283-8602; 83 Main St., Southampton, NY 11968) Open in summer: daily 10am–6pm; shorter hours rest of year. If you've been invited to a swish garden party, you're sure to turn heads if you arrive in one of these full iridescent taffeta skirts topped with a clingy silk top, and if you pour yourself into one of the store's wild flocked satin stretch capris in lime or red, you'll do the same on the dance floor.

Titano (631-287-4123; www.titanoonline.com; 22 Nugent St., Southampton, NY 11968) Open daily 10am–6pm. Everything in this store is imported from Italy. You'll find beautiful Egyptian cotton shirts for men, women, and children, as well as silk ties, fine knitwear, and accessories in their crisp and neat shop.

Tracy Tooker Hats (631-287-3956; 81 Job's Ln., Southampton, NY 11968) Open Mem. Day–Labor Day: daily 10am–6pm; May, Sept.–Dec.: weekends. Tracy Tooker is a hat designer who truly knows her discriminating Hamptons' customers. Celebrities looking for the ideal chapeau for an elegant event and those who want knock-'em-dead bonnets for the Hamptons' Classic Horse Show, all go to Tracy Tooker. (She even has a booth at the Horse Show.) Tracy also maintains shops in Manhattan and Palm Beach.

WATER MILL

De Bracieux (631-726-2605; Water Mill Sq., PO Box 1376, Water Mill, NY 11976) Open in summer: Thurs.–Sat. 10am–4pm. Owner: Wayne Young. After 25 years on Newtown Ln. in East Hampton, designer Wayne Young has moved to Water Mill. He still designs the simple but classic suits, blouses, and skirts for which he's noted. All fabrics are of natural fibers in subtle, earthy colors and are generally imported from Italy or England. Most of his business is custom, but you will find his shop in a little courtyard opposite Mirko's Restaurant.

WESTHAMPTON BEACH

Lon Sabella et Daniel (631-288-5988; 8B Moniebogue Ln., PO Box 1071, Westhampton Beach, NY 11978) Open daily 11am–5pm. This very stylish women's wear shop specializes in made-to-order and ready-to-wear fashions. There are beaded dresses, slinky black sheaths, filmy ball gowns, plus slacks outfits and jewelry.

Village Safari Clothiers, Ltd. (631-288-4541; 8D Moniebogue Ln., PO Box 1071, Westhampton Beach, NY 11978) Open daily 11am–5:30pm. Handsome men's clothing is displayed amid dark wooden antique furniture. You'll find sweaters, blazers, silk ties, linen shorts, and all of the necessary items for an elegant, summer garden party.

DECORATIVE ARTS, INTERIOR DESIGN, FURNITURE

BRIDGEHAMPTON

Cabbage Rose Interiors (631-537-9225; Main St., Bridgehampton, NY 11932) Open in summer: daily 10am–5pm; by appt. only rest of year. Owner: Barbara Morgan. This little boutique, above Country Gear, is a one-stop shop for all interior design needs. There are fine fabrics for upholstery, draperies, and bed coverings.

Country Gear (631-537-1032; 2408 Main St., PO Box 727, Bridgehampton, NY 11932) Open in summer: daily 10am–6pm. Designer Charles DiSapio's unique niche is appreciated by the most discriminating home owners. His shop is filled with fascinating, English and Irish country-style antiques that include harvest tables, fireplace mantels, and armoires. Although all of these are for sale, they are also used as models for his custom-designed work. Adapting a molding here or a finish there and using aged pine (generally 150–200 years old), he custom-designs libraries, entertainment centers, hutches, and armoires that won't be found anywhere else. Scattered throughout the shop are smaller, English antique accessories, such as metal bottle caddies, enamel kitchen boxes, mirrors, and birdcages.

Juan Garcia Habitat (631-537-2121; 2493 Main St., PO Box 1530, Bridge-hampton, NY 11932) Open year-round: daily 10am–5pm; closed Wed., Sun. This interior design studio has museum-quality antiques and a wide array of interesting fabrics. Among the antiques, you might find a hand-carved, mahogany four-poster bed or a round, mahogany tilt-top table (dining room-sized) with a carved pedestal base.

EAST HAMPTON

Lars Bolander (631-329-3400; 74 Montauk Hwy., East Hampton, NY 11937) Open May–Sept.: daily 10am–5pm; closed Tues., Wed. rest of year. Beautiful, very high-quality European and painted furniture is imported by Lars Bolander for his shop, located in the Red Horse Market. He also sells decorative objects, old prints, oil paintings, and does interior design.

Roberta East Linens (631-324-2518; www.robertaeastlinens.com; 62 The Circle,

East Hampton, NY 11937) Open Thurs.–Mon. 11am–5pm. Owner Debbie Gustin. The silky feel of fine Egyptian cotton sheets soothes us into a peaceful slumber. You can buy a lovely array of them here, as well as towels, quilts, down pillows, table linens, and shower curtains. There's also a nice selection of bedding for babies and children.

SAG HARBOR

C. B. Summerhouse, Ltd. (631-725-4700; 89 Division St., PO Box 1175, Sag Harbor, NY 11963) Open in summer: daily 11am–6pm; closed Tues., Wed.; fewer days rest of year. Owner: Cathleen B. Stewart. Ms. Stewart forsook a career in the stock market to open this delightful shop devoted to elegant and beautiful beds, bedding, pillows, and accessories.

Spilling over with unusual and interesting custom-designed furniture — and now even clothing — Headley Studio continues to entrance us.

Morgan McGivern

Headley Studio (631-725-1194; www.headleystudio.com; 97 Madison St., PO Box 10, Sag Harbor, NY 11963) Open in spring and summer: daily 11am–6pm; in fall and winter: daily 11am–5pm; closed Wed. Owner: Stephen Hadley. For loyal clients, Stephen has long been painting faux wood or marble finishes, as well as trompe l'oeil scenes on walls and furniture; you can buy some of his pieces in his studio/store. Recently, however, he's extended his creativity into designing his own line of glamorous but comfy clothing for ample-sized women. All of this, plus high-quality unusual gifts and housewares, can be purchased in his shop.

SOUTHAMPTON

Chez Morgan Home (631-287-3595; 53 Job's Ln., Southampton, NY 11968) Open Mon.–Fri. 10am–5pm, Sat. 10am–6pm, Sun. 11am–4pm. This design shop in a premier designer town has terrific furniture and decorator services. You might find a massive four-poster plantation bed, an ornate iron bed, a pine armoire, or a leather and wood daybed. Lush fabrics are used for upholstery and draperies.

WESTHAMPTON BEACH

Jeanne Leonard Interiors (631-288-7964; 10 Beach Rd., Westhampton Beach, NY 11978) Open Mon.–Fri. 9:30am–5pm, Sat. 10am–2pm. This impressive design store offers a wide range of fabrics, antique and painted furniture, paintings and prints, rugs, lamps, and pine furniture for sale. You might find a pine breakfront, a double-doored armoire, or a shell-designed corner cupboard. There are even wrought iron gates and fireplace screens. Ms. Leonard also provides both residential and commercial interior design services.

FACTORY OUTLETS

AMAGANSETT

Amagansett Square This very tasteful collection of cottages houses a variety of outlet stores, including Van Heusen, Le Sportsac, Bass, Sunglass Hutt, and Joan and David. The prices are much better than retail, especially when sales are underway.

Coach Store (The Factory Store) (631-267-3340; Main St., Amagansett, NY 11930); Coach Store (631-329-1777; 69 Main St., East Hampton, NY 11937) Open year-round: daily 10am–6pm. For leather handbags, briefcases, and wallets, plus T-shirts, sweats, and shorts, these shops has very reasonable prices.

SOUTHAMPTON

Dansk Factory Outlet (631-287-2093; 5 Main St., Southampton, NY 11968) Open Mon.–Sat. 10am–6pm, Sun. 11am–5pm. This large store features Dansk baking dishes, serving pieces, china, silver, glassware, wooden bowls, trays, and gift items. Prices are often 40-50 percent below retail.

John Rogers Collection Outlet (631-287-5567; 93 Main St., Southampton, NY 11968) Open Mon.–Sat. 10am–5:30pm, Sun. 12 noon–5pm. When John Rogers started importing and selling the fabulous Indonesian furniture that looks and feels so much like antique English colonial pieces, he had immediate success. Now he sells to major department stores and upscale catalog companies. Some of the factory seconds, however, are sold through his outlet store here.

Villeroy and Boch Factory Outlet (631-283-7172; 35 Main St., Southampton, NY 11968) Open Mon.–Thurs. 10am–5:30pm, Fri., Sat. 10am–8pm (6pm in winter), Sun. 12 noon–5pm. This factory outlet store of the well-known German tabletop designer offers porcelain, silver, glassware, and gifts at discounts of 40–70 percent off retail.

GALLERIES

A rt galleries abound in the Hamptons and are the site of many art shows. Opening receptions for the shows attract glittering crowds of artists, writers, and actors. The gallery scene is such an established institution in the Hamptons, that the avid gallery hopper may attend as many as five openings in one night. The following listings represent only a few of the better-known galleries.

BRIDGEHAMPTON

Elaine Benson Gallery (631-537-3233; Montauk Hwy., Bridgehampton, NY 11932) Open mid-May–mid-Sept.: daily 12 noon-6pm; closed Wed.; closed rest of year. This gallery was owned by perhaps the most influential art dealer in the Hamptons. Not only did Elaine Benson (who opened this gallery in 1964) devote almost 40 years to promoting Hampton artists (many undiscovered until she championed them), but she also raised many dollars for various charities through her art previews and events. Her gallery always contains a range of interesting, unusual art. Sadly, Ms. Benson passed away in 1998, and the gallery is now run by her daughter Kimberly Goff.

EAST HAMPTON

Ann Kolb Gallery (631-324-3443; 46 Main St., East Hampton, NY 11937) Open Thurs.–Mon. 10am–6pm. Specializing in fabulous museum-quality American crafts and folk art, this is a must-stop for any serious collector. On a recent visit, there was a highly detailed model of Yankee Stadium circa 1955 fashioned of wood and acrylic, among other amazing craft items.

Arlene Bujese Gallery (631-324-2823; www.arleneBujeseGallery.com; 66 Newtown Ln., East Hampton, NY 11937) Open year-round: Wed.–Mon. 11am–6pm. Owner: Arlene Bujese. This fine gallery carries an eclectic mix of contemporary art that might include an exhibition of paintings or long-lost photographs or etchings, and they are all by local artists.

Giraffics Gallery (631-329-0803; 79A Newtown Ln., East Hampton, NY 11937) Open in summer: daily 10am–6pm; rest of year: Mon.–Wed. 10:30am–12:30pm, Thurs. 10:30am–1pm, Fri.–Sun. 10:30am–5:30pm. This interesting gallery specializes in graphics, prints, and lithographs. It provides representation for such artists as James McMullan and Lynn Curlee. An exhibit might include stage set sketches by well-known theater designers, such as Tony Walton.

Lizan/Tops Associates (631-324-3424; www.lizantopsgallery.com; 66 Newtown Ln., East Hampton, NY 11937) Open in summer: Thurs., Fri., Sun., Mon. 11am–6pm, Sat. 10am–9pm; rest of year: Fri.–Sun. 10am–6pm. Owners: Arnie Lizan and Elizabeth Tops. Located in the back of 66 Newtown Ln., this shop is a bit difficult to find, but the search is worth the effort. These two esteemed Manhattan art dealers are especially well versed in nineteenth- and twentieth-century art, as well as contemporary American work. You'll find Long Island landscapes, old masters' prints, drawings, watercolors, architectural engravings, botanical prints, photography, and more.

Morgan Rank Gallery (631-324-7615; 4 Newtown Ln., East Hampton, NY 11937) Open in summer: daily 10am–5:30pm; shorter hours rest of year; closed Feb. Owner: Morgan Rank. This gallery specializes in American primitive art — mostly folk or naive art created by self-taught artists. Rank often scouts out his artists himself through word of mouth, and most have never exhibited commercially before. He was one of the first to promote Outsider Art. You can depend on finding highly original, unusual artwork.

Vered Art Gallery (631-324-3303; 68 Park Pl., East Hampton, NY 11937) Open in summer: daily 11am–6pm; closed Tues., Wed. rest of year; closed Thurs. in Jan. Owner: Ruth Vered and Janet Lehr. The Vered Gallery represents some of America's and Europe's most prestigious artists — Willem de Kooning, Wolf Kahn, Milton Avery, Pablo Picasso, Henri Matisse, Marc Chagall, Alfonso A. Ossorio, Thomas Moran, Childe Hassam, Larry Rivers, Alfred Stieglitz, and Andy Warhol, among others.

The Wallace Gallery in East Hampton specializes in museum-quality 19th and 20th Century American art.

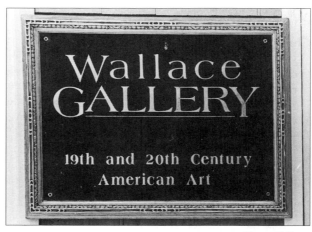

Morgan McGivern

Wallace Gallery (631-329-4516; 37A Main St., East Hampton, NY 11937) Open Mon.–Thurs. 10am–7pm; July–Aug.: Fri., Sat. 10am–11pm; closed Tues., Wed.

and shorter hours rest of year; closed Jan.–mid-Mar. Terry Wallace is an expert in museum-quality, nineteenth- and twentieth-century American art; he specializes in art from that period, created by Eastern Long Island landscape and maritime artists. In his shop, on a mews off Main St., you'll find fine oil paintings and watercolors, and at one time, I saw a tile painted by Thomas Moran, who was one of the members of the Tile Club, a group of nineteenth-century painters who made East Hampton their home in the summer.

Wally Findlay Galleries (631-329-9794; www.wallyfindlaygalleries.com; 2 Main St., East Hampton, NY 11937) Open Mon.–Sat. 10am–6pm; mid-Apr.–mid-Oct. only: Sun. 11am–5pm. Director: Edwin W. Laffey, Jr. The Wally Findlay Galleries (which were founded in 1870) are noted for selling fine museum-quality art. You'll find old masters, French and American impressionists, and contemporary European and American artists. The gallery, which opened in 2000 in East Hampton, joins the original in Manhattan, one in Chicago, and another in Palm Beach.

SAG HARBOR

Grenning Gallery (631-725-8469; 90 Main St. Sag Harbor, NY 11963) Open Thurs., Sun., Mon., Tues. 11am–6pm, Fri., Sat. 11am–8pm. Owner: Laura Grenning. Dedicated to the work of artists who employ a style and philosophy similar to that of the old masters, this gallery, located at the Sag Harbor Cinema, features realistic still lifes, landscapes, nudes, and portraits that have been painted from life. You will find beautiful paintings worthy of hanging in the most elegant homes.

SOUTHAMPTON

Chrysalis Gallery (631-287-1883; 2 Main St., Southampton, NY 11968) Open year-round: daily 10am–6pm. Owner: Agnes Ehrenreich. You'll find wonderful original oils, watercolors, and sculptures at this fine arts gallery on a prominent corner of the village, as well as prints by artists such as Michael Delacroix.

WESTHAMPTON BEACH

Paraskevas Studios (631-288-3812; jrkroll@aol.com; 83E Main St., Westhampton Beach, NY 11978) Open in summer: daily 5pm–10pm; call for hours and days rest of year. It all started rather simply. Michael Paraskevas created a character for *Dan's Papers* that he called Junior Kroll. Everyone loved it. Eventually his Mom wrote a story about Junior Kroll, and Michael illustrated it; it was published and sold very well. There are now 14 books, 4 TV shows, and this wonderful gallery where you can purchase drawings, books, and more. Don't miss this!

GIFTS

BRIDGEHAMPTON

Lisan & Co. (631-537-1260; 42 Snake Hollow Rd., PO Box 979, Bridgehampton, NY 11932) Open in summer: daily 10am–5pm; call for winter hours. Owner: Anna Moss. This charming shop in Bridgehampton Commons has unusual and fetching antiques, such as painted tables with a crackled glaze, decorative pottery, birdhouses, decorative pedestals, and mirrors.

EAST HAMPTON

Florence & Son (631-329-4444; 16R Newtown Ln., East Hampton, NY 11937) Open in summer: daily 10am–6pm; in winter: perhaps fewer days and shorter hours. Owner: Richard Feleppa. Follow the little brick path to the back of this building and your walk will be rewarded by a marvelous collection of Italian antiques and new imports. You'll find Venetian chandeliers, Tuscan pottery, Murano art glass, Florentine leathers, pretty Italian papers, and other luscious accessories for home and garden. Best of all — the prices are very competitive.

Rumrunner (631-324-3444; 14 Main St., East Hampton, NY 11937) Open in summer: daily 10am–11pm; in winter: shorter hours; **Rumrunner** (631-287-0583; 22 Main St., Southampton, NY 11968) Open year-round: daily 10am–6pm; **Rumrunner** furniture outlet center (631-537-8495; 14 Main St., Bridgehampton, NY 11932) Open in summer: 10am–11pm; call for hours rest of year. With great style, Rumrunner offers a selection of cleverly selected furniture, bright Italian and Portuguese dishes, replicas of old signs, and mechanical banks. There are also painted tiles, pillows, and cards. (Also see Rumrunner Kid in the section Children's Shops.)

MONTAUK

Claudia's Carriage House (631-668-5409; Main St., Montauk, NY 11954) Open in summer: daily 10am–10pm; in winter: daily 10am–6pm. Owners: Claudia and Brad Dickinson. If you don't find the gift you're looking for here, it probably isn't made. Choose from a selection of jewelry, dolls, children's clothing, stuffed animals, china, crystal, and lots of Christmas items — all charmingly displayed on perhaps an old sleigh, or a carriage, or even a buckboard. The salespeople are very helpful.

SAG HARBOR

Romany Kramoris Gallery (631-725-2499; www.kramorisgallery.com; 41 Main St., PO Box 2664, Sag Harbor, NY 11963) Open in summer: daily 10am–11pm /12 midnight; shorter hours rest of year. This eclectic collection of unusual items is like a blast from the '50s. The gifts range from blown glassware and shell lampshades to books, cards, and stationery. There are Christmas items, candles, and a garden full of statuary and distressed garden benches.

Sue's Gifts (631-725-7400; 20 Main St., PO Box 2392, Sag Harbor, NY 11963) Open in summer: daily 10am–8pm/9pm; rest of year: daily 10am–6pm; closed Tues. Robert Evjen and Sherna Mistry Evjen have collected a wonderful array of personalized gifts for adults and children. There are picture frames, coatracks, dishes, tableware, and Christmas items.

Youngblood (631-725-6260; 26 Madison St., PO Box 821, Sag Harbor, NY 11963) Open in summer: daily 10am–6pm; call for winter hours. This interesting shop carries gifts and treasures designed by nature's creativity. There are fossils, driftwood pieces, shells, rocks, and much more — all made into unusual decorative objects.

WAINSCOTT

Georgina Fairholme and Company (631-537-3732; 345 Montauk Hwy., PO Box 874, Wainscott, NY 11975) Open in summer: Wed.–Sun. 10:30am–4pm; in winter: fewer days and shorter hours. Brightly painted jardinieres, pretty découpage lamps, trays, and plates, and lovely botanical prints in colorful frames all make ideal hostess gifts or take-home presents for yourself.

WESTHAMPTON BEACH

O'Suzanna (631-288-2202; 108 Main St., Westhampton Beach, NY 11978) Open in summer: Sun.–Wed. 10am–6pm; Thurs.–Sat. 10am–10pm; fewer days and shorter hours rest of year. Owner Suzanne Marchisello travels the back roads of Italy every year, finding new ceramic designers whose work she features in her store. Many of the designs are her own, and most of her pieces won't be seen elsewhere. Come here to find bright, hand-painted Italian pottery in platters, vases, dishes, and plaques.

Pine Cone (631-288-8316; 1 Glovers Ln., Westhampton Beach, NY 11978) Open Mem. Day–Labor Day: Sun.–Thurs. 10am–8pm, Fri., Sat. 10am–12 midnight; rest of year: Thurs.–Mon. 12 noon–6pm. Owner: Judy Garry. This tiny shop has some very interesting pieces tucked into its small space. There are large collections of antique lead soldiers and ceramic teapots (some hand painted). All of the Limoges, Kosta Boda/Orrefors, Wedgwood, and Battersea dishes and figurines, as well as other porcelain lines, are discounted. There are also unusual dolls, picture frames, teddys, teddys, and more teddys, jewelry, brass candlesticks, cobalt glass vases, and more.

HANDCRAFTS

EAST HAMPTON

The Irony (631-329-5567; 53 Sag Harbor Rd., East Hampton, NY 11937) Open Tues.–Sat. 9am–5pm or by appt. Owner: Bob Blinker. If you would like a decorative wrought iron fence surrounding your house, just like the ones in New Orleans, or a lacy iron window box, Bob Blinker will make it for you.

Local Color (631-329-2700; 32 Park Pl., East Hampton, NY 11937) Open in summer: daily 10am–6pm; shorter hours rest of year. Located just off the parking lot behind Main St. and Newtown Ln., this ceramics studio provides "greenware" plates, mugs, boxes, toothbrush holders, and a variety of other objects for hand painting by artists and wanna-bes. All of their pieces are lead-free and dishwasher-safe. They will give you instructions on painting and glazing your piece, and then they will fire it for you. It's lots of fun for children and a great way to personalize your gifts.

SOUTHAMPTON

Claire Murray (631-287-3363; 40/40B Job's Ln., Southampton, NY 11968) Open year-round: daily 10am–6pm. What a welcome addition to the Hamptons' scene! Claire has long been one of our favorite designers. The beautiful handmade hooked rugs that are sold in her shop, located at Fountain Circle, are all designed in her distinctive creative style. They range from brilliant florals to home and garden designs. You'll also find a lovely selection of quilts, hand-painted boxes, stationery, dishes, and greeting cards.

Gayle Willson Gallery (631-283-7430; 43 Job's Ln., Southampton, NY 11968) Open in summer: Mon.–Sat. 11am–5pm, Sun. 12 noon–5pm; closed Tues. and sometimes Wed. rest of year. Owner: Gayle Willson. This store features art fabrics, wearable art, and contemporary, high-quality arts and crafts, including beautiful, handmade jewelry and clothing.

Hecho A Mano (631-283-7425; www.hechoamano.net; 46 Job's Ln., Southampton, NY 11968) Open in summer: daily 10am–6pm; in winter: fewer days and shorter hours. Hecho A Mano means made by hand in Spanish, so as you might imagine, everything in this store has been handmade. The quality is outstanding. You'll find beautiful pottery, oil paintings, silver pieces, hand-carved wood furniture, ironwork, ceramic work, hand-painted tiles — all distinctive accessories for a Hamptons' home.

Shinnecock Gallery (631-283-3937; 60 Job's Ln., Southampton, NY 11968) Open in summer: daily 10am–6pm; Shinnecock Trading Post (631-283-8047; Montauk Hwy., Shinnecock Reservation, Southampton, NY 11968) Open daily 7am–7pm. These interesting shops carry Native American arts and crafts that include pottery, dreamcatchers, sand paintings, sculptures, beaded belts, glassware, moccasins, and jewelry. The items have been assembled from a variety of American Indian tribes, and some especially lovely work comes from the Southwest.

HOUSEWARES & KITCHEN SHOPS

BRIDGEHAMPTON

King•Beck Fine Stationery, Ltd. (631-537-5115; www.kingbeck@peconic.net; 2454 Main St., PO Box 475, Bridgehampton, NY 11932) Open year-round: daily 10:30am–6pm. Since we love fine stationery, we were pleased to see that Alice King and Sandi Beck-Silverman opened this fine stationery shop on Main St. in Bridgehampton in 2000. There are unusual invitations, pretty pens, and a variety of fine stationery items that can be purchased or ordered.

Williams-Sonoma (631-537-3040; Bridgehampton Commons, Bridgehampton, NY 11932) Open in summer: Mon.–Sat. 10am–8pm, Sun. 11am–6pm; rest of year: Mon.–Sat. 10am–7pm, Sun. 11am–6pm. The addition of a new building at Bridgehampton Commons in 1994 brought this well-known kitchen store to town. Here you'll find terrific pots and pans, dishes, linen, silverware, glassware, knives, and such food staples as garlic oil, passion fruit vinegar, and coffee beans.

EAST HAMPTON

Curly Willow (631-324-1122; www.curlywillow.com; 55 Main St., East Hampton, NY 11937) Open in summer: daily 10am–6pm, later on weekends; closed Tues., Wed. rest of year. Owner: Denise Rebaudo. There are pots and pans, kitchen utensils, pottery, place mats and napkins, and even birdhouses here.

Home, James! (631-324-2307; 55 Main St., East Hampton, NY 11937) Open Mon.–Fri. 10am–5pm, Sat. 10am–6pm, Sun. 11am–5pm. If you're looking for a wonderful set of antique dishes, perhaps some new Spode, or a delicate French lace or handsome Irish linen tablecloth, you must come here. You will find a wide selection of elegant china, crystal, linens, and small antiques. And, if you're looking for expert interior design assistance, that's here, too.

SAG HARBOR

Sylvester & Co. (631-725-5012; Main St., Sag Harbor, NY 11963) Open in summer: daily 8am–9pm; closed Wed. and shorter hours rest of year. Owner: Linda Sylvester. This is a kitchenware shop with all of the items that you'd expect, but it also sells gourmet items, pottery, china, place mats, gardening baskets, cookbooks and gardening books, fresh coffee, muffins, cookies, and pastries. The coffeepot is on all day, and it's a town gathering spot.

SOUTHAMPTON

Fishs Eddy (631-287-2993; 50 Job's Ln., Southampton, NY 11968) Open in summer: daily 10am–10pm; shorter hours rest of year. This is a terrific place to purchase dishes for a party. Just as in the Manhattan stores, this great shop is stacked from floor to ceiling with dishes that are factory overruns or surplus orders. There are dishes with nautical motifs that were ordered for yacht clubs and bistro plates that were ordered for restaurants. One day, there were stacks of white plates with elaborate gold rims that had been ordered for the Helmsley Palace Hotel.

Table D'Art (631-204-9199; www.tabledart.com; 58 Job's Ln., Southampton, NY 11968) Open in summer: daily 10am–6:30pm; call for hours rest of year. Manager: Barbara Conway. You'll find hand-painted ceramic pottery, brightly patterned dishes in contemporary designs (including square shapes), candles, chess boards, and even jewel-like napkin rings for astonishingly reasonable prices.

Tabletop Designs (631-283-1313; 38 Job's Ln., Southampton, NY 11968) Open Mon.–Sat. 10am–6pm, Sun. 11am–5pm. Owner: Stephanie Queller. Ms. Queller carries a marvelous combination of antique and decorator china — all beautifully displayed as you might at your own dinner party. On one recent visit, I found some blue and white antique flo-blue plates with scalloped edges and some hand-painted dishes with gold rims. There are also silver flatware and serving pieces, napkins and place mats, and much, much more.

WESTHAMPTON BEACH

The Sea Shell (631-288-2285; 128 Main St., Westhampton Beach, NY 11978) Open in summer: Mon.–Sat. 10am–5pm; in winter: shorter hours. Owner: Mrs. A. J. Farrell. There's a fine selection of elegant china here that features a wide range of Herend china, including the delicate figurines, and also tableware created by talented artist Lynn Chase, who uses a palette of brilliant colors to create her dramatic porcelains.

JEWELRY

EAST HAMPTON

Gems of the Past (631-324-4367; 58B Park Pl., East Hampton, NY 11937) Open in summer: daily 11am–7pm, weekends 11am–10pm/11pm; in winter: only some weekends. Owner: Karen Adler. Ms. Adler, a graduate gemologist, has selected a wonderful collection of estate and one-of-a-kind jewelry. You will find diamond and ruby bracelets, gold watches, and for the most discriminating, there's a bird pin with a nine-carat black opal body embellished with six carats of diamonds. Also see a De Beers 2000 Hourglass filled with 2000 shimmering uncut diamonds.

You can buy far more than fine jewelry at London Jewelers. An extensive MacKenzie-Childs shop, an Alfred Dunhill humidor room, and a Tiffany jewelry department are only a few of the pleasures.

Morgan McGivern

London Jewelers (631-329-3939; 2 Main St., East Hampton, NY 11937) Open in summer: Mon.–Thurs. 10am–5:30pm, Fri., Sat. 10am–10pm, Sun. 11am–5pm; shorter hours rest of year. After transforming a great old building that was in need of considerable repair, the owners opened this very elegant shop in 1996. It offers a selection of fine jewelry, plus one of the largest collections of MacKenzie-Childs hand-painted furniture and dishes outside the couple's own shop in Manhattan. In addition, there's a Tiffany jewelry department and an Alfred Dunhill humidor room, where you can select fine cigars.

McCarver & Moser (631-324-7300; 27 Main St., East Hampton, NY 11937) Open in summer: Mon.–Fri. 10am–6pm, Sat. 10am–7pm, Sun. 12 noon-5pm; shorter hours rest of year. In this fine and very elegant jewelry and gift store, you will find a selection of art glass by Daum, Lalique, Steuben, and others, watches by Cartier, jewelry imported from Italy, and much more.

SOUTHAMPTON

Lee Gallery (631-283-9666; 49 Main St., Southampton, NY 11968) Open in summer: daily 11am–6pm; closed Tues., Wed. rest of year. Owner: Lee Elliot. This store displays and sells very elegant, handmade, nontraditional gold jewelry designed by Lee Elliot, as well as the work of Ray Tracey. You'll find handcrafted designs in fiber, wood, ceramics, and glass.

Rose Jewelry (631-283-5757; 57 Main St., Southampton, NY 11968) Open Mon.–Sat. 9:30am–5:30pm, Sun. 12 noon–5pm; Jan.–Mem. Day: closed Sun. Owner: Jan Rose. This very elegant jewelry shop carries unusual, hand-crafted rings, bracelets, and other jewelry, and an excellent selection of gifts.

WESTHAMPTON BEACH

Joan Boyce (631-288-1263; 116 Main St., Westhampton Beach, NY 11978) Open in summer: weekdays 10am–6pm, weekends 11am–10pm. Joan Boyce, who also has shops in Manhattan and Aspen, CO, is a jewelry designer of inter-national fame. She fashions elegant bracelets, earrings, necklaces, and rings from precious and semiprecious gems in her unmistakably graceful style.

OLD-FASHIONED EMPORIUMS

Hildreth's (631-283-2300; 51-55 Main St., Southampton, NY 11968) Open Mon.–Fri. 9am–6pm, Sat. 10am–6pm, Sun. 11am–5pm; Hildreth House & Garden (631-537-1616; 2099 Montauk Hwy., Bridgehampton, NY 11932) Open Mon.–Sat. 10am–6pm, Sun. 9am–4pm; Hildreth Clearance Center (631-283-8388; 22 West Main St., Southampton, NY 11968) Open Mon.–Sat. 10am–6pm, Sun. 10am–5pm. Owner: Henry Hildreth. This is the grand-daddy of Hamptons' department stores. Established in 1842, it's billed as "America's Oldest Department Store." This is still a general store, but one that sells all of the items necessary for today's home: thread, needles, fabric, furniture, bedding, towels, china, glassware, pots and pans, outdoor furni-ture, barbecues, etc. Don't miss the end-of-summer sale, when items are sold at a 40–80 percent discount.

Sag Harbor Variety Store (631-725-9706; 45 Main St., Sag Harbor, NY 11963) Open July–Aug.: Mon.–Sat. 9am–9pm, Sun. 9am–5pm; rest of year: Mon.–Sat. 9am–5:30pm, Sun. 9am–1pm. Remember the old five-and-dime stores — the ones with soda fountains and lunch counters, photo booths where you could have silly pictures taken, and shelves stacked from floor to ceiling with every delight imaginable? That tradition lives on in Sag Harbor. The photo booth and soda fountain may be missing, but how many of the old stores had two cigar-store Indians, guarding the entrance and an old Texaco pump, converted to a floor clock? The Sag Harbor Variety Store has been doing exactly the same thing for almost 75 years and that means selling pots and pans, fabric by-the-yard, sewing notions, candy, hats, cosmetics, jewelry, toys, and much more.

Thayer's Hardware & Patio (631-537-0077; 2434 Montauk Hwy., PO Box 790, Bridgehampton NY 11732) Open in summer: Mon.–Sat. 9am–5:30pm, Sun. 10am–3pm; in winter: closed Sun. Owner: Roger Thayer. You can buy garden and household tools, dishes, plus barbecues and terrific patio furniture in this great store.

PHOTO SHOPS

Many pharmacies, groceries, and shops sell film and handle photo processing. The following listing gives you the names of the camera stores in the Hamptons that specialize in meeting the needs of photographers. These stores not only help with your film and film-developing needs, but they also sell cameras and accessories.

BRIDGEHAMPTON

Hampton Photo Arts, Inc. (631-537-7373; Montauk Hwy., Bridgehampton, NY 11932) Open Mon.–Sat. 10am–6pm, Sun. 10am–2pm. Owner: Dave McHugh. Located in Bridgehampton Common, behind K-Mart, not only does this store carry a full line of cameras and photographic supplies, but they also sell art supplies and offer custom-framing.

EAST HAMPTON

Reed's Photo Shop & Studio (631-324-1067; 54 Newtown Ln., East Hampton, NY 11937) Open in summer: daily 9am–5pm; closed Oct.–Dec. on Sun., Jan.–May on Thurs., Sun. Owner: Jon Reed. This excellent photo shop processes film and sells cameras, accessories, and a variety of film. It is the place to bring print film for quick developing. The salespeople are accommodating and friendly.

SOUTHAMPTON

The Morris Studio (631-283-0085; 72 Main St., Southampton, NY 11968) Open year-round: Mon.–Sat. 9am–5pm, Sun. 11am–4pm. The Morris Studio has been around for over 100 years, so you know that they know what they're doing. A full-service photo shop, it processes film, sells cameras, film, and accessories, and also carries artists' supplies.

CHAPTER SIX
Developing Artistry
CULTURE

The Memorial Day observance in Southampton is accompanied by a cannon salute.

Over the last 100 years, cultural pursuits have played an increasingly important role in the lives of Hamptons' residents and visitors, but even as new artistic expression has flourished, appreciation for traditional art has not diminished. Instead, there is renewed and heightened interest in the history and heritage of the Hamptons.

Today, because of an active historic preservation movement in the Hamptons, there are nineteen historic districts on the South Fork — sixty-five houses, buildings, windmills, sites, and even a wrecked ship are listed on the National Register of Historic Places. This appreciation for the old, combined with the daring thrust of new expression, gives the Hamptons a unique place in history.

We often read about the artistic skill of painters and sculptors from the Hamptons, but we hear less about the skilled craftspeople and artisans, past and present. For instance, the Dominy family lived and worked in East Hampton from around 1750–1850. These skilled furniture makers, who were far more than local carpenters, obtained ideas and tools from Europe and Boston and are known for their tall-case clocks, chests, chairs, and the solid windmills scattered across the East End. Their artistry is appreciated as much today as it was in the 1800s, and examples of their work appear in several local museums. Furthermore, the value of their work is nationally recognized — their workshop and the tools they used are now part of the permanent collection at the Winterthur Museum in Delaware.

This dual interest in old and new also exists in the fine arts. Although the works of Thomas Moran, Childe Hassam, and William Merritt Chase continue to be respected, collected, and admired, the Hamptons embraced and nurtured the art of the abstract expressionists in the 1940s and 1950s. New forms of art continue to be embraced and encouraged today.

Artists of all genres are attracted to the Hamptons, as much by this spirit of welcome and encouragement as by the area's natural beauty. Prominent writers and playwrights who have chosen to live in the Hamptons include P. G. Wodehouse, Truman Capote, John Steinbeck, E. L. Doctorow, Ken Auletta, Peter Matthiessen, Linda Bird Francke, Kurt Vonnegut, Tom Wolfe, Wendy Wasserstein, and many more.

Recording artists, entertainers, singers, composers, newscasters, magazine editors, directors, and producers — all artists of a different nature — are also attracted to the Hamptons. A few include Steven Spielberg, Billy Joel, Donna Karan, Paul Simon, Kathleen Battle, Chevy Chase, Peter Jennings, Paul McCartney, Chuck Scarborough, Martha Stewart, George Plimpton, and Dick Cavett.

CALENDAR OF EVENTS

The following events take place on Long Island's South Fork every year. The **Long Island Convention and Visitors Bureau** (631-951-3440) publishes an excellent guide to Long Island, but for specific local information, you should call the following chambers of commerce on the South Fork:

East Hampton	631-324-0362
Hampton Bays	631-728-2211
Montauk	631-668-2428
Sag Harbor	631-725-2100
Southampton	631-283-0402
Westhampton Beach	631-288-3337

December–May

Seal Watching (631-369-9840) Sponsored by Riverhead Foundation for Marine Research and Preservation.

January/February

Hikes and walks are sponsored on the South Shore during Jan. and Feb. by several organizations. These include the *Long Island Greenbelt Trail Conference* (631-360-0753); the *Group for the South Fork* (631-537-1400); *The Nature Conservancy for the South Fork* (631-329-7689); and *The Nature Conservancy's Mashomack Preserve on Shelter Island* (631-749-1001).

Community Theatre Company and other companies (631-324-0806) Guild Hall, East Hampton. A series of theatrical productions take place in Jan. and Feb.

Student Arts Festival (631-324-0806) Guild Hall, East Hampton. This professionally curated show features art by students in East Hampton Township schools.

March

Members Exhibition (631-324-0806) Guild Hall, East Hampton.

Purim Carnival (631-324-9858) Jewish Center of the Hamptons, East Hampton; (631-725-0904) Temple Adas Israel, Sag Harbor.

St. Patrick's Day Parade (631-668-2428) Main St., Montauk.

St. Patrick's Day Parade (631-288-3337) Mill Rd. and Main St., Westhampton Beach.

April

Easter Egg Hunts Amagansett Firehouse, Amagansett; Hampton Library, Bridgehampton; Maidstone Gun Club, East Hampton; Sag Harbor Village; Parrish Art Museum, Southampton.

May

Dan's Papers Annual Potatohampton Minithon 10K (631-537-0500) Bridgehampton. Mem. Day weekend.

Meet the Writers Book Fair (631-537-3233) Elaine Benson Gallery, Bridgehampton. An annual event at which local writers sign and sell copies of their books to benefit the John Steinbeck writing program at Long Island University's Southampton Campus.

June

Blessing of the Fleet (631-329-0973) Takes place on a Sun. afternoon in Montauk. Fishing craft and private boats parade past a reviewing stand to receive a prayer for safety and a successful fishing season. Sponsored by Montauk Boatman's Assn.

Greater Westhampton Chamber of Commerce Craft Show (631-288-3337) Main

St., Westhampton Beach. This giant craft fair offers a wide variety of high-quality items.

Landscape Pleasures (631-283-2118) Southampton. Offers a tour of South Fork gardens and a series of seminars. Sponsored by Parrish Art Museum.

The Mighty Montauk Triathlon (631-668-2428) Consists of a 1-mile swim, a 20-mile bike race, and a 10K run.

Pianofest (631-329-9115) Piano recitals and concerts sponsored by Pianofest, Long Island University in Southampton.

Sag Harbor Cup Sailing Regatta (631-725-4604) Sag Harbor. Sponsored by Breakwater Yacht Club.

Southampton Rotary 8K Run (631-283-0402) Agawam Park, Southampton.

President Clinton visits East Hampton.

Morgan McGivern

July

All for the Sea (631-283-4000) Southampton College. Annual rock concert. Performers in the past have included Tina Turner, Crosby, Stills, and Nash, and The Allman Brothers Band.

Artist's Studio Tour East Hampton. Annual tour of up to 30 studios, homes, and gardens of East End Artists. This 3-day event includes a reception and garden party. Sponsored by Artists Alliance of East Hampton.

Boy's Harbor Fireworks Display (631-324-0362) Duke Dr. off Springy Banks Rd., East Hampton.

Fireworks Display (631-324-6868) Main Beach, East Hampton. Sponsored by East Hampton Volunteer Fire Department, at dusk.

Fourth of July Village Parade (631-283-2530) Southampton. Sponsored by combined veterans organizations.

Greater Westhampton Chamber of Commerce 5K Race (631-288-3337) Main St., Westhampton Beach.

Ladies Village Improvement Society Fair (631-324-1220) 95 Main St., East Hampton. Begins at 10am. Great for kids — games, contests, rides, home-baked goodies, an evening barbecue, and square dancing.

Mary Fritchie Outdoor Art Show (631-288-3337) Sponsored by Greater Westhampton Chamber of Commerce.

The Mercedes-Benz Polo Challenge (631-653-5252) Some of the world's most celebrated polo teams compete annually in the Hamptons. Sponsored by Bridgehampton Polo Club.

Music Festival of the Hamptons (800-644-4418) Snake Hollow Rd., Bridgehampton. Ten days of classical music, ranging from the Baroque to the Romantic periods, including chamber orchestras, a harp concert, children's and senior citizen's concerts, and much more, held under festival tents.

Opera of the Hamptons (631-728-8804) A series of operas (*La Boheme* and *Tosca*, for example) are performed at locations both on the North and South Forks.

Sag Harbor Historic House Tour (631-725-0401) Sag Harbor. Benefits John Jermain Memorial Library.

Sir Thomas Crapper 5-Mile Run (631-324-4572) Springs.

Parades are plentiful in the Hamptons.

Morgan McGivern

August

Artists and Writers Softball Game (631-324-0362) East Hampton. Well-known writers and artists compete in a very serious softball game.

Arts and Crafts Fair (631-725-0011) Annual Sag Harbor Arts and Crafts Fair.

Bridgehampton Chamber Music Festival (212-741-9403; 631-537-6368 in Aug. only) A series of 10+ concerts for young and old alike that take place in Bridgehampton.

The annual artists vs. writers softball game in East Hampton draws huge crowds to see the celebrity players.

Morgan McGivern

Dan's Papers **Annual Kite Fly** (631-537-0500) Sagg Main Beach, Sagaponack. Kites are judged in 24 categories.

Fisherman's Fair (631-324-5671) Held at Ashawagh Hall in Springs, traditionally on the second Sat. in Aug. Delectable food, annual art show, booths with crafts, children's games, and much more. Sponsored by Springs Improvement Assn.

Guild Hall Clothesline Art Sale (631-324-0806) 158 Main St., East Hampton. A popular sale of art created by local artists that is both framed and unframed (the unframed may be pinned to clotheslines).

Hampton Classic Horse Show (631-537-3177) Held in Bridgehampton at the end of Aug. and beginning of Sept. Sponsored by Hampton Classic Horse Show.

House and Garden Tour (631-537-1527) St. Ann's Episcopal Church, Main St., Bridgehampton. Tour of homes in the Hamptons sponsored by St. Ann's.

King of the Bays Regatta (631-298-9755) Sailing race in Noyack and Gardiner's Bays.

Lighthouse Weekend at Montauk Point (631-668-5340) Sponsored by Montauk Historical Society.

Long Island Barrel-Tasting Barbecue (631-369-5887) The annual wine tasting and barbecue, sponsored by Long Island Wine Council and *Wine Spectator* magazine, showcases East End wines and the cooking of local chefs.

Sand Castle Contest (631-324-6250) Atlantic Avenue beach, Amagansett.

September

Cartier Grand-Slam Tennis Tournament (631-537-0189) Sponsored by American Cancer Society.

Fit Hampton Triathlon (631-726-8700) 1-mile swim, 25-mile bike race, and a 6.2-mile run. Sponsored by Southampton Hospital.

Historic Sag Harbor "Harbor Fest" Weekend (631-725-0011) Includes tours, a parade, whaleboat races, and a concert. Sponsored by Sag Harbor Chamber of Commerce.

Historic Seaport Regatta and Breakwater International Regatta (631-725-4604) Sag Harbor. Sponsored by Breakwater Yacht Club.

Shinnecock Powwow (631-283-6143) Held on the Indian reservation in Southampton, this event includes 3 days of traditional dances, songs, and lots to do, see, buy, and eat.

October

The Shinnecock Powwow is an annual Labor Day week-end event on the Shinnecock Indian Reservation in Southampton.

Jason Green

Architectural House Tour (631-537-0120) In several villages. Sponsored by League of Women Voters.

East Hampton Chamber of Commerce Annual Georgica Jog 5K Run (631-324-0362) Part of the Fall Festival sponsored by East Hampton Chamber of Commerce.

Fall Festival on the Village Green (631-668-2428) Montauk. Includes a Clam Chowder Recipe Competition, hayrides, bike race, and pumpkin decorating. Sponsored by Montauk Chamber of Commerce.

Halloween Party (631-325-0200) Westhampton. For children and pets. Sponsored by Bide-A-Wee.

Hamptons International Film Festival (631-324-4600) Showings include new and art films. Stars and directors attend.

Montauk Annual Full Moon Bass Tournament (631-668-2428) Bluefish surf-casting contest; striped bass derby.

Pumpkin Trail and Halloween Activities (631-725-0011) Annual Sag Harbor Halloween Festivities. Sponsored by Sag Harbor Chamber of Commerce.

November

Country Christmas (631-283-0402) Southampton. Celebration with Santa coming to town. Sponsored by Southampton Chamber of Commerce.
Diver's Flea Market (631-283-4000) Southampton College. Sale of new and used diving equipment.
SweetPotatohampton (631-537-0500) Bridgehampton. Annual A.T. (after turkey) 8K run. Sponsored by *Dan's Papers.*
Turkey Day Run for Fun (631-324-4143) Montauk. Sponsored by East Hampton Town Recreation Dept.

December

Gallery of Trees (631-324-0362) East Hampton. Trees decorated by businesses and celebrities. Sponsored by East Hampton Chamber of Commerce.
Holiday Historic House and Inn Tour (631-324-0362) East Hampton. Sponsored by East Hampton Chamber of Commerce.
Sag Harbor Holiday Events (631-725-0011) Annual events include Santa's arrival and outdoor lighting, costumed carolers and horse and carriage rides. Sponsored by Sag Harbor Chamber of Commerce.
Santa Parade (631-324-0362) East Hampton. Sponsored by East Hampton Chamber of Commerce. Also, tree lighting (631-283-0402). Sponsored by Southampton Village Decorating Committee.
Santa Visits the Montauk Point Lighthouse (631-668-2544).

ARCHITECTURE

What a wealth of architectural attractions we have! Architectural styles for residential dwellings range from New England saltbox cottages to elegant 1700s manor houses. There are Federal-style buildings, high Greek Revival mansions, ornamented Victorians, and modern contemporaries.

Today, the Hamptons are noted for the distinctive modern houses that seem to rise in geometric curves and angles from the dunes and potato fields, as if from another world. Just as famed artists have left their mark on the East End, so have famed architects. The Hamptons have become a laboratory for innovative new ideas in architecture. George Nelson, Richard Meier, Andrew Geller, Jacquelin Robertson, Gwathmey/Siegel, Norman Jaffe, and Robert A. M. Stern are only a few of the contributors.

Several excellent books describe Hamptons' architecture. Architectural critic, Paul Goldberger's book, *The Houses of the Hamptons* (1986) is an excellent resource, as is *Hampton Style: Houses, Gardens, Artists* (1993) by John Esten and Rose Bennett Gilbert with photographs by Susan Wood, which provides an inside look through photographs and text into Hamptons' homes.

As Robert B. MacKay said in his introduction to the *AIA Architectural Guide to Nassau and Suffolk Counties, Long Island* (1992):

> *. . . few parts of the country can boast the range and depth of domestic architecture that can be found on Long Island. Perhaps because the Industrial Revolution bypassed the region for lack of falling water to power mill turbines, Long Island's built environment was not seriously affected by subsequent development from the seventeenth century until the post-World War II period, when the G.I. Bill and the growth of the aircraft industry sent thousands eastward on Robert Moses' parkways toward new suburban communities, such as Levittown. As a result, Long Island possesses close to 100 First Period buildings, the greatest concentration of surviving windmills . . . most of its eighteenth-century manorial seats and dozens of relatively intact nineteenth-century villages. . . . Long Island is also significant for its Modern and Post-Modern architecture, the South Fork in particular having served as an incubator for progressive domestic design for over a century.*

ART MUSEUMS

Some artists claim the light is better in the Hamptons than anywhere else — clearer, with a bluer sky and less haze. In an account of the first visit of the Tile Club to East Hampton in *Scribner's Monthly* in 1879, the writer claimed the light of the area was ideal, "The afternoon sky was filling with color, and the cumulus clouds that toppled from the horizon were turning to vast chryselephantine statue-galleries, ivory and gold." The area has also been praised for its peace and tranquility — the absence of noise, except for the occasional caw of a crow or the call of geese flying overhead. Whatever the reason, for more than a century, artists have been attracted to Long Island's South Fork.

The rich tapestry of art now enjoyed in the Hamptons can be traced to those first artists who came here in the 1800s and spread the word. When Thomas Moran, Winslow Homer, Childe Hassam, and their friends from the Tile Club made East Hampton their summer home, they set up their easels at the beach, on the village streets, and on the dunes at Montauk. Their paintings not only captured romantic fancy, but also brought more artists and residents to the area every summer. When one of their members penned an article in 1879 for *Scribner's Monthly* titled "The Tile Club at Play," complete with charming sketches, the summer migration to the Hamptons began in earnest.

William Merritt Chase arrived during this time and made Southampton his home. He established an acclaimed art school, where students painted *en plein air*, capturing the sea and dunes on their canvases. Thomas Moran, who painted many of America's national parks, loved East Hampton so much that he also made it his permanent home. The art of Moran and Chase was similar to the Barbizon School, which was located just outside Paris — romantic landscapes and sunsets, fields of flowers, and pretty women and children — and the Hamptons were christened "The American Barbizon."

The work of Jackson Pollock, who came to the village of Springs in 1945, was art of a different sort. Full of bold color and raw energy, it looked to some like little more than wild abandon put to canvas, but to others it represented a brilliant new technique — and abstract expressionism assumed new importance. Pollock, as did Moran before him, attracted other artists who appreciated the tranquility of the region, as well as its proximity to New York City. Robert Motherwell, Larry Rivers, Willem de Kooning, and Alfonso Ossorio were only a few of those who followed Pollock to the Hamptons. The Museum of Modern Art held summer art classes at Ashawagh Hall in the mid-1950s. Fairfield Porter, who gained increasing stature with a more realistic style, came to Southampton in 1949 and stayed until his death in 1975.

The following list is a representative sampling of exhibition art galleries in the Hamptons. For information about commercial art galleries, see Chapter Five, *Shopping.*

EAST HAMPTON

GUILD HALL
631-324-0806.
158 Main St., East Hampton, NY 11937.
Open: Mem Day–Labor Day:
    Mon.–Thurs. and Sat. 11am–5pm, Fri.

11am–6pm, Sun. 12 noon–5pm; Labor Day–Mem. Day: Wed.–Sat.
11am–5pm, Sun. 11am–5pm; closed Mon., Tues.
Admission: $5 suggested contribution.

Guild Hall has three large galleries where artwork is exhibited throughout the year. This marvelous institution has been encouraging artists in a variety of genres for almost 70 years. In addition to art and sculpture exhibitions, the Clothesline Art Sale, held in Aug., offers a place for both amateur and professional artists to exhibit and sell their work. There are literary readings by emerging and established writers, and it sponsors the H. R. Hays poetry series, in which readings by internationally acclaimed poets are conducted. Adult and children's art and writing workshops are offered throughout the year, and you can see musical and dance performances, hear cabaret and jazz artists, and attend plays at the John Drew Theatre.

SOUTHAMPTON

FINE ARTS GALLERY
631-283-4000.
239 Montauk Hwy., Southampton, NY 11968.

Open: Mon.–Fri. 1pm–5pm.
Admission: None.

The Fine Arts Gallery on Long Island University's Southampton Campus hosts a variety of art exhibits year-round, ranging from paintings and photography by students and faculty to works by a variety of local painters and sculptors.

THE PARRISH ART MUSEUM
631-283-2118.
25 Job's Ln., Southampton, NY 11968.
Open: Mid-June–mid-Sept.: Mon.–Sat.

11am–5pm, Sun. 1pm–5pm; mid-Sept.–mid-June: closed Tues., Wed.
Admission: $2 donation.

The Parrish Art Museum in Southampton was established in 1897 when its founder, Samuel Longstreth Parrish, hired architect Grosvenor Atterbury to build an addition to the existing Art Museum. The building, containing exhibition space and a concert hall, is located in the heart of the village beside the old Rogers Memorial Library building, which the Parrish will soon also occupy after the library's relocation to Cooper's Farm Rd. The Parrish collection of American art of the nineteenth and twentieth centuries is especially strong in paintings by William Merritt Chase and Fairfield Porter who spent much of their working life in the area. This fine museum also has a sculpture garden and an arboretum and offers lectures, concerts, changing exhibits, and children's programs in art and theater. Adult programs are also offered, including films, tours, musical performances, and more.

THE SOUTHAMPTON CULTURAL CENTER
631-287-4300.
2 Pond Ln., Southampton, NY 11968.

Open: Depends on exhibit or event.
Admission: Depends on exhibit or event.

The Southampton Cultural Center, on Pond Ln. in the heart of the village, across from Agawam Lake, exhibits artwork by members of the Southampton Artist's Association (a group of almost 300 artists) about four times yearly. It also sponsors workshops, seminars, and courses. This is a Village of Southampton facility.

CINEMA

Movie producers, directors, and actors call the Hamptons home (or at least their summer home), and a number of films have been shot on location here, so it's natural for local residents to have an avid interest in movies. As early as 1915, *The Sheik*, which featured Rudolph Valentino galloping across the dunes of Montauk, was filmed here. In 1932, *No Man of Her Own*, starring Clark Gable and Carole Lombard, was shot in Sag Harbor, as was *Sweet Liberty*, with Alan Alda in 1985. The 1988 movie, *Masquerade*, with Meg Tilly and Rob Lowe, was also filmed here. Every summer since 1988, HBO has screened a major television film at the East Hampton Cinema. The event attracts a bevy of stars, directors, and their friends.

In 1993, The Hamptons International Film Festival was inaugurated at which some 150 popular and art films were screened over a period of five days in October. Films are now shown at the East Hampton Cinema, and stars and directors are often on hand for the screenings and for lectures and symposia held at East Hampton's Guild Hall.

Hamptons' residents thus come by their appreciation of movies quite naturally. We have as much interest in seeing new movies the week that they come out as do New Yorkers, and our movie theaters don't disappoint us. Movies generally open here the same week that they do in New York City. Beware, however, we have often gone to the theater in East Hampton thirty minutes before show time, only to find that the film is sold out. It is advisable to buy the tickets early and then come back.

Loews Cineplex Hampton Arts (631-288-2600; Brook Rd., Westhampton Beach, NY 11978) A twin movie theater.

The Movie (631-668-2393; 3 Edgemere St., Montauk, NY 11954) A single-movie theater.

Morgan McGivern

Celebrities often come to the Hamptons for movie and TV film screenings.

Sag Harbor Cinema (631-725-0010; Main St., Sag Harbor, NY 11963) A single-movie theater that specializes in art and foreign films.

United Artists East Hampton Cinema (631-324-0448; 30 Main St., East Hampton, NY 11937) A six-plex movie theater.

United Artists Hampton Bays Theatre (631-728-8676; 119 West Montauk Hwy., Hampton Bays, NY 11946) A five-plex movie theater.

United Artists Southampton Theatre (631-287-2774; 43 Hill St., Southampton, NY 11968) A four-plex movie theater.

CULTURE COURSES

The Hamptons attract some of the finest art teachers, writers, photographers, and craftspeople who conduct summer and winter workshops, classes, courses, and seminars. Since many of these are arranged on short notice, it is important to watch the local newspapers every week for the list of scheduled events. In addition, posters announcing special courses will often appear in local stores and offices. The courses listed here are taught annually.

The Art Barge (Victor D'Amico Institute of Art) (631-267-3172; Napeague Meadow Rd., Napeague, NY 11930) Mem. Day–Labor Day. The Art Barge in Napeague is a great East End resource. It offers innovative, refreshing courses, as envisioned by its founder, Victor D'Amico, who was Director of Education at the Museum of Modern Art before beaching his unique barge in Napeague Bay. A wide range of classes are offered, especially in painting and drawing, but also in photography, papermaking, ceramics, sculpting, jazz, acting, and writing. There are also frequent play readings.

Bay Street Theatre (631-725-0818; Long Wharf, Sag Harbor, NY 11963) Throughout the year, this fine theatre company offers classes in acting and playwriting.

Guild Hall in East Hampton is the site of concerts, theatrical productions, art shows, and numerous classes for both adults and children. Here, the annual Clothesline Art Sale is in progress.

Morgan McGivern

Guild Hall (631-324-0806; 158 Main St., East Hampton, NY 11937) A variety of workshops and classes for adults and children are offered throughout the year, including courses in watercolor, figure drawing, photography, collage, and much more. Call for a complete schedule.

Long Island University, Southampton Campus (631-283-4000 ext. 349) A diverse and outstanding selection of courses are offered year-round. The following list represents several of the special workshops offered each summer and does not begin to scratch the surface. Call for a catalog.

Master Workshop in Art (631-283-4000 ext. 349) A renowned group of artists teach a creative course every summer for artists who have mastered the basic techniques. Studio space is provided for this 4-week living and working experience, and enrollment is limited. Interaction among the artists is a valuable component. Call for information.

Photography Workshop (631-283-4000 ext. 316) This is an annual workshop held by some of the nation's leading photographers who teach courses as varied as quality black-and-white printing, landscape and architecture in large-format photography, and electronic imagery and scanning photography. Call for a schedule.

Summer Writer's Conference (631-283-4000 ext. 423) This esteemed conference encompasses a variety of wonderful workshops, lectures, forums, and classes that are conducted by distinguished authors, poets, and playwrights. The workshops and classes include fiction writing, poetry, children's literature, screenwriting, and more. Call for a schedule.

Silvia Lehrer's Cookhampton (516-537-7831; Oliver's Cove Ln., Water Mill, NY 11976) Sylvia Lehrer has been writing the cooking column for *Dan's Papers* for some time; now she's also conducting great cooking classes in her home. Often Mrs. Lehrer will teach a cooking series herself on such subjects as the nuances of regional Italian cooking or the flavors of Provence. In these cases, the classes are hands-on and fully participatory in nature. Other times, she'll invite a well-known cookbook author, such as Giuliano Bugialli or a Hamptons' chef, to teach a demonstration class. In either case, the classes are instructional and lots of fun.

HISTORIC HOUSES, SITES, MUSEUMS & GARDENS

The Hamptons have a progressive and active historic preservation movement; therefore, many historic houses, museums, and sites have been identified and are open to the public. East Hampton and Southampton Towns currently have nineteen historic districts and sixty-five historic sites. In 1993, in recognition of it's "effective efforts to sustain the beauty of the historic village," the Village of East Hampton was awarded the Pillar of New York Award by the Preservation League of New York State.

The historic houses, sites, museums, and landmarks below are all open to the public. For an excellent history of East Hampton, with walking tours of Sag Harbor, East Hampton, Springs, Wainscott, Amagansett, and Montauk, a nature walk through Napeague, and three suggested bicycle tours, read *East Hampton, A History & Guide* (1985) by Jason Epstein and Elizabeth Barlow. In addition, there are excellent house and garden tours in East Hampton, Sag Harbor, and Southampton every year.

EAST HAMPTON TOWN

AMAGANSETT

EAST HAMPTON TOWN MARINE MUSEUM
631-267-6544; 631-324-6850.
Bluff Rd., Amagansett.
Mailing Address: 101 Main St., East

Hampton, NY 11937.
Open: July, Aug.: daily 10am–5pm;
  spring, fall weekends only by appt.
Admission: Adults $4; seniors and
  children $2.

The East Hampton Town Marine Museum, which overlooks the double dunes and Atlantic Avenue beach beyond, contains a fascinating collection of exhibits that describe and illustrate the history of whaling and fishing on the East End. There are dioramas, boats, tools, equipment, and explanations of the baymen's ongoing struggle with nature. An exhibit of haul seining illustrates the difficulty of this type of fishing; other exhibits describe shellfishing, harpooning, and the evolution of whaling. Outside, a series of displays are devoted to hunting in the Hamptons.

MISS AMELIA'S COTTAGE
631-267-3020.
Montauk Hwy. and Windmill Ln.,
  Amagansett.
Mailing Address: PO Box 7077,

Amagansett, NY 11930.
Open: Summer and fall only: Fri.–Sun.
  10am–4pm.
Admission: Adults $2; children $1.

This delightful cottage provides a view into the life of Miss Mary Amelia Schellinger, who occupied the cottage from 1841–1930. The house was built in 1725 by one of Miss Amelia's ancestors and was moved to its present site in 1794. It contains a collection of furniture made by the Dominy family, as well as other examples of furniture and objects typical of the area. For insight into life in the Hamptons during a very interesting period of time, *Miss Amelia's Amagansett* (1976) by Madeline Lee and a tour of Miss Amelia's house are highly recommended. The **Roy K. Lester Carriage Museum**, also located on the property, contains a fascinating collection of thirty carriages (several impeccably restored), including racing sulkies and sleighs and even a surrey with a fringe on top. The site is operated by the Amagansett Historical Association.

EAST HAMPTON

The East Hampton Historical Society conducts an award-winning walking tour of East Hampton's historic downtown year-round. Tours are led by an actor dressed in colonial costume. This knowledgeable guide delivers a spicy historical narrative about East Hampton's colorful past. For information, call 631-324-6850.

CLINTON ACADEMY
631-324-1850; 631-324-6850.
151 Main St., East Hampton.
Mailing Address: 101 Main St., East
  Hampton, NY 11937.

Open: July, Aug. 1pm–5pm; spring, fall
  weekends only by appt.
Admission: Adults $4; seniors and
  children $2.

Clinton Academy is a stately, three-story, brick and clapboard building that once housed the first chartered secondary school in New York State. Established in 1784, students came from as far away as the West Indies to attend this esteemed school to prepare for college. It was especially notable as it was one of the first schools to offer a coeducational program. Its graduates attended Harvard, Yale, and Princeton. The Academy is now one of East Hampton's primary historical museums, housing 12,000 articles that include furniture, clothing, textiles, ceramics, porcelains, tools, books, and photographs. It is operated by the East Hampton Historical Society.

HOME SWEET HOME
631-324-0713; 631-324-4150.
14 James Ln., East Hampton, NY 11937.

Open: Mem. Day–Labor Day: Mon.–Sat.
  10am–4pm, Sun. 2pm–4pm.
Admission: Adults $4; children $2.

Home Sweet Home, a 1650 saltbox house, was the boyhood home of John Howard Payne, author of the famous poem and song, "Home, Sweet Home," which presumably referred to this house. The house and all the furnishings have been impeccably restored. There is a very fine collection of English ceramics, including lustreware and blue Staffordshire china, American furniture, and textiles. The grounds include the 1804 Pantigo Windmill and a lovely garden. Home Sweet Home is operated by the Village of East Hampton.

HOOK WINDMILL
631-324-0713; 631-324-4150.
Montauk Hwy., East Hampton.

Mailing Address: 14 James Ln., East
  Hampton, NY 11937.
Admission: Adults $2; children $1.

This is one of the best surviving examples of the windmills that dotted the landscape of the East End for many years, grinding grain and sawing lumber, and helping the area prosper. Although eleven windmills still remain — more than in any other part of the United States — many are not open to the public. The Hook Windmill was built in 1806 by Nathaniel Dominy IV and is one of the finest examples of Dominy workmanship. Among the laborsaving devices constructed here are a sack hoist, a grain elevator, a screener to clean the grain, and bolters to sift the flour and cornmeal. The Hook Windmill is operated by the Village of East Hampton.

**LADIES VILLAGE IMPROVEMENT
 SOCIETY**
631-324-1220.
95 Main St., East Hampton, NY 11937.
Open: Apr.–Dec.: Tues.–Sat.

10am–5pm; Jan.–Mar.: Fri., Sat. only
10am–5pm.
Admission: None.
Special Features: Thrift shop and
 bargain books for sale.

Affectionately known as LVIS, this venerable organization is dedicated to the beautification and preservation of the parks, gardens, trees, and shrubs of East Hampton. It was founded in 1895, and every year its members supervise the planting of flowers at the entrances to the village; remind home owners to check their elm trees for Dutch elm disease; and maintain the village greens and the trees on village streets. To raise funds for its work, the Society holds a perpetual flea market, which includes an enormous selection of used books, and holds an annual fair that families consider one of the highlights of the summer season. The headquarters are located in the Gardiner Brown House, which dates to 1740.

LONGHOUSE RESERVE
631-329-3568.
Hands Creek Rd., East Hampton.
Mailing Address: PO Box 2386, East
 Hampton, NY 11937.

Open: Summer: Wed., 1st and 3rd Sat.
 each month 2pm–4pm; otherwise
 only open for lectures, tours, and
 special events.
Admission: Varies with events.

This is the laboratory and home of renowned designer Jack Lenor Larson. Events include tours, seminars, and workshops, as well as visual arts, dance, and musical performances. Mr. Larson, a textile designer, art collector, gardener, and philanthropist, said, "This is a dimensional, evolving study in lifestyle, built with the firm belief that we all learn best when experiencing visual arts in the 'full round'. . . as opposed to the media." Operated by the LongHouse Foundation.

MULFORD FARM
631-324-6869; 631-324-6850.
10 James Ln., East Hampton.
Mailing Address: 101 Main St., East
 Hampton, NY 11937.

Open: July, Aug. 1pm–5pm; spring, fall
 weekends only by appt.
Admission: Adults $4; seniors and
 children $2.

Mulford Farm was settled in 1680, and it remained in the Mulford family from 1712–1944. The farm, located in the heart of East Hampton, has been restored to its 1790s roots and provides an exceptional view of life on a prosperous, working eighteenth-century farm. This four-acre site includes the farmhouse with its original kitchen and implements, the original furniture, barn, and farm tools. Costumed guides give a narrated tour that includes an architectural history of East Hampton, as well as a look at early decorative arts and interior design. The tour also includes a living history exhibition where guides will demonstrate family activities, such as weaving and churning butter. Mulford Farm is operated by the East Hampton Historical Society.

The Osborn-Jackson House in East Hampton was built in 1740. It serves as the head-quarters of the East Hampton Historical Society.

Morgan McGivern

OSBORN-JACKSON HOUSE
631-324-6850.
101 Main St., East Hampton, NY 11937.

Open: Year-round: Mon.–Fri. 9am–5pm.
Admission: Adults $4; seniors and
    children $2.

The Osborn-Jackson house is a handsome 1740 Colonial that serves as head-quarters to the East Hampton Historical Society. It has been restored to the 1870s, and it contains exhibits that interpret the life of several generations of men, women, and children who lived there. At times, there are romantic evening lantern tours that help visitors recreate the mood and the ambience of the period.

TOWN HOUSE
631-324-6850.
149 Main St., East Hampton.
Mailing Address: 101 Main St., East
    Hampton, NY 11937.

Open: July, Aug. 1pm–5pm; spring, fall
    weekends only by appt.
Admission: Adults $4; seniors and
    children $2.

The Town House, a small structure built in 1731, is an excellent example of a one-room schoolhouse. The potbellied stove at the front, old school desks that contain children's scribbled notes, and early books and slates reveal how children were educated. The building, which also served as the town's original meeting hall, was moved several times. It now stands next to Clinton Academy, on Main St. in the heart of the village, and is operated by the East Hampton Historical Society.

Montauk

MONTAUK POINT LIGHTHOUSE MUSEUM

631-668-2544.
Montauk Hwy., Montauk.
Mailing Address: RFD #2, Box 112, Montauk, NY 11954.

Open: Year-round: summer hours generally 10:30am–6pm, later hours Sat. and holidays; shorter hours rest of year; call for schedule.
Admission: Adults $4; seniors $3.50; children $2.50; parking $5.

The Montauk Point Lighthouse is one of the most recognizable landmarks in New York State. Located at the state's easternmost tip, more than 100,000 people visit each year. Its construction was authorized by President George Washington in 1792 to warn ships of the large landmass they were approaching. Although originally built 297 feet from the steep cliffs, erosion during its 200-year history has eaten away all but the remaining 50 feet. Efforts are underway to stabilize the cliffs, although the lighthouse remains open. A museum at the base of the lighthouse contains exhibits and an interesting videotape narrated by Dick Cavett that describes the importance and function of lighthouses. Children (at least 41 inches tall) and adults can walk to the top of the tower for a spectacular view of the ocean. A snack bar, a large picnic area beside the parking lot, and many trails lead to the beach and across the bluffs. This landmark is operated by the Montauk Historical Society.

SECOND HOUSE MUSEUM

631-668-5340.
Second House Rd., Montauk.
Mailing Address: PO Box 81, Montauk, NY 11954.

Open: July–Columbus Day: daily 10am–4pm, closed Wed.; Mem. Day–June weekends only 10am–4pm.
Admission: Adults $2; children $1.

Second House Museum was the second house built to shelter the cattle and sheep tenders who spent their summers on the Montauk pasturelands. From 1661 until the 1920s, tenders herded settlers' cattle each summer to the verdant pastures in Montauk. It is said that cattle joined these great cattle drives from as far away as Patchogue. Second House was built in 1746 and is now the oldest building in Montauk. It's furnished with artifacts and beautiful period furniture, including lovely wicker and pine pieces. The original construction of handmade nails and pegged beams is still visible. It is operated by the Montauk Historical Society.

THIRD HOUSE MUSEUM

631-852-7878; 631-854-4949.
Montauk Hwy., Montauk, NY 11954.

Open: Mem. Day–Columbus Day: Wed.–Sun. 10am–5pm.
Admission: None.

Third House Museum was built in 1749. It is the third and final house constructed for the "cowboys" who watched over the cattle, sheep, and horses on the summer pastureland in Montauk. This large, rambling, wooden house is where Teddy Roosevelt stayed in 1898 when he and his Rough Riders returned sick and injured from the Spanish-American War in Cuba. The house is also headquarters for the Theodore Roosevelt County Park, which surrounds the museum. The **Pharaoh Museum**, containing Indian artifacts once belonging to the last family of the Montauk tribe to occupy the area, is in a wooden building on a hill behind Third House. Also on display are archeological tools and exhibits describing digging and dating techniques. Third House is operated by the Suffolk County Parks Dept.

Springs

It's been said of the ***Green River Cemetery*** that artists are "dying to get in." Ever since Jackson Pollock was buried here in 1956, other artists have been purchasing plots. Pollock's grave, in the back of the oldest section, is marked by a massive boulder called an *erratic*, which was deposited here as the glaciers receded some 15,000 years ago. Pollock's wife, Lee Krasner, who was also an artist, is buried in front of him. The cemetery is located on Accabonac Rd., almost to Old Stone Hwy.

Pollock-Krasner House and Study Center

Jackson Pollock's art studio (and also that of his wife Lee Krasner) in Springs is open to visitors.

POLLOCK-KRASNER HOUSE AND STUDY CENTER
631-324-4929.
830 Fireplace Rd., East Hampton, NY 11937.

Open: By advance reservation only May–Oct.: Tues., Fri., Sat. 11am–4pm; or by appt. for research or study groups.
Admission: $5.

Jackson Pollock's painting techniques were unique. Instead of using typical artists' paint, he preferred ordinary house paint. Instead of using artists' brushes, he devised several methods of splashing his canvas with color. He placed the canvas on the floor instead of on the wall; he sometimes poured directly from the can, or he spattered, dripped, or dribbled with a large brush, a stick, or a filled basting syringe, or he might apply the paint directly with his bare hands. Although his methods may have been considered primitive, the results that he achieved changed the face of American art; the critics called it abstract expressionism. This first, uniquely American, art technique gained acclaim and respect for American artists and put them on a par with their European contemporaries.

Pollock's barn studio was so drafty that he filled the wide cracks with rags in the winter, but it was here, between 1946–1956, that he created his greatest masterpieces. After Pollock's death in 1956, his wife Lee Krasner began using his studio, and she continued to paint here well into the 1980s. The farm on which they lived, overlooking the peaceful marshes and bay of Accabonac Creek, the barn studio, and the grounds are open to the public by appointment. The study center, which contains the artists' personal papers and a valuable oral history library, is open year-round. Operated by the Stony Brook Foundation.

SOUTHAMPTON TOWN

BRIDGEHAMPTON

CORWITH HOUSE
631-537-1088.
Montauk Hwy., Bridgehampton.
Mailing Address: PO Box 977,

Bridgehampton, NY 11932.
Open: Mid-June–mid-Sept.: Thurs.–Sat. 12 noon–4pm.
Admission: Voluntary donation.

The Corwith House, an historic 1820s home in Bridgehampton, contains interesting Colonial, Empire, and Victorian furniture and decor — all displayed in room settings. A former kitchen, which is set up as a washroom, reveals the difficulties of keeping all those white lace dresses clean and ironed. Upstairs rooms are devoted to lovely Victorian children's clothing, toys, and dolls. The Tractor Barn displays tractors and farm machinery, including a tall and unwieldy 1921 steam tractor. The Hildreth-Simons Machine Shop, on the same property, includes antique engines — all kept in working order. In the George W. Strong Wheelwright Shop, tools used to make wagons and sleds are displayed. The machine shop and the wheelwright shop are generally open only on special occasions. Operated by the Bridgehampton Historical Society.

QUOGUE

OLD SCHOOLHOUSE MUSEUM
631-653-4224.
Quogue St. East, Quogue.
Mailing Address: PO Box 1207,

Quogue, NY 11959.
Open: July 4–Labor Day: Mon., Wed.,
Fri. 2pm–5pm, Sat. 10am–12 noon.
Admission: None.

The Old Schoolhouse Museum provides a look at a much larger school-house than the one in East Hampton. When built in 1822, it was acclaimed as the "largest and best in Suffolk County." It is in pristine condition, with polished wood floors, a large fireplace, and a weathered shingle exterior. Used as a school and community meeting house until 1893, it now contains artifacts from Quogue's history, including photographs, dolls, toys, furniture, and more. Workshops, lectures, and exhibits are held in the museum in the summer. It is operated by the Quogue Historical Society.

SAGAPONACK

THE MADOO CONSERVANCY
631-537-8200.
618 Sagg Main St., Sagaponack.
Mailing Address: PO Box 362,

Sagaponack, NY 11962.
Open: May–Sept.: Wed.–Sat. 1pm–5pm.
Admission: $10.

The Madoo Conservancy was established to perpetuate the unique vision of artist Robert Dash, who created this lush and verdant garden on a two-acre plot of land that also contains his two studios and a wonderful collection of sheds, buildings, and outdoor sculptures. Near the entrance you'll encounter a whimsical gold and purple bench with a huge wheel at one end and wheelbarrow handles at the other, and as you meander along the paths, you discover an Oriental bridge crossing a little stream, a gazebo, arbors, and secret gardens. The gardens are continually in transition, as Mr. Dash adds and amends.

SAG HARBOR

Sag Harbor has many interesting old houses and buildings. The Society for the Preservation of Long Island Antiquities has developed a handy walking map to help you find and identify them. The map is on the inside of the brochure for the Old Custom House. Also, the Information Center, located in the old windmill at the entrance to Long Wharf, is a good resource.

THE OLD CUSTOM HOUSE
631-725-0250; 631-692-4664.
Garden St., Sag Harbor.
Mailing Address: PO Box 148, Cold
   Spring Harbor, NY 11724.
Open: Mem. Day–Columbus Day: Sat.,

Sun. 10am–5pm; July–Aug.:
Tues.–Fri. 10am–5pm; closed rest of
   year.
Admission: Adults $3; seniors and
   children $1.50.

The Old Custom House, on the corner of Main and Garden Sts. across from the Sag Harbor Whaling Museum, was originally the home of Henry Packer Dering who became the second customs collector of Sag Harbor in 1789. He later became the first postmaster as well, handling both duties from this home. The room that he used as his office is especially interesting. It has interior wooden shields that Mr. Dering could slide across the windows to prevent people from seeing inside when he was counting money. The building contains many pieces of furniture and decorative details that help us understand how a sophisticated family lived in the eighteenth century. It is operated by the Society for the Preservation of Long Island Antiquities.

SAG HARBOR WHALING MUSEUM
631-725-0770.
Main St., Sag Harbor.
Mailing Address: Box 1327, Sag Harbor,
  NY 11963.

Open: May–Sept.: Mon.–Sat. 10am–5pm,
  Sun. 1pm–5pm.
Admission: Adults $3; seniors $2; children
  $1.

The noble, Greek Revival mansion that is now the Sag Harbor Whaling Museum, was designed by Minard Lafever in 1845 for Benjamin Huntting, one of the earliest of Sag Harbor's whaling scions. The museum is entered through the jaws of a Right Whale. This is the Sag Harbor Historical Museum as well as one devoted to whaling. It features china, dolls, toys, a boat collection, ship models, whaling tools and artifacts, period furnishings, oil paintings, scrimshaw, and documents about Sag Harbor's glorious whaling days. Operated by the Sag Harbor Whaling and Historical Museum, it is located at the corner of Main and Garden Sts.

TEMPLE ADAS ISRAEL
631-725-0904.

Atlantic Ave., Sag Harbor, NY 11963.

In 1881, Joseph Fahys established a watchcase factory in Sag Harbor (it later became a Bulova Watch factory). As his business grew, he expanded his work force — eventually bringing some forty Jewish families to Sag Harbor directly from Ellis Island. Finding no place to worship, they built this synagogue in 1900, making it the first synagogue on Long Island.

THE WHALER'S CHURCH
631-725-0894.

Union St., at end of Church St., Sag
  Harbor, NY 11963.

This is the most magnificent church on the South Fork. Designed in 1844 by the well-known architect, Minard Lafever, it is set back from the street and has a broad platform of stairs that reach to the front door. Its impressive size, dignity, and stature command respect. This is a church that was meant to be noticed! It is sad that the magnificent 185-foot steeple tumbled off in the 1938

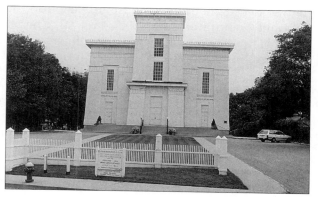

The magnificent Whaler's Church in Sag Harbor was built in 1844 and can hold up to 1,000 people.

Morgan McGivern

hurricane — what is left appears boxy and wanting, but there's good news on the horizon. A fund-raising effort is currently underway to raise money to fully replace the original steeple. One day, we'll see it just as it was designed! The interior holds up to 1,000 people, and its soaring, three-story height is truly inspirational. Concerts are often held here, and Presbyterian church services are conducted every Sun.

SOUTHAMPTON

Conscience Point is the spot where the first settlers from Lynn, MA, stepped from their boat in 1640 onto the land that became part of the first English settlement in New York State. A huge boulder set with a brass plaque marks the spot, located off North Sea Rd. in North Sea.

ELIAS PELLETREAU SILVERSMITH SHOP
631-283-2494.
Main St., Southampton.

Mailing Address: PO Box 303, Southampton, NY 11968.
Open: Call for information.
Admission: Voluntary donation.

The Elias Pelletreau Silversmith Shop is one of the few historic buildings still located on its original site although it now faces in a different direction. Built in 1686, the shop of this famous colonial silversmith is fully restored, exhibiting a workshop complete with tools. It is operated by the Southampton Colonial Society.

OLD HALSEY HOUSE
631-283-2494.
South Main St., Southampton.
Mailing Address: PO Box 303, Southampton, NY 11968.

Open: Reopening in 2001 following renovation. Call for hours.
Admission: Adults $2; children under 12 $.50.

The Old Halsey House (known as Hollyhocks for many years) is the oldest wooden frame saltbox house in New York State. Two rooms date from 1648 and the rest from 1653. This was a large home for its day, and it is still in excellent condition, with wide-plank floors, many fireplaces, and authentic seventeenth- and eighteenth-century furnishings. The acquisition of the furnishings was supervised by Henry Francis duPont, founder of the Winterthur Museum in Delaware, and many of the fine pieces are by renowned craftsmen. The grounds of the homestead contain colorful flower borders, an apple orchard, and an herb garden enclosed by privet hedges, which illustrates how it must have looked when the Halseys were living there. It is operated by the Southampton Colonial Society.

SOUTHAMPTON HISTORICAL MUSEUM
631-283-2494; 631-283-1612.
17 Meeting House Ln., Southampton.
Mailing Address: PO Box 303,
Southampton, NY 11968.
Open: June–Sept.: Tues.–Sat. 11am–5pm, Sun. 1pm–5pm; closed Mon.
Admission: Adults $3; seniors and students $2; children under 12 $1.

The Southampton Historical Museum is a collection of twelve buildings and thirty-five separate exhibits. The main house, a large, white, whaling captain's home, was built by Captain Albert Rogers in 1843. It contains many interesting exhibits, including china, glassware, and tole collections, a Shinnecock Indian exhibit, Revolutionary War artifacts, dolls, toys, and period clothing and furniture. Another building, an old New York schoolhouse (1850), contains the school's original desks, books, and maps. The Red Barn houses the Charles Foster collection of whaling instruments. It is set on a village street with a carriage shed, carpenter shop, blacksmith shop, the Corwith Drug Store, and a cobbler and harness shop. The Country Store is located in the pre-Revolutionary War barn where the British stabled their horses during the occupation of Long Island. It includes an old post office and general store. The complex is operated by the Southampton Colonial Society.

WATER MILL

WATER MILL MUSEUM
631-726-4625.
Old Mill Rd., Water Mill, NY 11976.
Open: Mem. Day–Labor Day: Thurs.–Sat. 11am–5pm, Sun. 1pm–5pm.
Admission: Donations accepted.

The Water Mill Museum is located in Southampton's original mill, which was constructed in 1644. This is a waterwheel mill rather than the wind-powered mills that are more prevalent. The museum exhibits the fully functional wooden gears, shafts, and restored wheel of this, the oldest operational mill on Long Island. Inside, the museum contains the tools of various local trades, such as farmers, blacksmiths, carpenters, spinners, weavers, and millers. Cornmeal ground at the mill is available for purchase. The museum is only open in the summer, but arts-and-crafts exhibits by local artists are also held in the summer. It is operated by the Ladies Auxiliary of Water Mill.

KULTURE FOR KIDS

Summertime in the Hamptons is packed with things for children to do. In addition to walking the nature trails and running on the beach (see Chapter Seven, *Recreation*), there are musical and art classes and performances geared especially to the younger set.

Bay Street Theatre Kidstreet (631-725-9500 box office; 631-725-0818 office; Bay St., Sag Harbor, NY 11963) A series of concerts for children that range from puppet shows to concerts of "Sesame Street" songs attract a bevy of children.

East Hampton Historical Society Summer Camp (631-324-6850) Ages 5–11. Children dress in costume and experience life in the seventeenth, eighteenth, and nineteenth centuries in a unique hands-on atmosphere. At the East Hampton Town Marine Museum in Amagansett, they will create a fish print T-shirt, handle a lobster trap, and work a trawler rig. At the Boat Shop in East Hampton, they'll talk to practicing fishermen, help restore a wooden boat, and learn how to make and sail a boat. In East Hampton's Town House and the Clinton Academy, they'll experience school life in the nineteenth century, while at Mulford Farm, they'll churn butter, card wool, and work on a loom. Call for information.

Guild Hall (631-324-0806; 158 Main St., East Hampton, NY 11937) May–Oct. Enjoyable workshops are conducted in drawing, sandpainting, mosaics, puppetry, soft sculpture, kite making, sculpting, and other artistic endeavors. Guild Hall also has a popular Kid's Fest every Wed. throughout the summer and periodically at other times. There are also theatrical productions just for children.

Kid's Kapers (631-287-4300; 2 Pond Ln., Southampton, NY 11968) Kid's Kapers is an entertainment series just for children that is held every Sat. morning in the summer and monthly the rest of the year at the Southampton Cultural Center.

Le Cercle Français (631-725-2128) This 7-week summer program offers classes in the French language, theater, cooking, manners, couture, and style. Classes are offered at Stella Maris in Sag Harbor for children from kindergarten through high school.

Westhampton Beach Performing Arts Center (631-288-2350) Special musical productions for kids have included *Cinderella, Pinocchio, Peter Pan, The Wizard of Oz*, and *Sleeping Beauty*.

LIBRARIES

L ibraries in the Hamptons are especially rich in local history; the *Long Island Collection* in the *East Hampton Library* encompasses one of the finest resources on Long Island for local research. Although the libraries allow unlimited use of the material on premises, several only permit residents to check out books; a nonresident library card can be purchased in some cases.

EAST HAMPTON TOWN

AMAGANSETT FREE LIBRARY
631-267-3810.
Main St., Amagansett.
Mailing Address: PO Box 726,
  Amagansett, NY 11930.
Open: Mon., Wed., Fri. 11am–5pm,
Tues., Thurs. 11am–8pm, Sat.
10am–5pm; closed Sun.
Fee: Library card free to year-round
  residents and taxpayers; honors cards
  from neighboring libraries; summer
  residents $25.

T he Amagansett Free Library was established in 1916 and is located in a building that dates from 1922. The Director Emeritus, Carleton Kelsey, is noted for his keen sense of local history. His book, *Amagansett, A Pictorial History 1680–1940* (1986), contains valuable photographs and historical material not found elsewhere.

EAST HAMPTON LIBRARY
631-324-0222.
159 Main St., East Hampton, NY 11937.
Open: Mon., Wed., Fri. 10am–7pm, Tues.,
  Thurs., Sat. 10am–5pm; *Long Island*
Collection: Mon.–Sat. 1pm–4:30pm.
Fee: Library cards are free to year-around
  residents and taxpayers of the East
  Hampton school district; nonresidents
  $50.

T he East Hampton Library was established in 1897, and it just keeps growing and getting better. The building is located on a parcel of land that once contained the home of Samuel Buell, East Hampton's third minister. The main building was designed in an Elizabethan style by Aymar Embury II in 1911. It has been expanded several times, in aesthetic and sympathetic architectural styles — once in 1946 by Embury himself — and again in 1999. It includes a local history and periodical room; a children's library where storytelling takes place; a video, record, tape, and CD lending library; a music listening room; and a large lending library. This is the repository of the *Long Island Collection*, most of which was donated by Morton Pennypacker, who was at one time historian of Suffolk County. The bequest has been bolstered by additional historic collections over the years, including the Thomas Moran Biographical Art Collection, and it contains an outstanding assemblage of books, prints, newspapers, genealogies, and much more. Dorothy King, who was the library historian for many years (and of great assistance when I was writing the first edition of this book), is extremely helpful and knows exactly where to find even the most obscure materials.

MONTAUK LIBRARY

631-668-3377.
Montauk Hwy., Montauk.
Mailing Address: PO Box 700, Montauk, NY 11954.
Open: Mon.–Wed., Fri. 11am–5pm, Sat. 10am–5pm, Sun. 2pm–5pm, evening hours Mon., Wed. 7pm–9pm.
Fee: Free to year-round residents and taxpayers of the Montauk school district; nonresidents $30 per year.

The Montauk Library, in a new building completed in 1991, has bright spaces for reading and an interesting collection that is especially strong on fishing and early Montauk history.

SPRINGS LIBRARY

No telephone.
Old Stone Hwy., East Hampton, NY 11937.
Open: Mon., Tues., Fri. 10am–12 noon, Wed. 10am–12 noon and 3pm–5pm, Sat. 9am–12 noon, evening hours Fri. 6pm–8pm.
Fee: $10.

The Springs Library is located in the small 1700s white clapboard house that was the former home of the Parsons family, one of the oldest Springs families. The library is not open full time and does not have a telephone, but it is an excellent resource for local Springs history.

SOUTHAMPTON TOWN

HAMPTON BAYS PUBLIC LIBRARY

631-728-6241.
Ponquogue Ave., Hampton Bays.
Mailing Address: PO Box AU, Hampton Bays, NY 11946.
Open: Mon., Tues., Thurs. 10am–9pm, Wed., Fri., Sat. 10am–5pm; mid-Oct.–mid-May: Sun. 1pm–5pm.
Fee: Free to full-time residents and taxpayers; summer residents $25 to borrow books ($20 refunded end of summer) or $40 to borrow videos and books ($35 refunded end of summer).

The Hampton Bays Public Library was established in the 1960s. It has a children's room where storytellers often read to children. You can borrow books, videos, CDs, books on tape, and music tapes, and there is an excellent lending book collection that is strong in art books.

HAMPTON LIBRARY IN BRIDGEHAMPTON

631-537-0015.
Main St., Bridgehampton.
Mailing Address: PO Box 3025, Bridgehampton, NY 11932.
Open: Year-round: daily 9:30am–5pm, except Wed., Sat. 9:30am–7pm; closed Sun.
Fee: Library card free to residents in Bridgehampton and Sagaponack school districts; $35 to nonresidents for books, with an additional fee of $25 for videos.

The Hampton Library is housed in a white shingled building built in 1876 and expanded in 1982. During the summer, the courtyard is the site of the library's popular *Fridays at Five*, a discussion series with local authors. In addition to lending books, the library has a music room, a children's room, a video library, and a selection of periodicals. Children's story hours are held on Sat. throughout the year.

JOHN JERMAIN MEMORIAL LIBRARY IN SAG HARBOR
631-725-0049.
Main St., Sag Harbor.
Mailing Address: PO Box 569, Sag Harbor, NY 11963.

Open: Mon.–Wed. 10am–7pm, Thurs. 10am–9pm, Fri., Sat. 10am–5pm.
Fee: Free to residents of Sag Harbor; accepts library cards from local libraries.

The John Jermain Memorial Library was built with funds donated by Mrs. Russell Sage in 1907. This imposing brick, two-story building houses a fine collection of books. The former library historian, Dorothy Zaykowski, wrote an excellent book, *Sag Harbor, The Story of an American Beauty* (1991), that chronicles the history of Sag Harbor.

QUOGUE LIBRARY
631-653-4224.
Quogue St. East, Quogue.
Mailing Address: Drawer LL, Quogue, NY 11959.

Open: Closed for renovation summer of 2000.
Fee: Free to residents of Quogue and those with library card within Suffolk County.

The Quogue Library is located in a charming 1897 building of weathered shingles on the same property as the Old School House Museum. The library sponsors summer programs for children and adults, as well as art events.

ROGERS MEMORIAL LIBRARY IN SOUTHAMPTON
631-283-0774.
91 Cooper's Farm Rd., Southampton, NY 11968.
Open: Oct.–May: Mon.–Thurs.

10am–9pm, Fri., Sat. 10am–5pm, Sun. 1pm–5pm; Mem. Day–Sept.: closed Sun.
Fee: Free to year-around residents or taxpayers of Southampton or Tuckahoe school districts; $50 nonresidents.

The Rogers Memorial Library was established in 1896 through a gift of Harriet Jones Rogers. For many years it resided on Job's Ln. in a wonderful and impressive, red Victorian brick building with an arched entrance, designed in the classic R. H. Robertson style, for which the architect was so famous. In the fall of 2000, however, the library moved to its equally impressive, new Hamptons' shingle-style building just off Windmill Ln. The new building is light and bright and extremely user-friendly — a wonderful place to peruse the extensive collection of books, as well as videos, tapes, and CDs. A Children's Reading Club sponsors popular storytelling activities. The old library will now be incorporated into the Parrish Art Museum, located next door.

WESTHAMPTON FREE LIBRARY
631-288-3335.
7 Library Ave., Westhampton, NY
11977.
Open: Mon.–Thurs. 9am–9pm, Fri.–Sat.
9am.–5pm, Sun. 1pm–5 pm.

Fee: Free to year-round residents and
taxpayers of Westhampton school
district; nonresidents $50; accepts
library cards from Suffolk County
libraries.

The Westhampton Free Library has much more than books. There's a lend-ing library of CDs, audio books, tapes, and videos, and activities, such as a Sun. bridge game, storytelling for children, a French club, and a book discussion group. The library contains an extensive village history collection, and it is fully handicap accessible.

MUSIC

Many musical events take place in the Hamptons, especially in the summer. The annual *All for the Sea* concert on Long Island University's Southampton Campus features top-name popular artists, such as Tina Turner and The Allman Brothers Band.

In addition, a *Fourth of July Music Festival*, sponsored by the East End Arts Council in Riverhead, features well-known artists, such as the Benny Goodman Alumni Orchestra and Richie Havens.

The Art Barge (631-267-3172) Napeague. Musical events, including blues, jazz, dance, and music performances, and much more, are performed at the Victor D'Amico Institute of Art.

Bridgehampton Chamber Music Festival (212-741-9403; 631-537-6368 in Aug. only) This marvelous chamber music festival has grown in stature and scope under the artistic direction of Marya Martin. During the month of Aug., an ambitious and star-studded series of concerts appeal to young and old alike. Most concerts are held at the Bridgehampton Presbyterian Church.

The Choral Society of the Hamptons (631-283-0404) This 100-voice choir con-ducts several concerts during the year with orchestral accompaniment. Their performances are always eagerly anticipated for their mix of classical music, opera, and show tunes.

Music Festival of the Hamptons (631-267-8293; 800-644-4418) This Hamptons-only outgrowth of the Newport Music Festival has grown since its inception in 1995 to include chamber music, piano recitals, children's concerts, and vocal events. It's under the distinguished leadership of Lukas Foss; some events take place in Bridgehampton, some in Guild Hall in East Hampton, and others in the Whaler's Church in Sag Harbor.

Opera of the Hamptons (631-728-7990) Various locations in Southampton. Year-round. Light opera is performed at dinner theaters, in wineries, and at Agawam Park.

Perlman Music Program (631-749-0740) This wonderful summer music program, which Itzhak Perlman established to teach musically gifted students, has moved to Shelter Island (see Chapter Ten, *Shelter Island*, for location and schedule).

Pianofest (631-329-9115; Fine Arts Theatre, Long Island University, Southampton Campus) June–July. This weekly series provides Hamptons' residents and visitors with a rare treat. Polished piano artists are selected by nomination and audition to attend a summer residential study program in the Hamptons. Often these students have already won prestigious competitions and are on the verge of launching concert careers.

Sag Harbor Chamber of Commerce Concerts (631-725-0011; Marine Park, Bay St., Sag Harbor) July–Aug. These free concerts might feature blues, jazz, or pop artists. Bring a blanket or a lawn chair.

Sag Harbor Community Band (631-725-9759; American Legion Post 388, Bay St., Sag Harbor) July–Aug. Free band concerts followed by dancing, with music by *Big Band East.*

Village of Southampton (631-287-4300) Agawam Park, Southampton. July–Aug. A variety of musical performances are sponsored by the Village of Southampton.

Westhampton Beach Performing Arts Center (631-288-2350) Westhampton Beach. A variety of musical performances by such entertainers as Marvin Hamlisch take place in this restored Art Deco building that was formerly a cinema.

Westhampton Cultural Consortium (631-288-0780) Village Green Gazebo, Westhampton Beach. July–Aug. Free concerts every summer include vocal, jazz, and classical music.

THEATER & DANCE

The Bay Street Theatre Festival is noted for its marvelous productions. Here Dianne Wiest and Mercedes Ruehl perform in the world premiere of Blue Light.

Gary Mamay

BAY STREET THEATRE FESTIVAL
631-725-1108 box office;
631-725-0818 office.
Bay St., Sag Harbor.

Mailing Address: PO Box 810, Sag
Harbor, NY 11963.
Open: Year-round.
Admission: $10–$42.

The Bay Street Theatre Festival in Sag Harbor opened with a bang in 1992, and it gets better every year. One of the principles is Emma Walton, daughter of Julie Andrews and Tony Walton. On occasion, her dad designs the sets, and sometimes her mom stars or helps with fund-raising benefits. Theatrical performances, play readings, pre–New York City openings, cabaret productions, and much more are presented in an intimate 330-seat professional theater throughout the year. The company also sponsors courses in drama, direction, and playwriting, and it has established a Young Playwrights curriculum in local schools that culminates in a student production.

**THE HAMPTON THEATRE
COMPANY**
631-653-8955.

Quogue Village Theatre, Jessup Ln.,
Quogue, NY 11959.
Open: Fall, spring.

The Hampton Theatre Company produces several plays during the fall and spring seasons, while the Quogue Junior Theatre Troupe produces several plays each summer. All are performed at the Quogue Village Theatre on Jessup Ave. in Quogue.

**JOHN DREW THEATRE OF GUILD
HALL**
631-324-4051.
Main St., East Hampton, NY 11937.

Open: Year-around.
Admission: Changes, depending upon
performance.

The John Drew Theatre of Guild Hall in East Hampton is the oldest playhouse on Long Island and sponsors theatrical productions, cabaret singers, poetry readings, and children's theater. During the summer, it teams up with several New York theater companies to hold readings and premier performances of productions before they head for the city.

**THE PLAYWRIGHTS' THEATRE OF
EAST HAMPTON**
631-324-5373; 718-434-6566.
LTV Studios, 75 Industrial Rd., East
Hampton.

Mailing Address: 30 Talmadge Farm
Ln., East Hampton, NY 11937
(summer); 666 East 19th St.,
Brooklyn, NY 11230 (winter).
Open: 4 weeks in late summer.

The Playwrights' Theatre of East Hampton conducts readings of new plays, but these are a far cry from ordinary play readings. Here, well-known dramatic artists, such as Tammy Grimes, Ben Gazzara, or Phyllis Newman, might be heard reading a play by Joyce Carol Oates or Lucy Wang, directed by respected Broadway directors. These events are followed by lively discussions and refreshments.

**WESTHAMPTON BEACH
 PERFORMING ARTS CENTER**
631-288-2350 office; 631-288-8519 fax.
Main St., Westhampton Beach.
Mailing Address: PO Box 631,

Westhampton Beach, NY 11978.
Open: July, Aug.
Admission: $15–$50, depending on
 performer.

Just as the decorative old Art Deco Westhampton Beach Cinema was sliding into a steep decline, a group of public-spirited citizens came to the rescue. With Herculean efforts that included fund-raising events and an immense amount of volunteer effort, the ornamented interior now shines, and a full schedule of live performances take place. You might see a Hamptons' version of *Forbidden Broadway* or performances by Claire Bloom, Ben Vereen, Marvin Hamlisch, Leslie Uggams, or Alan King, as well as a performance by the New York Theatre Ballet.

CHAPTER SEVEN
One of the Last Great Places
RECREATION

East Hampton's Main Beach is as popular today as it was when this scene was painted by Edward Lamson Henry in the 1880s.

The first Hampton settlers believed each day was placed before them in order to accomplish a goal — building a barn, tilling the soil, baking bread, tending a flock. Days were filled with hard work, and the concept of recreation was foreign. And yet, today, recreation is the Hamptons' chief attraction. An early morning walk along the beach with the spray from the crashing waves rising to meet the mist; a jog along the bay at dusk as the fiery setting sun leaves brilliant streaks of pink, orange, and red; a sail to Block Island, whisked along on bundling breezes; a quiet kayak trip through tall reeds, surprising a crane at its meal — these are only a few of the many joys to be experienced in the Hamptons.

The abundance and bounty of the waters surrounding the Hamptons attracts people who know that the best fishing, the best boating, and the best swimming in the United States is found right here. Hikers, bicyclists, horseback riders, and bird-watchers also have their favorite haunts, as have canoeists, golfers, tennis enthusiasts, and scuba divers.

Through the enlightened perseverance of The Nature Conservancy, The Peconic Land Trust, and Group for the South Fork, more land is in the public domain on the East End of Long Island than in almost any other place in America. The Nature Conservancy alone either owns or manages 25,000 acres, preserving them for us and our children to enjoy, appreciate, and gently use.

Everybody needs beauty as well as bread, places to play in and pray in, where Nature may heal and cheer and give strength to body and soul alike.

John Muir, *Yosemite*, 1942

AUTO RACING

Auto racing began in 1915 in Bridgehampton, when European-style road races were conducted along the narrow dirt streets and the adjacent fields. These races continued in one form or another until 1953 when the state banned car races through village streets for safety reasons. Now **Bridgehampton Road Race** (631-537-5830), an asphalt competition racecourse — 2.85 miles in length — is the site of an active season that runs from April–October when sports car, race car, formula Ford, motorcycle racing, and performance exhibitions take place. The track is located on Millstone Road, between Sag Harbor and Bridgehampton. Also, the **Long Island Motor Sports Park** (631-288-1555) on Old Country Road in Westhampton is the site of drag racing and other exhibitions on weekends in the summer.

BEACHES

The beaches are the glory of the Hamptons. They are clean, broad stretches of white sand that, in this writer's opinion, are the finest in the world. Unlike the beaches of France or Italy, for example, pesky flies and other bugs stay away. Unlike those in Hawaii and other Pacific beaches — often mere slips of sand hidden between rock cliffs or promontories — Long Island beaches seem never ending.

Don't be fooled into thinking that the best beaches are all on the ocean. When the fog hovers near the ocean until noon, head for the secret bay beaches, where you might bask in brilliant sunshine from early morning until late afternoon. In general, the bay beaches are less populated than those on the ocean, so if you seek solitude or prefer a lazy swim in calm waters unaccompanied by the crash of the ocean waves, the bay should be your choice. Everyone has their favorite beach, and there are enough to go around, so start your quest now for your own personal choice.

Beach rules are very strict in the Hamptons. Driving on beaches is permitted with a sticker, but generally in the summer, it is allowed only when swimmers and sunbathers are not using them. Signs posted at each beach give details about driving and also about when dogs are allowed on the beach (a controversial, ever-evolving issue). Check with town or village officials for the current rules.

Now for the tricky part — getting there. If you live within walking distance, walk! The next best mode of transportation is a bicycle; there are an abundance of bicycle racks at most beaches. If you must drive, be certain that you have the proper parking sticker. This is essential from Memorial Day to Labor Day. A parking sticker from East Hampton Town, for example, will not allow you to park at an East Hampton Village beach or a Southampton Village beach. Qualifications for resident and nonresident status vary from village to village, so check with the appropriate town hall before you go. Parking is available at several beaches on a daily use-fee basis, but generally a sticker is required. A resident sticker is free (in Southampton Town, $10); nonresident stickers may be purchased for the following fees.

Nonresident Parking Permit Sticker Fees

East Hampton Town	$125	631-324-4142
East Hampton Village	$160	631-324-4150
Quogue Village	$150	631-653-4498
Sag Harbor Village	$100	631-725-0222
Southampton Town	$100	631-283-6011
Southampton Village	$130	631-283-0247
Westhampton Beach Village	$225	631-288-1654

The following beaches are by no means a complete list, but they are the most popular choices.

EAST HAMPTON TOWN

AMAGANSETT

Atlantic Avenue (ocean beach) Rest rooms; telephones; parking with East Hampton Town resident or nonresident permit, or $10 per day. A broad ocean beach, Atlantic Avenue has a number of additional amenities. The concession stand in the former coast guard station is terrific. You can buy hamburgers, hot dogs, and great marinated chicken breast sandwiches, as well as old-fashioned comfort food desserts, such as ice-cream bars and Popsicles; you can also rent beach chairs and umbrellas. Known for years as asparagus beach (because so many singles stood in packs, surveying everyone else), this is now a very popular family beach, where you might find numerous volleyball games underway.

Fresh Pond (bay beach) Rest rooms; telephone; picnic tables; grills; nature trails; parking with East Hampton Town permit. Fresh Pond is a delightful spot at the end of Fresh Pond Rd. on Napeague Bay. Breakwaters create a sandy beach, and from a park bench, you can contemplate the tranquility of the scene and watch the gulls wheel over the fishing nets in the water. The preferred sun site is the sandy beach surrounding Fresh Pond; small, shallow pools of placid, clean water at the entrance to the larger pond are ideal for families with children.

Indian Wells (ocean beach) Rest rooms; telephones; mobile concession stand; parking with East Hampton Town resident permit. Indian Wells is near the spot where the Montauk Indians once came for fresh water. At the end of Indian Wells Hwy. in the middle of the Atlantic Double Dunes Preserve, the gleaming, white sand beach stretches as far as the eye can see. Unspoiled by development of any kind, this beach remains a favorite with sun lovers who want to pretend that they are on their own beach, on their own private island.

Lazy Point (bay beach) Boat launch; parking with East Hampton Town permit. Lazy Point, a protected point of land jutting into Napeague Harbor, is accessed through Napeague State Park. Surrounded by the tiny fishing cottages of the village of Napeague (no shops, just cottages), this beach is generally deserted, except for windsurfers who have found the bay breezes ideal for skittering across the water. Main Beach (631-537-2716), a surfing shop in Wainscott, rents windsurfing equipment from a truck on nice summer days.

Pretty girls are a common sight on Hampton beaches.

Morgan McGivern

EAST HAMPTON VILLAGE

Georgica Beach (ocean beach) Rest rooms; showers; lifeguard; parking with East Hampton Village permit only; bicycle racks. Located at the end of Apaquogue Rd. and Lily Pond Ln. in the heart of the estate section of East Hampton, Georgica Beach is one of the preferred ocean spots. With a backdrop of estates and mansions just beyond the dunes, this sparkling clean beach is underutilized.

Main Beach (ocean beach) Rest rooms; telephones; lockers and showers; lifeguards; tidal report; concession stand; beach chair and umbrella rental; parking with East Hampton Village permit, or $15 per day, weekdays only;

no daily parking permits available weekends and holidays. Main Beach, at the end of Ocean Ave., is consistently rated the number one beach in Hampton surveys. This broad expanse of pristine beach has it all, but it's also one of the most crowded. To bask in the glorious sun, to roll over and see the elegant mansions, to sit on the spacious, covered deck and gaze out to sea — this truly is summer heaven. Walk up to the pavilion and select a freshly sliced fruit cup, a tall glass of lemonade, a grilled hamburger, or an ice-cream cone from the Chowder Bowl. If you find that you've forgotten something, there's a shop that sells everything from aspirin and sunscreen to beach chairs.

Two Mile Hollow (ocean beach) Parking with East Hampton Village permit. This beach is located at the end of Two Mile Hollow Rd., almost on the village/town line. In the midst of a nature sanctuary, it is preferred by many village residents for its serene and peaceful surroundings. There's none of the mob scene of Main Beach here, but neither are there any facilities.

MONTAUK

Ditch Plains (ocean beach) Rest rooms; showers; lifeguard; mobile concession stand; parking with East Hampton Town permit. Noted for its great surfing, Ditch Plains is off Ditch Plains and DeForest Rds. The usual snacks and ice cream can be purchased from the Beach Dog, the mobile concession stand.

Gin Beach (bay beach) Rest rooms; lifeguard; mobile concession stand; parking with East Hampton Town permit. Broad and sandy, Gin Beach is at the end of East Lake Dr., near the jetty where boats enter Lake Montauk. It's great for fishing and for watching the boats coming and going in the harbor.

Hither Hills State Park (ocean beach) Camping (631-668-2554; reservations required); parking $7 per day. This park has one of the finest beaches on the ocean — a broad, 2-mile expanse of clean, white sand. You can camp beside the beach and take a swim as soon as you awaken in the morning and the last thing at night. See additional information in the section Parks & Nature Preserves.

NORTHWEST

Sammy's Beach (bay beach) Parking with East Hampton Town permit. Sammy's is a broad crescent of protected bay beach that overlooks Gardiner's Bay. It's a wonderful place for waterskiing and boating (the boats can come directly to shore), but because of the quick drop-off, it is not a great place for children to swim.

SPRINGS

Louse Point (bay beach) Boat launch; parking with East Hampton Town permit. At the end of Louse Point Rd., you will find a two-sided beach separating Napeague Bay from Accabonac Harbor. Most locals say, "Please don't tell anyone about Louse Point. The tourists will come." The harborside is picturesque, dotted with marshy islands filled with birds — a favorite place for egrets, cranes, and osprey. At one time, the area fostered a rich oyster bed.

Maidstone Park Beach (bay beach) Rest rooms; lifeguard; baseball field; picnic area; pavilion; parking with East Hampton Town permit. Maidstone Park Beach is one of the all-time great places to watch a sunset. The long, broad, sandy beach hugs the jetty into Three Mile Harbor; it is an excellent spot for watching the yachts go by. Local anglers find the fish are plentiful off the jetty.

SOUTHAMPTON TOWN

BRIDGEHAMPTON

Mecox Beach (ocean beach) Parking with Southampton Town resident or nonresident permit, or $10 per day. Mecox Beach is on the ocean at the end of Job's Ln. in Bridgehampton. A wooden walkway leads to the beach from the large parking lot. There are no rest rooms or food facilities.

W. Scott Cameron Beach (ocean beach) Rest rooms; showers; lifeguard; concession stand; parking with Southampton Town resident permit. This beach is on the ocean in Bridgehampton at the end of Dune Rd.

HAMPTON BAYS

Meschutt Beach (bay beach) Parking with Southampton Town resident or nonresident permit, a $5 fee for Suffolk County residents with a "Green Key Card," or $8 per day without a "Green Key Card." Meschutt Beach is a Suffolk County park, operated by the Town of Southampton. It is on North Hwy. where the Shinnecock Canal joins the Great Peconic Bay in Meschutt Park.

Ponquogue Beach (ocean beach) Rest rooms; lifeguard; parking with Southampton Town resident or nonresident permit, or $10 per day. Ponquogue Beach is on the ocean, on Dune Rd. in Hampton Bays at the end of the Ponquogue Bridge, bordered by Shinnecock County Park East and West.

Road H (ocean beach) Parking with Southampton Town parking permit. Road H, in the Shinnecock Inlet County Park East, is a favorite place for surfers and scuba divers. It's right beside the jetty from the ocean into Shinnecock Bay, where a rich supply of saltwater fish journey into the quiet bays to spawn.

Tiana Beach (ocean beach) Rest rooms; lifeguard; parking with Southampton Town permit, or $10 per day. Located on Dune Rd., Tiana is on that great expanse of ocean beach sandwiched between Shinnecock Bay and the ocean. The Town of Southampton Parks and Recreation Dept. conducts a series of classes (swimming, sailing, windsurfing) at Tiana Beach.

NOYACK

Foster Memorial (bay beach) Rest rooms; lifeguard; snack bar/restaurant; parking with Southampton Town permit, or $10 per day. Foster Memorial is on Long Beach, the stretch of land separating the inner harbors of Sag Harbor from Noyack Bay. The small snack bar/restaurant (open in summer only) serves pizza and is a welcome change from the food that you get at most mobile beach concessions. On the Noyack end of the beach, a special section has been reserved for powerboats, and it's a popular spot to water-ski.

QUOGUE VILLAGE

Quogue Village Beach (ocean beach) Rest rooms; bicycle path; parking with Quoque Village permit only. Located on Dune Rd., this beach is accessed by the Post Lane Bridge from the Village of Quogue. Due to erosion, the beach is considerably narrower here than in many other places, and drive-on beach access is no longer permitted.

SAGAPONACK

Sagg Main Beach (ocean beach) Rest rooms; showers; mobile concession stand; parking with Southampton Town resident or nonresident permit, or $10 per day (but very few daily permits sold). Sagg Main Beach, on the ocean at the end of Sagaponack Main Rd., is reached by passing through the sleepy village of Sagaponack. There are no designer boutiques here, just the local general store, where the food is homemade and excellent. Have the proprietors prepare a picnic lunch and head for the beach for a delightful al fresco outing.

SAG HARBOR VILLAGE

Havens Beach (bay beach) Rest rooms; lifeguard; picnic tables and grills; children's play area; parking with Sag Harbor Village permit only. Located on Bay St. in Sag Harbor Village, Havens Beach is part of the former Frank C. Havens estate. There are benches where you can watch the children playing on the sandy beach and the pleasure boats bobbing in the water beyond.

SOUTHAMPTON VILLAGE

Southampton Village beaches stretch from Mecox Bay to the Shinnecock Inlet, an unbroken line of broad, white, splendid sand. The village does not require permits for all of its beaches, but pay close attention to the signs as the authorities are very strict about where you park. In general, parking lots where permits are not required are short street ends (an exception is Main Beach South); specific parking spots are clearly marked. The village police patrol the beach parking lots regularly and will definitely give you a ticket or have you towed away if you are parked illegally. The advice is to go early. There are many more street ends than identified here.

Cooper Neck Beach (ocean beach) Rest rooms; concession stand; parking with Southampton Village permit, or $20 per day weekdays, $25 per day weekends and holidays. Located at end of Cooper Neck Ln., this is the main public beach for Southampton Village. It's a favorite with the high school crowd.

Dune Beach (ocean beach) Rest rooms; handicapped access; parking with Southampton Village permit. Located in Southampton Village, this beach is toward the end of Dune Rd., almost to the Shinnecock Inlet. There is a wooden deck for picnics and a boardwalk over dunes that are covered with sea grass to the ocean.

Old Town Beach (ocean beach) About 30 parking spaces, no permit required. Old Town Beach is uncrowded, perfect for relaxed reading or quiet contemplation. This is not a young person's beach; there are no rest rooms or food facilities.

South Main Beach (ocean beach) Parking lot at beach and in front of the Southampton Beach Club and St. Andrew's Dune Church, no permit required; parking lot next to Agawam Lake, Southampton Village resident parking only with permit ($55). This beach is located at the south end of Agawam Lake, next to the Southampton Beach Club.

WATER MILL

Flying Point Beach (ocean beach) Rest rooms; lifeguard; mobile concession stand; parking with Southampton Town resident or nonresident permit only. One of the most popular beaches in the Hamptons is located on the ocean on Flying Point Rd. On the way there, alongside Mecox Bay, you'll see baymen with handheld nets, plucking the fish from the rich waters.

WESTHAMPTON BEACH VILLAGE

Westhampton Beach Village maintains some of the finest beaches along the Atlantic Ocean, but village parking permits are required, and they're generally restricted to residents. They're free to taxpayers and can be purchased by residents of Remsenburg, Quogue, and Speonk. Even those who walk or bicycle to the beach must have a walk-on pass (obtained from the village offices) or a photo ID with a local address. For information about obtaining a permit, contact the village office (631-288-1654).

Lashley Pavilion (ocean beach) Rest rooms; showers; mobile concession; parking with Westhampton Beach Village permit only. Lashley Pavilion is located at the western end of Dune Rd. This beach generally handles the overflow from Rogers, although some people prefer it for its quieter crowd.

Rogers Pavilion (ocean beach) Rest rooms; lifeguard; concession stand; handicapped access; parking with Westhampton Beach Village permit. Rogers Pavilion is located at the end of the Beach Lane Bridge on Village Beach. At the excellent concession stand, they have fresh fruit, and the sandwiches are made with fresh, local produce.

BICYCLING

Cycling in the Hamptons.

Morgan McGivern

With miles of flat, paved roads, this is a cyclist's paradise. Although Montauk Highway has a broad, paved shoulder that is frequently used by bicyclists, in-line skaters, and joggers, the back roads offer the least traveled byways for leisurely cycling, and the bayside roads tend to be hillier than those near the beach. This writer's favorite short cycling trip is along Dune Road in Southampton, with outrageous mansions on the ocean side and the rich, marshy bird habitat on the bay side. Another favorite trip is to start in Bridgehampton and ride past the potato fields and horse farms of Sagaponack, continuing through the village of Wainscott and then on to East Hampton.

There's an excellent guide to bicycling the Hamptons, *Short Bike Rides on Long Island* (1989) by Phil Angelillo that includes about eight trips throughout the Hamptons, with maps and explicit directions. The chambers of commerce in East Hampton and Southampton have maps and information that include several suggested bicycle rides as well.

When bicycling through a village, be sure to observe the signs. In East Hampton Village, for example, bicycling is not permitted on the sidewalks in the main business district, but it is permitted on the street. In Southampton Village, bicycling is not permitted in the main business district, either on the streets or the sidewalks. If you plan to rent a bicycle, please remember to call ahead. Shops often run out of rental bicycles early in the day.

Bicycle touring in the Hamptons is increasing in popularity. **Brooks Country Cycling Tours** (212-874-5151) conducts several bicycle tours to the East End. These include a day trip to the North Fork and one to Shelter Island, as well as a longer trip to Shelter Island and Montauk, with stays at country inns.

Rotations Bicycle Center (631-283-2890) in Southampton sponsors diverse and interesting, weekend group bicycle rides for beginners, intermediate cyclists, and racing enthusiasts. The following shops have bicycles to rent, generally fairly basic 12-speeds or less, unless otherwise noted.

AMAGANSETT

Amagansett Beach & Bicycle (631-267-6325; Montauk Hwy. at Cross Hwy., Amagansett, NY 11930) $6/hour, $25/day English, hybrid, mountain, and children's bicycles.

EAST HAMPTON

Bermuda Bikes (631-324-6688; 36 Gingerbread Ln., East Hampton, NY 11937) $12/hour, $20/day, $120/week.

Espo's Surf & Sport (631-329-9100; The Old Barn, 57 Main St., East Hampton, NY 11937) $8/hour, $25/day.

Village Hardware (631-324-2456; 32 Newtown Ln., East Hampton, NY 11937) $6/hour, $18/day, $60/week, $100/month.

HAMPTON BAYS

P & M Bicycles & Equipment (631-728-6686; 38 E. Montauk Hwy., Hampton Bays, NY 11946) $15/day, $60/week.

MONTAUK

Montauk Bike Shop (631-668-8975; www.montaukbikeshop.com; 725 Montauk Hwy., Montauk, NY 11954) $5/hour, $30/day hybrids; $9/hour, $50/day full-suspension mountain bicycles.

Plaza Sporting Goods (631-668-9300; Main St., Montauk, NY 11954) $8/hour, $22/day English or mountain bicycles; $30/hour, $70/day mopeds.

SAG HARBOR

BikeHampton (631-725-7329; 36 Main St., Sag Harbor, NY 11963) $6/hour, $25/day mountain, hybrids, or cruisers. Tandem bicycles and in-line skates are also available.

SOUTHHAMPTON

Rotations (631-283-2890; 32 Windmill Ln., Southampton, NY 11968) $5/hour, $25/day.

WAINSCOTT

Cycle Path Bikes (631-537-1144; 330 Montauk Hwy., Wainscott, NY 11975) $25/day, $55/week hybrids; $35/day, $90 week mountain bicycles. They'll even deliver the bicycles to you if you're renting for more than several days.

WESTHAMPTON BEACH

Bike 'n Kite Ltd. (631-288-1210; 112 Potunk Ln., Westhampton Beach, NY 11978) $28/day, $65/week, $110/month. Rental includes helmet, lock, and rack.

BOATING & WATER SPORTS

More than 80,000 boats use Long Island's network of waterways every year. The quiet, tranquil bays between the North and South Forks or between the sandy barrier bar and the South Fork along the ocean provide many opportunities to fish, sail, participate in a variety of water sports, take a cruise, or to just bob quietly while soaking up the sun. Many marinas provide daily, weekly, and monthly moorage. In addition, boats can be rented, either for group charter or on daily, scheduled sails. Fishing charters and excursions are also readily available (see the section Fishing & Shellfishing).

BOATING

GROUP EXCURSIONS

EASTERN STAR
800-445-5942.
www.easternstarcruises.com.
E-mail: info@easternstarcruises.com.
Gardiner's Marina, Three Mile Harbor,
East Hampton, NY 11937.
Three-five night cruises to Block Is., Newport, and southern CT towns.
Rates: Depends on length of cruise; call for rates.

In the summer months, twelve lucky passengers at a time can climb aboard this sleek 85-foot yacht for three-five night cruises from East Hampton to several destinations. A gourmet chef prepares elegant meals accompanied by fine wines. You can choose a variety of activities that range from taking a guided kayak tour to just sitting in the gleaming mahogany and brass salon, while reading a good book. When the ship stays in port overnight, it operates as a floating country inn.

HARBOR TOURS
631-725-0397.
Long Wharf, Sag Harbor.
Mailing Address: PO Box 7, Sag Harbor,
　NY 11963.
Daily sight-seeing tours and sunset cruises.
Rates: 90-minute sight-seeing cruises:

adults $19, or 2 adults $35; children 5–12 $10; children under 5 free; 2-hour sunset cruises: adults $25; children 5–12 $15; children under 5 free; dinner cruises: $20 or $30 per person depending on where you choose to eat.

The *American Beauty* is a 45-foot wooden powerboat that docks at Sag Harbor's Long Wharf. It takes passengers on 90-minute sight-seeing tours of Sag Harbor and Peconic Bays accompanied by a history and nature guide who narrates the trip. There are three tours daily in summer. Dinner cruises combine a nautical journey from Sag Harbor to Southold on the North Fork and dinner at one of two restaurants. Depending on where you choose to eat, the evening will cost either $20 or $30 per person. The evening sunset cruises are romantic and inspirational. There's nothing like a view of the setting sun from the water.

VIKING FLEET
631-668-5709.
West Lake Dr., Montauk.
Mailing Address: RD 1, Box 259,
　Montauk, NY 11954.
Summer excursions to Block Is., Martha's
　Vineyard, and New London; also
　casino cruises.

Rates: Block Is. and New London: adults, $23 one way/$40 round-trip; children ages 5–12 $20; children under 5 free; bicycles $5/$7; Martha's Vineyard: adults $80 round-trip; children ages 5–12 $40; children under 5 free; bicycles $6; casino cruises $15; packages, including overnight stays available.

The Viking Ferry in Montauk offers several delightful options for boating excursions, including a daily trip to Block Island, Rhode Island, which leaves every morning at 9am and returns about 6:15pm. This trip takes about one hour and forty-five minutes each way and allows almost six hours on the island (an excellent place for biking and hiking). A less frequent sunset trip to New London, CT, leaves at 7pm and returns about 11pm. There's also once-a-year trips to Martha's Vineyard, as well as a July fireworks cruise, a wine cruise, and a fall foliage cruise. Casino cruises depart nightly at 7pm and return at 12:30am. These include opportunities to play slot machines, roulette, and table games. The $15 fare includes a $5 coupon to play and one cocktail.

WHITE SWAN HARBOR CRUISES
631-668-7878.
Gosman's Dock, Montauk.
Mailing Address: PO Box 2280,
　Montauk, NY 11954.

Seasonal tours of Lake Montauk.
Rates: Hourly harbor tour: adults, $12; seniors $10; children $8; marine life excursion $12 per person regardless of age.

This excursion company offers interesting 45-minute narrated tours of Lake Montauk every hour on the hour during the day on their 30-foot pontoon boat. In addition, they conduct an educational marine life excursion once a day, departing at 9am. During this 1-hour cruise, you can help pull lobster pots and crab traps, while a marine naturalist describes the various crustaceans you are seeing, as well as their habitat.

LAUNCHING RAMPS & PUBLIC MARINAS

Towns provide many launching ramps in this boat-oriented area, but they also require permits to use the ramps and to park. Contact town offices for requirements and maps showing locations of launching ramps. In addition, several of the towns provide marinas for transient use, sometimes for a fee and, in other cases, on a complimentary basis.

The *Town of East Hampton* has about 100 marina spaces available every season, but seldom on an overnight basis. Applications for space must be made to the Town Trustees, and then space is assigned at various locations throughout the town. Fees vary. Call the Town of East Hampton harbormaster (631-329-3078) for details.

The *Village of Sag Harbor* (631-725-2368) operates a marina at Marine Park on Bay Street in the village. There are slips for yachts, cruisers, and sailboats, and some of the largest yachts in the world dock here in the summer. Rates are $2 per foot, plus $6 for electric.

The *Shinnecock Canal County Marina* (631-852-8291) is run by the Suffolk County Parks and Recreation Department. It offers approximately fifty berths during the season on a first-come, first-serve basis. There are electric hookups, sanitary facilities, and showers. Rates are $30/day on weekdays, $35/day on weekends for Suffolk County residents; $45/day on weekdays, $55/day on weekends for nonresidents. The marina is located at the Shinnecock Canal, Hampton Bays.

The *Town of Southampton* (631-283-6000) offers town marina space in Eastport, East Quogue, Hampton Bays, Sag Harbor, and elsewhere, on a first-come, first-serve basis. A stay is generally limited to five to seven days, but there is no charge.

The *Village of Westhampton Beach* (631-288-1654) maintains Stevens Park Municipal Yacht Basin, on Library Avenue in the village, for public use. There are daily, weekly, monthly, and full-season rates and municipal launching ramps. The fees are $30 for up to thirty feet and $1 per foot beyond that, plus $4 for electric hookup. In addition, there are a limited number of boat parking spaces in the car parking lot behind Main St. These are complimentary, but are limited to two hours during the day and three hours at night.

PRIVATE MARINAS

The Hamptons have a variety of private marinas where boats can be moored. The following are only a few of those also available for public use.

EAST HAMPTON

East Hampton Point Marina (631-324-8400; 295 Three Mile Harbor Rd., East Hampton, NY 11937) Rest rooms; showers; laundry; pool; tennis; ship store; great sunset views; complimentary continental breakfast; van service; fine restaurant on premises with deck for watching spectacular sunsets; other restaurants within walking distance; 45 slips.

The Harbor Marina of East Hampton (631-324-5666; 423 Three Mile Harbor Rd., East Hampton, NY 11937) Rest rooms; showers; beach; spectacular views; electric; repair shop; gas; fishing supplies; gift shop; full pumping service "no discharge" marina; fine restaurant and bar on premise; 100 slips.

Tulla Booth

Maidstone Harbor is located on Three Mile Harbor Road in East Hampton.

Maidstone Harbor Marina (631-324-2651; 313 Three Mile Harbor Rd., East Hampton, NY 11937) Rest rooms; showers; pool; fine restaurant on premises; other restaurants within walking distance.

HAMPTON BAYS

Hampton Watercraft & Marina (631-728-0922; 134 Springville Rd., Hampton Bays, NY 11946) Rest rooms; electric hookups; 30 slips.

Jackson's Marina (631-728-4220; 6 Tepee St., Hampton Bays, NY 11946) Rest rooms; showers; electric hookups; cable TV; fishing supplies; repairs; gas; 240 slips.

MONTAUK

Gone Fishing Marina (631-668-3232; East Lake Dr., Montauk, NY 11954) Small shop on premises; 180 slips.

Montauk Marine Basin (631-668-5900; West Lake Dr., Montauk, NY 11954) Rest rooms; showers; electric hookups; charter boats; fishing equipment; about 25 slips.

Montauk Yacht Club Resort Marina (631-668-3100; Star Island Rd., Montauk, NY 11954) Rest rooms; showers; laundry; three pools; tennis; fully equipped health club, cable TV; two restaurants; 225 slips.

Star Island Yacht Club & Marina (631-668-5052; Star Island Rd., Montauk, NY 11954) Rest rooms; showers; laundry; pool; weekend entertainment; picnic area; fishing charters; fishing supplies; bar and grill; about 100 slips.

Uihlein's Marina (631-668-3799; West Lake Dr. Ext., Montauk, NY 11954) Showers; many restaurants and shops within walking distance; 10 slips.

West Lake Fishing Lodge (631-668-5600; West Lake Dr., Montauk, NY 11954) Rest rooms; showers; charter boats; fishing supplies; bar and restaurant; 100 slips.

SAG HARBOR

Baron's Cove Marina (631-725-3939; West Water St., Sag Harbor, NY 11963) Rest rooms; showers; laundry; cable TV; access to pool; many restaurants and shops within walking distance; 84 slips.

Waterfront Marina (631-725-3886; Bay St., Sag Harbor, NY 11963) Rest rooms; showers; many shops and restaurants within walking distance; 65 slips.

CANOEING & KAYAKING

You can explore quiet ponds, inlets, and bays in the Hamptons by canoe. Here a fisherman casts his line in Hook Pond — overseen by a tree-shrouded mansion.

Morgan McGivern

In a serene pond shaded by overhanging trees, you sit quietly in your canoe as you watch a crane feeding. Suddenly, a graceful osprey swoops to the water, dives, and emerges with a fish in its talons, then departs. This image is the reason that canoeing and kayaking are so popular in the Hamptons. There are hundreds of secluded, interconnecting ponds, streams, and bays in which these and other images emerge again and again.

Local groups often sponsor nature trips to visit bird and animal sanctuaries. The trips are educational, interesting, and fun. Watch the local newspapers for expeditions sponsored by the Group for the South Fork and The Nature Conservancy.

Amagansett Beach & Bicycle (631-267-6325; Montauk Hwy. at Cross Hwy., Amagansett, NY 11930) Also rents kayaks: single kayaks $15/hour, $35/half-day, $55/full day; double kayaks $25/hour, $55/half-day, $75/full day.

Main Beach Surf & Sport (631-537-2716; Hwy. 27, Wainscott, NY 11975) Rents canoes and kayaks either for individual use or for organized excursions. Main Beach is located across the street from the northern tip of Georgica Pond. The Pond provides a delightful paddle past The Creeks, one of the great estates of the Hamptons, as well as many other fabulous estates. The rich, marshy borders of the pond are feeding grounds for a variety of birds. Main Beach is also the location of **East End Kayak Tours** (800-564-4386) where you can sign up for a group kayak tour or rent a kayak on your own. Single kayaks and canoes $45/half-day, $65/full day; double kayaks $60 half-day, $75/full day.

Offshore Surf & Sport (631-287-2979; 46 Job's Ln., Southampton, NY 11968) Rents and sells surfboards, kayaks, and wakeboards. Single kayaks $40/half-day, $55/full day; double kayaks $50 half-day, $65 full day.

Puff & Putt (631-668-4473; Main St., Montauk, NY 11954) Rents canoes, rowboats, and pedal boats for use on Fort Pond. Canoes, single kayaks, pedal boats $12/half-hour, $20/hour; double kayaks $15/half-hour, $25/hour.

SAILING

Sailing is as popular in the bays and lakes of the Hamptons as it is in Narragansett or San Francisco Bay. Headwinds make the bays ideal for sailboat racing, and the annual Sag Harbor Cup Regatta starts the sailing season every June. Favorite local places to sail are Mecox Bay in Bridgehampton, Napeague Bay off Lazy Point, and Quantuck Bay in Quogue.

For sailboat rentals and instruction, there are only a few options available. (It's the insurance, we're told.)

Puff & Putt (631-668-4473; Main St., Montauk, NY 11954) Rents sailboats, such as Triumphs, Sunfish, lasers, a catamaran, or a 15-foot Dayfish, by the hour for use on Fort Pond; they also rent pedal boats, rowboats, and canoes. For landlubbers, there's a miniature golf course and a video room.

Tompkins Yacht Sales & Sag Harbor Sailing School (631-725-5100; yacht-world.com\sailsagharbor; Bay St., Sag Harbor, NY 11963) Rents 21-foot and 23-foot sailing sloops; they also charter other sloops and offer sailing lessons.

Uihlein's (631-668-3799; West Lake Dr. Ext., Montauk, NY 11954) Rents cruisers, sailboats, powerboats, and jet skis; they also organize group excursions.

Windsurfing Hamptons (631-283-9463; 1686 North Hwy. (Rte. 27), Southampton, NY 11968) Instruction and Sunfish rental.

WATER SPORTS

JETSKIING, SURFING, WATERSKIING & WINDSURFING

Surfers ride the Hamptons' waves.

Morgan McGivern

Surfing is a tremendously popular sport in the Hamptons. Witness the surfers out at 6am along Dune Road in Westhampton Beach or at Ditch Plains Beach in Montauk, but be aware that no surfing is allowed within 100 feet of public-bathing beaches. Although the waves may not equal the height or intensity of those pounding Hawaii's beaches, they provide challenging and exhilarating rides, especially after storms. Hamptons' surfing has gained such acclaim that the U.S. Surfing Association has considered holding the U.S. Amateur Surfing Championships at Ditch Plains. The *Eastern Surfing Association* (631-668-5040) in Montauk sponsors amateur surfing contests all year.

Waterskiing is permitted in Noyack Bay at Foster Memorial beach. The Town of East Hampton also has designated a section of Three Mile Harbor, from Settlers Landing at the end of Hands Creek Road to Sammy's Beach, for waterskiing. Within Three Mile Harbor, the water is generally glassy smooth.

East End Jet Ski (631-728-8060; 9 Canoe Place Rd., Hampton Bays, NY 11946) Just off the beaches of Shinnecock Bay in Hampton Bays at the Mariner's Cove Marine, 1- or 2-person jet skis are available for rent. The rate is

$50/half-hour and includes instruction and fitted life preserver. Plenty of thrills are available at speeds of up to 40 mph.

Espo's Surf & Sport (631-329-9100; The Old Barn, Main St., East Hampton, NY 11937; summer only) Rents surfboards, boogie boards, and water skis.

Main Beach (631-537-2716; Montauk Hwy., Wainscott, NY 11975) This store provides one-stop shopping for surfers, windsurfers, and all those who enjoy water-related sports. In addition to providing a daily surf report (631-537-SURF), Main Beach rents and sells surfboards, boogie boards, paddle skis, canoes, and kayaks. In the summer, it sets up a satellite mobile windsurfing shop with rental equipment at Lazy Point Beach on Napeague Harbor. No reservations are necessary.

Offshore Surf & Sport (631-287-2979; 46 Job's Ln., Southampton, NY 11968) Rents and sells surfboards, kayaks, and wakeboards. Surfboards $50/24-hour day.

Plaza Sporting Goods (631-668-9300; Main St., Montauk, NY 11954) Rents surfboards, fins, and a variety of other sporting equipment. Surfboards $8/hour, $22/day.

Sunrise to Sunset (631-283-2929; 21 Windmill Ln., Southampton, NY 11968) Rents surfboards and boogie boards. Surfboards $50/24-hour day; boogie boards $10/day.

Uihlein's Marina & Boat Rental (631-668-3799; West Lake Dr. Ext., Montauk, NY 11954) Ski boats and skis for up to 4 people can be rented for skiing on Lake Montauk ($100/hour).

SCUBA DIVING & SKIN DIVING

For those who like to dive for sunken treasure or explore shipwrecks, many underwater opportunities quietly await in the waters surrounding the Hamptons. Shipwrecks dot the ocean floor from Amagansett to the Montauk Lighthouse, but some of the finest diving is further offshore. About forty miles off Montauk lies the wreck of the *Andrea Doria*, which sank in 1956 after a collision with the *Stockholm*. Because of its depth and poor visibility, however, this is considered a very dangerous dive. Wrecks of numerous other ships, though, are scattered along the coast.

There are less hazardous diving sites in Napeague Bay and off Block Island, as well as on the South Shore near the Shinnecock Inlet and the Ponquogue Bridge. Visibility is good along the South Shore, where divers can see tropical fish in the summer and other fish and shellfish year-round.

One must take a course and become certified in order to scuba dive; the course usually takes about four weeks.

Weight-N-Sea Scuba School (631-329-9073) Run by certified PADI instructor Paul Casciotta, this school gives lessons in open-water and rescue diving, either in a group or individually. Lessons generally take place on Fort Pond Bay in Montauk from May–Nov. Paul is an experienced diver who knows the local waters. He'll take people in his small, 2-person boat to nearby dive sites, such as the old World War II navy dock in Fort Pond Bay.

EQUESTRIAN ACTIVITIES

HORSEBACK RIDING

The Hampton Classic Horse Show, held in Bridgehampton every year, draws the best riders in the East.

Jason Green

DEEP HOLLOW RANCH
631-668-2744.
Montauk Hwy., Montauk.
Mailing Address: PO Box 835,
   Montauk, NY 11954.
Open: Year-round.

Rates: $40/1.5-hour trail ride; $50/2-hour beach ride; BBQ plus entertainment: adults $35; children $15.
Directions: Located on Montauk Hwy., 3 miles east of Montauk.

Established in Montauk in 1658, this is the oldest cattle ranch in the U.S., and thus it claims to be the home of the first American cowboys. It is still in operation, although not as a cattle ranch; but there certainly are cowboys in residence. The owner, Rusty Leaver, first came to the ranch as a child in 1963. Deep Hollow Ranch offers trails on 4,000 acres of Suffolk County and New York State parklands that include picturesque beach rides along the Atlantic Ocean. Groups of 6–7 people leave the ranch daily on the hour; western saddles are used. Deep Hollow offers riding lessons, using both English and Western saddles. Pony rides and a petting farm entertain the small tikes, and a pony camp, where children aged 5–9 can learn to ride and care for horses, is offered in the summer. Also in the summer, there's a Texas-style family barbecue that includes BBQ beef, corn on the cob, grilled local fish, and homemade pies, eaten to the accompaniment of a singing cowboy. There are also roping lessons, a play about Native Americans, horseshoe pits, and a hay-bale jungle gym for the kids.

RITA'S STABLES
631-668-5453.
West Lake Dr., Montauk.
Mailing Address: Benson Dr., Montauk,
NY 11054.
Open: Year-round.
Rates: $20/.5-hour trail ride; $30/

1-hour trail ride; BBQ: adults $25;
children $15.
Directions: Located 1 mile east of
Montauk village. Turn left onto West
Lake Dr. at Montauk Downs sign and
take first right after little white house.

R ita's Stables has two locations: one in Montauk and at Sears Bellows Park in Hampton Bays. At the Montauk location, there are trail rides, pony rides, and a petting farm for children, as well as a 6pm BBQ nightly by reservation only. This also includes wagon rides, fishing, and more. Inquire about group rates and the summer pony camp.

SEARS BELLOWS STABLES
631-723-3554.
Sears Bellows County Park, Re. 24,
Hampton Bays.
Mailing Address: PO Box 14, Benson Dr.,
Montauk, NY 11954.
Open: Year-round, 9am–6pm.

Rates: $20/.5-hour trail ride; $30/1-hour
trail ride; $45/1.5-hour lake ride.
Directions: Located on Rte. 24, bet.
Hampton Bays and Riverhead at Sears
Bellows County Park; entrance beside
The Big Duck.

S ears Bellows Stables, in Sears Bellows County Park in Hampton Bays, offers approximately 20 miles of groomed trails that twist through the wild pine barrens region (recently recognized by New York State as worthy of preservation) and wind past ponds and streams. Organized rides vary in length; a maximum of 6 participants can choose either English or Western saddles.

The above stables are the only ones offering hourly trail rides. For those who want to take lessons, especially in dressage, hunting, and jumping, the following stables offer instruction.

Clearview Stables (631-283-0073; Long Springs Rd., Southampton, NY 11968)
East End Stables (631-324-9568; Oak View Hwy., East Hampton, NY 11937)
Quantuck Bay Farm (631-288-0303; 607 Main St., Westhampton Beach, NY 11978)
Rosewood Farm (631-287-4775; 100 Majors Path, Southampton, NY 11968)
Sagpond Farm (631-537-2879; Narrow Ln., Sagaponack, NY 11962)
Stony Hill Stables (631-267-3203; Town Ln., Amagansett, NY 11930)
Swan Creek Farms (631-537-0662; Halsey Ln., Bridgehampton, NY 11932)
Topping Riding School (631-537-0948; Gibson's Ln., Sagaponack, NY 11962)

POLO

Bridgehampton Hunt & Polo Club, Inc. (631-537-1110; 206 Millstone Rd., Bridgehampton, NY 11932) Now in new facilities on the South Fork (they used to be headquartered at the Big E in Jamesport), this private polo club has exhibition games from mid-May–Oct. The games, which are generally played on Wed. and Fri. nights at 5pm and on Sat. and Sun. at 10am, are open to the public on a complimentary basis. This is a terrific place to spread a blanket on the lawn and enjoy a gourmet picnic with a bottle of Long Island wine, while watching the "Sport of Kings." For those who want to learn to play, clinics are sometimes offered.

FAMILY FUN

Events and activities for children take place year-round in the Hamptons. In the spring, summer, and fall, hikes along the beaches and nature trails and bicycle rides along the back roads open a world of adventure and ideas to children's inquisitive minds. Also consult Chapter Six, *Culture*, for music and art classes, as well as Chapter Nine, *North Fork*, for additional activities in that area. The following are just a few of the planned activities available to children in the Hamptons.

Pathfinder Country Day Camp at Montauk (631-668-2080; Montauk, NY 11954) This camp offers swimming, boating, tennis, and crafts for children ages 4–12 in summer only.

Quogue Wildlife Refuge (631-653-4771; Old Main Rd., Quogue, NY 11959) Guides lead children on well-marked trails, as they explain about the animals, birds, ponds, marshes, and plants along the way. There are tame deer, hundreds of ducks, and several endangered bird species, including an American bald eagle at the refuge. If you make arrangements in advance, you can also see the nature center and the rescued animals being nursed back to health.

Suffolk County Farm and Education Center (631-852-4600; Yaphank Ave., Yaphank, NY 11980) The center offers a glimpse of life on a farm 100 years ago. Operated by Cornell Cooperative Extension Service, this is a fully operational farm with pigs, sheep, goats, beef cattle, and other farm animals. An 1870 hay barn is a typical example of beam and peg construction and is often the starting point for hayrides. There's a grassy picnic area in the gardens.

FISHING & SHELLFISHING

The Hamptons, and particularly Montauk, which is considered the "Sportfishing Capital of the World," are noted for outstanding fishing. Over thirty of the world fishing records (registered in the International Game Fish Association Record Book) have been caught at Montauk. In 1993, for example,

The rocky beach just below the Montauk Point Lighthouse is a popular place to fly-fish, especially for striped bass.

Morgan McGivern

a 561-pound bluefin tuna, a 536-pound dusky shark, a 321-pound mako, and a 284-pound bluefish were only a few of the prizes. Seasonal tournaments attract anglers from all over the world. Cash prizes, trophies, and world records often reward the dedicated.

Rules for fishing are distinctly different for saltwater fish, where no permit is required, and for freshwater fish, where a license is necessary. For saltwater fishing, you can surf cast for the illusive, but remarkable, striped bass. Some enjoy the challenge of bagging a big game fish while fishing offshore from a "party boat," with groups as large as 100 people, all vying for the catch of the day; others prefer a charter boat that generally takes six or fewer people; and the rest fish from their own yachts. The offshore lure is for tuna, marlin, mako, swordfish, and shark. Inshore fishing, closer to home base, will net such prizes as bluefish, striped bass, blackfish, cod, flounder, fluke, mackerel, pollock, porgy, sea bass, weakfish, and whiting.

Fishing for freshwater fish in the local ponds is a much more complicated proposition. New York State requires a fishing license, which can be obtained from any of the town offices, but you must be a resident to obtain one. With the license, you'll get a state booklet advising where fishing is permitted, if you live in East Hampton Town. If, on the other hand, you live in Southampton Town, there's one more step to take. Since the Town Trustees claim ownership over fish in local ponds, you are allowed to fish only if accompanied by a guide licensed by the Town Trustees. Call the Trustees for a list of their approved guides. For more information about the license, contact the **Town of East Hampton** (631-324-4142), **Shelter Island** (631-749-0291), or **Southampton** (631-283-6000). For a list of licensed guides, call the Southampton Trustees (631-283-6000 ext. 259). For excellent booklets and maps about freshwater fishing on Long Island, contact the **New York State Department of Environmental Conservation** (631-444-0273).

A shellfish license is required for harvesting shellfish from Hampton waters, and the times and quantities are strictly regulated. Contact the appropriate town for a license (see telephone numbers above); you must be a resident to apply. The New York State Department of Environmental Conservation (631-444-0475) maintains a list of prohibited areas. It will also advise about pollution levels and water quality. The Department operates a hot line (631-444-0480) that gives recorded information about any areas unsafe for harvesting due to storms or other temporary problems.

At the *Shellfish Hatchery* (631-668-4601), which is located off Edgemere Road in Montauk, clams, oysters, and scallops are cultivated and then seeded in nearby ponds and bays for harvesting. Group tours can be arranged with advance notice. The hatchery is operated by the Town of East Hampton.

CHARTER BOATS

Charter fishing boats are very sophisticated these days. They take a maximum of six passengers and are equipped with fish finders, radar, and satellite navigation. The following charter boats are piloted by experienced captains who know exactly where to find fish. If you call *ProSport Charters* (631-668-2154), they will reserve a boat for you. Otherwise, you can call one of these fishing boats directly.

Abracadabra (631-668-5275) Captain Ray Ruddock will take anglers on excursions for shark, tuna, marlin, bass, bluefish, and fluke.

Blue Fin IV (631-668-9323) This custom-built Montauk sportfishing boat has sophisticated electronics and a large cabin and is piloted by a second-generation captain, Michael Potts.

Daybreaker (631-668-5070) Captain Mike Brumm pilots his 38-foot sportfisherman from Montauk to the Continental Shelf.

Fishhooker (631-668-3821) Offshore and inshore charters of half-day or full-day duration are captained by Otto Haselman.

Florence B (631-324-6492) This new 35-foot sportfisherman will take you to the quiet bays or offshore with Captain Jeff Picken.

Oh, Brother Charter Boat (631-668-2707) Fishing offshore for shark, tuna, and marlin or inshore for bass and bluefish is offered with Captain Robert Aaronson.

Star Island Yacht Club & Marina (631-668-5052) A number of fishing boats are chartered out of this marina. They'll be pleased to give you the telephone numbers of several captains.

Venture (631-668-5052) Captain Barry Kohlus operates a 41-foot Hatteras, built for sportfishing.

PARTY BOATS

Flying Cloud (631-668-2026; Montauk Harbor, Montauk, NY 11954) Captain Fred will take up to 80 fisher people on half-day fishing trips on his 70-foot party boat. The fare of $30 for adults includes rod, tackle, bait, and anything else you might need. There are discount rates for senior citizens and children. Located behind Dave's Grill.

Lazybones in Montauk (631-668-5671; Johnny Marlin's Dock, 144 Jefferson Ave., Montauk, NY 11954) Offers fishing trips twice daily, mid-Apr.–Nov., on a 50-foot cruiser. The boat can accommodate 35 people and concentrates on the gentle, inshore waters. Only soda and beer are sold on board. From Apr.–July, they look for flounder and blackfish; from July–Sept., the catch is fluke; from Sept.–Nov., the quest is for striped bass; adults $30; children aged 12 and younger $15.

Marlin V (631-668-2818; Salivar's Dock, off Flamingo Rd., Montauk, NY 11954) Marlin V is a 65-foot boat offering two half-day fishing trips daily, and night fishing some nights from 7pm–1am. It has enclosed lounges, sundeck, modern fish-finding equipment, and knowledgeable crew; adults $55 night trips/adults $30 half-day trips.

Viking Fishing Fleet (631-668-5700; West Lake Dr., Montauk, NY 11954) This is the largest party boat operator in Montauk. The trips range from a half-day for fluke fishing to all-night trips for night bluefish and striped bass to three-day offshore trips. Half-day trips run 8am–12 noon and 1pm–5pm. Viking boats have full restaurants on board, sundecks, and rest rooms. Half-day fares include rod, reel, bait, tackle, and lessons. Night-fishing trips depart at 7pm and return at 1am. The $62 charge for night-fishing includes rod, reel, and bait. The half-day fares for adults range $32–$45, and children's fare ranges $15–$22.

FLYING, GLIDING, SKYDIVING

Except for the Wright Brothers' first flight, most of the historic events in aviation history took place on Long Island. Glenn Curtiss experimented with his "pusher plane" in Garden City in 1909 and steadily expanded his company, building record-breaking racing planes during the 1920s. Charles Lindbergh launched his famous *Spirit of St. Louis* in 1927 from Long Island's Roosevelt Field, giving Long Island the title "the cradle of aviation." In the 1940s, Grumman Aircraft Engineering Corporation, headed by Leroy Grumman, who grew up in Huntington, watching the Curtiss aircraft spiraling through the skies, became a major military aircraft manufacturer. Today, although little aircraft manufacturing remains on Long Island, flying, gliding, and skydiving are enjoyed as recreational activities.

FLYING

Sound Aircraft Flight Enterprises (631-537-2202; East Hampton Airport, Wainscott, NY 11975) Sight-seeing rides for up to 3 people, $135/hour; instruction available.

GLIDING

Sky Sailors Gliders School (631-288-5858; Suffolk County Airport, Westhampton Beach, NY 11978) Birds do it and so can you. If you've never taken a glider flight, you are missing a fabulous experience. Half-hour glider flight (with licensed pilot at the controls) $153/1 person, $163/2 persons.

SKYDIVING

For those who love to sky dive or have a secret yearning to try, *Skydive Long Island* has the only student jump center on Long Island. They train in the morning for an afternoon jump; $210 instruction and first jump solo; $225 instruction and first jump tandem (beside an instructor); $80 jumps thereafter. They're located at *Spadaro's Airport* (631-878-5867; Montauk Hwy., East Moriches, NY 11940).

GOLF

Much of golf's early history in the United States took place in the Hamptons. The first golf course (only six holes) was laid out on a lawn in Yonkers in 1888, but the Hamptons were not far behind. In 1891, the Shinnecock Hills Golf Club in Southampton became the first professionally planned course in the United States. The twelve-hole course was laid out by the Scottish golfer, Willie Dunn, while the exquisite clubhouse was designed by the renowned firm of McKim, Mead, and White. In 1896, the Shinnecock Hills Golf Club hosted the second U.S. Open and also the U.S. Amateur Championship. The Open was held here again in 1986 and in 1995.

Other clubs were not far behind. The Maidstone Club in East Hampton was established in 1890 as a tennis club, but soon had its own eighteen-hole golf course. The National Golf Links of America, in Southampton, was established in 1908 along the lines of St. Andrew's in Scotland.

Most golf in the Hamptons is still played on private courses. If you're lucky enough to belong to one of the private clubs or have friends that do, have a great time! Otherwise, the following courses are available to the general public. Also consult Chapter Nine, *North Fork*, for additional courses.

BARCELONA NECK
631-725-2503.
Barcelona Neck Preserve (off Rte. 114),
  bet. East Hampton and Sag Harbor.
Mailing Address: Sag Harbor Golf Club,
  Golf Club Rd., Sag Harbor, NY 11963.

Open: Year-round, dawn to dusk.
Size: 9 holes; par 35; 2,900 yards.
Rates: $12 weekdays; $18 weekends.
Directions: Located 1 mile south of Sag
  Harbor on Rte. 114.

This course, which is managed by the Sag Harbor Golf Club, has a small clubhouse that sells soft drinks, beer, snacks, hamburgers, and hot dogs. The land is owned by The Nature Conservancy and is also laced with hiking trails. Soft-spike shoes only, please.

MONTAUK DOWNS GOLF COURSE
631-668-5000.
Fairview Ave., Montauk (in Montauk
  Downs State Park).
Mailing Address: RR 2, Box 206A,
  Montauk, NY 11954.
Open: Year-round, 6am–7pm.
Size: 18 holes; par 72; 6,860/6,402 yards.

Rates: $30 weekdays before 4pm/$16
  after 4pm; $36 weekends before
  4pm/$19 after 4pm; $3 additional fee
  for a reservation.
Directions: Located 1 mile east of
  Montauk village. From Montauk Hwy.,
  turn left onto West Lake Dr. and follow

This golf course, within Montauk Downs State Park, is a rare state treasure. Built in the 1920s by Carl Fisher as part of his grand scheme to turn Montauk into the "Miami of the North," the golf course was redesigned in the 1960s by Robert Trent Jones and Rees Jones. This has been rated one of the finest public courses in the U.S. You'll find lockers, showers, pro shop, resident pro, and much more; instruction is available. The restaurant in the clubhouse serves lunch and dinner with nightly entertainment and sometimes is used for theatrical productions. Six tennis courts and two swimming pools complete the facility.

POXABOGUE GOLF COURSE AND
  DRIVING RANGE
631-537-0025.
Montauk Hwy., Bridgehampton.
Mailing Address: PO Box 890,
  Wainscott, NY 11975.
Open: Apr.–Nov., 7am–6pm.

Size: 9 holes; par 30; 1,706 yards.
Rates: Golf course: $25 Mon.–Thurs.;
  $35 Fri.; $50 Sat., Sun.; driving range:
  $8/1 bucket 55 balls; $13/2 buckets;
  $18/3 buckets.
Directions: Located on Montauk Hwy.,
  2 miles east of Bridgehampton.

Poxabogue Golf Course includes a pro shop, driving range, and restaurant for hungry and thirsty golfers; it is consistently rated as one of the favorite breakfast spots on the South Fork. The course is especially appreciated by those with limited time; it has six par 3 and three par 4 holes.

HIKING & RUNNING

Hiking trails are described in the section Parks & Nature Preserves. For a book on hiking, read *Short Nature Walks on Long Island* (1993) by Rodney

& Priscilla Albright. It lists fourteen walks on the South Fork, with maps and specific directions.

Jogging and running are also favorite pastimes in the Hamptons. Montauk Highway's broad shoulder attracts many joggers, as do the side roads. When school is not in session, local high schools also have running tracks that are available for public use.

NIGHTLIFE

Nightlife in the Hamptons is frenetic in the summer. From bikini contests to free ladies' drinks, giveaways, and theme parties — the clubs compete for business. The following are only a few of the many clubs that pack them in. Most stay open until 2am or even 4am on weekends, which allows employees of restaurants, sports shops, and visitors from New York City to participate. The clubs listed here are noted for their entertainment, their celebrity DJs, and many serve food, as well. Although not listed here, many restaurants also offer live music on weekend nights. It's best to check the newspapers.

AMAGANSETT

The Stephen Talkhouse continues to pack in the crowds to listen to top name bands and entertainers.

Morgan McGivern

Stephen Talkhouse (631-267-3117; Main St., Amagansett, NY 11930) This is the place to go for music, music, music. It's been around since 1832, so it's got the formula down pat. The rather small room is intimate. For name entertainers, such as Richie Havens or Kris Kristofferson, the cover charge can climb as high as $100, but most of the time it ranges from $20–$40, and some evenings it's as low as $5. At the casual indoor/outdoor restaurant, you can get burgers or steak, but the focus is definitely on the entertainment. Stephen Talkhouse is also noted for the stars who drop by unannounced. Paul McCartney, Paul Simon, Billy Joel, Jimmy Buffet, G. E. Smith, and many more have been known to stop in for quick jam sessions with their friends. There's often a waiting line on weekends, so plan ahead.

BRIDGEHAMPTON

Bridges (631-537-9105; 964 Sag Harbor-Bridgehampton Tpke., Bridgehampton, NY 11932) This very pretty club/restaurant, owned by John Lock and Jeff Bernstein, serves up wonderful food, as well as live music. Every Thurs., Fri., and Sat., there's jazz with dinner, and every Fri., that's followed by a dance party that begins at 10pm. You can dance to classic tunes from the '70s, '80s, and '90s spun by a DJ. On Sun. morning, there's a great brunch with entertainment, featuring gospel singers, and every once in awhile, there will be a cabaret show in the evening. Best of all, there are happy hours and prix fixe dinners that make this an affordable evening out.

Wild Rose Cafe (631-537-5050; Sag Harbor-Bridgehampton Tpke., Bridgehampton, NY 11932) This popular place is on summer and winter. Billed as the "Speakeasy for the '90s" and a great favorite with year-round residents, the Lone Sharks play danceable rock on Thurs., live music from rock to blues to jazz is played on Fri. and Sat., and Sun. is open-mike night. There's food, but the scene and the setting, which includes shelves of books, overstuffed sofas, stained glass lamps, and, tin ceiling, as well as entertainment, are the primary reasons to go.

EAST HAMPTON

N/V (631-329-6000; 44 Three Mile Harbor Rd., East Hampton, NY 11937) This very classy nightclub cum lounge opened in 1999 and has been packing them in ever since. There are shiny, coppery-colored walls inside and a terrific outdoor bar. In the club, you'll hear music ranging from reggae to hip-hop. Call in advance to get details about the evening entertainment. Sometimes, they host celebrity-studded product launches; other times, they host parties for gays. It has a separate restaurant, Tsunami, where fine fusion cuisine is served. (see Chapter Four, *Restaurants & Food Purveyors*).

HAMPTON BAYS

CPI (631-728-4121; Montauk Hwy. at Shinnecock Canal, Hampton Bays, NY 11946) CPI (Canoe Place Inn) has an old history and a young crowd. It served as the summer home of New York's Governor Al Smith and bedded, at various times, Franklin Roosevelt, Helen Hayes, Albert Einstein, Cary Grant, and many others. Today, CPI begins swinging by 10pm and keeps up a jived pace until the wee hours. It's so large that it can hold 1,000 people in its three distinct lounges. The music ranges from '50s music to rock. Live bands, $1 drinks, cash prizes for winners of bikini contests — it just goes on and on. The VIP lounge features comedy and karaoke! $20 admission charge.

MONTAUK

Lakeside Inn (631-668-6900; 183 Edgemere Rd., Montauk, NY 11954) A DJ pumps out '70s, '80s, and '90s tunes, salsa, and more nightly after 10pm. In addition, there's a bocci court and league play, plus a weekly luau.

Nick's (631-668-4800; 148 South Emerson Ave., Montauk, NY 11954) And now for something different! Some nights you can perform in a karaoke contest, other nights there might be a "Who Wants to be a Millionaire"-style game show; the rest of the time, there's a DJ spinning discs.

SOUTHAMPTON

Conscience Point (631-204-0600; 1976 North Sea Rd., Southampton, NY 11968) Open Mem. Day–Labor Day weekends only. This is a very classy operation, with live music that features the classics, rock, rhythm and blues, and reggae. The main lounge, designed by Manhattan designer Cynthia Rowley features velvet banquettes, and there's a Green Room and a VIP lounge as well. The club attracts a star-studded clientele of models and social swingers, who wear their slinkiest duds and come to be seen.

Jet East (631-283-0808; 1181 North Sea Rd., Southampton, NY 11968) Open Mem. Day–Labor Day, Thurs.–Sun. This East End rendition of the Manhattan and Miami clubs is opulent and ultraelegant, and it's exclusively VIP. Some nights, someone like Tommy Hilfiger might host a party (read lots of supermodels); other nights, there may be a product launch. It helps to arrive with a celeb in hand or to look knockout gorgeous (either male or female) to get past the velvet ropes. DJs spin the standards.

Tavern (631-287-2125; 125 Tuckahoe Ln., Southampton, NY 11968) This old-timer had a face-lift and offers both inside and outside (patio) space. DJs spin tunes for the chic crowd.

PARKS & NATURE PRESERVES

The Hamptons are blessed with an enlightened and environmentally aware population, both among the permanent and the summer residents. The Nature Conservancy, a national environmental organization, owns many areas in the Hamptons, and because of their perseverance, we can walk along trails that skirt marshes and dunes and that overlook bays and the ocean, realizing we would not have the privilege had they not persevered. The Nature Conservancy publishes a pamphlet, *The Nature Conservancy South Fork Shelter Island Preserve Guide* (1990), which is available at most bookstores and chamber of commerce offices, that describes each of its properties. The organization owns or manages thirty preserves on the South Fork and is responsible, along with the Group for the South Fork and the Peconic Land Trust, for the preservation of some 25,000 acres of open space and farmland on Long Island, including about 8,000 acres on the South Fork.

Because of the sensitive nature of the land and its plant and animal inhabitants, many areas are only open to the public when accompanied by a guide. Listed here are only a few of the areas where visitors are welcomed throughout the year. For more areas, watch for announcements in local newspapers or call **The Nature Conservancy** (631-329-7689), the **Group for the South Fork** (631-537-1400), or the **Long Island Greenbelt Trail Conference** (631-360-0753).

In addition to those within preserves or parks, there are currently five official hiking trails on Long Island, ranging in length from 3.7 miles to 47 miles, managed by the **Long Island Greenbelt Trail Conference**. Most meander in a north/south direction across the width of the island, but it has long been a dream of Long Island residents to create a hiking trail from Rocky Point to Montauk Point — one of roughly 100 miles in length that would be the region's version of the Appalachian Trail. Recently that dream has come closer to reality. The New York state legislature passed a bill protecting the Pine Barrens region of central Long Island that opens the way to the creation of the **Paumanok Path**. For more information, contact the **Long Island Greenbelt Trail Conference** (631-360-0753) in Smithtown, or on weekends in the summer, stop at the **Pine Barrens Trail Information Center** (631-369-9768) to pick up a map. In addition, the **Southampton Trails Preservation Society** and the **East Hampton Trails Preservation Society** are constructing trails. Those trails that already lie within the two townships are the **Red Creek Trail**, the **Long Pond Greenbelt**, and the ten-mile **Northwest Path**. Organized hikes and walks are sponsored by these organizations.

Suffolk County residents who wish to camp or to use the county parks should purchase a "Green Key Card." The price is $20 for three years and entitles residents to reduced fees for parking, camping, and other activities. The card can be purchased at the entrance to the parks, but be sure to bring proper identification, proving you are a full-time county resident. Call **Suffolk County** (631-854-4949) for details.

EAST HAMPTON TOWN

EAST HAMPTON

East Hampton Village Nature Trail No fee. The trail is a delightful area in the heart of East Hampton and is accessed from David's or Huntting Ln. Ducks and swans, often with their babies, happily paddle about in the tiny pond;

birds and small animals hustle in and out of the underbrush along the wooded paths. It's a popular spot for parents and children.

MONTAUK

Hither Hills State Park (631-668-2554) Reservations required for campsites (800-456-CAMP); $16 per night, $8 reservation fee, $7 parking (day use only). This park has 168 tent and trailer campsites, hiking trails, rest rooms, camp store, children's play area, and picnic area. It is situated on 1,700 acres overlooking 2 miles of ocean beach in Montauk. Nightly entertainment includes movies, children's summer theater, concerts, square dancing, games, and lots of fun. A variety of trails bisect this vast acreage, making available a wealth of scenic vistas, ponds, dunes (including the walking dunes), and marshes. The state park is adjacent to Hither Woods Preserve and the County Nature Preserve.

Montauk Point State Park (631-668-3781) $5 parking fee. With over 700 acres, hiking and nature trails, and snack and gift shop, this park adjoins Theodore Roosevelt County Park and includes the Montauk Point Lighthouse (fee and under different management). Some trails near the lighthouse are currently closed, as efforts are made to stabilize the cliff from ongoing erosion. (See detailed information about the Montauk Point Lighthouse Museum in Chapter Six, *Culture.*) Many other hiking and nature trails are open, however, and some overlook the ocean where it's easy to see why so many shipwrecks have taken place here. Surf fishing is a popular sport, especially for striped bass.

Theodore Roosevelt County Park (631-852-7878) $13 per night camping county residents/$23 noncounty residents; $75 annual fee for outer beach permit for Suffolk County residents (plus "Green Key Card")/$200 annual fee noncounty residents; outer beach nightly camping fee $12 Suffolk County residents/$20 noncounty residents. On 1,185 acres, the park has picnic areas, campsites, hostel for cyclists, and 3.5 miles of nature trails. The park headquarters and the Pharaoh Indian Museum are located in Third House; the rest of the park is off East Lake Dr. in Montauk. There is camping space for about 400 families on the 3 miles of beach, but campers must use 4-wheel drive, self-contained vehicles. A trailer park with access to the beach is also available. A 3-mile nature trail meanders through a wooded, swampy area with wildflowers, ferns, and a variety of birds, turtles, and animals.

NORTHWEST

Cedar Point County Park (631-852-7620) $13 per night camping county residents/$23 noncounty residents; $10 deposit rowboat rental, $6 first hour and $4 each hour after or $30 per day. This park has 190 tent and trailer campsites, rest rooms, hot showers, camp store, playground, basketball and volleyball courts, baseball diamond, nature trails, and free movies in summer. It is located on a 608-acre point that juts into Northwest Harbor and points toward Shelter Island and Sag Harbor. The old stone lighthouse on its tip was built in 1868 to guide whaling ships to their home port of Sag Harbor. When built, the light was actually on an island; the landmasses were joined together during the 1938 hurricane. One of the most interesting trails is the beach walk to the lighthouse, where, in early summer, a barrier protects the nesting area of endangered birds, such as terns, plovers, and giant ospreys.

SPRINGS

Merrill Lake Sanctuary The Nature Conservancy owns this property of about 30 acres, within the Accabonac Harbor Preserve (one of the primary spots on the East End for bird-watching). You may see ospreys nesting as their young hatch in late June and early July or graceful herons feeding in the marshy lagoons, as well as a variety of other animal and plant life. The entrance is well marked, off the Springs Fireplace Rd.

SOUTHAMPTON TOWN

BRIDGEHAMPTON

Long Pond Greenbelt This is a 6.2-mile trail, threading past a chain of ponds and wetlands. It is in the heart of the Atlantic Flyway, making it rich with bird life. Managed by The Nature Conservancy, trails lead into the area from Sag Harbor's Mashashimuet Park.

HAMPTON BAYS

Sears Bellows County Park (631-852-8290) $13 per night camping county residents/$23 noncounty residents. This Suffolk County park has 70 tent and trailer campsites, bicycle hostel, rest rooms, showers, nightly lectures and movies, picnic area, lake swimming, hiking trails, rowboat rentals, freshwater pond fishing, and horseback riding. Access is from Bellows Pond Rd., off Rte. 24 in Flanders.

QUOGUE

Quogue Wildlife Refuge (631-653-4771) Run by the New York State Dept. of Environmental Conservation, this is a marvelous place to acquaint children with various species of birds. They'll love all the ducks, the turkey that gobbles as they enter, and the tame deer. There's a nature center with exhibits and a sanctuary where staff take care of injured and orphaned animals. Guides lead exploratory walks. A resident population of Canada geese make the refuge their permanent home, and children delight in seeing the baby geese march across the grass in the spring. The 7 miles of trails are well marked, and there are benches along the way. Access is off Old Main Rd., near the Long Island Rail Road tracks in Quogue.

A monarch butterfly lights on seaside goldenrod at Morton National Wildlife Refuge in Noyack.

Jason Green

SAG HARBOR

Morton National Wildlife Refuge (631-286-0485) Run by the U.S. Fish and Wildlife Service, this 187-acre preserve is a temporary home to migratory waterbirds. A self-guided nature trail explains what you are viewing; a map may be obtained from The Nature Conservancy (631-329-7689). The entrance is off Noyack Rd., west of Sag Harbor.

ROLLER BLADING

Roller blading is currently as popular as bicycling. A favorite spot to practice the sport is Long Beach in Sag Harbor, especially in the evening when there's a blazing sunset. Watch the local newspapers for places to freestyle.

Amagansett Beach & Bicycle (631-267-6325; Montauk Hwy. at Cross Hwy., Amagansett, NY 11930) Rentals $25/day, including pads and helmet.
Espo's Surf & Sport (631-329-9100; The Old Barn, Main St., East Hampton, NY 11937) Rates $7/hour, $15/day.
Rotations Bicycle Centers (631-283-2890; 32 Windmill Ln., Southampton, NY 11968) Rentals $35/day, including pads and helmet.

Quiet pathways and few cars make the Hamptons popular with roller bladers.

Morgan McGivern

SWIMMING

East Hampton Town and Southampton Town conduct numerous swimming classes, ranging from beginners' classes to lifesaving courses, each summer at the town beaches. With many miles of bay and ocean, most swimming areas have been listed under the section Beaches. There are few public swimming pools or places to swim in fresh water in the Hamptons.

Emma Rose Elliston Park (631-283-6000; Big Fresh Pond, off Millstone Brook Rd., North Sea) This park, for Southampton Town residents only, has a tiny beach on Big Fresh Pond with rest rooms, lifeguard, and picnic area. It's within a beautifully maintained park.

Montauk Downs County Park (631-668-5000) This park has two pools that are open long hours, and an excellent array of classes are taught every summer.

Trout Pond Noyack Road This pond, in Noyack, is rated locally as the favorite freshwater swimming spot in the Hamptons, but beware! There are no lifeguards, and signs, posted by the Town of Southampton warning NO SWIMMING, are placed there for a reason. The depth of the pond is uneven and hard to predict, but since there's not much beach, children generally paddle about on rafts or in inner tubes.

TENNIS & RACQUET SPORTS

The Meadow Club of Southampton, the first tennis club in the Hamptons, was established in 1887. The club now has more grass courts than any other on the East Coast, as well as smooth croquet lawns, all hidden away behind privet hedges. The Maidstone Club of East Hampton, not far behind, opened in 1891. Although a golf course was built at Maidstone, tennis continues to be the main interest of many of its members.

In the Hamptons, there are many more courts at private clubs than in public places, and most clubs, private and public, are open primarily in the summer. Several Hamptons' villages, though, provide public tennis courts, but the fees and access vary from village to village. It's best to check first.

PRIVATE CLUBS

Although the following are membership clubs, they also offer short-term playing opportunities to nonmembers.

EAST HAMPTON

Buckskill Tennis Club (631-324-2243; Buckskill Rd., East Hampton, NY 11937) 10 Har-tru courts; $40 per hour; pro shop; clubhouse.

EAST QUOGUE

Sportime in the Hamptons (631-653-6767; County Rte. 104 and Dune Rd., East Quogue, NY 11942) 26 courts (4 indoor Har-tru courts, open year-round); rates range according to day and time; swimming pool; basketball and racquetball; fitness equipment. Offers adult tennis camps with special packages that include tennis instruction.

MONTAUK

Hither Hills Racquet Club (631-267-8525; Montauk Hwy. at Napeague, bet. Amagansett and Montauk, Montauk, NY 11954) 5 Flex-pave courts; $20 weekdays/$30 weekends per hour.

QUOGUE

Racquet Club of Quogue (631-653-9828; Montauk Hwy. and Lamb St., Quogue, NY 11959) 10 Har-tru courts; $30 per hour after 12 noon.

SOUTHAMPTON

Nort-sea Racquet Club (631-283-5444; 655 Majors Path, Southampton, NY 11968) 10 Har-tru courts; $50 per hour when courts available. Offers instruction and will arrange games with varied-level players.
Triangle Tennis Club (631-287-3052; 411 Hampton Rd., Southampton, NY 11968) 3 all-weather courts; $40 per hour; reservations required day in advance.

WESTHAMPTON BEACH

East Side Tennis Club (631-288-1540; Montauk Hwy., Westhampton Beach, NY 11978) 12 Har-tru courts; $25 per hour; game room; clubhouse; volleyball.
Westhampton Tennis & Sport Club (631-288-6060; 22 Depot Rd., Westhampton Beach, NY 11978) 24 Har-tru courts and 4 all-weather courts under a bubble. Membership only in summer. From Oct.–May per hour rental $25-$64.

PUBLIC TENNIS COURTS

AMAGANSETT

Abrahams Path Park (631-324-2417; Abrahams Path, Amagansett, NY 11930) 4 courts; $8 per hour; rest rooms; attendant on duty; reservation required day of play.

BRIDGEHAMPTON

Bridgehampton High School (631-537-0271; Montauk Hwy., Bridgehampton, NY 11932) 2 courts for public use; weekdays no fee; weekends $10 Bridgehampton residents, $20 nonresidents; attendant on duty.

EAST HAMPTON

East Hampton High School (631-329-4143; 2 Long Ln., East Hampton, NY 11937) 6 courts; $12 fee; attendant on duty; sign up each morning.

Herrick Park (631-329-4143; Park Pl., East Hampton, NY 11937) 3 courts; $12 fee; lights for night use; attendant on duty. Easily accessed from Park Pl. (parking lot behind shops on Main St. and Newtown Ln.).

John Marshall Elementary School (631-329-4143; 30 Church St., East Hampton, NY 11937) 2 courts for public use; $12 fee; attendant on duty; sign up each morning.

MONTAUK

Lions Park (631-324-2417; Essex St., Montauk, NY 11954) 3 courts for public use; $8 per hour; attendant on duty; reservation required day of play.

Montauk Downs State Park (631-668-5000; Fairview, off West Lake Dr., Montauk, NY 11954) 6 Har-tru courts; $12 per hour; attendant on duty; rest rooms; showers; lockers; golf course; two swimming pools; restaurant.

SAG HARBOR

Mashashimuet (631-725-4018; Main St., Sag Harbor, NY 11963) 8 courts for public use (2 all-weather and 6 clay); hard courts $20 per hour; clay courts $25 per hour; attendant on duty. Although this is a membership organization, sometimes there are courts available on an hourly basis, and seasonal memberships are reasonable. Managed by Hampton Tennis Company for the Parks and Recreation Assn. of Sag Harbor.

SOUTHAMPTON

Southampton High School (631-283-6800; Leland Ln., Southampton, NY 11968) 5 courts for public use; weekdays no fee; weekends $12/hour; first-come, first-serve.

SPRINGS

Springs Recreation Area (631-324-2417; off Old Stone Hwy., Springs, NY 11937) 3 courts for public use; $8 per hour; attendant on duty; reservation required day of play.

WESTHAMPTON BEACH

Westhampton Beach High School (631-288-3800; Oneck Ln., Westhampton Beach, NY 11978) 8 courts for public use; no fee; sign up with attendant on duty. Preference given to district residents.

WHALE WATCHING

The *Viking Line* (631-668-5709) offers Whale Watch Cruises during the summer, departing from the Viking Dock in Montauk. A naturalist is always on board to explain what you are seeing. The trip is conducted in July and August only, as this is when the whales are migrating and it's most likely you'll see them. The trips depart at 10:30am and return at 5pm on Thursday, Friday, and Saturday; there's often a bonus sighting of dolphins, seabirds, and other marine life. Prices for the trips are $36 adults, $31 senior citizens, $18 children 5–12, and children under 5 free, but the cruise is long, and it is not recommended for children under 5. Reservations are required. See Chapter Nine, *North Fork*, **Atlantis Marine World** for an additional whale-watching trip.

CHAPTER EIGHT
Practical Matters
INFORMATION

We promised a complete guide to the Hamptons, and it certainly wouldn't be complete without the following basic, though essential, information. We hope that whether you are a longtime resident or a tourist, you will turn first to this guide for accurate and complete information.

Insider's tip: In East Hampton, people with a 324 prefix often give their telephone number using the last four digits only.

Morgan McGivern

East Hampton's village hall is located in this house formerly occupied by Lyman Beecher and his family when he was minister of East Hampton. (Harriet Beecher Stowe had not been born yet, however.)

For local **time**, call **631-976-1616.**
For local **weather**, call **631-976-1212.**
For **extended weather** forecast, call **631-976-8888.**

AMBULANCE, FIRE, POLICE

Throughout Suffolk County, the emergency number is 911, but most small villages have their own fire and police departments that can be reached at the following local numbers.

Town	Fire	Ambulance	Police
Amagansett	631-267-3300		
Bridgehampton	631-324-4477		
East Hampton Town		631-324-0024	631-324-0024
East Hampton Village	631-324-0124		631-324-0777

Hampton Bays	631-924-5252		631-728-3400
Montauk	631-668-5695		631-668-3709
North Haven			631-725-3030
North Sea	631-283-3629		
Quogue			631-653-4175
Sag Harbor	631-324-6550	631-725-0058	631-725-0058
Southampton Town	631-283-0056	631-728-3400	631-728-3400
Southampton Village	631-283-0056	631-287-0558	631-283-0056
Westhampton Beach	631-288-3444		631-288-3444

For other emergencies, please consult the following list or your telephone directory.

Emergency	**911**
AIDS Hot Line	631-952-2083; 800-462-6786
Child Abuse Hot Line	800-342-3720
Coast Guard	
(South Shore)	631-395-4400
Domestic Violence Hot Line	800-942-6906
FBI	631-501-8600
General Fire, Rescue, and	
Emergency Number	631-924-5252
LIPA (light company)	
Emergency	631-755-6000
Poison Control	631-542-2323
Rabies Hot Line	631-853-3000
Rape Hot Line	631-360-3606
Red Cross	631-924-6911
Runaway Hot Line	800-231-6946
Runaway Youth Shelter	631-329-6109
Southampton Hospital	631-726-8200
State Police	
(in Hampton Bays)	631-728-3000
Suicide and Crisis	
Counseling	631-751-7500

AREA CODES, CHAMBERS OF COMMERCE, TOWN GOVERNMENT & ZIP CODES

The area code for all of Suffolk is 631. Frequently called nearby area codes are as follows:

Location	Area Code
New York:	
Nassau County	516
Manhattan	212, 646, 917
Brooklyn, Bronx, Queens, Staten Island	718, 917
Westchester County	914
Connecticut:	
Western Coastal Connecticut	203
Eastern Connecticut	860

CHAMBERS OF COMMERCE

East Hampton Chamber of Commerce (631-324-0362; 79A Main St., East Hampton, NY 11937) Open May–Dec.: 10am–4pm; Jan.–Apr.: 3–4 days a week, usually Wed.–Sat. at 10am–4pm.

Hampton Bays Chamber of Commerce (631-728-2211; 20 East Montauk Hwy., Box 64, Hampton Bays, NY 11946) Open Fri., Sat. 10am–5pm.

From the multitude of bays and harbors on the East End to the villages near the ocean, a welcome is extended to all.

Jason Green

Montauk Chamber of Commerce (631-668-2428; Main St., The Plaza, Montauk, NY 11954) Open May–Oct.: Mon.-Fri. 10am–5pm, Sat. 10am–3pm, Sun. 10am–2pm; Oct.–Apr.: Mon.–Fri. 10am–4pm.

Sag Harbor Chamber of Commerce (631-725-0011; 55 Main St., PO Box 2810, Sag Harbor, NY 11963) Open July–Aug.: daily 9am–5pm; rest of year by telephone or mail.

Southampton Chamber of Commerce (631-283-0402; 76 Main St., Southampton, NY 11968) Open Mon.-Fri. 9am–5pm, Sat. 9am–4pm.

Greater Westhampton Chamber of Commerce (631-288-3337; 173 Montauk Hwy., Westhampton Beach, NY 11978) Open in summer: Mon.–Sat. 10am–4pm; in winter: Mon.–Fri. 10am–2pm.

O n the East End, town government is the predominant local lawmaking and enforcement agency, but, within each town, individual incorporated villages and even smaller hamlets are self-governing. The incorporated villages generally have legal and law enforcement influence within their boundaries (and this includes maintaining their own police force), but the hamlets depend upon the town for these services. Most villages have a village hall where local business is conducted. Beach permits for village beaches, for example, are issued by the village, while permits for the town beaches are issued at the town office.

TOWN OFFICES

East Hampton Town Office (631-324-4143; 159 Pantigo Rd., East Hampton, NY 11937)

East Hampton Town Satellite Office (631-668-5081; Main St., Montauk, NY 11954)

Southampton Town Office (631-287-5740; 116 Hampton Rd., Southampton, NY 11968)

VILLAGE OFFICES

East Hampton Village Office (631-324-4150; 86 Main St., East Hampton, NY 11937)

North Haven Village Office (631-725-1378; 335 Ferry Rd., Sag Harbor, NY 11963)

Quogue Village Office (631-653-4498; Jessup Ave., PO Box 926, Quogue, NY 11959)

Sag Harbor Village Office (631-725-0222; Main St., PO Box 660, Sag Harbor, NY 11963)

Southampton Village Office (631-283-0247; 23 Main St., Southampton, NY 11968)

Westhampton Beach Village Office (631-288-1654; Sunset Ave., PO Box 991, Westhampton Beach, NY 11978)

ZIP CODES

Town, Village, Hamlet	Zip Code
Amagansett	11930
Bridgehampton	11932

East Hampton	11937
Eastport	11941
East Quogue	11942
Hampton Bays	11946
Montauk	11954
North Haven	11963
Quogue	11959
Remsenburg	11960
Sagaponack	11962
Sag Harbor	11963
Southampton	11968
Speonk	11972
Wainscott	11975
Water Mill	11976
Westhampton	11977
Westhampton Beach	11978

BANKS, FOREIGN EXCHANGE, 24-HOUR ATMS

If you arrive in the Hamptons with currency from another country, be assured that you will not be stranded. Most banks will cash traveler's checks, and Cook Travel, Inc. converts foreign money into American traveler's checks. In addition, Chase Manhattan Bank in Southampton has a foreign money exchange and will be able to convert most currencies.

Chase Manhattan Bank (631-935-9935; 60 Main St., Southampton, NY 11968) Open Mon.–Thurs. 9am–3pm, Fri. 9am–6pm.

Cook Travel, Inc. (631-324-8430; 20 Main St., East Hampton, NY 11937) Open Mon.–Fri. 9:30am–5:30pm, Sat. 10am–5pm. Also (631-283-1740; 30 Nugent St., Southampton, NY 11968) Same hours.

Why is it that we seem to run out of cash at the most inopportune times? In an effort to ease the panic, we are listing banks that serve the Hamptons and also the cards they accept at their Automatic Teller Machines (ATMs). In this electronic age, we're never far from our money once we learn how and where to access it.

EAST HAMPTON TOWN

AMAGANSETT

North Fork Bank and Trust (631-267-6000; 100 Montauk Hwy., Amagansett, NY 11930) ATM: Cirrus, Honor, MC, NYCE, Pulse.

EAST HAMPTON

Apple Savings Bank (631-324-6500; 50 Montauk Hwy., East Hampton, NY 11937) ATM: Cirrus, NYCE.

The Bank of New York (631-324-0800; 66 Main St., East Hampton, NY 11937) ATM: Cirrus, Honor, MC, NYCE, Plus, Pulse, V.

North Fork Bank and Trust (631-324-7230; 40 Newtown Ln., East Hampton, NY 11937) ATM: Cirrus, Honor, MC, NYCE, Pulse.

The Suffolk County National Bank (631-324-2000; 351 Pantigo Rd., East Hampton, NY 11937; 631-324-3800; 100 Park Pl., East Hampton, NY 11937) ATM: AE, Cirrus, D, Honor, MAC, MC, NYCE, Plus, Pulse, V.

MONTAUK

The Bank of New York (631-668-5771; Main St., Montauk, NY 11954) ATM: Cirrus, Honor, MC, NYCE, Plus, Pulse, V.

Bridgehampton National Bank (631-668-6400; 1 The Plaza, Montauk, NY 11954) ATM: AE, Cirrus, D, Honor, MAC, MC, Plus, V.

The Suffolk County National Bank (631-668-4333; West Lake Dr., Montauk, NY 11954; 631-668-5300; Montauk Hwy., Montauk, NY 11954) ATM: AE, Cirrus, Honor, MAC, MC, NYCE, Plus, Pulse, V.

SOUTHAMPTON TOWN

BRIDGEHAMPTON

Bridgehampton National Bank (631-537-1000; 2200 Montauk Hwy., Bridgehampton, NY 11932) ATM: AE, Cirrus, D, Honor, MAC, MC, Plus, V.

HAMPTON BAYS

The Bank of New York (631-728-0100; 47 West Montauk Hwy., Hampton Bays, NY 11946) ATM: Cirrus, Honor, MC, NYCE, Plus, Pulse, V.

HSBC Bank (631-728-6555; 248 West Montauk Hwy., Hampton Bays, NY 11946) ATM: Cirrus, NYCE.

North Fork Bank and Trust (631-728-6500; 93 East Montauk Hwy., Hampton Bays, NY 11946) ATM: Cirrus, NYCE.

The Suffolk County National Bank (631-728-2700; Montauk Hwy., Hampton Bays, NY 11946) ATM: Cirrus, Honor, MC, NYCE, Pulse, V.

SAG HARBOR

Apple Bank for Savings (631-725-2200; 800-525-1524; 516-472-4545 customer service; 138 Main St., Sag Harbor, NY 11963) ATM: Cirrus, MC, NYCE, V.

North Fork Bank and Trust (631-725-3500; Main St., Sag Harbor, NY 11963) ATM: Cirrus, Honor, NYCE, Pulse.

The **Suffolk County National Bank** (631-725-3000; 17 Main St., Sag Harbor, NY 11963) ATM: AE, Cirrus, Honor, MAC, MC, NYCE, Plus, Pulse, V.

SOUTHAMPTON

Astoria Federal Savings Bank (631-283-0100; 65 Nugent, Southampton, NY 11968) ATM: Honor, NYCE, Plus, Pulse.

Bridgehampton National Bank (631-283-1286; 425 County Rd. 39, Southampton, NY 11968); 631-287-5880; 94 Main St., Southampton, NY 11968) ATM: AE, Cirrus, D, Honor, MAC, MC, Plus, V.

Chase Manhattan Bank (631-935-9935; 60 Main St., Southampton, NY 11968) ATM: Cirrus, MAC, MC, NYCE, Plus, Pulse, V.

HSBC Bank (631-283-2700; 25 Nugent St., Southampton, NY 11968) ATM: Cirrus, MC, NYCE, Plus, V.

North Fork Bank and Trust (631-283-8300; 46 Windmill Ln., Southampton, NY 11968) ATM: AE, Cirrus, Honor, NYCE, Pulse, V.

The Suffolk County National Bank (631-283-3800; 295 North Sea Rd., Southampton, NY 11968; Branch) ATM: AE, Cirrus, MC, NYCE, Plus, Pulse, V.

WATER MILL

The Suffolk County National Bank (631-726-4500; Montauk Hwy., Water Mill, NY 11976) ATM: Cirrus, MAC, MC, NYCE, Plus, Pulse, V.

WESTHAMPTON BEACH

Astoria Federal Savings Bank (631-288-2200; 71 Sunset Ave., Westhampton Beach, NY 11978) ATM: Cirrus, MC, V.

The Bank of New York (631-288-2220; 154 Main St., Westhampton Beach, NY 11978) ATM: Cirrus, Honor, MC, NYCE, Plus, Pulse, V.

North Fork Bank & Trust (631-325-0500; Montauk Hwy., Speonk, NY 11972; ATM only at 43 Main St., Westhampton Beach, NY 11978) ATM: AE, Cirrus, Honor NYCE, Pulse, V.

The Suffolk County National Bank (631-288-4000; 144 Sunset Ave., Westhampton Beach, NY 11978) ATM: Cirrus, MC, NYCE, Plus.

ADDITIONAL ATMS

At press time, the following cash machines (not located in banks) were in operation.

BRIDGEHAMPTON

King Kullen Grocery Store (631-537-8103; Bridgehampton Shopping Plaza,

Bridgehampton, NY 11932; only available during store hours) ATM: AE, Cirrus, D, MC, NYCE, Plus System, V.

HAMPTON BAYS

King Kullen Grocery Store (631-728-9621; 268A West Montauk Hwy., Hampton Bays, NY 11946; only available during store hours) ATM: AE, Cirrus, D, MC, NYCE, Plus System, V.

SOUTHAMPTON

Southampton Hospital (631-726-8200; 240 Meeting House Ln., Southampton, NY 11968) ATM: Cirrus, NYCE.

Southampton Town Hall (631-287-5740; 116 Hampton Rd., Southampton, NY 11968) ATM: Cirrus, MC, NYCE, Plus, V.

Waldbaums (631-283-0045) Main St., Southampton, NY 11968) ATM: Cirrus, MAC, MC, NYCE, Plus, Pulse, V.

CLIMATE, WEATHER, TIDES

The climate in the Hamptons is generally moderate and mild, with cooling ocean breezes in the summer and brisk winds in the winter. For the daily weather report, call **631-976-1212**; for the extended local forecast, call **631-976-8888**. The following temperature and precipitation figures are average.

Month	Average Temperature	Average Precipitation in Inches
January	29.9	4.18
February	31.1	3.85
March	38.2	4.11
April	46.5	3.97
May	56.2	3.82
June	65.5	3.59
July	71.5	3.00
August	71.0	3.45
September	64.1	3.46
October	54.0	3.39
November	45.0	4.53
December	35.2	4.31

* Based on the daily averages collected by the National Oceanic and Atmospheric Administration in Bridgehampton.

Montauk's rocky promontory has been the site of numerous shipwrecks.

Morgan McGivern

Tidal information along the ocean and, to a lesser extent, in the bays is essential to a relaxed, enjoyable day. If you're sunning by the ocean, the beach generally is wide enough so that you can just move further back if the water starts to lap your toes. If, on the other hand, you are hiking or picnicking, you will not want to be stranded on a sandbar; and if you are boating, you will want to know the time of high and low tides in order to successfully navigate your way back to the dock. The Coast Guard can inform you of coastal weather conditions and give you tidal information; it's wise to call them before heading out to sea. Three Coast Guard stations serve the Hamptons and can give weather and tidal reports.

Coast Guard Group Moriches (631-395-4400) Remsenburg and Westhampton Beach.

Coast Guard Station Montauk (631-668-2773) Eastern tip of the South Fork.

Coast Guard Station Shinnecock (631-728-0343) Westhampton Beach to about 15 miles east of the Shinnecock Canal.

COMPUTER, INTERNET, FAX & BUSINESS SERVICES

You're in the Hamptons on vacation, but someone from the office calls. Your expertise is needed. Instead of returning to the office, perhaps the work can be accomplished right here. The following businesses specialize in organizing and doing the routine jobs, so that you can concentrate on what you do best.

The Boating Channel (631-725-4440; www.boatingchannel.com; 2615 Deerfield Rd., Sag Harbor, NY 11963) This is an Internet channel for boaters.

Charde Computer Service (631-537-4264; 631-324-2064; 350 Montauk Hwy., Wainscott, NY 11975) Owner John Charde and his staff are experts in advising about upgrades, removing bugs, and giving computer lessons.

East Hampton Business Service (631-324-0405; 19 Railroad Ave., East Hampton, NY 11937) This is a one-stop shop for all business needs, including typing, word processing, typesetting, developing mailing lists, creating printouts from floppy disks, copying (including color), blueprints, fulfillment and mailing house services, fax service, bookkeeping, accounting, and mailboxes. (This book was done with their invaluable help.)

Hamptons Online (631-287-6630; www.hamptons.com) This is a Hamptons on-line service, providing Internet and World Wide Web access, local information, educational seminars, and support services.

Montauk Printing and Graphics (631-329-1270; 78 Park Pl., East Hampton, NY 11937; 631-668-3333; 771 Montauk Hwy., Montauk, NY 119540) You can have great printing and graphics done here, as well as color and black-and-white copies.

Southampton Packaging & Shipping Services (631-283-5660; 22 Jaggar Ln., Southampton, NY 11968) This service provides packaging, mailing, messenger service, copying, fax, and mailboxes.

South Shore Computer Works (631-324-7794; 34 Pantigo Rd., East Hampton, NY 11937) Expert advice on upgrades, plus they have rental computers; they will do on-site service calls for repairs.

HANDICAPPED SERVICES

New York State Department of Environmental Conservation publishes an accessibility guide to all state recreational facilities. *Opening the Outdoors to People with Disabilities* can be obtained by calling 518-457-2344.

Suffolk County publishes a brochure describing accessibility to its county parks and golf courses. Also, a Suffolk County Green Key Card with a handicapped designation entitles its holder to free weekday admission to all county parks and reduced fees for activities. Contact the *Suffolk County Office of Handicapped Services* (631-853-8333 voice; 631-853-5658 TTY).

The *Town of East Hampton* provides various services in the *Disabilities Office* (631-267-2153), part of the *Department of Human Services.* For example, transportation in a handicapped accessible bus is provided for doctors' visits, shopping, etc. The office also provides wheelchairs with fat, rubber tires for beach use.

HOSPITALS & MEDICAL SERVICES

Prime Care (631-728-4500; 240 West Montauk Hwy., Hampton Bays, NY 11946) Open Mon., Tues., Thurs., Fri. 8am–6pm, Sat. 8am–4:30pm, closed Wed., Sun. Walk-in medical office.

Southampton Hospital (631-726-8200; 240 Meeting House Ln., Southampton, NY 11968) 194 beds; 115 doctors on staff; 550 full-time employees; surgical, maternity, pediatrics, ambulatory, outpatient, and emergency departments; radiology; full laboratory services. Hampton Eye Physicians and Surgeons also use the hospital's operating facilities.

KENNELS

You've been invited to a country house for the party of the season, and you find that your host is allergic to pets. Yet, you never leave your darling behind. What to do? If a Hamptons' kennel is the answer for you, here are several suggestions. Remember, however, that advance reservations are a must.

East Hampton Veterinary Group (631-324-0282; 800-287-3484; 22 Montauk Hwy., East Hampton, NY 11937) Boarding and full veterinary services. Kennels are sized to the dog, and cats are kept in their own facility.

Olde Towne Animal Hospital (631-283-0611; 380 County Rd. 39, Southampton, NY 11968) Full-service veterinary hospital that also boards pets.

Cat in a basket.

Morgan McGivern

Westhampton Kennels (631-288-3535; 49 Tanners Neck Ln., Westhampton, NY 11977) Cat and dog boarding and full grooming services. Located on over four acres, private kennels are sized to the dog, each with an indoor and outdoor run. You can bring your own food and medication and be assured of 24-hour supervision. According to the owner, this is the pet resort of the Hamptons.

If these are not right for you, there is another kennel in Bridgehampton, run by Robin Foster. She takes pets only on referral from animal clinics and hospitals, however. Not a kennel, but an animal rescue agency, the *Animal Rescue Fund* (631-537-0400; Daniel's Hole Rd., Wainscott, NY 11975) rescues and cares for injured and abandoned animals; they also have an adoption service. Should you find a stray animal, take the animal to the ARF. If you feel like taking a walk, you could also stop by at ARF, and they will lend you a dog who would love the companionship. You can both stroll along ARF's dog-walking trail.

Bide-a-wee (631-325-0200; Old Country Rd., Westhampton, NY 11977) operates both an animal shelter/adoption service and a clinic, offering a full range of veterinarian services. They also provide pet training and pet therapy. There's a pet cemetery, and they'll arrange a memorial service and/or bereavement counseling as well.

LATE-NIGHT FOOD SERVICES

GROCERIES

Brent's Amagansett General Store (631-267-3113; Montauk Hwy. at Cross Hwy., Amagansett, NY 11930) Open 24 hours weekends in summer.

King Kullen (631-537-8103; Bridgehampton Common, Montauk Hwy., Bridgehampton, NY 11932; 631-728-9621; 260 West Montauk Hwy. and Terrace Rd., Hampton Bays, NY 11946) Open 24 hours in summer, except Sun.

7-Eleven (631-728-5130; 53 West Montauk Hwy., Hampton Bays, NY 11946; 631-653-9889; Montauk Hwy., East Quogue, NY 11942; 631-725-3931; Main and Water Sts., Sag Harbor, NY 11963; 631-283-8511; 10 County Rd. 39, Southampton, NY 11968; 631-288-9755; 61 Sunset Ave., Westhampton Beach, NY 11978; 631-288-3446; Montauk Hwy. and Mill Rd., Westhampton Beach, NY 11978) Open 24 hours year-round.

Waldbaums (631-324-6215; Newtown Ln., East Hampton, NY 11937; 631-283-0045; Jagger Ln. and Main St., Southampton, NY 11968) Open 24 hours in summer, except Sun.

RESTAURANTS

East Hampton Bowl (631-324-1950; 71 Montauk Hwy., East Hampton, NY 11937) Open weekdays 10am–12 midnight, weekends 10am–3am. Snack bar serves pizza, nachos, etc.

Hampton Bays Diner and Restaurant (631-728-0840; Montauk Hwy. and Flanders Rd., Rte. 24, Hampton Bays, NY 11946) Open 24 hours in summer; Oct.–Apr.: Sun.–Thurs. 6am–12 midnight, Fri., Sat. 24 hours.

McDonald's (631-283-6777; 307 North Sea Rd., Southampton, NY 11968) Open 24 hours.

Salivar's (631-668-2555; 470 West Lake Dr., Montauk, NY 11954) Open 24 hours. This diner has never changed, either in decor or in the food that it offers. Late-night party goers and early morning anglers can get burgers, chili, or breakfast.

Southampton Princess Diner (631-283-4255; Montauk Hwy. at County Rd. 39, Southampton, NY 11968) Open Sun.–Thurs. 6am–11pm, Fri., Sat. 24 hours.

Stephen Talkhouse (631-267-3117; Main St., Amagansett, NY 11930) Open weeknights until 12 midnight, in summer Fri., Sat. until 3am; shorter hours rest of year. Serves hamburgers, seafood, and salads.

LATE-NIGHT FUEL & SERVICES

Should you find yourself stranded, either because of car trouble or lack of gas, the following numbers may help.

For *AAA members*, the emergency number is 800-AAA-HELP day or night. For those who are not members of AAA, the following garages and gas stations are open late (and early in the morning) to provide fuel and road service.

CAR TOWING & REPAIR

B & B Auto Service (631-668-1195 days; 631-668-2217 nights; Edgemere Rd., Montauk, NY 11954)

Bays Auto Repairs (631-728-0650; 192 West Montauk Hwy., Hampton Bays, NY 11946)

Joe's Garage (631-283-2098; 1426 North Sea Rd., Southampton, NY 11968)

North Main Street Citgo (631-324-8671; 150 North Main St., East Hampton, NY 11937)

Village Auto Body (631-728-1500; 82 Old Riverhead Rd., Hampton Bays, NY 11946)

EARLY MORNING & LATE-NIGHT FUEL

Independent Gas Station (631-283-7670; 1630 North Hwy., Southampton, NY 11968) Open 6am–10pm; next to B & M Automotive.

North Main Street Citgo (631-324-8671; 150 North Main St., East Hampton, NY 11937) Open 6am–10pm in summer; 6am–8pm off-season.

LAUNDROMATS

On vacation, washing machines and dryers are not always readily available. The following laundromats have been selected because they are clean, well maintained, and conveniently located.

Sag Harbor Launderette (631-725-5830; 20 Main St., Sag Harbor, NY 11963) Large, very clean, well lit; attendant on duty.

Southampton Village Launderette (631-283-9708; 34 Nugent St., Southampton, NY 11968) Very clean, well-lit; attendant on duty.

Tony's Tubs (631-728-1046; 218 West Montauk Hwy., Hampton Bays, NY 11946) Very clean, new; attendant on duty; will help carry laundry to and from your car.

MEDIA

NEWSPAPERS & MAGAZINES

Dan's Papers (631-537-0500; www.danspaper.com; Montauk Hwy., Bridgehampton, NY 11932) An irreverent, tongue-in-cheek, tabloid-style paper, carrying current local news and unabashedly plump with the editorial opinions of its owner, Dan Rattiner. It's over 30 years old and claims to have the largest circulation in the Hamptons. Free and available throughout the area.

East Hampton Star (631-324-0002; www.easthamptonstar.com; 153 Main St., East Hampton, NY 11937) A venerable newspaper that's been in business since 1885, mostly in the able hands of the Rattray family, who still steer the ship. It covers business and events in a no-nonsense, professional manner for the Town of East Hampton and beyond.

The Hampton Catalog (631-725-2351; PO Box 2668, East Hampton, NY 11937) A glossy, slick catalog with lush ads for clothing, gifts, cars, services, and more.

Hamptons Magazine (631-283-7125; www.hamptons-magazine.com; 5 Main St., Southampton, NY 11968) Free, glossy, upscale, full-color magazine, published in the summer only. Fashion news, what's happening at the clubs, and gossip.

The Independent (631-324-2500; 74 Montauk Hwy. at Cove Hollow Rd., in the Red Horse Market, PO Box 5032, East Hampton, NY 11937; Southampton Independent (631-287-2525; 33 Flying Point Rd., Southampton, NY 11968) Tabloid-style paper that was launched in 1993; they report local news and views.

Sag Harbor Express (631-725-1700; Main St., Sag Harbor, NY 11963) The first newspaper on Long Island, the *Long Island Herald* was established in Sag Harbor in 1791. Although the *Sag Harbor Express* is not a direct descendent, it's certainly close, and it recently celebrated its 175th year.

Southampton Press (631-283-4100; 135 Windmill Ln., Southampton, NY 11968) Established in 1897, this newspaper offers complete news, business, and events coverage in Southampton Town.

RADIO

WBAB-FM and **WHFM-FM 95.3** (631-283-9500; 33 Flying Point Rd., Southampton, NY 11968) Popular and rock music.

WBAZ-FM 101.7 and **WBSQ 102.5** (631-765-1017; 44210 County Rte. 48, Southold, NY 11971) Light, adult contemporary music — "Z-Lite on the Bays."

WBEA BEACH-FM 104.7 and **WEHM-FM 96.7** (631-267-7800; 249 Montauk Hwy., PO Box 7162, Amagansett, NY 11930) Popular music.

WBLI-FM 106.1 (631-732-1061; 3090 Rte. 112, Medford, NY 11763) Popular music.

WLNG-AM 1600 and **WLNG-FM 92.1** (631-725-2300; 1692 Redwood Causeway, Sag Harbor, NY 11963) Popular music, local news, and information.

WPBX-FM 88.3 (631-287-8830; 239 Montauk Hwy., Long Island University, Southampton Campus, Southampton, NY 11968) Classical, jazz, and progressive music.

WWHB-FM 107.1 (631-728-9229; 252 West Montauk Hwy., Hampton Bays, NY 11946) Affiliated with WNEW, New York. Classic rock music.

TELEVISION

LTV, CH 27 (631-537-2777; 75 Industrial Rd., Wainscott, NY 11975) Community access cable for the East End.

WVVH, CH 58, UHF CH 23 (631-537-0273; 75 Industrial Rd., Wainscott, NY 11975) Commercial TV for the East End.

POST OFFICES

Amagansett (631-267-3344; Montauk Hwy., Amagansett, NY 11930)
Bridgehampton (631-537-1090; Main St., Bridgehampton, NY 11932)
East Hampton (631-324-0790; 7 Gay Ln., East Hampton, NY 11937)
East Quogue (631-653-5360; Bay Ave., East Quogue, NY 11942)
Hampton Bays (631-728-0371; Ponquogue Rd., Hampton Bays, NY 11946)
Montauk (631-668-2218; South Edison St., Montauk, NY 11954)

Quogue (631-653-4121; 6 Midland Ave., Quogue, NY 11959)
Remsenburg (631-325-0550; 137 Main St., Remsenburg, NY 11960)
Sagaponack (631-537-1140; 542 Main St., Sagaponack, NY 11962)
Sag Harbor (631-725-0108; 21 Long Island Ave., Sag Harbor, NY 11963)
Southampton (631-283-0268; 29 Nugent St., Southampton, NY 11968)
Speonk (631-325-0430; 323 Montauk Hwy., Speonk, NY 11972)
Wainscott (631-537-3636; 357 Montauk Hwy., at North West Rd., Wainscott, NY 11975)
Water Mill (631-726-4811; 670 Montauk Hwy., Water Mill, NY 11976)
Westhampton (631-288-2828; 408 Mill Rd., Westhampton, NY 11977)
Westhampton Beach (631-288-1238; 170 Main St., Westhampton Beach, NY 11978)

REAL ESTATE

If you've come to the Hamptons for a visit and just can't bear to return to your old home, you may wish to consult one of the following real estate firms, who will be pleased to assist you with either the rental or purchase of a home. The following is a list of some of the top househunters.

Allan M. Schneider & Associates (631-267-3900; 140 Main St., Amagansett, NY 11930; 631-537-3900; 1936 Montauk Hwy., Bridgehampton, NY 11932; 631-324-3900; 51 Main St., East Hampton, NY 11937; 631-725-1500; Main St. at Madison, Sag Harbor, NY 11963; 631-283-7300; 99 Job's Ln., Southampton, NY 11968; 631-287-6700; 570 Noyac Rd., Southampton, NY 11968)
Dayton-Halstead Real Estate (631-537-6900; 2450 Montauk Hwy., Bridge-hampton, NY 11932; 631-324-0421; 78 Main St., East Hampton, NY 11937)
Dunemere Associates (631-324-6400; 37 Newtown Ln., East Hampton, NY 11937; 631-287-4900; 60 Windmill Ln., Southampton, NY 11968)
Sotheby's International Realty (631-537-6000; Main St., Bridgehampton, NY 11932; 631-324-6000; 631-324-7400; 6 Main St., East Hampton, NY 11937)
Tina Fredericks (631-324-4418; Georgica Rd., East Hampton, NY 11937)

CHAPTER NINE
From Vines to Wines
NORTH FORK

Although the North Fork of Long Island is not part of the Hamptons and is distinctly different in character, it has a fascinating history and numerous attractions of its own. Its burgeoning wine industry leads to comparisons with the early days of the Napa Valley. And as the wine industry grows, so do the tourist facilities. Old, established restaurants are thriving, and chefs in new restaurants are testing new ground.

Suzi Forbes Chase

Summer sunlight illuminates North Fork grapes that are almost ready for harvest.

Interesting bed-and-breakfasts and inns are housed in gingerbread Victorian homes — remnants of the North Fork's days as a whaling port and transportation hub.

The North Fork is approximately twenty miles shorter than the South Fork, with the tip, Orient Point, approximately 120 miles from New York City. The trip can be made in 2.5 hours from Manhattan and in less time from Connecticut. The North Fork has more of a permanent, year-round population than do the Hamptons; therefore, you're less likely to find shops and restaurants closed after Labor Day. In fact, a number of restaurants are open for lunch and dinner throughout the year. Visit the North Fork, and you'll be pleasantly surprised. It's a trip you'll undoubtedly want to repeat over and over again.

Although this chapter cannot identify all of the North Fork's many attractions, we have attempted to include the very best.

HISTORY

*My manner of living is plain, and I do not mean to be put out of it. A glass of
wine and bit of mutton are always ready.*

George Washington

The early history of the North Fork is closely tied to that of the South Fork.
Yet, although the South Fork has now acquired a cachet of social promi-
nence, with large homes replacing potato fields and duck farms, the North
Fork remains stubbornly rural, clinging to its water and land resources for sus-
tenance. The winds, however, are shifting. As the local wine industry gains
recognition, so does the region. Where scattered, homegrown restaurants once
lured folks out for dinner after church on Sunday, a variety of fine, gourmet
restaurants now beckon a sophisticated clientele.

Southold's history is almost as old as Southampton's. They were both settled
in 1640, probably only a few months apart. Actually, a friendly rivalry exists
over which was settled first. The truth lies buried in the records, or the absence
of them — Southold's are not as complete as Southampton's. It is established,
however, that Southold's settlers organized the oldest church society in New
York State.

It's also true that the intrepid traveler George Washington came through
Greenport in 1757, bound for Boston to secure his commission as commander-
in-chief of the Virginia troops from Governor Shirley of Massachusetts prior to
the American Revolution. Already recognized as a fine seaport, Greenport
offered the most desirable route to Boston from Virginia. Fortunately,
Governor Shirley fully concurred with Washington's appointment and made
his trip worthwhile. Journeying to Greenport, Washington and his entourage
stayed at a country house owned by Lieutenant Constant Booth and took the
ferry the next day to New London, Connecticut. He thus avoided crossing
eighteen rivers on horseback in the freezing winter months. The house where
Washington stayed was moved from Greenport some years ago to the nearby
hamlet of Orient, where it is maintained today by the Oysterponds Historical
Society.

Almost 100 years after George Washington's trip, there were still few
bridges across the rivers that separated New York from Boston, the United
States' two great northern cities, and travel by water was preferred to the
bumpy, dusty stagecoaches. Greenport thus became an important transportation hub. In 1844, the Long Island Rail Road established its northern terminus
in Greenport, thereby making the journey even shorter. Following along
George Washington's path, travelers came to Greenport by railroad. They then
boarded steamers for an overnight trip to Boston, complete with dinner, dancing, and gambling.

Because of its water orientation, the North Fork's commercial enterprises traditionally have been linked to the water — fishing, shipping, and boatbuilding. Jamesport had a thriving commercial fishing industry in the mid-1800s, and the first submarines purchased by the U.S. Navy in 1900 were built in New Suffolk.

The whaling and shipbuilding industries flourished in Greenport, where many large sailing ships were built. By the late 1800s, 286 sailing vessels and seventy-three fishing boats made Greenport their home. As merchants and shipbuilders grew wealthy, they built grand Victorian homes, many of which still remain.

The advent of Prohibition didn't slow down the North Fork. It's said that the coastal villages of the East End prospered substantially during this time, not only from the moonshine itself, but also from servicing and repairing the boats of both bootleggers and revenuers. Often the vessels of bootleggers and revenue agents would be repaired side by side.

In the 1930s, Greenport gained distinction of another type. The sailing master for three successful America's Cup defenders lived in Greenport. Although the ships were headquartered in Newport, Rhode Island, Captain George Monsell brought all of the crews to Greenport to sign their contracts. One of the skippers and a first mate lived here, as well. Those were heady days when the *Enterprise* won the race in 1930, the *Rainbow* in 1934, and the *Ranger* in 1937.

What is most tempting about Greenport is the waterfront, that long, ragged fringe of wharves, boatbuilder's yards, and sail lofts from which one looks out across the harbor to the wooded bluffs of Shelter Island. Of course, the whalers in these waters have long since become completely extinct, and those square-rigged ships that sailed from here direct to the West Indies for molasses are also long since dead and gone.

William Oliver Stevens, *Discovering Long Island*, 1939

Even if whaling ships no longer docked in Greenport, it was still an important shipbuilding center, and other North Fork villages had developed thriving oyster and scallop industries. Peconic Bay scallops are still considered sweeter and more tender than those harvested elsewhere, making them prized by chefs around the world.

The beauty of the North Fork cannot be denied. Pure, unspoiled bays, inlets, and creeks to the south and majestic Long Island Sound to the north are linked together by miles of flat, rich farmland. Villages remain true to their New England roots with treasured old houses and buildings looking much as they did a century ago.

Fortunately for us, community-spirited citizens recognized the importance of preserving some of their oldest and most historic buildings. In Mattituck, Cutchogue, Southold, and Orient, buildings have been moved from locations where they were endangered and settled into clusters around a village green where they are open to the public. In Greenport, the Stirling Historical Society also maintains several buildings, and there's an interesting walking tour past historic, old homes.

TRANSPORTATION

This chapter does not repeat the information contained in Chapter Two, *Transportation*, but it does identify specific ways to reach the North Fork.

BY BUS

Suffolk County Transit (631-852-5200; www.sct-bus.org) $1.50, with additional charge of $.25 for each transfer; seniors and the handicapped $.50. Operates buses Mon.–Sat. throughout Suffolk County to North Fork and as far east as Orient Point Ferry. You can pick up schedule and fare information from local chamber of commerce offices. **Please note:** Exact fare is required, as drivers do not carry change.

Sunrise Coach Lines (631-477-1200; 800-527-7709) $16 one-way; $31 round-trip. This company runs coach bus service between North Fork and Manhattan, with about 3 trips each way per day, stopping at most towns from Riverhead to Greenport. Departures, depending on day, leave 5:30am–7pm and arrive in New York City between 8am–9:30pm. The latest bus from Manhattan is at 9:45pm, arriving 11:45pm. There's also a stop in Queens, both ways. These clean, bright buses are equipped with rest rooms.

BY CAR

From New York, the trip to the North Fork is infinitely easier than to the Hamptons. The Long Island Expressway (I-495) terminates in Riverhead, the gateway to the North Fork. It is from this point that two fingers of land — one reaching North and East and the other South and East — separate and grow wider, enclosing the Peconic Bay. The first of the North Fork wineries is no more than a half-hour from the end of the Long Island Expressway.

BY FERRY

A pleasant way to travel from Connecticut is via the *Bridgeport/Port Jefferson Steamboat Company* ferry to the North Shore of Long Island, followed by a drive along Rte. 25A to the North Fork, less than an hour's trip along a meandering, rural road. For reservations and information, call 631-473-

The Cross Island Ferry runs between Orient Point on the North Fork and New London, Connecticut, in about 90 minutes.

Suzi Forbes Chase

0286 on Long Island. Another route is via the **Cross Sound Ferry** from New London, Connecticut, to Orient Point on the eastern tip of the North Fork. For information and reservations, call 860-443-5281 in Connecticut. The third ferry route is from North Haven on the South Fork to Shelter Island, then by a second ferry from Shelter Island to Greenport: *North Ferry* (631-749-0139) and *South Ferry* (631-749-1200). All of these routes are described in detail in Chapter Two, *Transportation*.

BY TRAIN

The **Long Island Rail Road** (718-217-5477 in New York; 631-231-5477 in Suffolk County; 516-822-5477 in Nassau County) runs trains to the North Fork on its North Shore branch, although travel is rather infrequent. Three or four trains leave and arrive at Riverhead daily, but only two continue on to Greenport; on weekends, there are only two trains to Riverhead. If someone can pick you up in Ronkonkoma, however, the options are increased to over twenty trains per day. The fare is $15.25 one-way during peak hours; $10.25 off-peak times to both Riverhead and Greenport.

RENTAL CARS

Most national car rental companies have offices at Long Island Islip/ MacArthur Airport, approximately twenty-five miles from Riverhead. In addition, the following companies are located on the North Fork.

Enterprise Rent-A-Car (631-369-6300; 1076 Rte. 58, Riverhead, NY 11901)
Pam Rent-A-Car (631-727-7020; Ramada Inn, Rte. 25, Riverhead, NY 11901)
Rent-A-Wreck (631-477-9602; 631-477-9607; 72365 Main Rd., Greenport, NY 11944)

TAXIS & LIMOUSINES

Classic Limousine Service of Eastern Long Island (631-727-5003; 56 Union Ave., Riverhead, NY 11901)

Keri Taxi (631-727-0707; 800-727-5374; 434 Osborne Ave., Riverhead, NY 11901) 24-hour service; all new cars; drivers are conscientious.

Maria's Taxi (631-477-0700; 43375 Rte. 48, Southold, NY 11971)

Southold Taxi (631-765-2221; 800-698-2944; Rte. 48, Southold, NY 11971) 24-hour service; limousines, vans, wagons, and cars; take both large and small groups; package delivery.

WINERIES

When men drink, then they are rich and successful and win lawsuits and are happy and help their friends.

Quickly, bring me a beaker of wine, so that I may wet my mind and say something clever.

Aristophanes

People in California, New York, and Europe are talking about Long Island's East End wines. There hasn't been this much excitement in the wine world since the Napa, Sonoma, and Alexander Valleys of California began serious production. In the twenty-five years of East End wine production, the number of wineries has grown to twenty-four on the North Fork and three on the South Fork. As the awards for the wines accumulate, the number of visitors to the tasting rooms increases, and so do the sales. That's good news for other businesses, too. New gourmet restaurants, caterers, motels, bed-and-breakfast establishments, gift shops, and wineshops are flourishing. Therefore, it seems natural to begin this chapter with a description of the wineries.

In the last ten years, the North Fork has gained a respected position in the wine industry. It all started when a local farmer, John Wickham, planted the first grapes on the North Fork in the early 1960s; he sold them at his farm stand to home winemakers. Alex and Louisa Hargrave were the first commercial pioneers; they planted vinifera vines in 1973 and produced their first wines in 1977. Modern, award-winning wineries that rival California's Napa Valley are now the sites of guided tours and tastings, along with a variety of courses and events.

Wine production, however, is still so small that some wineries depend on a mobile bottling truck that travels from winery to winery to handle that part of the operation. And, others are opting to join Russell Hearn, the winemaker at Pellegrini, in the custom-crush winery that he is building in Mattituck. First reported by Frank Prial in the *New York Times* (July 26, 2000), Premium Wine

Group is patterned after the highly successful Napa Wine Company. Lieb Family Cellars, who are partners with Mr. Hearn, for example, will produce, age, bottle, and label their wines here instead of building their own winery. The stature and respect that Mr. Hearn has earned on the North Fork give these growers confidence that their wines will be produced with the same integrity as if they were doing all the work themselves.

To put the production in perspective, there are still only 2,200 acres of land planted in grapes on the East End, while more than 6,000 acres are planted in potatoes, the North Fork's largest crop. Frank Prial says that annual wine production is estimated at a mere 300,000 cases, about the same as for one medium-sized California winery.

For anyone interested in wines, now is the time to visit. The enthusiasm and excitement are contagious. When you visit an East End winery, you're likely to meet the owner and the winemaker, who are often the same person. You'll find that most of today's wineries are family enterprises run by hardworking vintners who are absolutely serious about their wines. They will share their belief in the region, their dreams for their vineyards, and their growth objectives for their winery. In a few years, as demand and production grow, some of this personal contact inevitably will be lost.

In fact, the times are already changing. The wine world has taken note! In 1998 and 1999, investors with deep pockets purchased several of the wineries and have plans for major expansions. A new enterprise called Raphael Vineyards will be a one-wine winery — Merlot — and the owner is currently, as we go to press, building a spectacular Mediterranean-style winery reputed to be costing about $6 million.

An excellent book about North Fork wines, *The Wines of Long Island, Birth of a Region* (2000) by Philip F. Palmedo and Edward Beltrami, is recommended reading for anyone visiting the East End wineries. It is a comprehensive guide (newly updated in 2000) to the history of winemaking on the East End and includes profiles of the wineries, the owners, and the winemakers. A comprehensive guide to East Coast wines, including an analysis of those on Long Island is *Wineries of the Eastern States* (1999) by Marguerite Thomas; this book highlights some of the region's wineries and includes interviews with winemakers and ratings for the wines. For up-to-the-minute information about local wines, call the **Long Island Wine Council** (631-369-5887; 104 Edwards Ave., Calverton, NY 11933).

Should you wish to take a guided tour of the wineries, several companies have started businesses to comply. ***Vintage Tours*** (631-765-4689; PO Box 143, Peconic, NY 11958) offers a comfortable fifteen-passenger, air-conditioned van. Personable Jo-Ann Perry will provide a picnic lunch and escort you to several fine wineries. **Long Island Wine Tours** (631-924-3475; 30 Artist Dr., Middle Island, NY 11953) offers luxury motor coach wine tours from Manhattan (or any destination) to the North and South Fork. The all-day tour includes visits to three to five wineries, a video program describing American winemaking, and a catered buffet lunch.

This section is neither a comprehensive guide to the wineries nor does it analyze the wines. We have identified each winery and hope to enhance your visit to this very special place by describing the settings and suggesting lodgings, restaurants, and cultural and recreational attractions. So, buy some cheese, a baguette of French bread, perhaps a sandwich, and plan a day of wine tasting. Actually, you should plan several days, with a leisurely stop for lunch at a winery, perhaps on a deck overlooking the vineyards.

There are three excellent wineries also located on the South Fork. For information about South Fork wineries, see Chapter Four, *Restaurants & Food Purveyors.*

BEDELL CELLARS
631-734-7537.
www.bedellcellars.com.

Main Rd. (Rte. 25), Cutchogue, NY 11935.
Open: Daily 11am–5pm.
Fee: None.

Kip Bedell began producing wines here in 1985, and by 1998, he had thirty-two acres planted. Bedell bottles approximately 8,500 cases of wine per year. Consistently winning awards, especially for the Merlot, this winery is modern and efficient. A full range of wines are available for sampling on a complimentary basis in the showroom. If available, the Reserve Merlot is a prize that should be purchased. Group tours can be arranged. In 2000, the winery was sold to Michael Lynne, a Time Warner executive, but Kip Bedell is remaining as the winemaker.

This handsome building, which is sheathed in natural shingles houses the sleek new tasting room at Bidwell Vineyards.

Suzi Forbes Chase

BIDWELL VINEYARDS
631-734-5200.
North Road (Rte. 48), Cutchogue, NY 11935.

Open: Daily 11am–6pm.
Fee: $1 per customer.

Bidwell bottled its first wines in 1986. It now has thirty-three acres of vines planted and produces about 8,000+ cases annually. The winery is run by Robert, Kerry, and James Bidwell; the winemaker is Bob Bidwell. Group tours can be arranged with advance notice. A handsome two-story, green-shingled tasting room was built in 1998; it has soaring ceilings and tiled floors. French park tables and chairs provide places to sip the wines, and there's a grassy picnic area outside. Call for summer and fall schedule of live music.

B & L FARMS
631-734-2225.
www.alexandervineyards.com.

8850 Bridge Ln., Cutchogue, NY 11935.
First grapes planted in 2000; wines not
produced yet.

L eslie Alexander, the owner of the Houston Rockets, has been quietly planning his winery for several years. He originally purchased eighty-six acres, then added an additional sixty-eight acres in Mattituck and Cutchogue. He has been preparing for his vines by carefully tilling the soil and adding nutrients. In 2000, he planted the first five acres in Cabernet Sauvignon. Overseeing the operations is Greg Sandor, operations manager, who has degrees in viticulture from Fresno State and Cornell. The plans are to plant an additional fifty acres in 2001 and fifty more acres in 2002. A tasting room and winery — and the wine itself — are still a few years off, but Alexander intends to concentrate on Bordeaux-style red wines and will make estate-bottled wines only. Stay tuned! This promises to be a winery to watch!

Previously known as Hargrave Vineyards, where the first commercial vineyards were planted on the North Fork, the winery is now known as Castello di Borghese/Hargrave Vineyards.

Suzi Forbes Chase

CASTELLO DI BORGHESE/
HARGRAVE VINEYARDS
631-734-5111.
www.castellodiborghese.com.
North Rd. (Rte. 48) at Alvah's Ln.,
    Cutchogue.

Mailing Address: PO Box 957, Cutchogue,
    NY 11935.
Open: Daily 11am–6pm.
Fee: None.

T his is where it all began. Alex and Louisa Hargrave were the first to believe that Long Island's North Fork could produce great wines, and they were right. After many years of hard work, they sold their winery in 1999 to Marco and Ann Marie Borghese, an Italian couple with a royal pedigree. The winery currently has thirty acres of vines planted on the eighty-acre estate, and it produces more than 8,500 cases a year in a variety of wines. Mark Terry is the winemaker. Hargrave is particularly noted for its red wines — Cabernet Sauvignon, Pinot Noir, and Merlot, but it produces a nice Chardonnay also. No formal tours are conducted at present, but the tasting room was undergoing expansion in 2000 to accommodate more visitors. A lovely pergola was also being added so that guests can enjoy al fresco tastings and picnics. In the former conference room, visitors can now enjoy art exhibitions.

COREY CREEK VINEYARDS
631-765-4168.
www.coreycreek.com.
Main Rd. (Rte 25), Southold.

Mailing Address: PO Box 921, Southold, NY 11971.
Open: Daily 11am–5pm.
Fee: None.

The thirty acres in Southold that Joel and Peggy Lauber called Corey Creek Vineyards were planted with vines in 1981, but the grapes were originally sold to local wineries. Now these mature vines are yielding grapes for estate-bottled wines, and the Laubers sold the winery in 1999 to Michael Lynne, a Time Warner executive (they're staying on to run it, however, until January 1, 2001). Corey Creek produced its first bottles of Chardonnay in 1993, and it immediately earned rave reviews. If you see a bottle for sale in a wineshop, buy it. It's outstanding! Also available are a Reserve Chardonnay and a Merlot, and there are plans for a Pinot Noir and a Gewürztraminer. Production has now reached 4,000 cases annually, and demand far outstrips the supply. A beautiful, natural-sided wood building was completed in 1997 to house a handsome tasting and sales room. This is a great spot for a picnic as a huge deck overlooks the vineyards.

DZUGAS VINEYARD
631-765-3692.
4400 North Rd. (Rte. 48), Southold, NY 11971.

Tasting room to open fall 2000 or spring 2001.

Although some of the new winery owners are building grandiose tasting rooms, Donna and Stephen Dzugas have much more humble plans. They proudly call themselves a mom-and-pop venture and raptly describe their hand-hewn log tasting room, built by Native Americans from an Iroquois tribe in Oneida, NY. It even has a tasting counter carved from a bent log that extends from the wall. And there's another difference, as well. This is a true working farm, where children are welcome to pet the ponies and llama, see the sheep and chickens, and take an old-fashioned hayride — at least when all is completed.

As far as the wine is concerned, however, this is a very serious endeavor. They have ten acres of grapes planted (some were planted in the early 1980s by one of the earliest growers) — five acres are in Chardonnay and five are in Merlot. Most of their grapes are sold to Bedell Cellars and are blended into Bedell wines, but for the last few years, about 25 percent have been reserved for estate Dzugas wines. They painstakingly hand-prune the vines and personally pick off grapes that have shriveled — and although this is highly labor-intensive work, it is a labor of love. Kip Bedell has been making wine for them, and although production is small, their wine has attracted the attention of prominent wine authorities. Until the tasting room opens, you can taste and purchase the wine at Ternhaven Cellars in Greenport, or you can buy it at local wineshops.

GALLUCCIO ESTATE
 VINEYARDS/GRISTINA WINERY
631-734-7089.
www.gristinavineyards.com.
24385 Main Rd. (Rte. 25), Cutchogue.

Mailing Address: PO Box 1269,
 Cutchogue, NY 11935.
Open: Daily 11am–5pm.
Fee: Most wines complimentary; reserve
 wines $2 each.

This classy winery offers classy wines in a classy setting. It is located in a gray-stained building, reminiscent of a New England farmhouse, with a huge fireplace inside and a broad deck with tables and chairs, surrounded by a white fence, outside — all made for lingering. The spacious, manicured lawns leading up the driveway set the tone. Gristina was purchased from the founding Gristina family in 2000 by Vincent Galluccio, but he has retained Adam Suprenant as the winemaker; Rob Hensult is the vineyard manager. The first Gristina wines were produced in 1988. Although no tours are offered, a selection of wines can be sampled. There are currently thirty acres planted (the new owner is planting more), and the annual production is 6,000 cases (with plans to expand to about 15,000 cases).

JAMESPORT VINEYARDS
631-722-5256.
www.jamesport-vineyards.com.
Main Rd. (Rte. 25), Jamesport.

Mailing Address: PO Box 842, Jamesport,
 NY 11947.
Open: Daily 10am–6pm.
Fee: None.

This winery is partly new and partly old. Rising from the ashes of the defunct North Fork winery and with grapes from a Cutchogue vineyard planted by Ronald Goerler, Sr. and his son, Ron, Jr. in 1982, the first Jamesport Vineyards wines were produced in 1987. Jamesport is the largest producer of Sauvignon Blanc, but makes a variety of other wines, including a Champagne made with Pinot Noir and Chardonnay grapes. There are currently forty-five acres planted on the sixty-acre estate, and the annual production is 5,000 cases. The winemaker is Sean Capiaux. The winery is located in a 200-year-old, cedar shake, potato and hay barn with soaring ceilings.

LAUREL LAKE VINEYARDS
631-298-1420.
www.laurellakewines.com.

3165 Main Rd. (Rte 25), Laurel, NY 11948.
Open: Daily 10am–6pm.
Fee: None.

In 1993, Michael McGoldrick purchased thirty-five acres that had been partially planted in Chardonnay vines in 1980, and he bottled his first Laurel Lake Vineyards wines in 1994. But that was just the beginning. In 1997, he built a beautiful gray wooden winery with dormers and front and side porches that offer spots for quiet relaxation and picnics. Inside there's a soaring ceiling with a skylight, a window for viewing the stainless steel tanks and barrels, and a hospitality area for tastings and sales. In 1999, Mr. McGoldrick sold the winery to a partnership, and there are now plans for expansion. In addition to Chardonnay, the winery is now producing Cabernet Sauvignon and Riesling, and they are planting more vines on the thirty-five-acre estate. Current production is approximately 5,000 cases annually. Rolf Achterberg is the winemaker, and Jim Eller is the general manager.

LENZ VINEYARDS
631-734-6010.
www.lenzwine.com.
Main Rd. (Rte. 25), Peconic.
Mailing Address: PO Box 28, Peconic, NY
  11958.

Open: May–Oct.: daily 10am–6pm;
  Nov.–Apr.: daily 10am–5pm.
Fee: 7 wines complimentary; 4 additional
  wines $2 each.

L enz, located in a rose-stained wood building, has an interesting entrance that is shaped somewhat like a hopper. The property is surrounded by a split rail fence, and grape vines cover the rustic, colonnaded porch. Although the first vines were planted in 1980, the current winemaking team — owners Peter and Deborah Carroll, winemaker Eric Fry, vineyard manager Sam McCullough, and general manager Tom Morgan — was assembled in 1990. There are sixty acres of vines in production, and the average annual yield is 9,000 cases. There is no outside deck or scheduled tours. People come from miles around to buy the Gewürztraminer. The Pinot Noir, Cabernet Sauvignon, and Chardonnay are award winning, and the sparkling wines are refreshing and graceful.

LIEB FAMILY CELLARS
631-734-1100.
www.leibcellars.com.
North Rd. (Rte. 48) at Cox's Neck Ln.,
  Mattituck.

Mailing Address: PO Box 907, Cutchogue,
  NY 11935.
Tasting room to open fall 2000.

L ieb Family Cellars is an excellent example of the next generation of wines that we can expect to see produced on Long Island. The family (Mark and Kathy Lieb, plus "uncles, aunts, and cousins," according to Mark) purchased a fifty-acre farm in Cutchogue some years ago that had been planted in 1982 with grape vines, making it one of the oldest vineyards on the North Fork. Until 1997, they sold all their grapes to other wineries, but in that year they began making their own wines. When they released their 1997 Merlot in 2000, it was made with such finesse that it immediately won rave reviews, as has the Lieb Cellars Pinot Blanc Reserve 1998. The family plans to release a Pinot Blanc and a Champagne in 2000. Their intention is to remain small and to concentrate on producing only fine reserve wines. Rather than building their own winery, they are partners with Russell Hearn in the Premium Wine Group custom-crush winery, which will open in the fall of 2000. Their wines will be produced there, but they plan to open their own tasting room in the fall of 2000. They eventually hope to produce between 3,000 and 4,000 cases annually.

MACARI VINEYARDS AND WINERY
631-298-0100.
www.macariwines.com.
150 Bergen Ave. (just off Rte. 48),
   Mattituck.

Mailing Address: PO Box 2, Mattituck,
   NY 11952.
Open: Daily 11am–5pm.
Fee: 4–6 wines $2 per person.

One of the most exciting new ventures on the North Fork is taking place near the former Mattituck Hills Winery. In 1995, 105 acres of farmland were planted by the Macari family in a combination of Merlot, Chardonnay, Cabernet Franc, and Viognier. Several years later, they purchased the adjacent five acres of mature vines from Mattituck Hills. By 1998, they had opened an impressive, natural cedar-sided building, which has a stone foundation and a spacious covered deck. This is a great place to hold an event or to just sit at the black wrought iron tables overlooking the vineyards and sip the wine.

This thoroughly modern winery is fully computerized, yet the vines are tended with the utmost concern for the environment. The Macari family make their own fertilizer and use absolutely no herbicides or chemicals in caring for their vines. The first wines were offered in 1997, and winemakers José Montilla and Charles Girard say current production ranges from 6,000–10,000 cases annually. This team is committed to producing the very highest quality wines. The Macaris have one of the largest farms on the North Fork — a total of almost 350 acres — and there are plans to plant grapes on an additional eighty acres. Tours of the beautiful Macari farmstead can be arranged by advance notice.

MARTHA CLARA VINEYARDS
631-298-0075.
www.marthaclaravineyards.com.

2595 Sound Ave. (Rte. 48), Mattituck, NY
   11952.
Tasting room to open fall 2000.

When a friend of mine moved to Seattle, she made me promise to send her a care package of Entenmann bakery products once a month. Now folks will be making similar requests for his wines. Robert Entenmann planted a broad selection of red and white grapes on some of his acreage on the North Fork several years ago, and in 2000, his first white wines were released. They're getting rave reviews, especially the Viognier and the dry Alsatian-styled wines of Riesling, Gewürztraminer, and Semillion; a 1997 Merlot is scheduled to be released in 2000. For now, Roman Roth, the winemaker at Sagpond Vineyards in Sagaponack, is producing the wines for Entenmann, and he plans to use the new custom-crush winery, Premium Wine Group, that Russell Hearn is building as soon as it's complete in the fall of 2000. But future plans for this winery are expansive. Entenmann plans to open a historic brown barn on the property in the fall of 2000 that will contain an ornate old bar to be used as a temporary tasting counter. Plans on the drawing board include a fabulous $4-million tasting room (incorporating the historic barn) that will include a round tasting bar, an outdoor patio, and a demonstration kitchen equipped for TV coverage. After that, a $3-million winery will be built. Although current production is small, Entenmann projects the winery will eventually bottle 20,000 cases annually.

OSPREY'S DOMINION WINERY
631-765-6188.
www.ospreysdominion.com.
44075 Main Rd., Peconic.
Mailing Address: PO Box 275, Peconic,
    NY 11958.

Open: Mem. Day–Thanksgiving:
    Mon.–Sat. 10am–6pm, Sun. 12
    noon–6pm; rest of year: Mon.–Sat.
    10am–5pm, Sun. 12 noon–5pm.
Fee: None.

When Bud Koehler and Bill Tyree purchased seventy acres in Peconic that had been planted with grape vines in the 1980s (and sold to other wineries), they acquired mature vines that allowed them to offer their own estate wines. They subsequently added an additional twenty acres, and the winery's current annual production is 16,000 cases. A handsome, yellow stucco retail and tasting outlet was built in 1996, where such classics as Chardonnay, Riesling, Merlot, Cabernet Franc, Meritage, and Cabernet Sauvignon may be tasted and purchased. Winemaker Peter Silverberg also makes a hot spiced wine, similar to a mulled wine, and light, crisp peach and strawberry wines (they call this "strawberry shortcake in a glass"). The latter was created for the annual Mattituck Strawberry Festival. The general manager is Deborah Wilm, the vineyard manager is Tom Stevenson, and the tasting room manager is Dorian Harkoff. Osprey's Dominion also makes excellent grape jellies and vinegars, and you can buy sweatshirts, books, picnic backpacks (perfect for bicyclists), and gift baskets. A pretty patio overlooks the vineyards. Additional weekend attractions include hayrides and art shows.

PALMER VINEYARDS
631-722-9463.
www.palmervineyards.com.
108 Sound Ave. (Rte. 48), Aquebogue.
Mailing Address: PO Box 2125,
    Aquebogue, NY 11931.

Open: May–Oct.: daily 11am–6pm;
    Nov.–Apr.: daily 11am–5pm; self-
    guided tour.
Fee: 2 wines complimentary; additional
    tastings $.50–$3 each.

Owner Robert Palmer has a New York advertising agency, so promotion is his field. Not only are Palmer wines distributed in twenty-three states and four foreign countries, but they are also offered on American Airlines. Palmer Vineyards is one of the largest North Fork producers, bottling 22,000 cases annually; there are 100+ acres planted. Winemaker Tom Drozd produces outstanding wines. One of the finest is a reserve Chardonnay, but the Sauvignon Blanc, Gewürztraminer, and White Riesling are also excellent. Visitors (there can be many as 500 a day) love the look and feel of this user-friendly winery.

Clear, informative signs lead visitors on a self-guided tour past windows for viewing the tank, cask, and bottling rooms. The tasting and sales room contains an oak bar and several oak and wrought iron Victorian booths that were once part of an authentic, eighteenth-century pub in England. An inviting deck, which overlooks the vineyards, is made for relaxing. There's even a small gift shop where T-shirts, caps, and books are sold. In the summer, food demonstrations are held on the deck, as well as concerts and special events.

PAUMANOK VINEYARDS
631-722-8800.
www.paumanok.com.
1074 Main Rd. (Rte. 25), Aquebogue.
Mailing Address: PO Box 741,
    Aquebogue, NY 11931.

Open: May–Oct.: Mon.–Sat. 11am–6pm,
    Sun. 12 noon–6pm; Oct.–May:
    Mon.–Sat. 11am–5pm, Sun. 12
    noon–5pm.
Fee: Most wines complimentary; some
    select wines $2.

The vines for Paumanok Vineyards, owned by Charles and Ursula Massoud, were first planted in 1983. Although the first vintage was bottled in 1991, it was produced by grapes on mature vines. Although Charles was originally the winemaker, Ryan Leeman was hired for that position in 1999. The winery currently produces about 7,000 cases annually from their fifty-three acres of vines. The tasting room is spacious, with a glass viewing window overlooking the tank and barrel rooms below. Guided tours are offered when sufficient people have assembled. The large, outdoor deck is a wonderful place for picnics, and in the summer, a series of concerts called Sunset in the Vineyards, takes place here. The Harvest Festival in the fall is also a must, and a program of Christmas carols in Dec. is enchanting.

PECONIC BAY WINERY
631-734-7361.
www.peconicbaywinery.com.
31320 Main Rd. (Rte. 25), Cutchogue.
Mailing Address: PO Box 818, Cutchogue,
    NY 11935.

Open: Mon.–Fri. 11am–5pm; in season:
    Sat., Sun. 11am–6pm; in winter: Sat.,
    Sun. 11am–5pm.
Fee: Some wines complimentary; others
    nominal fee $1-$2.

Ray Blum, the original owner of Peconic Bay, planted his first grapes in 1979 and produced his first wines in 1984, so he was one of the first winemakers here. Although he sold the winery in 1999 to Paul and Ursula Lowerre, it continues to produce a fine selection of wines. There are now about fifty acres in production on the 250-acre estate, and the winery bottles around 6,000 cases a year. The winemaker is Greg Gove, and the general manager is Matthew Gillies. The winery's estate Chardonnay is excellent, but for an ambrosial dessert or after-dinner wine, the Vin de I'lle Blanc is smashing; it's more like a Barsac than a Sauterne. A pretty patio covered by an awning has been added to the tasting room by the new owners, and there also is a small gift shop. Summer concerts include folk and pop singers, as well as jazz.

PELLEGRINI VINEYARDS
631-734-4111.
www.pellegrinivineyards.com.
2300J Main Rd. (Rte. 25), Cutchogue, NY
  11935.

Open: Daily 11am–5pm; self-guided tour.
Fee: Most wines complimentary; others
  $6 for 3 glasses.

It's always an advantage if you can purchase land that is planted with mature grape vines. In the case of Bob and Joyce Pellegrini, they bought thirty acres in 1988 that had been planted in 1982, enabling them to produce their first wines in 1991, and they've been adding additional acreage ever since. In 2000, they purchased an additional sixty acres, bringing their total acreage to approximately 120, which will enable them to grow all their own grapes and produce estate wines. By 1997, production had increased to 10,000 cases annually. The winemaker is Russell Hearn. The Pellegrini winery opened in 1993 in a sensational building; it's shaped like a cloister, with a grassy inner courtyard circled by a brick and flagstone walkway. Inside, vaulted ceilings and a multitude of windows create a light-filled space. There's a tasting counter on one side and tables and chairs by the windows; outside there's a deck for picnics or for lounging. A loft overlooking the room could be used for musicians as events unfold below. This is a winery built for visitors. Self-guided tours may be taken throughout the day, or visitors may watch the winery workers from a balcony above the tank and barrel rooms. Special events sometimes take place in this wonderful space.

PINDAR VINEYARDS
631-734-6200.
www.pindar.net.
Main Rd. (Rte. 25), Peconic.

Mailing Address: PO Box 332, Peconic,
  NY 11958.
Open: Daily 11am–6pm.
Fee: None for most wines.

Dr. Herodotus Damianos, who also owns Duck Walk Vineyards on the South Fork, is of Greek descent (Pindar was an ancient Greek poet), and the distinctive labels on his bottles are derived from Greek mythology. Pindar's first vines on the 350-acre spread were planted in 1979, and the first release was bottled in 1983. When the winery first opened, the huge white stucco building seemed to rise from the neat rows of vines like a mirage in the desert, but over the years we've gotten used to it. This is the largest winery on the North Fork with some 80,000 cases produced annually, and the tasting and sales room is built to accommodate visitors. There are scheduled tours of the winery, and there can be as many as 2,000 visitors a day in the summer and up to seventy people per tour, so the best time to go is in the winter or spring. Pindar's Mythology, a red wine blend, has received much praise and is a must for sampling, as are the Cabernet Sauvignon, Chardonnay, and a refreshing Summer Blush that includes cranberry juice. Mark Friszolowski is the winemaker. There's a delightful outside pavilion that makes a terrific place for a picnic or just for summer sipping.

The gleaming white exterior of Pindar Vineyards' sales and tasting building in Peconic reflects owner Herodotus Damianos's Greek roots.

Suzi Forbes Chase

PUGLIESE VINEYARDS
631-734-4057.
www.pugliesevineyards.com.
Main Rd. (Rte. 25), Cutchogue.

Mailing Address: PO Box 467, Cutchogue, NY 11935.
Open: Daily 10am–5pm.
Fee: None.

The Puglieses planted their first vines in 1980 and made their first wines in 1986. They now have thirty-six acres planted and produce almost 5,000 cases of wine annually, including Chardonnay and Merlot, as well as a sparkling wine. If packaging can sell a product, the Puglieses will sell a lot of wine. Lovely, hand-painted bottles are decorated by Patricia Pugliese, who is the winery owner with her husband Ralph. Their son, Peter, is the winemaker. Their Blanc de Blanc Champagne, made of 100 percent Chardonnay, is outstanding. Tastings are proudly offered at the winery. Rows of gift baskets with hand-painted bottles and glasses line a table in the tasting room, ready to be given as house gifts to lucky East End hosts. (Call in advance to order a personalized gift basket.) Picnic tables are set up under a grape arbor overlooking a pond and offer one of the most appealing places to sip and relax on the North Fork.

RAPHAEL
631-765-1100.
39390 Main Rd., Peconic.

Mailing Address: PO Box 17, Peconic, NY 11958.
Tasting room to open spring 2001.

Throughout 2000, those of us who drove down Main Rd. in Peconic were fascinated by the mammoth, Spanish-style building rising from a roadside field. Turns out, it's the $6-million tasting room and winery of Raphael, an enterprise of John Petrocelli, a New York commercial builder. This winery will rival the finest in California. But it's not all show — this is a thoroughly well-thought out venture. Several years ago, Petrocelli planted forty-two of his sixty acres of land in mostly Merlot grapes, and he intends to produce only a Merlot wine. For his winemaker, he hired Richard Olsen-Harbich, who has been making wines on Long Island since the early 1980s, and he also hired Paul Pontallier, the managing director of Château Margaux, as his consulting winemaker. All three men are banking on the similarities of the North Fork's climate and soil to those of Bordeaux. About 700 cases of the 1999 vintage will be produced in 2000, but production will probably never exceed 5,000 cases. The visitor's center/winery is projected to open by Mem. Day, 2001. Not only will it include a handsome tasting room and winery, but also test kitchens and rooms where official wine comparisons can take place.

SCHNEIDER VINEYARDS
631-727-3334.
www.SchneiderVineyards.com.

2248 Roanoke Ave., Riverhead, NY 11901.
Tasting and sales room not built yet.

Bruce and Christiane Baker Schneider have been producing their own wines since 1994 by personally selecting grapes from the finest vineyards on the North Fork and by hiring respected vintner Kip Bedell to produce their wines for them. But in 2000, they advanced their operation a notch by purchasing a twenty-two-acre potato farm in Riverhead. They planted their first seven acres in Cabernet Franc grapes (their signature wine), and they hired Sean Capiaux as their winemaker. Although their state-of-the-art winery is still on the drawing board, we continue to expect great things from this couple. Bruce had apprenticed in Burgundy vineyards so he knows what he's doing. They currently produce about 1,350 cases annually of Merlot and Cabernet Franc wines, and they offered their first Chardonnay in 1999. The *Wine Spectator* said of their 1994 Cabernet Franc, "Bright in flavor, serious and lush in texture." In 1999, they began producing a Potato Barn White and a Potato Barn Red, both of which are blended wines that are light and drinkable now. Until the sales room opens, wines may be ordered directly from the Schneiders, or they can be purchased at local and Manhattan wineshops. They also are offered at some of the finest restaurants in Manhattan.

TERNHAVEN CELLARS
631-477-8737.
331 Front St., Greenport.

Mailing Address: PO Box 758, Greenport, NY 11944.
Open: Fri.–Sun. 11am–6pm.

This tiny boutique winery, which opened its doors in the summer of 1998, is located in the heart of Greenport. It's obvious from this plain-Jane tasting room that the emphasis is on wine, not window dressing. Specializing in hand-crafted Bordeaux-style wines, the owner Harold Watts planted his five-acre parcel, Wesley Hall Vineyard, which is located in Cutchogue, in 1985 in a combination of Merlot, Cabernet Sauvignon, and a small amount of Cabernet Franc, from which he makes a Claret; he also makes a Rosé that he calls Harbor Rose. Watts produced his first wines in 1994, and his production is currently at about 600–700 cases a year; he believes his top production will be about 1,000 cases a year. The tasting and sales room offers a view of the barrel room.

LODGING

*Always In' is a handsome
Colonial tucked away in a
wooded setting far from
the crowds.*

Suzi Forbes Chase

ALWAYS IN' BED & BREAKFAST
531-765-5344.
www.northfork.com/AlwaysIn.
14580 Soundview Ave., Southold.
Mailing Address: PO Box 1018, Southold,
NY 11971.
Innkeepers: Marguerite and Jay
Schondebare.
Open: Year-round.
Price: Moderate.
Credit Cards: None.

Special Features: Nonsmoking inn; full
breakfast; air-conditioning; adults only;
no pets; Trinket, a Jack Russell Terrier
on premises.
Directions: From North Rd. (Rte. 48)
traveling east, turn north (left) in
Southold onto Horton's Ln. at traffic
light. At stop sign, turn east (right) onto
Soundview Ave. Inn is on right about .3
mile, before Lighthouse Rd.

Should you wish to combine your visit to local wineries with a relaxed stay
at an elegant B&B, this delicious spot offers all the amenities — a superbly
quiet location, beautifully landscaped grounds, gourmet breakfasts, and
friendly, caring innkeepers. The white, center hall colonial has a handsome living room on one side with a polished oak floor, a white wooden fireplace mantel, and a daffodil yellow sofa. On the other side, a pretty dining room has a
table covered with a lace tablecloth and set with Lenox or antique
Haviland/Limoges china; at every place, you will find a handwritten quote that
has been selected especially for you. Breakfast will be inventive. Marguerite,
who is a marvelous cook, may start the meal with pears poached in Bedell's
raspberry wine and follow that with coffee-rum-cinnamon French toast topped
with ice cream. Of course, there will be homemade muffins or scones.

There are two rooms in the B&B, and they share a decorator tile bath,
embellished with striped ivory paper and located off the hallway. In both
rooms, you'll drift away to sleep on a cloudlike feather bed and find a fluffy
terrycloth robe to wear when padding across the hall. Tally-Ho, one of the

guest rooms, has sponged walls and grape vines painted at chair rail height. A pretty quilt covers the bed. Hunt pictures hang on the walls and riding gear is used as decoration. In a corner, Marguerite has dressed a fox-headed clothing tree in traditional hunting garb. The other guest room, Serengetti, has an African theme (the couple's daughter studied in Africa). In this room, Marguerite painted a mural of an African sunset on the wall above the bed and has kept her daughter's scrapbook filled with letters and snapshots for guests to review. In the closet, there's a surprise. A huge stuffed gorilla offers his greetings in Swahili — *habri*.

The Belvedere, with its wraparound porch and enchanting rooftop belvedere, contains fabulous frescoes painted on 11.5-foot ceilings in the double parlors and entry.

Suzi Forbes Chase

THE BELVEDERE
631-765-1799.
www.northfork.com/belvedere.
3070 Peconic Ln., Peconic, NY 11958.
Innkeepers: Lee and Marie Beninati.
Open: Year-round.
Price: Expensive.
Credit Cards: AE, MC, V.

Special Features: On 2 landscaped acres; wraparound porch; smoking outside only; air-conditioning; continental-plus breakfast; children over 14 welcome.
Directions: Traveling east on Rte. 48, turn right onto Peconic Ln. in Peconic. Inn is on left.

Who would ever have thought that a Victorian as beautiful and elaborate as the best either Cape May or San Francisco has to offer would be tucked away on the North Fork of Long Island, but here it is. This elaborately embellished painted lady has a pale brown exterior with brick-colored shutters and ivory trim. In addition to the gingerbread that drips from the porches, the house is also crowned with a tall belvedere. The inside is even more beautiful than the exterior. Fabulous frescoes have been painted on the 11.5-foot ceilings, as well as on the walls of the entry hall and the double parlors (both have pretty marble fireplaces). The entry doors and pocket sliding doors have etched glass. In remarkably good shape, the house has obviously been lovingly tended through the years so that when Lee and Marie purchased it in 2000, they only needed to add their gracious antique furniture and upgrade the baths to convert it to a B&B.

They opened with two rooms, but plan to add a third. The Green Room has an elegant sage green damask spread on the wood and brass bed and a working fireplace; its bath has a pretty claw-foot tub painted with ivy leaves and a great pedestal sink. The Azalea Room has yellow walls and a yellow metlassé spread on a bed with a green moiré headboard; its pretty bath has bead board walls. The charming innkeepers owned a restaurant previously. Lee is a great chef, and Marie is a pastry chef. Breakfast, which may be served in the parlor or on the wraparound porch, includes fresh fruit and juices, plus perhaps a quiche or French toast, as well as freshly baked croissants, popovers, or breads. Cappuccino and espresso are also available.

COEUR DES VIGNES L'HOTEL
631-765-2656.
www.coeurdesvignes.com.
57225 Main Rd., Southold, NY 11971.
Innkeepers: George and Donna Marie
  Pavlou.
Open: Year-round.
Price: Moderate.

Credit Cards: AE, D, DC, MC, V.
Special Features: Restaurant on premises;
  smoking on outside porch only; air-
  conditioning; continental breakfast;
  children accepted.
Directions: Traveling east on Main Rd.,
  pass through Southold. Inn is on left.

George and Donna Marie Pavlou offer overnight lodging in four charming rooms above their restaurant, Coeur des Vignes (heart of the wines). The handsome, columned building was completely renovated in 1999 to create these rooms. You will find sleigh beds dressed in pretty linens, a tray of cordials, and interesting wall decor. I was especially intrigued by the framed needlepoint (actually petit point) pictures made by Donna Marie's father. Every room has an impeccably clean, modern private bath. A continental breakfast that includes freshly baked croissants, rolls, fruit, and juice is served.

HOME PORT BED & BREAKFAST
631-765-1435.
www.northfork.com/homeport.
2500 Peconic Ln., Peconic.
Mailing Address: PO Box 333, Peconic,
  NY 11958.
Innkeepers: Pat and Jack Combs.
Open: Year-round.

Price: Moderate.
Credit Cards: None.
Special Features: Continental-plus
  breakfast; children accepted; no pets.
Directions: From Main Rd. traveling east,
  turn left onto Peconic Ln. B&B is on
  right.

The Combs, who hark from a family of baymen who settled the North Fork in 1640, have converted their gracious 1876 Victorian farmhouse, with its five lovely fireplaces, into a comfortable bed-and-breakfast. It's filled with interesting antiques, such as the Victorian headboard and marble-topped Victorian dresser in the Gold Room and the four-poster bed in the Peach Room. All three guest rooms have semiprivate baths and are decorated with Waverly fabrics. A magnificent 1840s mahogany breakfront in the South Room, one of the common rooms, is stunning. There's a cozy fireplace in the dining room to take the chill off cool winter mornings. The Teddy Roosevelt

Room, which is filled with fishing and hunting gear, as well as a superb collection of Teddy Roosevelt memorabilia, pictures, and books, shouldn't be missed. Examples of Mr. Combs' exquisite duck decoys and those of his son, Michael, might be on view (carving has been a family pastime for six generations), if they haven't all been sold. Ask about the special fly-fishing classes.

Shorecrest contains some of the most beautiful interior woodwork of any bed and breakfast on the East End.

Dustin Chase

SHORECREST
631-765-1570.
E-mail:jbarnes1@optonline.net.
54300 North Rd., Southold, NY 11971.
Innkeepers: John and Susan Barnes.
Open: Year-round.
Price: Moderate–Very Expensive.
Credit Cards: AE, MC, V.
Special Features: Full breakfast; 1 block from beach; air-conditioning in guest rooms; smoking outside only; 2-night minimum weekends in summer; beautifully landscaped grounds; children over 12 welcome; a cat and a dog in owners' quarters only.
Directions: From Riverhead, follow Sound Ave. (Rte. 48) west for about 16 miles to Southold. Continue on Rte. 48 past Southold Town Beach. Inn is on right about 300 feet beyond beach and behind tall hedge.

This fabulous and elegant B&B, which opened in 1999, has some of the most beautiful woodwork of any inn on the East End, and also the loveliest antiques. On the outside, it's a typical weathered-shingle cottage with white trim, but inside, the wide, thick crown and door moldings, 10.5-foot ceilings, and elaborate detailing over the doors and windows mark it as very special. The living room contains a massive fireplace mantel, as well as antique love seats, a pretty ladies writing desk, and a sofa; original paintings hang on the walls. The Captains Sitting Room, which is lined with bookcases, offers comfortable chairs for reading or watching TV, and the Sunroom includes antique wicker furniture in a sunny setting that overlooks the beautiful gardens. The Rose Room, located on the first floor, contains a beautiful four-poster bed and an elaborately framed, huge round mirror; it has a beautiful tiled bath. Two additional rooms are located upstairs (a fourth will be added eventually). The East Room has a four-poster bed and an antique dresser, while the West Room has a bed with a blue-and-white quilt and pretty framed antique French drawings on the walls. These rooms share a bath.

A full breakfast, presented on elegant antique or period china, is served in the formal dining room by candlelight at 9am. The breakfast features local produce and products and might include fresh fruit or berries with local peach or strawberry wine, cinnamon-raisin toast with local jams, freshly baked scones, and an herb-cheese omelette with local eggs and bacon.

TOP O' THE MORNING

631-734-5143.
26350 Main Rd., Cutchogue, NY 11935.
Innkeepers: Patty and Tommy Monahan.
Open: Apr.–mid-Jan.
Price: Moderate.
Credit Cards: None.
Special Features: On .25 acre adjacent to golf course; continental breakfast; air-conditioning; nonsmoking B&B; 2-night minimum weekends in summer; children accepted; Irish hospitality.
Directions: From west, follow Main Rd. (Rte. 25) to Cutchogue. B&B is on right.

Opened in 1997, this thoroughly charming B&B offers its guests a terrific time. Tommy will crank up the old Victrola or put some rolls into the player piano, and folks can participate in impromptu sing-alongs into the night. Patty was a professional singer, and she'll set a lively and entertaining pace. The pretty Victorian farmhouse was built in 1910, and its clapboard is now painted a mellow yellow, while the elaborate gingerbread stands out in white. Antique wicker tables and chairs sit on the broad front porch, sharing space with pots of flowers. In addition to the music room, there's a living room with a sofa upholstered in red and white, and a Victorian hall tree. The guest rooms are bright and inviting: one has a verdigris iron bed, wide-plank pine floors, and very pretty rose wallpaper; another features violet colors and has a pretty curlicued wicker side table. Each room has its own bath. One has a green tile floor, white tile walls, a pedestal sink, and a platform tub with brass fixtures. The third room includes a carved four-poster bed, an antique armoire, and teal carpeting; its beautiful bath has a pedestal sink, a white tile floor, and a shower. Generally, there's a continental breakfast, but on Sun., Patty fixes a hearty Irish breakfast that often includes Irish soda bread.

TREASURE ISLAND BED & BREAKFAST

631-477-2788.
14909 Main Rd., East Marion.
Mailing Address: PO Box 337, East Marion, NY 11939.
Innkeepers: Norman and Marjorie Whitehead.
Open: Year-round.
Price: Very Expensive.
Credit Cards: AE, MC, V.
Special Features: On 6 acres; waterfront; bird-watching; air- conditioning; full breakfast; beach passes and towels provided; smoking on outdoor terraces only; not appropriate for children; no pets.
Directions: Follow Rte. 25 (Main Rd.) or

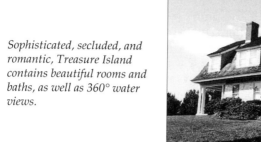

Sophisticated, secluded, and romantic, Treasure Island contains beautiful rooms and baths, as well as 360° water views.

Dustin Chase

Rte. 48 (Sound Ave.) beyond Riverhead for about 20 miles to Greenport. In Greenport, Rte. 48 merges into Rte. 25. Continue east on Rte. 25 for another 2.5 miles to causeway. B&B is up first driveway on left.

This unique waterfront estate is located on the causeway to Orient Point, where it is almost surrounded by Dam Pond. To the north is Long Island Sound and Truman Beach, while on the south there's Orient Harbor and Gardiner's Bay. Situated on a slight hill, the bed-and-breakfast offers glorious sunset views, opportunities for abundant bird-watching, and romantic vistas of the starry skies from the columned porch and the terrace. Norm Whitehead summered here at his grandparents' estate while he was growing up, and he remembers they named it Treasure Island, either because his grandmother found some lovely antique pieces of furniture in the attic, or because they found some money buried in the yard. Today, this lovely "island" is a spot that we can all treasure.

The Whiteheads made extensive renovations before converting the home to a bed-and-breakfast. There are three spacious guest rooms. A suite on the main floor has a bedroom with a soundside view and a sitting room overlooking the bay. This room is furnished with a matching antique Eastlake Victorian bedroom suite, and it has its own private bath, beautifully finished with antique slatelike tiles and Corian countertops. The other two rooms are on the second floor, and both are furnished with Victorian antiques (one has a beautiful wicker chaise); they share one full and one half hall bath. A continental breakfast is served in a corner of the spacious living room, and guests often sit on the terrace or the glass-enclosed porch to watch the fascinating assortment of birds and animals parading by.

RESTAURANTS & FOOD PURVEYORS

RESTAURANTS

ALDO'S TOO
631-477-2859.
136 Front St., Greenport, NY 11944.
SUSHI AT ALDO'S
631-477-1699.
105 Front St., Greenport, NY 11944.
Owner: Aldo Maiorana.

Sushi Chef: Guan Yin Chen.
Cuisine: Japanese.
Serving: L, D.
Open: Year-round.
Price: Inexpensive–Moderate.
Credit Cards: AE, MC, V.
Special Features: Outside patio.

Aldo began his enterprise as a baker, and he continues to bake great breads and biscotti. You can try them at his café called Aldo's Too, which is a pleasant place to go for breakfast. It's just across the street from his original restaurant. It seems Aldo is always trying something new, and in 2000, he transformed his former bistro into a sushi spot. Eventually, Aldo will begin adding items from his own menu as well. The charming building, with its pressed tin ceiling is now sleek and crisp with marine blue tablecloths and nautical pictures on the walls.

One of the finest dining experiences on the North Fork will be found at this Contemporary American hideaway in the Brewer Yacht Yard in Greenport.

Suzi Forbes Chase

ANTARES CAFE
631-477-8839.
2530 Manhanset Ave., Greenport, NY 11944.
Owner/Chef: Matthew Murphy; co-owner Kim Pino.
Cuisine: Contemporary American.
Serving: D, (L, July 4–Oct. only), BR Sat., Sun.
Open: Mar.–Dec.

Price: Expensive.
Credit Cards: D, DC, MC, V.
Special Features: Deck dining.
Directions: From Main St. in Greenport (Rte. 25), turn right onto Champlin Pl. At end, turn right onto Manhanset Ave. Brewer Yacht Yard is just beyond Stirling Harbor Marina. Restaurant is on right in boatyard.

Located in the Brewer Yacht Yard, this wonderful addition to the North Fork dining scene offers Contemporary American fare that's served with finesse. Trout is crusted with Parmesan and served with fennel and an orange salad; saddle of lamb comes with a side of creamy polenta and a variety of chutneys. The restaurant's name is adopted (we are told on the menu) from the name for the brightest star in the constellation Scorpio. It is a "red supergiant star, 9,000 times more luminous and 700 times the size of our sun." To bring the image home, the stucco walls of the tiny cathedral-ceilinged dining room are painted a bright glossy red and embellished with bright posters. The white tablecloths and tall white napkins offer a dramatic contrast. This newcomer is certainly a bright star in the North Fork constellation.

Bistro Blue offers upscale American bistro fare overlooking the water.

Suzi Forbes Chase

BISTRO BLUE
631-477-3940.
www.bistroblue.com.
1410 Manhanset Ave., Greenport, NY
11944.
Owners: Jeffrey Baruch, Daniel Giannini,
Jerry Simonetti.
Manager: John De Rosa.
Chef: Jerry Simonetti.
Cuisine: American Bistro.
Serving: L, D.
Open: Mem. Day–Labor Day: daily; fewer
days rest of year; in winter: closed.

Price: Expensive.
Credit Cards: AE, D, MC, V.
Special Features: Waterfront dining;
fireplace; outdoor deck; boat dock; jazz
on weekends.
Directions: From Main St. in Greenport
(Rte. 25), turn right onto Champlin Pl.
At end, turn right onto Manhanset Ave.
Stirling Harbor Marina is on right in .25
mile. Drive past scores of boats in
drydock to restaurant, on the water at
end.

Located in Stirling Harbor Marina, Bistro Blue's setting can't be topped. It sits at water's edge, surrounded by manicured lawns with views of the harbor filled with classy yachts and with the village of Greenport beyond. For many years, Porto Bello occupied this special spot, but when they moved to a roadside location in 1999, these partners were quick to fill the space. It's now a more casual, lively, and innovative place that spotlights fresh seafood with zesty accoutrements.

CLAUDIO'S RESTAURANT
631-477-0627.
111 Main St., Greenport, NY 11944.
Cuisine: Seafood.

Serving: L, D.
Open: Mid-Apr.–Jan. 1.
Price: Moderate–Expensive.
Credit Cards: MC, V.

In 1870, Manuel Claudio opened Claudio's Tavern. The restaurant has been in the same family ever since (Bill Claudio manages it now), making it the oldest restaurant in America to be owned continuously by the same family. The incredible, 10-foot-high Victorian bar was salvaged from an old hotel in New York in 1885 and brought to the tavern by barge. The decor is a riot of beveled mirrors, stained glass, and carved wood. Claudio's history includes interesting interludes with bootleggers who incorporated trapdoors and dumbwaiters in their operations. The food is as fresh as seafood can be and includes lobster, shrimp, scallops, and perhaps sea bass.

COEUR DES VIGNES
631-765-2656.
www.coeurdesvignes.com.
57225 Main Rd., Southold, NY 11971.
Owners: The Pavlou family.
Chef: Aristodemos Pavlou.
Cuisine: French.
Serving: L, D.

Open: Daily; closed Tues.
Price: Moderate–Very Expensive.
Credit Cards: AE, MC, V.
Special Features: Guest rooms available; extensive list of Long Island wines.
Directions: Traveling east on Main Rd., pass through Southold. Restaurant and inn are on left.

This fine French restaurant, which opened in 1998, is romantic and charming. There are three intimate dining rooms — one with beamed ceilings — and all have lacy curtains on the windows. Chef Pavlou is a graduate of the Cordon Bleu in Paris. The menu might include braised sweetbreads or a rack of lamb with pine-kernel herb butter crust. For dessert, if it's available, you must try the Saragelie, a dessert that the Chef's grandmother used to make in Cyprus. It consists of a thin homemade pastry that is wrapped around an almond and cinnamon filling, baked in the oven, then finished with a citrus-honey syrup. The wine list includes a lovely selection of Long Island wines, as well as French, California, and Italian.

DALY'S OLD MILL INN
631-298-8080.
West Mill Rd., Mattituck, NY 11952.
Owner: Jeremiah Daly.
Cuisine: American and Seafood.
Serving: L, D.
Open: May–Dec.
Price: Inexpensive–Expensive.

Credit Cards: AE, MC, V.
Special Features: Outdoor waterfront dining; fireplace; entertainment; boat dock.
Directions: From Rte. 48, travel north on Cox Neck Rd. to West Mill Rd. Follow West Mill Rd. to end.

Down by Mattituck Creek, a little inlet that feeds into Long Island Sound, stands an historic old mill that is built on pilings suspending it over the creek. With its red-shingled exterior and attractive little deck filled with tables overlooking the tiny, local fishing fleet, there is little hint of its bawdy Prohibition days when rumrunners stealthily paddled underneath by night to hoist their bounty through trapdoors into the kitchen. The old beams, posts, barnwood walls, and bare wood floors look much as they did originally, and the huge brick fireplace in the taproom continues to warm its inhabitants. The dining room, however, is much more refined and offers watery views from its large windows. This is serious food — a mix of fish of the day, which is purchased from local fishermen, and meat that includes a rack of lamb and a boneless duck à l'orange, as well as chicken and pastas. There's a good selection of Long Island wines, plus wines from California and Europe. On weekend evenings, there's also live entertainment.

GREENPORT TEA COMPANY
631-477-8744.
119A Main St., Greenport, NY 11944.
Owner: Adrienne Noonan.
Cuisine: American Continental.
Serving: L, HT; BR (weekends only).

Open: Mar.–Dec.; closed Tues.
Price: Inexpensive.
Credit Cards: AE, D, MC, V.
Special Features: Wheelchair access;
  outside sidewalk seating.

There's nothing like the Greenport Tea Company, either in the Hamptons or in Manhattan. The Victorian building with its high ceilings is an enchanting spot. Shelves on one wall hold teacups and saucers, teapots, and gourmet food products available for purchase. Tea is served in china cups and from antique teapots — each one different. The food is also unique: clam pie, shepherd's pie, soups, salads, corn bread, and Irish brown bread. You can also get a glass of local wine or a beer to wash it all down. Best of all, however, is high tea, served from tiered serving trays, laden with the best fresh scones that you'll ever eat; an old, Irish recipe is responsible for these moist and tender morsels. A variety of finger sandwiches changes with the season; there may be salmon, tomato, or cucumber, but they're always made-to-order and finished with freshly chopped parsley garnishing the edges. The bottom tier is reserved for luscious fresh lemon tarts, minipastries, and fresh fruit. It's the sort of place where our grandmothers took our mothers after a day of shopping. Do ask Adrienne's husband Bill to play the old Victrola for you.

ILE DE BEAUTE
631-477-2822.
www.IledeBeaute.com.
314 Main St., Greenport, NY 11944.
Owner/Manager: Jeannette Charvet.
Chef: Jerry Mohr.
Cuisine: French Crêperie.

Serving: L, D.
Open: Year-round: daily.
Price: Expensive.
Credit Cards: AE, D, DC, MC, V.
Special Features: Patio dining.
Directions: On Main St. (Rte. 25) at
  Front St.

In a lovingly restored Victorian house in Greenport, this French restaurant and crêperie opened in 2000. The creamy clapboard house has black shutters and pretty black wrought iron light standards. You can sit at tables under umbrellas on a patio in front or in one of two interior dining rooms with Venetian-tiled fireplaces. Upscale and romantic, the menu features crêpes (you can watch them being made) with more than fifty choices of fillings, as well as serious dinner entrées. There's a tiny Victorian bar in the entry where you can order mixed drinks, or wine or beer from the extensive selection.

JAMESPORT COUNTRY KITCHEN
631-722-3537.
Main Rd. (Rte. 25), Jamesport, NY 11947.
Owner/Manager: Matthew Kar.
Chef: Matthew Kar.

Cuisine: American.
Serving: L, D.
Open: Year-round: closed Tues.
Price: Moderate.
Credit Cards: AE, MC, V.

Matthew Kar prides himself on featuring the wines and produce of the North Fork in his cuisine. The wine list contains more than seventy-five varieties, primarily from Long Island, and the prices range from $14–$43. This is an excellent place to sample local wines with food prepared from local ingredients. The menu is well priced and changes every week to reflect the freshest local produce. It relies on simple, straightforward dishes, but with interesting, fresh twists. For, example, a Caesar salad can be ordered for lunch either plain, with grilled shrimp, or with thinly sliced, grilled filet mignon. An entrée that included a wedge of salmon had an herbed crust, with a light, herb-caper butter drizzled over the top. Reservations are absolutely necessary at this popular restaurant. Even though the casual country decor doesn't match the sophistication of the food, the wines, or the knowledgeable service, this restaurant is a real sleeper.

LEGENDS
631-734-5123.
www.northfork.com/legends.
835 First St., New Suffolk.
Mailing Address: PO Box 321, New Suffolk, NY 11956.
Owners: Dennis and Diane Harkoff.
Chefs: Kevin Bolinski and Mike Reilly.
Cuisine: American.
Serving: L, D, LN.

Open: Year-round.
Price: Moderate.
Credit Cards: AE, D, MC, V.
Special Features: Best sports bar on the East End; entertainment some nights.
Directions: From Rte. 25 in Cutchogue, turn south at light onto New Suffolk Rd. and drive 1.5 miles to blinking light. Turn left onto Main St., then left onto First St. Restaurant is on left.

Divided into two sections, Legends has a sophisticated, upscale restaurant on one side with fresh flowers, candles gracing the linen tablecloths, and soft music playing. Sports memorabilia (see an autographed Mickey Mantel uniform) and pictures of sports figures line the walls, and a polished racing scull hangs from the cathedral ceiling. On the other side, the café has tables along the windows and a raised sports bar that includes twenty-two television monitors. You can actually watch both figure skating and football at the same time without so much as craning your head. The menu includes an extensive seafood selection, pork chops, steak, chicken — and even grilled marinated alligator. All except a very few of the wines are from the North Fork and are available both by the glass and by the bottle; also there's a vast selection of more than 200 beers from twenty-six countries. Desserts include a chocolate-peanut butter pie and a walnut roll. This lively place has a happy hour on weekdays from 4pm–7pm, entertainment most Thurs. nights in summer, and nightly dinner specials, such as Mon. night prime rib for $12.95.

PORTO BELLO
631-477-1717.
74825 Main Rd., Greenport, NY 11944.
Owner: Francesca Divello.
Chef: Robert Howie.
Cuisine: Northern Italian.
Serving: D.

Open: Year-round.
Price: Expensive.
Credit Cards: AE, MC, V.
Special Features: Wheelchair access; outside patio dining.
Directions: On Main Rd. (Rte. 25) at Moores Ln.

Porto Bello has been a North Fork favorite since it first opened in the Stirling Harbor Marina in 1991. Now in new digs on Main Rd. (we miss that fabulous view), it sports a pretty interior of dark green walls and bentwood chairs. A bar on one side is separated from the formal dining room by a wall, and there's a patio for outside dining, although street noise could be troublesome. There's nothing troubling, however, about the food — fresh pastas and luscious, traditional northern Italian dishes, such as pollo alla griglia and vitello di scaloppine Marsala. The most popular dessert is a tiramisù.

ST. TROP CAFE - A BISTRO BY THE BAY
631-734-7888.
17475 Main St., New Suffolk.
Mailing Address: PO Box 38, New Suffolk, NY 11956.
Owners: Kathy and Michel Estienne.
Chef: Delia Wilbur.
Cuisine: North Fork Regional with French/Mediterranean flair.
Serving: L, D.
Open: Year-round: closed part of Feb., Mar.

Price: Inexpensive–Moderate.
Credit Cards: AE, MC, V.
Special Features: Wheelchair access; nonsmoking restaurant; waterfront dining.
Directions: From Rte. 25 in Cutchogue, turn south at light onto New Suffolk Rd. Drive 1.5 miles to blinking light. Turn left onto Main St. Restaurant is on left at end of street. Park in the boatyard.

This pretty waterside bistro takes full advantage of its setting. A row of windows stretches all along the waterside of both dining rooms (one with a fireplace), and there's a spacious outside deck at a lower level so as not to obstruct the view from the dining rooms. All tables overlook a marina on Peconic Bay. Marine blue tiles brighten the dining room, which is further enhanced by white tablecloths at night. Michel Estienne hails from Marseilles, and the seafood items on his menu reflect an especially light touch. One dish that's not light, however, is the fallen chocolate soufflé, which nevertheless should not be missed. Throughout the day, you can get wraps, burgers, pastas, and salads, as well as full meals.

THE SEAFOOD BARGE
631-765-3010.
62938 Main Rd. (Rte. 25), Southold, NY 11931.
Owner: Richard Ehrlicht.
Chef: Scott Jaffe.
Sushi Chef: David Huang.
Cuisine: Seafood and Sushi.

Serving: L, D.
Open: Daily.
Price: Inexpensive–Very Expensive.
Credit Cards: AE, D, MC, V.
Special Features: Wheelchair access; nonsmoking restaurant; waterfront dining.

Since being dubbed "the best restaurant on the North Fork" by the *New York Times*, The Seafood Barge, located at Port of Egypt Marina, has been packed, and it deserves to be. As one might expect, the entrées include a variety of fresh seafood that ranges from lobsters to sushi. One of my favorites, however, is the pepper-crusted swordfish, served with five-potato hash and baby bok choy. The setting is crisp and bright with royal blue tablecloths topped by butcher paper, white plates, and a bottle of wine on every table to serve as a reminder of the excellence of East End wines; the wine list includes over eighty wines, and 90 percent are from Long Island. The restaurant overlooks green lawns that slope to the boats in the marina beyond.

THE WILD GOOSE
631-734-4145.
4805 Depot Ln., Cutchogue, NY 11935.
Owners: Frank and Barbara Coe.
Chef: Frank Coe.
Cuisine: Seasonal and regional local North Fork cuisine.

Serving: L, D, BR (Sun. only).
Open: Year-round.
Price: Expensive.
Credit Cards: D, DC, MC, V.
Directions: From Rte. 48, turn right onto Depot Ln. Restaurant is on right in about 1/4 mile.

Ebullient and loquacious, Frank Coe seems to have found his niche in this formerly seedy bar-turned upscale restaurant. He'll tell you that he and his wife Barbara spent weeks on their hands and knees peeling away years of gunk to uncover the gleaming brass foot rail on the bar and the oak floors in the three dining rooms. They cleaned the tin ceiling in the bar, the wainscotted walls in one room, and the knotty pine in another, and then they sponge-painted the walls of the third in a mellow yellow. (They're still working on the exterior.) Frank's culinary pedigree is impeccable. He has worked in the kitchens of Daniel and Le Bernardin in Manhattan, and his menu reflects a distinct French influence. (Although born in Ireland, his mother was a pastry chef in Lyon, France.) You might order an appetizer of smoked eel and fois gras, for example, then dine on magret of free-range duck with a cherry-brandy sauce accompanied by a pyramid of wild rice and a fricassée of vegetables. Those veggies, by the way, will most likely have come from the herb and vegetable garden that Frank planted behind his new spot.

CAFES

Bruce's Cafe (631-477-0023; 208 Main St., Greenport, NY 11944) Open in summer: daily 8am–6pm; in winter: closed several days. Owner: Bruce Bollman. Choose from over thirty varieties of coffee and a gourmet array of cheeses and pâtés, as well as candy from the **Greenport Fudge Factory**, which has its own counter where you can buy fudge in a variety of flavors. This little café with its tin ceiling, tile floor, Victorian fretwork, and marble-topped tables is a popular local spot. For breakfast, you can have freshly baked pear-raisin or other varieties of muffins, or perhaps an omelette; in the afternoon, there are salads, sandwiches on homemade bread, and ice-cream concoctions that can be eaten at tables outside under the awning. Naturally, cappuccino and espresso are available, and this is the ideal place to put together a winery tour picnic.

Modern Snack Bar (631-722-3655; 628 Main Rd. (Rte. 25), PO Box 930, Aquebogue, NY 11931) Open daily lunch and dinner; closed Mon. Far more than a snack bar, this North Fork institution offers humble decor but terrific food. You can get Long Island duck or bay scallops accompanied by mashed turnips (a signature dish) and Long Island wines. Or, you can stop as you drive by to pick up one of their homemade pies.

The Star Confectionery, with its ornate tin ceiling, beautiful Victorian lighting fixtures, oak booths, and hexagon-tiled floor offers a wonderful journey into yesteryear — and you can still get an old-fashioned ice -cream soda at the counter.

Suzi Forbes Chase

Star Confectionery (631-727-9873; 4 East Main St., Riverhead, NY 11901) Open Mon.–Sat. 7am–5pm. Owners: The Meras family. You can step back to circa 1911 in this wonderful, old-fashioned soda fountain and luncheonette — all in perfect condition. The elaborate stained glass over the front windows, the tin ceiling, the hexagon-tiled floor, the old soda counter with its tiny stools, and the oak booths are all exactly as they were when this place originally became an ice-cream parlor in 1911. Remarkably, it's remained in the same family since 1920, and they obviously take great pride in its beauty and eats. You can get a banana split made with homemade ice cream, juicy hamburgers, or a grilled cheese sandwich, among other old favorites. There's even a candy counter stocked with homemade candies (for the holidays, they even make their own chocolates). This is a treasure not to be missed.

FOOD PURVEYORS

A trip to the North Fork in June yields U-pick, farm-fresh strawberries — in the fall, apples. Throughout the summer, farm stands are filled with fresh fruit, flowers, and vegetables. The following are only a few of the excellent resources on the North Fork that frequently lure restaurateurs and food shop owners from Manhattan.

For fresh-from-the-farm produce and flowers, as well as delectable pies, head for Briermere Farm.

Suzi Forbes Chase

Briermere Farm (631-722-3931; 4414 Sound Ave., Riverhead, NY 11901) Open in summer: daily 8am–6pm; in winter: shorter hours. The fresh vegetables and fruits from the farm are displayed on a covered porch at this roadside stand, but those in the know never stop here without also going inside to the bakery. This is where you can buy the same fabulous pies that are served in several fine local restaurants. All of the cream pies are "to die for," but I can never resist the raspberry cream pie or the blueberry-peach cream pie. I usually call to reserve one in advance if I know I'm coming that way, because they quickly sell out; also, if you've ordered in advance, you don't need to stand in the long line — just tell the clerk at the produce counter, and he or she will fetch it for you.

Crescent Duck Farm (631-722-8700; Edgar Ave., PO Box 1150, Aquebogue, NY 11931) No retail outlet, call for availability. At one time in the 1960s, there were sixty duck farms in the South Fork village of Quogue alone, and Long Island duckling gained a nationwide reputation. Now Crescent Duck Farm is the only one remaining on either the North or the South Fork. This farm has been in the Corwin family since the 1600s, and they have been raising ducks used by the finest East Coast restaurants since 1908.

George Braun Oyster Co. (631-734-6700; Main Rd., PO Box 971, Cutchogue, NY 11935) Open daily 8am–6pm. George Braun is often rated the best fish market on the East End by local residents. Founded in 1928, the company is the Cadillac of seafood markets, offering homemade clam or lobster pies and a wide selection of fresh fish and shellfish. Most local restaurants and many restaurants in Manhattan are supplied by George Braun. For the freshest Peconic Bay scallops, striped bass, flounder, oysters, and clams, this is the place to come.

Golden Earthworm Organic Farm (631-722-3302; 633 Peconic Bay Blvd., South Jamesport; mail: PO Box 871, Jamesport, NY 11947) Open growing season (end of May–mid-Nov.): Thurs. 11am–5pm, Fri., Sat. 9am–5pm, Sun. 9am–3pm. Owners: Matthew Kuszynski and Esther Wells. This 20-acre farm is certified 100 percent organic (no synthetic fertilizers or pesticides or genetically modified organisms) so what they grow is good for the soil and good for you. Throughout the season you will find the freshest produce grown (tomatoes, mesclun, apples, berries, onions, potatoes), and it comes direct from the field to you. You can also get handmade soaps and several other locally made products here.

Orient Country Store (631-323-2580; 930 Village Ln., PO Box 387, Orient, NY 11957) Open Mon.–Sat. 7:30am–5:30pm, Sun. 8:30am–5pm. This quaint store is a throwback to another era. It has its original wooden floors and a three-stool counter in the back for coffee or a sandwich. The prices are old-fashioned, too. A huge Reuben sandwich, for example, is still $2.50. It's next door to the old post office, where wooden floors, old-fashioned brass stamp windows, and brass mailboxes with combination locks continue to prevail.

Sang Lee Farms (631-734-7001; 25180 Rte. 48, Peconic, NY 11958) Open daily 9am–6pm. Not only does the North Fork have great growing conditions for grapes, but also for other produce. In 1999, this roadside stand opened to sell the Oriental vegetables and produce grown on this farm. You can get fresh mesclun, bok choy, napa cabbage, guy lon, and more.

Wickham's Fruit Farm (631-734-6441; Main Rd. (Rte. 25), Cutchogue, NY 11935) Open Apr.–Dec.: Mon.–Sat. 9am–5pm. It was John Wickham who first experimented with grape growing in the 1950s, providing the start of the North Fork's prized industry. Today, the family grows a variety of fruit that includes apples, peaches, nectarines, pears, apricots, cherries, grapes, raspberries, strawberries, and melons. Call the farm to find out about U-pick days for apples, blackberries, raspberries, strawberries, and cherries. You also can buy delicious fruit pies, fruit breads, jams and jellies, and apple cider at the farm stand in season.

Will Miloski's Poultry Farm (631-727-0239; 4418 Rte. 25, Calverton, NY 11933) Open Feb.–Dec.: Wed.–Mon. 8:30am–5:30pm; closed Tues. Raises free-range chickens, ducks, geese, and turkeys, as well as supplying venison, pheasants, and buffalo. This is where many local restaurants get their meats. You can get homemade frozen chicken and turkey pot pies, fruit pies, and fresh eggs, as well as ready-to-go rotisseried chickens and other BBQ meats.

WINESHOPS

Claudio's Wines and Liquor (631-477-1035; 219 Main St., Greenport, NY 11944) Open in summer: Mon.–Thurs. 10am–7:30pm, Fri., Sat. 10am–9:30; in winter: Mon.–Thurs. 9am–6:30pm, Fri., Sat. 9am–8pm. Owner: Harvey Katz. An excellent selection of Long Island wines, as well as other wines.

Peconic Liquors (631-734-5859; Main Rd., PO Box 901, Cutchogue, NY 11935) Open daily 9am–8pm. Owners: Beverly Cierach and Cindy Richards. Located in King Kullen Shopping Plaza, this shop features an outstanding selection of local wines. Drop by for a friendly chat and guidance in making your selections from the knowledgeable owners.

Showcase Wine & Liquor (631-765-2222; 46455 Rte. 48, Southold, NY 11971) Open Mon.–Thurs. 9am–7pm, Fri., Sat. 9am–8pm. Owner: Corinne Ferdenzi; Manager: Mike Ricciardi. This very attractive and well-organized shop offers the largest selection of Long Island wines on the North Fork.

SHOPPING

This new Polo Ralph Lauren Store opened in 2000 in the Tanger Factory Outlet Center in Riverhead.

Dustin Chase

Like an explosion, the ***Tanger Factory Outlet Center*** (631-369-2732; 800-4-TANGER; 1770 West Main Rd., Riverhead, NY 11901; on Rte. 25 at end of I-495, the Long Island Expressway) has hit the shopping scene. Open Mon.–Sat. 10am–9pm, Sun. 10am–7pm. Opened in 1994, by 1996, there were almost seventy outlet stores, and by 1997, another forty to fifty were added — by 2000, the number had escalated to 170. The shops currently range from The Gap and

Reebok to Brooks Brothers, Barneys, Lenox, Royal Doulton, The J. Peterman Co., Ann Taylor, and a gorgeous new Polo Ralph Lauren building that opened in the fall of 2000.

ANTIQUES

Antiques and Old Lace (631-734-6462; 31935 Main Rd., Cutchogue, NY 11935) Open daily 11am–5pm. Owners: Gene and Pat Mott. You'll find 5,000 square feet of space in this shop filled with interesting furniture that ranges from armoires to curved glass china cabinets to oak rolltop desks, as well as Oriental rugs, clocks, baskets, art glass, and more.

The Furniture Store Antiques (631-477-2980; 214 Front St., Greenport, NY 11944) Open daily 12 noon–5pm. Owners: Jay and Miz Johnson. Vintage clothing and linen, china and glassware, jewelry, and furniture are all sold here. Don't miss the hallway with all of the old tools or the back room that may have an old woodstove.

Jan Davis Antiques/L. I. Doll Hospital (631-765-2379; 45395 Main Rd., PO Box 1604, Southold, NY 11971) Open in summer: daily 12 noon–5pm; closed Tues., Wed.; in winter: shorter hours. Owner: Jan Davis. This quality road-side shop was built as a country store in 1856. Today, you'll find Victorian furniture, light fixtures, sterling silver candlesticks, glassware, and dolls that range from bisque to Mme. Alexander. Jan expertly repairs dolls, so you'll find several in the back room being elegantly coiffed or gowned.

Kapell Antiques (631-477-0100; 400 Front St. (Rte. 25), Greenport, NY 11944) Open daily 9am–5pm. Owner: David Kapell. This shop is located in a great old building that houses a real estate agency run by Mr. Kapell, who is also the mayor of Greenport. The antiques are of the highest quality and include massive desks, dining room tables, a giant old scale, ship models, paintings, folk art, early tools, and an impressive selection of vintage Steinway pianos. Don't miss the monthly flea markets!

The Pickwick Shop (631-765-3158; 45475 Main Rd. (Rte. 25), Southold, NY 11971) Open year-round: daily 11:30am–5:30pm; closed Tues., Wed. Owner: Roberta Hering. This little shop has a mix of all sorts of things from furniture to Wedgwood china.

BOOKS

Burton's Bookstore (631-477-1161; 43 Front St., Greenport, NY 11944) Open year-round: Mon.–Sat. 10am–5pm, Sun. 12:30pm–4:30pm. Owner: George Maaiki. This complete bookstore carries a wide selection of hardbound and paperback books, greeting cards, and calendars.

GALLERIES & GIFTS

The colorful window displays of imported hand-painted ceramic vases, urns, and cachepots irresistibly lure you into The Doofpot in Greenport.

Suzi Forbes Chase

The Doofpot (631-477-0344; 308 Main St., Greenport, NY 11944) Open May–Dec.: daily 10am–5pm; shorter hours rest of year. Owners: Maryanna Zovko and Jaap Hilbrand. Located in Stirling Sq., this unique shop carries a marvelous array of brilliant, hand-painted ceramic vases, cachepots, urns, wall frescos, and tables, selected by the owner and imported from Italy and Spain. You'll also find luminous Venetian glass and chandeliers.

The Down Home Store (631-734-6565; 37070 Main Rd., Cutchogue, NY 11935) Open Mar.–Dec.: Mon.–Sat. 10am–5pm, Sun. 11am–5pm; closed Tues. Owner: Terry Hofer. Once you see the marvelous array of handcrafted items in this shop, you will come back again and again. You will find elegantly painted furniture in faux finishes, plus furniture hand-painted with flowers and wildlife. There are small rugs, dried herb wreathes, hammocks, teddy bears, birdhouses, china, and splatterware.

Gazebo Gallery (631-477-1410; 124 Main St., Greenport, NY 11944) Open in summer: 9am–6pm; weekends only spring, fall; closed Nov.–Mar. Owner: Jane Schumacher. Jane is a local artist who specializes in oil and watercolor paintings, featuring flowers and seascapes. Her wonderful, luminous, brilliantly hued and detailed paintings can be purchased in a variety of sizes at her shop.

Island Artists Gallery (631-477-3070; 429 Main St., Greenport, NY 11944) Open daily 12 noon–5:30pm. This co-op artists' gallery sells works made by local artists. You will find watercolors, oils, stained and etched glass, and art in a variety of other mediums.

Jamesport Country Store (631-722-8048; Main Rd. (Rte. 25), Jamesport, NY 11947) Open daily 10am–5:30pm. Owner: Howard Woldman. This great old brick building with wooden floors houses a terrific little country store that carries such items as beach plum jam and honey, wicker, baskets, candles,

Although in her 80s, Jane Schumacher's floral and landscape paintings are as luminous as ever. She opened her delightful gallery 30 years ago, and devoted collectors continue to arrive to purchase her latest pieces.

Dustin Chase

and most other things that you think a country store should carry, except groceries, of course.

Old Town Arts & Crafts Guild (631-734-6382; 28265 Main Rd. (Rte. 25), Cutchogue, NY 11935) Open July–Aug.: Mon.–Sat. 10am–5pm, Sun. 12 noon–5pm; weekends rest of year; closed: mid-Dec.–mid-May. This co-op of North Fork artists was founded in 1948 and displays and sells members' high-quality art that includes knit work, patchwork quilts, jewelry, oil and watercolor paintings, toys, carved wooden items, ceramics, and pottery.

Preston's Outfitters and Preston's Ship and Sea Gallery (631-477-1990; www. prestons.com; 102 Main St., Greenport, NY 11944) Open daily 9am–6pm. Owner: George Rowsom. Located on Preston's Wharf, Preston's Ships Chandlery has been outfitting ships and their sailing crews since 1883. Today, nautical needs are still supplied, as well as clothing. In addition, a marvelous shop full of nautical gifts brings shoppers from miles around. There are ship models, hundreds of paintings and prints, scrimshaw, Nantucket baskets, shells, and so much more. If it's a nautical object, it's likely Preston's will have it. If you can't get here in person, call to receive the catalog.

Southold Historical Society Gift Shop (631-765-5500; 54325 Main Rd., Southold, NY 11971) Open Mem. Day–Christmas: Tues.–Sat. 10am–4pm. You'll find interesting items here that you won't find elsewhere. Pretty white lace parasols, lovely lined baskets, T-shirts, books, quilts, pottery, and antiques, such as a roll-armed wicker rocker. Many of the items are new, but the antiques are in excellent condition. **The Treasure Exchange** (631-765-1550), a consignment shop across the street, sells items such as antique furniture, silver, and china.

Sweet Indulgences (631-477-8250; 200 Main St., Greenport, NY 11944) Open in summer: daily 10am–6pm, except Fri., Sat. 10am–9pm; shorter hours rest of year. Don't let the name fool you! Angela Oliveri and Frank Deroski have filled their charming shop with wonderful gifts and craft items, including collectible Santas, candles, and much more, as well as Godiva chocolates and lots of other candies.

HOUSEWARES

Cookery Dock (631-477-0059; 132 Main St., Greenport, NY 11944) Open in summer: daily 10am–5pm. Owner: Arlene Marvin. This fine cooking shop has all of the things that we need to be great cooks, including pots and pans, pot holders, cookbooks, and much more.

PHOTOGRAPHY SHOPS

Camera Concepts (631-727-3283; 21 East Main St., Riverhead, NY 11901) Open Mon.–Sat. 10am–5:30pm. This full-service camera shop carries video cameras and supplies as well as still cameras. They also process film and carry one of the largest selections of telescopes on Long Island.

Mike Richter Photography (631-477-0479; 207 Main St., Greenport, NY 11944) Open in summer: Mon.–Sat. 9am–6pm, Sun. 11am–4pm; shorter hours rest of year. From cameras to film, frames to gifts, this shop has it all. Mike is also available for special photography assignments.

CULTURE

CALENDAR OF EVENTS

Especially during the summer and fall, the wineries hold events that range from dinners to concerts, from theatrical productions to poetry readings and murder mystery events. The *Long Island Wine Council* (631-369-5887) puts out a weekly newsletter listing the events. You can also check the local newspapers or call the wineries for their individual schedule.

March

Easter Egg Hunt (631-298-5248) Every year on the Sat. before Easter, Mattituck Historical Society holds its popular Easter Egg Hunt.

May

Antique and Classic Boat Show (631-477-2100) For 20 years, Greenport has featured more than 40 wooden boats of all styles in its Classic Boat Show. Call East End Seaport Maritime Museum for information.

Memorial Day Parade (631-765-5500) Southold Historical Society holds a Founder's Day weekend that includes a parade and Civil War encampment.

June

The Mattituck Strawberry Festival (631-298-2222) Eagerly awaited each year, the festival is sponsored by Mattituck Lions Club. There are over 250 booths, featuring arts and crafts, as well as strawberry shortcake for everyone.

July

Antiques Show and Sale Sponsored by Cutchogue/New Suffolk Historical Council, this show (now in its 38th year) takes place on the village green in Cutchogue. There are almost 100 dealers, as well as a bake sale.

Croquet Tournament (631-323-2480) Orient. Held in late July or early Aug., this annual event is sponsored by Oysterponds Historical Society.

Fourth of July Parades There are parades on the Fourth of July in New Suffolk and Southold.

Gem, Mineral, and Jewelry Show Mattituck. This annual event, now in its 20th year, is held at Mattituck High School on the last weekend in July.

Greenport Carnival Greenport. This carnival ends with a fireworks display on both Sat. and Sun. of Independence Day weekend.

July 4th Music Festival (631-727-0900) This all-day, annual event in Riverhead has featured such national artists as the Benny Goodman Orchestra and Richie Havens. Sponsored by East End Arts Council.

Mattituck Street Fair (631-298-1452) The village of Mattituck has a street fair on historic Love Ln., the second Sat. in July every year.

Opera in the Hamptons (631-728-8804) A series of opera performances (*La Boheme* and *Tosca*, for example) are performed both on the North and the South Forks.

August

Cutchogue Library Annual Book Sale (631-734-6360) Once a year Friends of the Cutchogue Free Library hold a book sale.

Ice-Cream Social (631-765-5500) Southold. Southold Historical Society holds an ice-cream social that includes hayrides, face painting, and of course, ice cream.

Outdoor Arts & Crafts Show (631-734-6382) Cutchogue. Now almost 50 years old, this event takes place on the village green. Members of Old Town Arts and Crafts Guild display and sell their work using snow fences as props.

Polish Festival Riverhead has been noted for this 2-day festival for a number of years. Booths serve kielbasa and funnel cakes. Polish crafts abound, and the Polka Festival attracts hundreds of avid dancers.

September

Craft Fair (631-765-3161) Local crafts are displayed and sold. Sponsored by Greenport/Southold Chamber of Commerce.

Harvest Festival Mattituck Chamber of Commerce holds an annual Harvest Festival and Clam Chowder Contest each year in Sept.

Historic Seaport Regatta (631-477-2121) An annual sailing event in early Sept. between Greenport and Sag Harbor.

Jazz Festival (631-744-7697) Annual Jazz Festival sponsored by The Arts in Southold town and held at Southold High School.

Maritime Festival and Fishing Tournament (631-477-0004) This festival is held annually in Greenport Harbor and includes a wooden boat parade and regatta, wine and seafood tasting, and much more. Sponsored by East End Seaport and Marine Foundation of Greenport.

November

Christmas Open House (631-323-2655) Cutchogue. In late Nov., Old Town Arts and Crafts Guild holds this annual event.

December

Christmas House Tour (631-323-2480) Orient. Sponsored yearly by Oysterponds Historical Society.

MOVIES

Mattituck Cinemas (631-298-4400; Main Rd. (Rte. 25), Mattituck, NY 11952) Open year-round: every night. Located in the Mattituck Plaza near the A&P, this is an eight-plex theater, showing first-run movies.

Village Cinema Greenport (631-477-8600; 211 Front St., Greenport, NY 11944) Open Apr.–Dec.: every night, with matinees on weekends; Dec.–Apr.: may be open only on weekends. This is a four-plex theater, showing first-run movies.

MUSEUMS & OTHER SITES

CUTCHOGUE

CUTCHOGUE-NEW SUFFOLK HISTORICAL COUNCIL
631-734-7122.
Main Rd., Cutchogue, NY 11935.

Open: July–Aug.: Sat.–Mon. 1pm–4pm; shorter hours rest of year.
Fee: None.

Located on the village green, this interesting collection of historic buildings was assembled through a community effort that began in 1959 with a query from the Smithsonian Institution about North Fork Indians. Mounting one of the finest historic preservation efforts on the East End, community-spirited citizens moved and restored the buildings now included in this complex.

The oldest building is the circa 1649 Old House, which is one of the oldest houses in New York State. It is furnished with handcrafted furniture and accessories of the period, creating a unique example of how early East End settlers lived. The Wickham Farmhouse, which dates to 1704, served as a Wickham family home for more than 250 years. It is a double Cape Cod-style farmhouse, furnished with a variety of eighteenth- and twentieth-century antiques. The Old Schoolhouse was built in 1840 and served as a one-room school until 1903. The Carriage House dates to the early nineteenth century and now contains an old carriage and the council's information center.

ORIENT

This former village inn serves as the headquarters of the Oysterponds Historical Society in Orient.

Dustin Chase

**OYSTERPONDS HISTORICAL
   SOCIETY**
631-323-2480.
Village Ln., Orient, NY 11957.

Open: Tours June–Sept.: Thurs., Sat., Sun.
   2pm–5pm.
Fee: Adults $3; children $.50.

The Oysterponds Historical Society in the delightful hamlet of Orient, which is a designated National Historic District, includes a variety of nineteenth-century buildings. In the former village inn, the parlors, dining room, and kitchen are furnished in a style that reflects a range of periods from 1790-1940; there is also a marvelous toy and train collection. The Old Point Schoolhouse was built in 1873 and contains a library of historical documents. The Amanda Brown Schoolhouse serves as the Beach Plum Museum Shop, where society members sell craft items. One of the most interesting buildings in the collection, the Webb House, is an authentic "George Washington Slept Here" structure, since he rested in the house in 1757 when traveling to Boston to receive his commission to lead the Virginia troops into battle prior to the American Revolution. The house was then owned by Lt. Constant Booth and was located in Greenport. This beautiful building was later moved to this site and expertly restored. The society sponsors frequent walking tours of the village, a holiday house tour, an annual croquet tournament, and numerous cultural events, such as Gilbert and Sullivan musicals and plays.

RIVERHEAD

ATLANTIS MARINE WORLD
631-208-9200.
www.atlantismarineworld.com.
431 East Main St., Riverhead, NY 11901.

Open: In summer: daily 9am–8pm; rest of year: daily 9am–6pm.
Fee: Adults $11.50; seniors over 62 $10; children 3-11 $9.

In partnership with the Riverhead Foundation for Marine Research and Preservation (631-369-9840) and the Cornell Cooperative Extension's Marine Division, Atlantis Marine World, which opened in 2000, includes a live coral reef, tanks of sharks, seals (there's a show), and several touch tanks. The setting is designed to conjure visions of the lost city of Atlantis so you walk through passageways that look like coral reefs with colorful fish tanks on either side. There's a little cylinder of sea horses, a submarine simulator, and more. Atlantis also operates the *Atlantis Explorer*, an excursion boat that takes participants on a 2.5-hour environmental tour of the Peconic River and Flanders Bay. A naturalist explains the ecosystem, and guests participate in trap pulls, plankton tows, and more. The cost is adults $17 and seniors and children under 12 $15.

The mission of the Foundation is to treat and release wounded or stranded marine life, and you can view the turtles, dolphins, whales, porpoises, and seals that they are assisting in one area of the aquarium. This is a wonderful place for children to become acquainted with the fragility of the sea and the sea creatures and environmental concerns associated with the ocean. During the whale migration season in summer, the Foundation also sponsors bus trips to Plymouth, MA, where you are guaranteed to see whales. Price for trip: adults $69; seniors $64; children 12 and under $59.

THE BIG DUCK
631-852-8292.
Rte. 24, Riverhead.
Mailing Address: PO Box 144, West Sayville, NY 11796.

Open: Mid-May–mid-Sept.: daily 10am–5pm; mid-Sept.–Christmas: selected weekends only.
Admission: None.

Recognized as one of the most famous examples of roadside art in America, this gigantic white duck measures 30 feet long and 20 feet high. It was built in 1931 to attract customers to the Big Duck Ranch. The inside was a salesroom where clients could purchase Peking duck, otherwise known as Long Island Duckling. Today, it's a tourist information center, where Long Island gifts and "duck-a-bilia" are sold. Operated by the Friends for Long Island's Heritage.

**HALLOCKVILLE MUSEUM FARM
　AND FOLKLIFE CENTER**
631-298-5292.
6038 Sound Ave. (Rte. 48), Riverhead, NY
　11901.

Open: Apr.–mid-Dec.: Tues.–Sat. 12
　noon–4pm; by appt. rest of year.
Fee: Adults $4; children and seniors $3.

Peter Hallock was one of the first settlers on the North Fork, and this was his
family homestead. The farm, which is on the National Register of Historic
Places, was in the Hallock family for almost 200 years, and it's remained virtually intact. Children and adults will see how a turn-of-the-century farm operated. Included are the 1765 Hallock Homestead, furnished as it would have
been from 1880-1910, with shoemaker's shop, smokehouse, workshops, large
English-style barn, and outhouse. The Museum Farm is also home of the
Suffolk County Folklife Center. Craft demonstrations, festivals, school programs, and special summer camps take place here; they might include decoy
carving, whittling, quill pen making, fishnet mending, or horseshoeing. The
Hallock family still gathers at the family farm once a year for the annual picnic.

**SUFFOLK COUNTY HISTORICAL
　SOCIETY**
631-727-2881.
300 West Main St., Riverhead, NY 11901.

Open: Tues.–Sat. 12:30pm–4:30pm;
　research library open Wed., Thurs., Sun.
Fee: None.

The Suffolk County Historical Society is the second-oldest historical society
on Long Island. The museum, research library, archives, and education
programs offer a glimpse into the rich life of Suffolk County. In addition, the
Weathervane gift shop has unusual gift items that include historical books and
maps, as well as genealogical supplies.

SOUTHOLD

CUSTER INSTITUTE
631-765-2626.
Bayview Rd., Southold, NY 11971.
Open: Every Sat. night at dusk, or call

Barbara Latuna (516-722-3850) for appt.
　and schedule of events.
Fee: Donation.

The Custer Institute is an astronomical observatory with an auditorium,
library, and small museum. It is open to the public every Sat. night to observe
stars, planets, and meteors. Concerts, classic films, art exhibits, lectures, and other
cultural events are held year-round, and an astronomy jamboree, which includes
lectures, solar viewing, and stargazing, is held every fall.

**HORTON POINT LIGHTHOUSE AND
　NAUTICAL MUSEUM**
631-765-2101.
Lighthouse Rd. at Long Island Sound,
　Southold.

Mailing Address: PO Box 1, Southold, NY
　11971.
Open: Mem. Day–Columbus Day: Sat.,
　Sun. 11:30am–4pm.
Fee: Donation suggested, adults $2.

The Horton Point Lighhouse was built in 1857 and continues to protect ships from the hazardous shoreline.

Suzi Forbes Chase

Although construction was not completed until 1857, the Horton Point Lighthouse was commissioned by President George Washington in 1790. It served as one of the links in the chain of lighthouses that guided ships through the treacherous inlets and rocky points of Long Island Sound. The light was removed from the lighthouse in 1933 and installed on a tower nearby, but it was reinstalled in 1990 as part of the renovation of the lighthouse. Although the light continues to serve its original function and is maintained by the U.S. Coast Guard, the museum in the base is operated by the Southold Historical Society. The Nautical Museum contains sea chests, paintings, maps, ships' logs, and other remnants of the active North Fork shipping trade. A climb up the stairs to the tower to see the light will be rewarded by a fine view of Long Island Sound.

SOUTHOLD HISTORICAL SOCIETY
631-765-5500.
54325 Main Rd. (at Maple Ln.), Southold.
Mailing Address: PO Box 1, Southold, NY 11971.
Open: In summer only: Wed., Sat., Sun. 1pm–4pm; gift shop in Prince Bldg. on Main St., open May–Christmas: Thurs.–Sat. 10am–4pm; The Treasure Exchange, consignment shop, open May–Nov.: Thurs.–Sat. 10am–4pm.
Fee: $2 donation suggested.

The Southold Historical Society maintains and operates a collection of buildings in the center of Southold that includes the 1900 Ann Currie Bell Hallock House & Buttery; 1750 Thomas Moore House; 1842 Cleveland Grover Gagen Blacksmith Shop; Downs Carriage House circa 1840; Pine Neck Barn circa eighteenth century; and Bay View School circa 1822. There's a wonderful millinery display of nineteenth- and twentieth-century hats and fabrics, and you'll learn about spinning and weaving, scrimshaw, old ovens and fireplaces, and so much more. The society maintains its headquarters in the ornate Prince Bldg. on Main St., where its delightful gift shop is located. The Treasure

Exchange, a consignment shop, is located on the museum grounds and sells antique furniture, silverware, and china. Events such as garden tours and ice-cream socials are held on occasion.

SOUTHOLD INDIAN MUSEUM
631-765-5577.
Bayview Rd., Southold.
Mailing Address: PO Box 268, Southold, NY 11971.

Open: Year-round: Sun. 1:30pm–4:30pm; Sat. also, Mem. Day–Labor Day.
Fee: Adults $2; children $.50.

The Southold Indian Museum was organized in 1925 and is now incorporated by the Long Island Chapter of the New York State Archaeological Association. The museum is noted for its extensive collection of local Algonquin Indian artifacts, many of which were found on the North Fork of Long Island. There are several items that date more than 10,000 years ago. The collection includes not only arrowheads and spears, but it also displays many pieces of pottery unearthed nearby. In a dramatic illustration of how advanced this agrarian society was when the first English settlers arrived in 1640, an exhibit of various corn types illustrates the farming techniques used.

MUSIC, THEATER, CULTURAL EVENTS

Glenn Horowitz-Bookseller

The Greenport Brass Band was formed in 1851 as part of the New York State Militia. They were so popular in the early 1900s that folks came out on steamers from New York City to hear the concerts.

The North Fork made musical history with the **Greenport Brass Band,** which was formed initially in 1851 as part of the New York State Militia. Their popularity was so great in the early 1900s that folks would come to Greenport on a steamer from New York City just to listen to the concerts. The concerts are still held every Friday at 8pm in the summer and continue to draw crowds.

The wineries sponsor a number of interesting cultural activities during the summer. Palmer Vineyard, for instance, sometimes has a *Victorian Murder Mystery,* which is performed by the Wild Thyme Players; a winery tour is included. At other times, a popular poetry series called *Voices on the Vine* is held. *Summer Showcase Outdoor Concerts* take place weekly throughout the summer at the Silversmiths Corner on Town Green in Southold. Past events have included performances by The Bay Chamber Players, North Fork Fiddler and Friends, Barber Shop Harmony, and Clinton Church Gospel Choir.

The *North Fork Community Theatre* presents summer theatrical productions in a church in Mattituck and *Opera of the Hamptons* features opera performances in July.

RECREATION

AIRPLANE RIDES

Sea Island Seaplane Tours (631-477-3730; Mitchell Park Marina, Greenport, NY 11944) You can take a narrated seaplane tour of the North Fork and Shelter Island in this 5-passenger plane. The cost for a 15–25-minute ride is adults $36; children 12 and under $21.

AUTO RACING

Riverhead Raceway (631-842-RACE; 631-727-0010; www.riverheadraceway.com; Rte. 58, Riverhead; mail: PO Box 148, Lindenhurst, NY 11757) Admission: adults $16–$25; $5 children 6–12; complimentary under 6. Rev your engines because every Sat. night, there's a NASCAR stock car race, plus demolition derbies, school bus races, monster truck events, and more.

BEACHES, PARKS, NATURE PRESERVES

Just as on the South Fork, car parking permit stickers are required at all town and village beaches. In Riverhead Town, which includes Aquebogue and Jamesport, an annual parking permit sticker is $10/day and $75/year for nonresidents. In Southold Town, the parking fee is $8.66 daily/$32.48 season. A nonresident season pass can be obtained for $108.25. The following beaches and many more are open to the public.

Indian Island County Park (631-852-3232; Riverside Dr. (Rte. 105), Riverhead, NY 11901) This 274-acre Suffolk County Park at the mouth of the Peconic River is rich with birds and wildlife that nest among the trees and marshes. The park contains 150 campsites, which cost $13/night for county residents with a Suffolk County "Green Key Card" ($20, good for 3 years); $23 nonresidents. There are also group camping areas, picnic areas, hiking trails, long stretch of sandy beach (no lifeguard), and a playground for children. In addition, canoeing, fishing, and bird-watching are encouraged.

Orient Beach State Park (631-323-2440; Rte. 25, Orient, NY 11957) $7 parking Mem. Day–Labor Day. Consistently rated as the best beach on the North Fork, this is far more than just a beach. There's a concession stand that serves local seafood and where you can participate in barbecues on the weekends, bathhouse with showers and rest rooms, playground, and picnic area with grills. This long spit of land, jutting 4 miles out into Gardiner's Bay, is packed with swimmers and picnickers in summer. For those who like to walk, a hike from the parking lot along Long Beach to the point will pass ponds, marshes, and numerous birds (sometimes osprey on nests on high poles and sometimes terns or plovers in cordoned-off areas) and will end at a new lighthouse.

BICYCLING

Bicycling on the North Fork is a pleasure. The land is flat, and the road shoulders are wide. There are relatively few cars and lots of roads to explore and sites to see. The following shops rent bicycles and provide parts and repairs.

Bike Stop (631-477-2432; 200 Front St., Greenport, NY 11944) Open daily 10am–5pm. Rents new mountain bicycles $18/half-day, $22/full day; tandem bikes $30/half-day, $40/full day.

Country Bike Time Shoppe (631-298-8700; 6995 Main Rd. (Rte. 25), Mattituck, NY 11952) Owner: Greg Williams. Rents mountain bicycles $15/half-day, $22/day, $65/week. Expanded into a spacious new building in 1997, this is one of the largest bicycle shops in Suffolk County.

BOATING, CANOEING, FISHING

Eagle's Neck Paddling Company (631-765-3502; www.eaglesneck.com; 49295 Main Rd., Southold; mail: PO Box 83, Peconic, NY 11958) This company has kayaks for sale and to rent and provides paddling instructions. They also conduct guided kayak tours that include instructional lectures about the surrounding wildlife, geology, or stargazing. In addition, they offer a 2.5-hour sunset tour every Fri. and Sat. Rental fees: single kayak $25/half-day, $37/full day; double kayak $40/half-day, $60/full day. Guided tours range $45–$50.

Historic Schooner *Mary E* (631-477-8966; Preston's Dock, Greenport, NY 11944) Although the *Regina Maris* is no longer docked at Greenport (it's now undergoing restoration in Glen Cove), there is a tall ship in port that takes folks on cruises in the harbor. There are three sailings daily in summer, including a champagne sunset cruise. Prices for 2.5-hour sailing: adults $25; children $12.50.

Peconic Paddler in Riverhead rents a variety of canoes and kayaks for excursions along the Peconic River or in the bay.

Suzi Forbes Chase

Peconic Paddler (631-369-9500; 631-727-9895; www.peconicpaddler.com; 89 Peconic Ave., Riverhead, NY 11901) Open daily 8am–5pm; closed Tues. $45 per canoe/4–5-hour trip; $13/1 hour or $21/2 hours. Sea kayaks (depending on make) range $29–$69/day, $15–$29/hour. Weekly rates available also. Owner: Jim Dreeben. Peconic Paddler sells a wide variety of kayaks (over 400 in stock) and canoes; also has an extensive fleet available for rent. They will provide instructions, and they also make several trips a day to a spot 8 miles up the Peconic River, where they will put the canoe or kayak in the water and then let you drift back down at your own pace. In addition, they rent sea kayaks for adventures on Peconic Bay and in a nearby bird sanctuary. Many people take along a picnic lunch and make a day of it.

Peconic River Cruises (631-369-3700; www.PeconicRiverCruises.com; Riverhead Village Dock, PO Box 458, Riverhead, NY 11901) Open Apr.–Dec. You can have lunch, dinner, or brunch on this 111-foot authentically reproduced paddle wheeler as you cruise the Peconic Bay and Long Island Sound. Rates range $36.95–$51.95 (latter is for dinner/dance cruise with live entertainment). Several times during summer, there are also cruises to Greenport and to Sag Harbor; they are all-day cruises that do not include lunch and cost $24.95.

The Roadhouse (631-727-9856; 631-878-7937; 1111 West Main St. (Rte. 25), Riverhead, NY 11901) Open Mem. Day–Labor Day: daily. $35/day per canoe. You can rent canoes at a roadside stand situated next to this riverside pub. They will drive you and your canoe to a drop off either 9 miles up the river or 4.5 miles up, and you can spend a lazy day lollygagging along a tranquil and beautiful section of the Peconic River. You'll see birds and flowers and will be sheltered by overhanging trees. Then come back to The Roadhouse for a waterfront picnic or a burger. There are also outdoor picnic tables beside the river.

MARINAS

Brewer Yacht Yard (631-477-9594; 500 Beach Ave., Greenport, NY 11944) Part of the Brewer Yacht Marina network, a series of fine marinas located throughout New England and Long Island. Greenport has 200 slips and provides electric hookup, laundry, swimming pool, showers, rest rooms, and acclaimed sailing school. The Greenport Sailing School employs an instructor certified by the American Sailing School who teaches classes to beginning and advanced sailors on a variety of sailboats. The marina sponsors races, regattas, and trips to other member marinas. This is also the home of **Antaras Cafe** (see the section Restaurants & Food Purveyors), which is open Mar.–Dec.

Stirling Harbor Marina (631-477-0828; 1410 Manhanset Ave., Greenport, NY 11944) This is an exceptional marina and includes a full gym, aerobics classes, manicurist, masseuse, pedicurist, delivery of the *New York Times*, full laundry facilities (will do laundry for you and deliver to your boat), rest rooms, electric and cable hookup, and full repair services. There's also a fine Italian restaurant, **Bistro Blue** (see the section Restaurants & Food Purveyors), which is open mid-Apr.–Oct.

CHILDREN'S ACTIVITIES

Frank Field's Miniature Railroad For location, call or stop by North Fork Tourist Information Center (631-477-1383; Main Rd., Greenport, NY 11944). On a wooded piece of land on Middleton Rd. in Greenport, Frank Field gives complimentary rides to children on his marvelous miniature railroad every Sun. and holidays in summer.

Greenport Carousel (631-447-3000; Front St., Greenport, NY 11944) This is the temporary location until Greenport Waterfront Park is completed. When Grumman Aerospace Corporation employed thousands of people on Long Island, they maintained a lovely park on the North Shore where summer picnics, baseball games, and other recreation took place. The centerpiece of the park was a handsomely carved carousel. After the park closed, the ornate carousel sat idle for many years; its future sometimes debated, but often forgotten until the village of Greenport obtained it. Today's children can now ride the carousel in summer, but tomorrow's children will ride it in a handsome new domed pavilion that will be completed in 2001 as part of the wonderful new Greenport Waterfront Park. A competition to design the park, which will have a boardwalk, promenades, a pavilion for the celebrated carousel, and much more, attracted submissions from more than 300 recognized architects from around the world. Work will be completed in time for summer 2001.

Long Island Game Farm (631-878-6644; Chapman Blvd., PO Box 97, Manorville, NY 11949) Open Mem. Day–Columbus Day: daily 10am–6pm; briefly for Fall Harvest Festival and during Christmas holidays. Adults $12.95; seniors 60+ $7.95; children age 2–11 $10.95; children under 2 free. Open since 1970, there are train rides on a restored 1860s train, carousel, pony rides, in-the-wild animal show, and petting bambiland. Call for special events.

Splish Splash Water Park (631-727-3600; 2549 Middle Country Rd., Riverhead, NY 11901) Open Mem. Day–Labor Day: July–Aug. daily 9:30am–7pm; weekends only rest of season. Adults $24.95; seniors 62+ and children under 48 inches $16.95; parking $6. There are lockers, showers, and food facilities at this 40-acre water park, and the rides range from screechers to tame rides safe for small fry. There's a wave pool, cliff-diver ride, giant twister, shotgun falls, mammoth river rapids, plus soak city and lazy river ride. Be sure to come in bathing attire that has no buckles or other decor that might get caught.

GOLF

Cherry Creek Golf Links (631-369-8983; 631-369-7425; 800-883-5674 reservations only; www.cherrycreeklinks.com; 900 Reeves Ave., Riverhead, NY 11901) This 18-hole, par 73, 7,187-yard course opened in 1996 and includes a driving range, practice bunker, putting green, restaurant, and pro shop. It contains the only par 6 hole on Long Island. $20/weekdays, $25/weekends 9 holes; $35/$45 18 holes.

Indian Island Country Club and Golf Course (631-727-7776; 631-727-0788 restaurant; Riverside Dr. (Rte. 105), Riverhead, NY 11901) The manicured greens and gated entrance look more like an exclusive private club than a public golf course. Beautifully maintained by Suffolk County Dept. of Parks, Recreations, and Conservation, it's an 18-hole, par 72, 6,508/6,055-yard course with pro shop, clubhouse, lockers, showers, rental clubs and carts, and a very good restaurant serving breakfast, lunch, and dinner. The club and course are part of Indian Island County Park. $20/weekdays, $23/ weekends Suffolk County residents with 3-year pass; $30/weekdays, $35/weekends nonresidents.

Island's End Golf & Country Club (631-477-0777; Main Rd., PO Box 2066, Greenport, NY 11944) This golf course is actually part of a private club, but nonmembers are able to play for a fee. It's an 18-hole, par 72 course with driving range, pro shop, clubhouse, snack bar, restaurant, and rental clubs and carts. $34/weekdays, $40/weekends nonmembers.

Long Island National Golf Club (631-727-4653; 1793 Northville Tpke., Riverhead, NY 11901) Opened in 1999, this dramatic course, which was designed by Robert Trent Jones, Jr., features a spectacular natural-shingled clubhouse faced with massive white columns in a style similar to that designed by Stanford White for Shinnecock Hills. There's a lovely restaurant and bar, plus an extensive golf shop. The course is challenging to say the least, as it includes rolling hills with roughs similar to St. Andrews and three large lakes. It features 18 holes with a par 71 and extends over 6,800 yards. $50 early-bird play 9 holes; $110 18 holes.

HORSEBACK RIDING

Hedgewood Farm (631-298-9181; Main Rd., Laurel, NY 11948) This farm has a 12-acre riding facility where hunt seat equitation and western pleasure riding are taught. They have a lighted indoor arena that permits year-round lessons, conduct escorted trail rides, if given advance notice, and offer pony rides.

Hidden Lake Farms Riding School (631-765-9896; North Rd. (Rte. 48), Southold; mail: PO Box 269, Peconic, NY 11958) On this 95-acre spread, riders can learn to ride English-style and to fox hunt ("riding to the hounds"). Three large outdoor rings, pony camp, cross-country course, trails to the beach, and lighted indoor arena make this a very versatile school. Group and individual lessons can be arranged, plus escorted trail rides.

Hillcrest Sport Stable (631-369-1176; 1219 Middle Rd., Riverhead, NY 11901) This facility offers lessons in jumping, equitation, and dressage. They have an indoor arena, plus jumping ring and hunt course.

SCUBA DIVING

Hampton Dive Center (631-727-7578; 369 Flanders Rd. (Rte. 24), Riverhead, NY 11901) Hampton Dive Center is a scuba diving school that offers courses leading to scuba diving certification; courses are taught twice a week for 4 weeks and cost $149. Once certification is earned, they regularly take members on dives. Generally, the dives are nearby, either off the jetties on the South Fork or off boats nearby in the ocean, but they also sponsor diving trips to the Caribbean and other spots. You can rent scuba equipment, and they allow nonmembers to accompany them on local dives, which generally cost about $20 per trip.

Sound View Scuba Center (631-765-9515; North Rd. (Rte. 48), Southold, NY 11971) This full-service, year-round company offers sales of scuba diving equipment, as well as instruction leading to certification (cost $270). They also sell and rent kayaks, water skis, and wakeboards.

INFORMATION

EMERGENCY NUMBERS

In both Riverhead and Southold Towns, the **Police** and **Fire Emergency Number** is **911**.

AREA CODES

The area code for all Suffolk County is **631**. Frequently called nearby areas are as follows:

Location	Area Code
New York:	
Manhattan	212, 646
Brooklyn, Bronx, Queens,	
Staten Island	718
Nassau County	516
Westchester County	914
Connecticut:	
Western Coastal Connecticut	203
Eastern Connecticut	860

CHAMBERS OF COMMERCE

North Fork Tourist Information Center (631-477-1383; Main Rd. (Rte. 25), Greenport, NY 11944) Open May–Columbus Day weekend: daily 10am–4pm. Operated by North Fork Promotion Council Inc., PO Box 1865, Southold, NY 11971.

Riverhead Chamber of Commerce (631-727-7600; 540 East Main Rd., Riverhead, NY 11901) Open year-round: Mon.–Fri. 8:30am–4:30pm; Mem. Day–Labor Day: Sat. 8:30am–12 noon.

TOWN & VILLAGE OFFICES

Greenport Village Office (631-477-0248; 631-477-2385) 236 Third St., Greenport, NY 11944)

Riverhead Town Office (631-727-3200; 210 Howell Ave., Riverhead, NY 11901)

Southold Town Office (631-765-1800; 53095 Main Rd., Southold, NY 11971)

ZIP CODES

Town, Village, Hamlet	Zip Code
Aquebogue	11931
Cutchogue	11935
East Marion	11939

Town, Village, Hamlet	Zip Code
Greenport	11944
Jamesport	11947
Laurel	11948
Mattituck	11952
New Suffolk	11956
Orient	11957
Peconic	11958
Riverhead	11901
South Jamesport	11970
Southold	11971

BANKS WITH ATM MACHINES

Only the banks that have ATM machines have been listed below. Other banks are also located on the North Fork.

CUTCHOGUE

North Fork Bank and Trust Co. (631-734-6500; Main Rd., Cutchogue, NY 11935) ATM: Cirrus, Honor, MC, NYCE, Pulse.
Suffolk County National Bank (631-734-5050; 31525 Main Rd. (Rte. 25), Cutchogue, NY 11935) ATM: AE, Cirrus, D, Honor, MAC, MC, NYCE, Plus, Pulse, V.

GREENPORT

North Fork Bank and Trust Co. (631-477-0036; 230 Main St., Greenport, NY 11944) ATM: Cirrus, Honor, MC, NYCE, Pulse.

JAMESPORT

North Fork Bank and Trust Co. (631-722-3396; Main Rd., Jamesport, NY 11947) ATM: Cirrus, Honor, MC, NYCE, Pulse.

MATTITUCK

Bridgehampton National Bank (631-298-0190; Main Rd., Mattituck, NY 11952) ATM: AE, Cirrus, D, Honor, MAC, MC, Plus, V.
North Fork Bank and Trust Co. (631-298-5000; headquarters: 9025 Rte. 25, Mattituck, NY 11952; branches: 631-298-8884; 245 Love Ln. and 631-298-8882; 10095 Main Rd., Waldbaum Shopping Plaza, both in Mattituck, NY 11952) ATMs at both branches: Cirrus, Honor, MC, NYCE, Pulse.
Suffolk County National Bank (631-298-9400; 10900 Main Rd., Mattituck, NY 11952) ATM: AE, Cirrus, D, Honor, MAC, MC, NYCE, Plus, Pulse, V.

RIVERHEAD

North Fork Bank and Trust Co. (631-727-6353; 140 E. Main St., also 631-369-1333; Rte. 58, Roanoke Plaza, both in Riverhead, NY 11901) ATM: Cirrus, Honor, MC, NYCE, Pulse.

Suffolk County National Bank (800-841-4000; Rte. 58 and Northville Tpke., Riverhead, NY 11901) ATM: AE, Cirrus, D, Honor, MAC, MC, NYCE, Plus, Pulse, V.

SOUTHOLD

Bridgehampton National Bank (631-765-1500; 54970 Main Rd., Southold, NY 11971) ATM: AE, Cirrus, D, Honor, MAC, MC, Plus, V.

Fleet Bank (800-841-4000; 51300 Main Rd., Southold, NY 11971) ATM: Cirrus, MC, NYCE, V.

North Fork Bank and Trust Co. (631-765-2800; 54375 Main Rd., Southold, NY 11971) ATM: Cirrus, Honor, MC, NYCE, Pulse.

BUSINESS SOLUTIONS

The Ink Spot (631-765-3625; 175 Boisseau Ave., Southold, NY 11971) For color or black-and-white printing, fax service, blueprints, typesetting and design, or four-color printing, this is the place.

North Fork Internet (631-323-1446; home.northfork.net; E-mail: info@north-fork.net) These folks host a North Fork web site, will do individual web site development, or provide technical assistance.

HOSPITALS & MEDICAL SERVICES

Central Suffolk Hospital (631-548-6000; 1300 Roanoke Ave., Riverhead, NY 11901) Full-service hospital.

Eastern Long Island Hospital (631-477-1000; Manor Pl., Greenport, NY 11944) Small hospital with full services.

MEDIA

RADIO

WBAZ-FM 101.7 (631-765-1017; 44210 County Rd. 48, Southold, NY 11971) "The music of the beach" or "The Light on the Bays" plays light, popular music.

WRIV-AM 1390 (631-727-1390; 40 West Main St., Riverhead, NY 11901) Adult contemporary music.

NEWSPAPERS

Newsday (631-727-7335; 209 West Main St., Riverhead, NY 11901) This is the East End news bureau for Long Island's newspaper.

Suffolk Life **Newspapers** (631-369-0800; 1461 Rte. 48, Riverhead, NY 11901) *Suffolk Life* is the primary weekly newspaper of Riverhead and North Fork. It is published in 34 different editions and has a circulation of 488,000. It has been published continuously for almost 40 years.

Times/Review **Newspapers** (631-298-3200; www.timesreview.com; 7785 Main Rd., PO Box 1500, Mattituck, NY 11952) This local company is publisher of the *Suffolk Times* (covering Southold Township) and the *News-Review* (covering Riverhead Township), as well as *North Fork Vacation Guide, Shelter Island Vacation Guide, The Wine Press,* and *Tanger Times*.

Traveler Watchman **Newspapers** (631-765-3425 main office; Traveler St., PO Box 725, Southold, NY 11971; 631-727-1992 satellite office; 436 East Main St., Riverhead, NY 11901) General coverage weekly.

POST OFFICES

Aquebogue (631-722-4668; Main Rd. (Rte. 25), Aquebogue, NY 11931)
Cutchogue (631-734-5222; 240 Griffing St., Cutchogue, NY 11935)
East Marion (631-477-1570; 9165 Main Rd. (Rte. 25), East Marion, NY 11939)
Greenport (631-477-0038; 131 Front St., Greenport, NY 11944)
Jamesport (631-722-3778; 1451 Main Rd. (Rte. 25), Jamesport, NY 11947)
Laurel (631-298-4511; 2168 Main Rd. (Rte. 25), Laurel, NY 11948)
Mattituck (631-298-4230; 140 Love Ln., Mattituck, NY 11952)
New Suffolk (631-734-7343; 375 First St., New Suffolk, NY 11956)
Orient (631-323-2515; 980 Village Ln., Orient, NY 11957)
Peconic (631-765-3772; 2575 Peconic Ln., Peconic, NY 11958)
Riverhead (631-727-2335; 21 West Second St., Riverhead, NY 11901)
South Jamesport (631-722-4452; 70 Second St., South Jamesport, NY 11970)
Southold (631-765-2677; 710 Travelers St., Southold, NY 11971)

CHAPTER TEN
A Charming Green-Clad Island
SHELTER ISLAND

S helter Island is actu- ally a well-kept local secret. Merely one half-mile from the South Fork and one mile from the North Fork of the eastern end of Long Island, it is nevertheless remote and secluded — an ideal haven. In fact, most people who regularly come here hope that the rest of the world will never hear about Shelter Island's charms. Covering an area of approximately eight thousand acres,

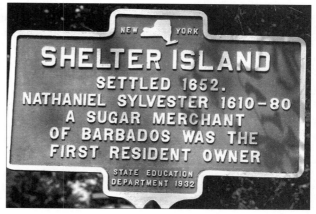

Suzi Forbes Chase

Shelter Island was settled in 1652.

Shelter Island is six miles long and four miles wide. It boasts of famous artists, writers, and performers who seek isolation in a beautiful setting.

HISTORY

As Long Island stretches out her arms to the Atlantic, she gathers within her embrace a little group of islands. Largest and fairest among them, fertile and beautifully wooded, is Shelter Island, lying in the waters of Gardner's [sic] and Peconic Bays, separated from Greenport and the northern arm of Long Island Sound by about a mile of sunny water, and on its southern side looking across Sag Harbor, and the long, low line which stretches away to Montauk.

From an 1889 brochure for Prospect House,
reprinted by *The Grapevine of Shelter Island Heights*, 1987

S helter Island's history includes a mixture of entrepreneurial enterprise, independence, and tolerance. This island was chosen by James Farrett, the personal representative of the Earl of Stirling, as his own land grant. It appears that he inspected it as early as 1638, but he never actually occupied the island. In 1641, he sold Shelter Island to a merchant, Stephen Goodyear, who subsequently sold it in 1651 to four businessmen with interests in the Barbados sugar industry.

Nathaniel Sylvester was one of those businessmen. After returning to England and marrying, he sailed with his bride in 1652 to their new home. Although they suffered shipwreck and lost many of their possessions, the manor house they built on Shelter Island, along with its surrounding gardens, must have been as fine as many in England. The Sylvester Manor House, although changed over the years, is still owned by members of the Sylvester family.

Prior to the Sylvesters' arrival, the Manhanset tribe, led by their *sachem*, Pogatticut (brother to the sachems of the Montauks of East Hampton, the Shinnecocks of Southampton, and the Corchaugs of the North Fork) ruled Shelter Island. Pogatticut and his people voluntarily left the island shortly after the Sylvesters arrived.

It was apparent from the beginning that the Sylvesters were peaceable people with open minds. For about five years in the mid-1600s, persecution of members of The Society of Friends (Quakers) was particularly severe in Massachusetts. Many were imprisoned, whipped, tortured, branded with hot irons, and banished from their homes. Those fortunate few who found their way to Shelter Island were treated by the Sylvesters with sympathy and understanding. They were given food, protection, clothing, and permission to practice their religion. Quaker church services are still held weekly on Shelter Island.

From 1660–1673, a tug-of-war took place between the British and the Dutch over Long Island. Eventually Shelter Island, not immune to the conflict, was confiscated by the Dutch. It was regained later by Nathaniel Sylvester, at a cost of 500 pounds, but only after the Dutch landed on the island with 500 men, surrounded his house, and demanded payment, merely days before they again surrendered the territory to the British.

Other families of importance soon joined the Sylvesters. William Nicoll became the first Supervisor of Shelter Island in 1726 and occupied the estate left to him by his father. The Havens family came shortly thereafter in 1742 and purchased an estate of 1,000 acres from Nathaniel Sylvester. By 1769, the house that James Havens' father, William, had built was used as a school by day and a tavern by night, as well as a home, serving such concoctions as a mug of flip, a brandy sling, and a nip of grog to wayfarers. In 1795, Jonathan Havens was elected to serve in the new Congress of the United States, representing the district that contained Shelter Island.

The Dering name emerges in 1760 when Mary Sylvester, who had married Thomas Dering in 1756, inherited Sylvester Manor from her father and consequently moved her family into the manor house. The Sylvester, Nicoll, Havens, and Dering families were cultured people who cherished family life on the island. In 1743, the first church was built, and by 1791, a school had been established.

The Havens' homestead was built in 1742 and now serves as a museum.

Jason Green

Around 1800, Timothy Dwight, President of Yale College, journeyed the length of Long Island and included Shelter Island in his travels. He observed that, "To the credit of the inhabitants, especially of the principal proprietors, it ought to be observed that they have customarily made considerable exertions to support schools and obtain the preaching of the gospel."

Shelter Island (along with Gardiner's Island) had one of the finest stands of white oak found on the East Coast. These trees were especially prized after the magnificent forests of Connecticut and Massachusetts were exhausted. In the mid-1800s, a shipyard was established on Shelter Island; the massive trunks necessary for keels and masts were cut from the area known as the "Great Woods."

Throughout Shelter Island's history, religion has played an important role. In 1871, the highest point of land on the Island became the home of The Shelter Island Grove and Camp Meeting Association of the Methodist Episcopal Church. They called the area Prospect, and summer visitors began arriving in numbers. The handsome Prospect House, a colonnaded Victorian hotel with a piazza encircling the building, overlooked the harbor toward Greenport and accommodated up to 300 guests. Although the hotel is gone, the restaurant, where communal meals were held, is the nucleus of the present Chequit Inn. Some of the charming Victorian cottages and the fine houses built by the prominent citizens of the day now form the delightful village of Shelter Island Heights.

TRANSPORTATION

Shelter Island remains a quiet, peaceful retreat, secluded and hidden, and yet accessible to both the North and South Forks by a ten-minute ferry ride. Although the grand Victorian hotels are no longer here, newer, smaller hotels

Suzi Forbes Chase

Secluded Shelter Island retains a wealth of handsome mansions with spectacular water views.

and inns now provide lodging. You'll find excellent restaurants, interesting shops, and an abundance of recreational options.

Part of the delight of Shelter Island is its island status and the necessity of reaching it by boat. The ferries that putt back and forth are efficient throwbacks to an earlier age. There are no amenities here, just a drive- or walk-on, open-decked ferry that shuttles between the island and the North or South Forks. Both ferries operate year-round, but trips are much more frequent in the summer.

North Ferry (631-749-0139) From Shelter Island 5:40am–11:45pm. From Greenport 6am–12 midnight. $7 one-way for car and driver; $8 for same day, round-trip; $1 for each additional passenger; bicycles $3 one-way/$4 round-trip.

South Ferry (631-749-1200) From North Haven 6:05am–1:50am. From Shelter Island 6am–1:45am. $7 one-way for car and driver; $8 round-trip; $1 each for passengers; bicycles $2 one-way, $3 round-trip, $1 each rider.

For those traveling to Shelter Island from Manhattan, the North Shore branch of the **Long Island Rail Road** may be an option, although its schedule is limited. There are generally three or four trains during the week and two trains on the weekends. The Greenport station, however, is merely steps from the Shelter Island ferry dock, and after a short water ride, you'll be in Shelter Island Heights.

For taxi service, contact **Shelter Island Go'Fors Taxi** (631-749-4252; 1 Thomas Ave., Shelter Island, NY 11964).

This hand-stenciled sign seems to direct turtles to cross here.

TOURS

If you'd prefer to see the island in a more active fashion, there are great cycling roads. Or, you might want to meander along the country roads in the company of others. If the latter is your choice, call *Brooks Country Cycling Tours* (212-874-5151). They offer a cycling tour of Shelter Island, combined with a jaunt to Montauk and followed by a trip over to Block Island. The four-night adventure includes stays in B&Bs and some meals. Or, for a shorter, one-day trip, sign up to cycle about twenty-six miles around the island, with time for a swim before heading back home.

LODGING

In addition to the following listings, an old-fashioned, longtime resort offers all-inclusive lodging and meals. The *Pridwin Hotel* (631-749-0476), with manicured lawns and a private dock and beach, is on eight acres overlooking Crescent Beach on Shore Road and has fifty rooms.

AVALON MANOR AT CHASE CREEK
631-749-2502; 800-501-3997;
   fax: 631-749-2506.
www.avalonmanor.com.
E-mail: info@avalonmanor.com.
18 Sylvan Rd., Shelter Island.
Mailing Address: PO Box 1947, Shelter
   Island, NY 11964.
Innkeepers: Deborah Vecchio and Melissa
   Palermo.
Open: Year-round.

Price: Inexpensive–Very Expensive.
Credit Cards: MC, V.
Special Features: Full breakfast; overlooking water; swimming pool;
   smoking outside only; children over 12
   welcome; no pets.
Directions: From Rte. 114, turn onto West
   Neck Rd. and follow for about 1/4 mile
   to Sylvan Rd. Turn onto Sylvan Rd. and
   follow to end. Inn is at end of private
   driveway.

Avalon Manor offers charming guest rooms, beautiful baths, and delightful common rooms, as well as a quiet, secluded setting overlooking placid Chase Creek.

Suzi Forbes Chase

Shelter Island is growing up. Frumpy boardinghouses are out; classy B&Bs are in. A case in point: Following an extensive renovation of a tired but gracious manor house by sisters Deborah Vecchio and Melissa Palermo and their husbands, lovely Avalon Manor opened for business in 1999.

The broad porch across the front of the house is the ideal spot to curl up with a good book, listen to the birds sing, and appreciate the views of the pond. (Chase Creek is actually a wide body of water, not a tiny creek.) The oak-floored entrance foyer is so wide it accommodates a dramatic double staircase. On one side, there's a wonderful living room with an oak floor, a fireplace, and cozy conversation areas. A basket holds antique linens and pillows, which are for sale. On the other side, the formal dining room includes an elegant table and a breakfront. But the heart of the main floor is the spectacular kitchen, which features an oak floor, granite counters, and a brass and iron French baker's rack filled with a birdhouse collection. The four guest rooms, all with private en suite baths, are upstairs. The Cherub Suite, decorated in wine colors, has a fireplace, a balcony overlooking Chase Creek, and a canopy bed with twisted columns. In the bath, there's a claw-foot tub. The lively yellow Tea Room has a beautiful, puffy quilt on the bed and piles of pretty pillows, while the Mashomack Room has a giant twig bed and is decorated in autumn colors.

A full breakfast of perhaps an individual egg, sausage, and cheese soufflé, plus strawberry bread or chocolate chip muffins, is served in the kitchen, allowing the guests to interact with Debby and Melissa while they prepare the meal. The inn is located on a little more than two and one-half acres, and it has a private, fenced pool in back.

CHEQUIT INN AND RESTAURANTS

631-749-0018; fax: 631-749-0135.
www.shelterislandinns.com.
23 Grand Ave., Shelter Island Heights.
Mailing Address: PO Box 292, Shelter
  Island Heights, NY 11965.
Special Features Inn: Nonsmoking inn;
  continental buffet breakfast; telephones;
  TV available.
Innkeepers: Linda and James Eklund.
Chef: Justin Dwyer.
Cuisine: New American.
Open: Year-round.
Price: Inexpensive–Very Expensive.
Credit Cards: AE, MC, V.
Special Features Restaurant: Dining Room
  has porch with view; terrace under the
  trees; Catchall has TVs and pool table.
Directions: From South Ferry, travel north
  on Rte. 114, following signs to North
  Ferry. After crossing bridge to Shelter
  Island Heights, take Chase Ave. up hill.
  Inn is straight ahead. From North Ferry,
  inn is on right, about 4 blocks after
  exiting ferry.

This large, white, 1872 Victorian inn sits proudly on the only commercial street in Shelter Island Heights. In 1994, Linda and James Eklund, also owners of the Ram's Head Inn, purchased this venerable old inn. The lobby is filled with old wicker, a huge oak library table, a wood-burning fireplace, and a spacious porch that overlooks the village. There are thirty-five rooms (all with private baths). Those on the third floor of the main building are bright and cheerful and have carpeted floors, painted furniture, and such whimsical touches as old sleds used for coffee tables. Rooms in the weathered gray Summer Cottage behind the main building have endearing little quirks. Suite 7–8, for example, has an interesting little room with a sink and a wicker chair (sort of a sitting room/bath), and the rest of the bathroom is located between this room and the bedroom. The furniture in the bedroom is painted white (some has stenciling), and there are antique beds. There are more rooms in Cedar House across the street.

The dining room, on the second floor of the hotel, overlooks the village and has a broad porch that is used for dining in the summer. It's a romantic restaurant with exceptional food. When weather permits, lunch is served on an outside terrace under the trees. The Catchall is a renovated bistro on the inn's lower level. It offers a relaxed, casual spot for lunch and dinner, where you can watch a sporting event on TV or play pool.

DERING HARBOR INN AND MICHAEL ANTHONY'S RESTAURANT

631-749-0900; fax: 631-288-6001;
  restaurant: 631-749-3460.
13 Winthrop Rd., Shelter Island.
Mailing Address: PO Box 3028, Shelter
  Island Heights, NY 11965.
Manager: John M. King III.
Chef: Michael Anthony.
Cuisine: New American.
Open: May–Oct.: July, Aug. restaurant
  open every night; fewer nights rest of
  season.
Price: Moderate–Very Expensive.
Credit Cards: AE, MC, V.
Special Features Inn: Limited wheelchair
  access; saltwater pool; fireplaces in
  some rooms; tennis, volleyball,
  basketball, badminton; air-
  conditioning; nonsmoking rooms; cable
  TV; kitchenettes in most rooms;
  restaurant on premises; children
  welcome; no pets.
Special Features Restaurant: Fireplace;
  patio dining.
Directions: From Rte. 114, travel east on
  Winthrop Rd. Inn is on left.

The Dering Harbor Inn sits high on the bluff overlooking Dering Harbor and the boats in the marinas. It's a 1960s-style building, with a massive, double-sided, stone fireplace separating the cavernous lobby from the dining room. Rooms are located in one- and two-story, gray-stained buildings with decks overlooking Dering Harbor. This is a co-op, so all of the suites and villas have kitchens. Decor will vary, but most rooms are spacious and well appointed in a Caribbean-meets-the-Hamptons style. Room 7, for example, is a single-level unit with a fireplace, screened-in porch, full kitchen, and a lovely view; steps from the deck lead to a private stretch of lawn. In all, there are twenty-five rooms with private baths. The grounds are lovely, with two tennis courts and a saltwater pool that appears to be suspended over the bay. Michael Anthony's Restaurant, which opened in 1997, has received excellent reviews. It is open for dinner only.

HOUSE ON CHASE CREEK
631-749-4379.
www.chasecreek.com.
E-mail: chasecreek@mindspring.com.
3 Locust Ave., Shelter Island Heights.
Mailing Address: PO Box 364, Shelter
  Island Heights, NY 11965.
Innkeepers: Bill and Sharon Cummings.
Open: Year-round.
Price: Inexpensive–Moderate.

Credit Cards: AE, MC, V.
Special Features: Overlooking water;
  continental breakfast; nonsmoking
  B&B; not appropriate for children
  under 12.
Directions: From Rte. 114 in Shelter Island
  Heights, turn onto Locust Ave. by little
  bridge. Inn is on right in about 2 blocks,
  on corner of Locust Ave. and Meadow
  Pl.

This little gem of a B&B is located in the heart of Shelter Island Heights, but it's on a superbly quiet street that even in the height of summer offers a peaceful and quiet refuge. You might relax on the wicker porch swing or on the park bench down by Chase Creek (a wide body of water that resembles a pond more than a creek). When you enter the parlor of the inn, you won't fail to admire the antique sofa and chairs, which have backs inlaid with mother of pearl. There are three guest rooms, and they all have private baths. There are iron beds, an antique pedestal tub, wood floors, and marble vanities. A continental breakfast is served on a sunny, wicker-filled porch.

OLDE COUNTRY INN AND
  RESTAURANT
631-749-1633.
11 Stearns Point Rd., Shelter Island
  Heights.
Mailing Address: PO Box 590, Shelter
  Island Heights, NY 11965.
Innkeepers: Jeanne and Franz Fenkl.
Chef: Marcel Iattoni.
Cuisine: New French-Italian.
Open: Year-round.
Price: Inexpensive–Very Expensive.
Credit Cards: MC, V.
Special Features Inn: Wheelchair access;

nonsmoking inn; full breakfast; library
  with fireplace; piano; intimate bar; not
  recommended for children under 12; no
  pets.
Special Features Restaurant: Fireplace;
  outdoor dining; pavilion.
Directions: From Shelter Island Heights,
  take New York Ave. to West Neck Rd.,
  turning right toward Crescent Beach. In
  .2 mile, continue straight ahead onto
  Shore Rd. when West Neck Rd. turns
  left. Turn left onto Stearns Point Rd. at
  next intersection. Inn is on left.

The historic Shelter Island House, built as a hotel in 1886, and perched high on the cliff above Crescent Beach was renovated and opened as a bed-and-breakfast inn by innkeepers Jeanne and Franz Fenkl in 1994. Polished oak floors are a crisp backdrop for lovely Victorian furniture. There's a library with a fireplace, a piano, and lots of Victorian furniture. The tiny Victorian pub has another fireplace and doubles as an evening dining room. The guest rooms include iron and brass beds, an exquisite old Victorian coatrack, marble-topped dressers, and upholstered Victorian chairs. Each of the rooms has a private bath with a pedestal sink, built-in shelves, and a tiled tub surround. Two of the rooms have Jacuzzis, and one has a soaking tub. There's also a separate cottage.

Breakfast, either eaten in the pretty breakfast room or on one of the decks, might include crêpes with orange liqueur, omelettes, or waffles with sour cream and fresh berries. In 1996, the Fenkls teamed up with Chef Marcel Iattoni to serve winter dinners at tables set up in the living room. The restaurant proved to be so popular that they built a romantic dining room with another fireplace and a spacious, covered outdoor pavilion. Now the restaurant is open year-round, and the food is so good that reservations are an absolute must. Only dinner is served, but it's served with panache and style. Don't miss it!

The Ram's Head Inn, located on remote Ram Island overlooking Coecles Harbor, has lovely guest rooms and a gracious dining room. In summer, guests can also dine on a flower-edged terrace.

Suzi Forbes Chase

RAM'S HEAD INN AND RESTAURANT
631-749-0811; fax: 631-749-0059.
www.shelterislandinns.com.
108 Ram Island Dr., Shelter Island.
Mailing Address: PO Box 638, Shelter Island Heights, NY 11965.
Owners: James and Linda Eklund.
Cuisine: New American.

Open: Year-round.
Price: Inexpensive–Very Expensive.
Credit Cards: AE, MC, V.
Special Features Inn: Nonsmoking inn; overlooks water; telephones; TV available; tennis; boating; sauna; exercise room; continental buffet breakfast; children welcome; no pets.

Special Features Restaurant: Fireplace; terrace dining in summer; jazz Sun. evening in summer.
Directions: From South Ferry, travel north on Rte. 114 for 1.3 miles to Cartwright Rd.; Rte. 114 makes sharp left turn, but Cartwright Rd. continues straight ahead. In 1.5 miles, turn right onto Ram Island Rd. at Stop sign. In 0.7 mile, turn right onto Ram Island Dr. and continue for almost 2 miles to Ram's Head Inn, on right.

For the ultimate getaway, nothing compares to the Ram's Head Inn, which stands on an isolated bluff overlooking Coecles Harbor. The fireplace in the lobby offers a warm welcome in the winter, and the pretty sunporch, with its woodstove, green wicker furniture with floral cushions, brick floor, and games at the ready, make this a year-round retreat. The broad, outside terrace overlooks four and one-half acres of manicured lawns that slope to the tennis court and beyond to 800 feet of private beach. There are Adirondack lawn chairs, small boats for guests to use, an old-fashioned swing hanging from a tree, and hammocks strategically placed in shady groves. The exercise room is equipped with bicycle and step equipment and a sauna. The seventeen rooms are fresh and bright, with wicker and white-painted furniture interspersed with antiques; colorful fabrics are used for bedspreads and curtains. At present, only nine rooms have private baths. Special holiday weekend packages sometimes include a dramatic production, with the guests playing some of the roles.

The buffet breakfast includes muffins, sweet rolls, cereal, juice, fruit, and beverages. The wonderful restaurant is the most romantic on Shelter Island. There are polished oak floors topped with Oriental rugs and handsome oil paintings that softly glow in the candlelight. It's magical. In the summer, French doors open to a terrace for outside dining.

Sunset Beach attracts a chic and lively crowd who love its beachside setting and the Mediterranean cuisine served in the waterside restaurant.

Dustin Chase

SUNSET BEACH RESORT AND RESTAURANT
631-749-2001; fax: 631-749-1843; restaurant: 631-749-3000.

35 Shore Rd., Shelter Island.
Mailing Address: PO Box 278, Shelter Island Heights, NY 11965.
Owner: Andre Balazs.

General Manager: Kim Alley.
Chef: Terry Harwood.
Cuisine: Continental with Asian
  influences.
Open: Mid-May–Sept.
Price: Expensive–Very Expensive.
Credit Cards: AE, DC, MC, V.
Special Features Resort: Beach across
  street; pond; sundecks; TV; telephones;
  bicycles; paddleboats; children and pets

welcome.
Special Features Restaurant: Spectacular
  water views.
Directions: From Rte. 114, travel west on
  West Neck Rd. toward Crescent Beach.
  When West Neck Rd. turns left,
  continue straight ahead on Shore Rd.
  Follow Shore Rd. to beach. Resort is on
  left.

This neat little motel has occupied its prestigious spot across from Shelter Island's premier beach for many years, but it used to be furnished with old-fashioned vinyl chairs and formica-topped tables. All that changed in 1997 when Andre Balazs added this outpost to his collection of boutique hotels. (He is also the owner of Chateau Marmont and The Standard in Hollywood and The Mercer in Manhattan.) Following a thorough makeover, the outside has been transformed from dull brown to a lively combination of white, marine blue, and yellow. Best of all, the rooms are bright and inviting, decorated in a beachy/casual minimalist style with white walls, carpeted floors, and private baths. In every room, you'll find a TV and VCR, robes, air-conditioning, telephone, and minibar stocked with drinks. But what you'll love most are the enormous private decks with beautiful water views (the beach is about 200 feet away). There are pretty gardens on the property with a little pond as a centerpiece, and there are paddleboats and mountain bikes for the use of the guests, as well as the sandy beach across the street. The waterfront bistro and bar is located on three levels (two are covered and one is open-air). There are bright, tropical-patterned, oilcloth tablecloths, strings of little lights, and wonderful food. As might be imagined, Sunset Beach is attracting a star-studded cast.

ADDITIONAL BED & BREAKFAST ESTABLISHMENTS

When I wrote the first edition of this book in 1994, there were very few inns and bed-and-breakfasts on Shelter Island that I felt I could positively recommend. Happily that condition has changed. Today, in addition to the places above that are distinguished in the quality of their decor and the excellence of their baths, as well as their general ambience, setting, and the professionalism of their innkeepers, the following bed-and-breakfasts are taking guests as well. These establishments are, in general, more basic than those with full listings above, and they may have baths across the hallway instead of in the room. Nevertheless, they are clean and bright and offer an alternative to those above.

Beach House (631-749-0264; address and directions given when reservation made; mail: PO Box 648, Shelter Island Heights, NY 11965) Owner Jan Carlson offers 4 guest rooms with private baths in her contemporary waterfront home. There are antique beds and spectacular sunset views from the beach. Moderate–expensive; no credit cards; continental breakfast; non-smoking B&B; children over 14 welcome.

Candlelite Inn (631-749-0676; 3 South Ferry Rd. (Rte. 114), PO Box 237, Shelter Island, NY 11964) Owners John Sieni and Michael Bartholomew have created a thoroughly unique bed-and-breakfast in the pretty yellow-and-white Victorian that they laboriously restored in 1999. Most of the main floor is devoted to their hair salon (although there is a living room with TV for guests to use and a kitchen where breakfast is served), but on the second floor, there are 5 bedrooms: 2 have bathrooms en suite; 3 have private baths just across the hall. The baths are terrific — all done in tile. But the finest accommodation is the private cottage in back, which has a spacious bedroom and a tiled bath with a whirlpool tub. A full breakfast is served on Sat., Sun. only, and the B&B is only open to overnight guests on Wed.-Sat. nights. Expensive–very expensive; no credit cards; nonsmoking B&B; not appropriate for children or pets.

Captain Bennett House (631-749-0460; 28 Congdon Rd., PO Box 456, Shelter Island Heights, NY 11965) The Captain Bennett House, which is still located on 5 acres, dates to 1810, and at one time served as the main house of a summer camp. Today, it's owned by James and Linda Eklund, who also own the Ram's Head and Chequit Inns. There are 3 rooms, all with private baths. Inexpensive–moderate; credit cards: AE, MC, V; continental breakfast; not appropriate for children or pets.

Stearns Point House (631-749-4162; 7 Stearns Point Rd., PO Box 648, Shelter Island Heights, NY 11965) This former farmhouse has a front porch with a ceiling fan and polished pine floors inside. All 4 bedrooms have private baths. Owner Jan Carlson has decorated it with wicker and floral chintz. Expensive; no credit cards; continental breakfast; nonsmoking B&B; inquire about children and pets.

Two South Ferry (631-749-3208; 2 South Ferry (Rte. 114), PO Box 714, Shelter Island, NY 11964) Owner: Chris Gross. A wing was added to this hospitable 1930s farmhouse to create 4 bedrooms with private baths. A spacious common room offers ample seating, as well as a breakfast table that is supplied with homemade breads for the continental breakfast in the morning, as well as snacking all day long. Coffee and tea are ready for sipping. Inexpensive–moderate; no credit cards.

RESTAURANTS & FOOD PURVEYORS

RESTAURANTS

PLANET BLISS EATERY & MARKET
631-749-0053; fax: 631-749-0092.
23 North Ferry Rd., Rte. 114, Shelter
Island, NY 11964.
Owners: Julie O'Neill and Sebastian Bliss.
Chef: Sebastian Bliss.

Cuisine: American Regional.
Serving: L, D, BR (Sun. only).
Open: Year-round: in summer:
  Wed.–Mon.; fewer days rest of year.
Price: Inexpensive–Moderate.

Credit Cards: None.
Special Features: Broad porch and small
  patio for outside dining; wine and beer
  served; juice bar; natural foods market.
  directions: On Rte. 114 at Duvall St.

This building once served both as Shelter Island's first general store and a post office. The funky decor still includes the old wooden meat cases and counters that have settled into the well-trod floors, plus stained glass windows and antique furniture — it's a comfortable, homey, even kitschy atmosphere — all spiced up with bright orange wainscot walls. From the first week it opened in April 2000, people clamored for the chef's delicate crab cakes, his mussels in a lemongrass broth, and his grilled chicken that he marinates for four days in a rosemary/thyme/lemon broth. There's a lovely wine list that includes some interesting local wines, as well as some organic wines, and the selection of smoothies and juices is terrific. If you'd rather prepare your own meal, stop here anyway to pick up some of the natural foods they sell in the grocery section.

FOOD PURVEYORS

Stars, The Market/Coffee Cellar (631-749-3484; 17 Grand Ave., Shelter Island Heights, NY 11965) The Market open in summer: daily 9am–9pm; Coffee Cellar open in summer: daily 6:30am–10pm; both open fewer days and shorter hours rest of year. Owner: Cheryl Hannabury. Upstairs, The Market has a terrific gourmet grocery, with cheeses, vinegars, oils, and pastas, as well as a deli with sandwiches, salads, quiches, and bakery goods; there are tables inside and along the sidewalk. Downstairs, the Coffee Cellar has a selection of café lattés, mochas, cappuccinos, etc. (both hot and iced), plus bakery and dessert goods. After a play or a concert, this is the place for breakfast or dessert.

The Tuck Shop (631-749-1548; Menantic and West Neck Rds., Shelter Island, NY 11964) Open Mem. Day–Labor Day. Owner: Patricia Sulahian. You can tuck into more than thirty flavors of hard and soft ice cream at this nice little ice creamery.

SHOPPING

Books & Video (631-749-8925; 17 Grand Ave., Shelter Island Heights, NY 11965) Open daily 10am–8pm. Owner: Paul Olinkiewicz. This is the only bookstore on Shelter Island, but they sell old and new books and both hard-bound and paperback. There's a small selection of used, local history books. They also rent videos.

Cornucopia (631-749-0171; 27 West Neck Rd., Shelter Island, NY 11964) Open year-round. Owner: Jordan Eichhorn. You'll find an array of gifts at this little spot, ranging from baby things and Christmas ornaments to stained glass, toys, games, cards, and candy.

Fallen Angel Antiques (631-749-0243; 631-749-7801 messages only; Washington St., Shelter Island Heights, NY 11965) Open Mem. Day–Columbus Day. Owner: Joan Markell. Located in the Chequit Annex, known as Cedar House, this shop is a delightful, little treasure trove of quilts, silver, prints, wearable art, and other specialty items.

Hap's Iron Works (631-749-0200; 3 Midway Rd. South, PO Box 730, Shelter Island, NY 11964) Call for hours. Hap Bowditch, Jr. is a man of many talents, but today his interests lie with metal crafting. You cannot fail to recognize his domaine, as you will see a field invaded by a mermaid and a whaling vessel furiously being rowed as it tilts in a storm, among other metal works. He also makes smaller garden sculptures. You can buy his work at his gallery, or he will create iron sculptures to your specifications.

The Island Gallery (631-749-0733; 8 Grand Ave., Shelter Island Heights, NY 11965) Open June–Aug.: long weekends 10am–5pm; spring and fall: Sat., Sun. 10am–5pm; closed rest of year. This artists' cooperative has been in business for over twenty-five years, attesting to the commitment and expertise of its members. It exhibits lovely art, from watercolor to sculpture, that includes local landscapes, flower gardens, houses, animals, and more.

Showtime *by acclaimed sculptor Peggy Mach, who lives and works on Shelter Island*

Peggy Mach

Peggy Mach Gallery (631-749-0247; 631-749-2215; 21 North Ferry Rd., Shelter Island, NY 11964) Open Sat., Sun. 11am–5pm. Once you see one of Peggy Mach's sculptures, you won't be satisfied until you own one. Her subjects are so lyrical and so poignant that you almost feel as if you can talk to them, and they certainly "talk to you." Her subjects include dancers, clowns, lovers, and executives, sculpted in clay and stone and cast in bronze. Ms. Mach's work is included in important private and museum collections throughout the world, and she lives and works on Shelter Island.

The Whale's Folly (631-749-1110; Bridge St., Shelter Island, NY 11964) Open Mem. Day–Columbus Day only: Fri.–Mon. 10am–5pm. The handcrafted items in this store are very special. Vivid watercolor paintings by Island artist, Olive Reich, are for sale, as well as wicker furniture, pretty china platters, and painted wicker baskets.

CULTURE

CALENDAR OF EVENTS

April

Easter Egg Hunt (631-749-0107) Sponsored by Shelter Island Heights Fire Department Auxiliary.
Easter Sunrise Service Sponsored by all Shelter Island churches.

May

Memorial Day Parade Sponsored by Shelter Island American Legion Post.

June

Shelter Island 10K Run (631-749-RUNN) Annual event begins at 5:30pm, but activities lead up to the event all afternoon.

July

Fireworks Show (631-749-0399) Sponsored by Shelter Island Chamber of Commerce.

August

Annual Arts and Crafts Show (631-749-0399) Sponsored by Shelter Island Chamber of Commerce and Fire Department Country Fair, Shelter Island.
Annual Shelter Island Heights Firemen's Chicken Barbecue (631-749-0107).
King of the Bays Regatta (631-298-9755) Sailing race in Noyack and Gardiner's Bays.

September

Historical Society Fair, Shelter Island (631-749-0025) Sponsored by Shelter Island Historical Society.

October

5K Co-ed Run (631-749-0399) Sponsored by Shelter Island Chamber of Commerce.
Halloween Party and Parade (631-749-0184) Sponsored annually by Shelter Island Fire Department.

December

Christmas Tree Lighting (631-749-0399) Town Hall, Shelter Island.

CULTURAL ATTRACTIONS

Haven's House and Barn and Manhanset Chapel Museums (631-749-0025; Havens House, 16 South Ferry Rd., Shelter Island, NY 11964; Manhanset Chapel, 24 North Ferry Rd., Shelter Island, NY 11964) Operated by the Shelter Island Historical Society, this interesting old home with its period rooms is open Mem. Day–Labor Day: Fri., Sat., Sun. 11am–3pm.
Perlman Music Program (631-749-0740; 73 Shore Rd., Shelter Island, NY 11964) An outgrowth of the Hamptons Summer Music Festival, Itzhak Perlman has developed a summer program for musically gifted students of the violin, viola, cello, and piano. Students are individually selected by Mr. Perlman, and they participate in extensive individual classes. The public is encouraged to attend the rehearsals and performances (where Peconic Lodge used to be) that include full orchestras and a choral component. The performances are held every Fri. night from early July–mid-Aug. Don't miss this chance to hear budding Itzhaks and Midoris before they become famous.
Shelter Island Public Library (631-749-0042; fax 631-749-1575; State Rd., Shelter Island, NY 11964) In this lovely local library, there is a children's room where there's a Tues. story hour for children and a library of local history books. An Author Luncheon in June attracts interested parties, and there's a summer-long book sale. Call for hours.

RECREATION

BICYCLING

Shelter Island is an especially popular destination for cyclists. The minimal amount of traffic makes the roads relatively safe, even though there are no shoulders. The roads are fairly level, except for several significant exceptions, such as Shelter Island Heights. Many people ferry their own bicycles over to the island, but if you prefer to rent a bicycle, the following firm has bicycles for rent.

Piccozzi's Bike Shop (631-749-0045; Bridge Rd., Shelter Island Heights, NY 11965) Mountain bicycles, English varieties, and tandem bicycles. $18/full day, $14/half-day 3-speed bicycles; $22/full day, $18/half-day mountain bicycles.

BOATING

BOAT RENTALS

Shelter Island Kayak Tours (631-749-1990; Rte. 114, at Duvall's Rd., Shelter Island, NY 11964) This company provides kayak rentals and guided tours of the abundant waters surrounding Shelter Island, including nature areas that contain a wealth of bird and fish life. They offer two 2-hour tours a day leaving 9:30am and 5:30pm at $45 per person. You can also rent a kayak for your own tour: $13/hr single kayak; $15/hr double kayak.

MARINAS

Coecles Harbor Marina & Boatyard (631-749-0700; Harbor Ave., on Coecles Harbor, Shelter Island, NY 11964) This full-service marina and repair shop has 40 slips, ship's store, snack bar, swimming pool, and offers sailboat and bicycle rentals.

Island Boatyard and Marina (631-749-3333; 63 South Menantic Rd., Shelter Island, NY 11964) This full-service marina has 75 slips for boats measuring 16 feet–50 feet. It's on 20 acres of wooded grounds that include a swimming pool, the Shipwreck Bar, Alfred's Place Restaurant, barbecues, volleyball, game room, and laundromat.

Piccozzi's Dering Harbor Marina (631-749-0045; Bridge St., Shelter Island Heights, NY 11965) Docking is provided in 35 slips for boats up to 160 feet in length. There are rest rooms, hot showers, electric hookups, barbecues, laundromat, game room, and bicycles for rent.

GOLF

Shelter Island Country Club (631-749-0416; 631-749-8841; Goat Hill, Shelter Island Heights, NY 11965) 9 holes; par 35; 2,900 yards; clubhouse open to the public; small pro shop; resident pro; full-service restaurant. This is one of the most challenging courses on the East End; it meanders over steep hillsides near the lovely community of Shelter Island Heights. The classy clubhouse, with its broad porches, was built in 1898 and is set high on a hill with a commanding view of the bays. The course opened in 1902, making this the sixth oldest, continuously operating golf course in the U.S. It was a private club until 1940.

Shelter Island Whale's Tale (631-749-1839; Manhanset Rd. and Ram Island Rd., Shelter Island, NY 11964) 18-hole miniature golf course, plus tennis court, game room, and ice-cream shop that serves hard and soft ice cream and yogurt.

HORSEBACK RIDING

Hampshire Farms & Equestrian Center (631-749-0156; Bowditch Rd., Shelter Island, NY 11964) This 85-acre center offers riding instruction on an individual or group basis in hunting, jumping, and dressage, as well as summer youth programs; a large, indoor, lighted arena permits lessons year-round. The four outside rings and cross-country course provide experience for hunters and riders. They also offer escorted trail rides if notified in advance.

PARKS & NATURE PRESERVES

Mashomack Preserve, on over 2,000 acres of land, is owned by The Nature Conservancy and is open to the public. This is a map identifying the trails.

Dustin Chase

Mashomack Preserve (631-749-1001) Entrance about 1 mile from the South Ferry. Over 2,000 acres; woods; marshes; freshwater ponds; tidal creeks; occupies almost one-third of Shelter Island. In the late 1970s, The Nature Conservancy successfully launched the largest fund-raising effort in its history. They took title to this land in January 1980. Referred to as "The Jewel of the Peconic," this preserve contains one of the largest concentrations of nesting osprey, which, until recently, were almost extinct, as well as a wide variety of other birds, animals, and plants. Excellent maps and brochures are available at the visitor's center for the nature trails and hikes, which range from 1.5 miles to an 11-mile loop. Educational and recreational activities are provided, from canoe trips to bird-watching expeditions, and there's a children's program. The old Nicoll Manor House, a ten-bedroom Victorian mansion with four fireplaces, is used primarily by staff for preserve programs, fund-raising events, and environmental meetings.

INFORMATION

EMERGENCY NUMBERS

In case of emergency, call **911.**

Police   631-749-0600
Fire
  Shelter Island   631-749-0184   Shelter Island Heights   631-749-0107

TOWNS & VILLAGES

Shelter Island Chamber of Commerce (631-749-0399; www.shelter-island.org; 47 West Neck Rd., Box 598, Shelter Island, NY 11964)
Shelter Island Town (631-749-0291; 44 North Ferry Rd., Shelter Island, NY 11964)
Village of Dering Harbor (631-749-0020; Shore Rd., Dering Harbor, NY 11965)

POST OFFICES

Shelter Island Heights Post Office (631-749-1115; 6 Grand Ave., Shelter Island Heights, NY 11965) Open weekdays 8am–5pm, Sat. 9am–1pm.
Shelter Island Post Office (631-749-0250; 45 North Ferry Rd., Shelter Island, NY 11964) Open weekdays 8am–5pm, Sat. 9am–1pm.

BANKS

The Bank of New York (631-749-0440; 48 North Ferry Rd., Shelter Island, NY 11964)
North Fork Bank and Trust (631-749-1300; 20 West Neck Rd., Shelter Island, NY 11964) ATM: Cirrus, Honor, MC, NYCE, Pulse.

CHURCHES

Our Lady of the Isle Roman Catholic Church (631-749-0001; 5 Prospect Ave., Shelter Island, NY 11964)
St. Mary's Episcopal Church (631-749-0770; St. Mary's Rd., Shelter Island, NY 11964)
Shelter Island Friends Meeting (631-749-0555; 631-324-8557; Rte. 114, Shelter

Island, NY 11964) In the woods at Quaker Martyr's Monument, Sylvester Manor, Shelter Island.

Shelter Island Presbyterian Church (631-749-0805; 631-749-0642; 32 North Ferry Rd., Shelter Island, NY 11964)

Union Chapel was the center-piece of the Shelter Island Grove and Camp Meeting Association of the Methodist Episcopal Church in the 1870s. Services are still held here in the summer.

Suzi Forbes Chase

Union Chapel in the Grove (631-749-1164; Shelter Island Heights, NY 11965) Interdenominational services, Sun. 10am (summer only).

FAX & BUSINESS SERVICES

The Executive Option (631-749-3101; fax: 631-749-3102; 71 North Menantic Rd., Shelter Island, NY 11964) Typing, word processing, copying, fax services, internet access, meeting space, and other office services; also a full-service print shop.

Shillingburg & Associates (631-749-3028; 4 West Neck Rd., Shelter Island, NY 11964) These computer folk will design a web site, as well as offer computer lessons and training.

LATE-NIGHT CAR REPAIR

Piccozzi's Service Station & Garage (631-749-0045; Bridge Rd., Shelter Island, NY 11964)

NEWSPAPERS

Shelter Island Reporter (631-749-1000; 50 North Ferry Rd., PO Box 756, Shelter Island, NY 11964) Weekly newspaper, reporting the news of Shelter Island.

IF TIME IS SHORT

In my opinion, every trip to New York City, especially if it's in the summer, should include a visit to the Hamptons. I love the energy of the city — the "can do" attitude — the feeling that anything is possible. But I also appreciate the slower pace, the tranquility, and the beauty of the Hamptons. I admit to a certain prejudice, however, about both places, and I know it's difficult for many who live beyond New Jersey to believe that such a profound contrast to Manhattan's hurried pace and masses of people is so close at hand. So, come and see for yourself. A day in the Hamptons will convince you to come again and to stay longer.

HISTORY

If you're a history buff, a walk through most of the Hamptons' villages will include seeing buildings that date to the early seventeenth century. The **Southampton Historical Museum**, just off Main Street in *Southampton*, is composed of a collection of twelve buildings and thirty-five individual exhibits that range from an authentic village store to Revolutionary War artifacts. In *East Hampton*, **Mulford Farm** provides a glimpse of life on a working farm in the seventeenth century. Throughout the villages, picturesque windmills offer poignant reminders of the area's agricultural origins.

RECREATION

Traveling through the Hamptons by bicycle is an excellent way to see the countryside. The roads are relatively flat, and major highways have wide shoulders. In addition, opportunities for nature lovers abound. The **Long Pond Greenbelt** (a 6.2-mile trail) in *Bridgehampton* threads its way along a chain of ponds and wetlands in the heart of the Atlantic Flyway, making it a rich resource for bird-watching. In *Montauk*, **Hither Hills State Park**, a 1,700-acre preserve, includes two miles of ocean beach. There are campgrounds, picnic sites, nightly entertainment, movies, and a vast network of hiking trails.

BEACHES

The beaches of the Hamptons are glorious — broad, wide strips of fine, clean, white sand that stretch for miles, bordered on one side by the relentlessly steady surge of the ocean and on the other side, bordered either by sandy dunes covered with sea grass or magnificent mansions. If you can only go to one beach, I suggest **Main Beach** in *East Hampton*. It's within walking and bicycling distance of the town, and if you have a car, there's a parking lot where you can park for a fee. (Be sure to call 631-324-4150 to find out if parking is permitted on the day you want to go.) In addition, there are bathrooms, changing facilities, and a fine snack bar.

THE NORTH FORK

The North Fork of Long Island is a sleeper. This is where most of the East End wineries are located, and it's an easy two-hour drive from Manhattan. Furthermore, as the popularity of the wineries has increased, sophisticated bed-and-breakfasts and restaurants have opened to accommodate a more demanding class of tourist. I highly recommend a trip to Long Island's North Fork now, before it becomes as overcrowded as the South Fork.

If there is only time for a day trip, my suggestion would be to leave early enough to have time to visit two wineries, have lunch, and then visit two more wineries before heading back to the city. Start the tour at **Palmer Vineyards** in *Aquebogue*. The self-guided tour is interesting, and the tasting room includes remnants of an authentic British pub. Musical events often take place on the weekends. Next, stop at **Pellegrini** in *Cutchogue*, which has a winery building that is reminiscent of a cloister. You might have lunch at **The Seafood Barge**, in *Southold*, which offers fresh-from-the-sea fish dishes and a superb harbor view. At **Antaras** in *Greenport*, you'll sample fabulous Contemporary American cuisine in a sophisticated setting. If your mood is more casual, you might eat at the **Greenport Tea Company** in *Greenport*, where you can get great soups and meat pies or partake of a high English tea. As an alternative, you may wish to eat a picnic lunch and enjoy a local vintage on the deck of one of the wineries. Before leaving the North Fork, stop at the spectacular **Pindar Vineyard**s winery in *Peconic* and at **Peconic Bay Wineryz** in *Cutchogue*. At the latter, sample the ambrosial dessert wine, Vin de I'lle, and you'll be in a mellow mood for your return journey.

If there's time for an overnight stay, I highly recommend three bed-and-breakfasts. **The Belvedere** (631-765-1799) in *Peconic* opened in 2000. Although the outside, which drips with Victorian gingerbread is beautiful, the stunning frescos in the double parlors and entrance hall are breathtaking; it has two beautiful guest rooms. **Treasure Island** (631-477-2788) in *East Marion* offers spectacular water views in four directions, as well as antique-filled guest rooms and baths finished with Corian. **Shorecrest** (631-765-1570) in *Southold* has retained its elaborate, polished interior woodwork.

THE SOUTH FORK

LODGING

If there's time for just one night in the Hamptons, I would suggest one of the following inns, although the choice was difficult. Please note that I have included only inns that are open year-round; there are many wonderful places to stay that are closed during the winter months.

EAST HAMPTON

East Hampton Point (631-324-9191; 295 Three Mile Harbor Rd., East Hampton, NY 11937) For those who seek total privacy, these charming cottages are the solution. Each is an individual suite, often on two levels, that includes a kitchen and a private deck. Baths are spacious, and most have skylights and Jacuzzis. The cottages are connected by brick pathways and are bordered by abundant flower beds. There's a pool, marina, restaurant with a spectacular harbor view, tennis court, and exercise facility located in a former chapel.

The J. Harper Poor Cottage (631-324-4081; 181 Main St., East Hampton, NY 11937) This transformation of an East Hampton Main St. mansion into a very elegant bed-and-breakfast took place in 1996. The architecture and decor feature William Morris designs, and the fabrics and wallpapers were imported from England. Each of the five guest rooms is generously proportioned and has elegant tiled baths (several with Jacuzzis) and fireplaces. There's a lovely courtyard in back that overlooks an expansive formal garden.

SOUTHAMPTON

1708 House (631-287-1708; 126 Main St., Southampton, NY 11968) This was another newcomer to the Hamptons' inn scene in 1996 — a restoration of an old boardinghouse that had fallen on sad days. Each of the nine guest rooms and three cottages is spacious and luxurious. They are furnished with antiques from the owner's antique shop and decorated with Ralph Lauren fabrics. In the brick-floored wine cellar, wine and cheese are served in the evening.

RESTAURANTS

Selecting a few restaurants from the many excellent choices was almost as difficult as choosing a few places to stay. I have selected the following partly to offer choices in location, cuisine, and setting.

EAST HAMPTON

The Laundry (631-324-3199; 31 Race Ln., East Hampton, NY 11937) The setting is relaxed, attractive, and cosmopolitan; the food is consistently good. The menu includes a wide variety of options, allowing diners to choose an appetizer, salad, or three- or four-course dinner. This restaurant is a local favorite.

Nick & Toni's (631-324-3550; 136 North Main St., East Hampton, NY 11937) Lights! Camera! Action! It's always a "scene" at Nick & Toni's. Sophisticated but charming, this outstanding restaurant is so popular that summer reservations should be made weeks in advance. A star-studded, svelte clientele likes to nosh on chewy Tuscan bread, juicy, flavorful meats from the wood-burning oven, and luscious desserts. It's worth every penny.

Turtle Crossing (631-324-7166; 221 Pantigo Rd., East Hampton, NY 11937) Here you'll get great BBQ in an unpretentious little café. You can order an overflowing platter of spit-roasted chicken or smoked ribs, doused in delicious sauces, which the *New York Times* has acclaimed as the best BBQ on Long Island. Don't leave without having a fat square of warm bread pudding with Jack Daniel's sauce.

EAST QUOGUE

Stone Creek Inn (631-653-6770; 405 Montauk Hwy., East Quogue, NY 11942) This elegant restaurant, in a pretty, white-shingled building, serves French/Mediterranean cuisine. The chef was raised in France, and although he uses fresh local ingredients, he adds a dash of France to each of his dishes. Several fireplaces heighten the sense of romance.

MONTAUK

Dave's Grill (631-668-9190; 468 Flamingo Rd., Montauk, NY 11954) For fresh-from-the-boat seafood, Dave's can't be beat. Ditto for Thurs. night dinners with live jazz. This is a casual and engaging restaurant with an enclosed patio for summer dockside dining. Don't miss the desserts. The chocolate bag is an outrageous combination of chocolate and caramel sauces, ice cream, and bananas, enclosed in a chocolate crust shaped like a bag.

SAG HARBOR

American Hotel (631-725-3535; 25 Main St., Sag Harbor, NY 11963) This is the Hamptons' most celebrated French restaurant. Fine French/American cuisine is served in an elegant setting that includes a fireplace in one room and a glass ceiling in another. An exceptional wine list has won the highest awards year after year, and the selection of cigars was renowned long before cigar smoking became chic.

WATER MILL

Mirko's Restaurant (631-726-4444; Water Mill Sq., Water Mill, NY 11976) Mirko and Eileen Zagar have been winning rave reviews for their hideaway restaurant for more years than they would like to admit, but their longevity attests to their total dedication to offering a memorable dining experience to their guests. The Continental cuisine reflects Mirko's Yugoslavian background.

Robert's (631-726-7171; 755 Montauk Hwy., Water Mill, NY 11976) Robert Durkin won our hearts years ago with his Bridgehampton restaurant and wine bar called Karen Lee's. But in 1999, he closed that restaurant and opened this new, chic spot in a charming pre-Revolutionary War building. His Coastal Italian menu is terrific.

Index

LODGING BY PRICE CODE

Price Codes

Inexpensive	Up to $100
Moderate	$100–$150
Expensive	$150–$200
Very Expensive	$200 and up

EAST HAMPTON TOWN

Inexpensive–Moderate
Cozy Cabins, Wainscott, 65

Inexpensive–Expensive
Snug Harbor Motel and Marina, Montauk, 65

Inexpensive–Very Expensive
East Hampton House, East Hampton, 44
Montauk Manor, Montauk, 53
Peri's B&B, Montauk, 55
Sea Crest on the Ocean, Amagansett, 40
The Surf Club, Montauk, 55

Moderate–Expensive
1770 House, East Hampton, 50

Moderate–Very Expensive
B&B on Cove Hollow, East Hampton, 42
The Gansett Green Manor, Amagansett, 38
Gurney's Inn Resort & Spa, Montauk, 52
The Hedges Inn, East Hampton, 45
The Hermitage, Amagansett, 39
The Huntting Inn, East Hampton, 45
Lenhart Cottages, Montauk, 64
Montauk Yacht Club Resort & Marina, Montauk, 54
Ocean Colony Beach & Tennis Club, Amagansett, 39
White Sands Motel on the Ocean, Amagansett, 64

Expensive
Snug Country Cottage, East Hampton, 51

RESTAURANTS BY PRICE CODE

RESTAURANTS BY CUISINE

SHOPPING

The East End

Long Island Sound

25 Orient

Greenport

Peconic
Southold

48 25

Cutchogue

Mattituck New Suffolk

Jamesport

South
Jamesport

105 25

43 → Riverhead

I-495

104

24

27

31

80

27A

Westhampton
Beach

Quogue

27A

Hampton Bays

Southampton

27

Water Mill

Sagaponack

Bridgehampton

Sag Harbor

114

Wainscott

East Hampton

27

Amagansett

27

Montauk

Shelter Island

Gardiner's Island

Little
Peconic
Bay

Great
Peconic
Bay

Robin's Island

Atlantic Ocean

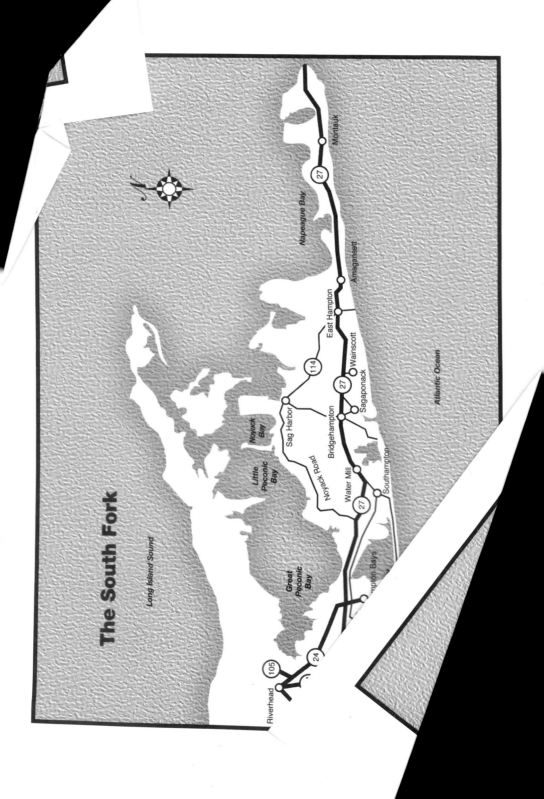

The South Fork

Long Island Sound

Great Peconic Bay

Little Peconic Bay

Noyack Bay

Napeague Bay

Atlantic Ocean

Riverhead
105
24

Southampton

Water Mill
27

Noyack Road

Bridgehampton

Sag Harbor
114

Sagaponack
27

Wainscott

East Hampton

Amagansett

27

Montauk

Hampton Bays

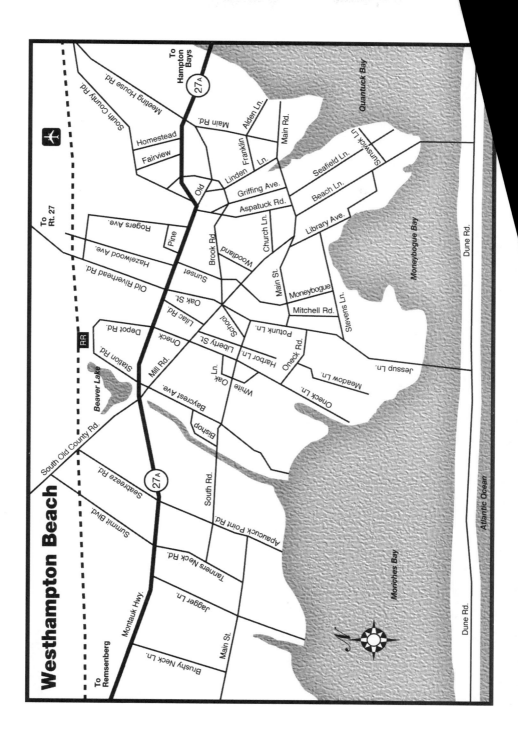

Westhampton Beach

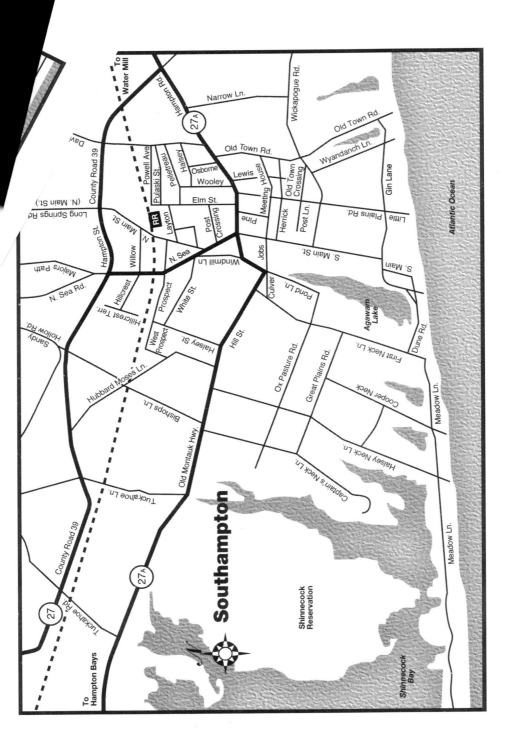

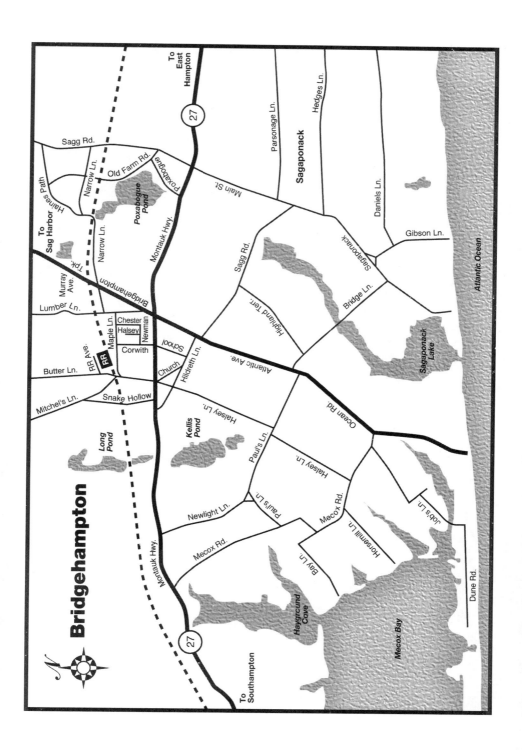

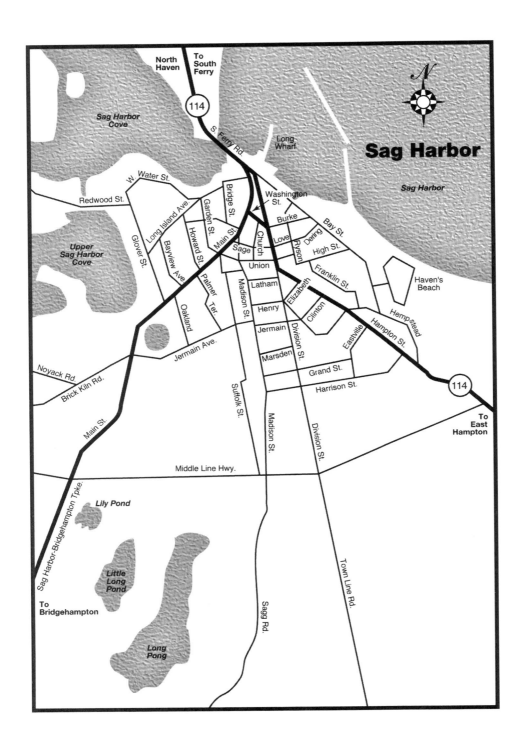

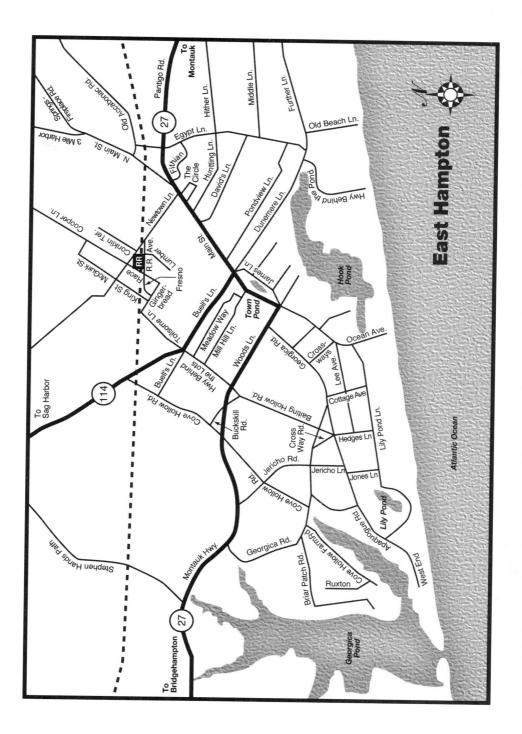

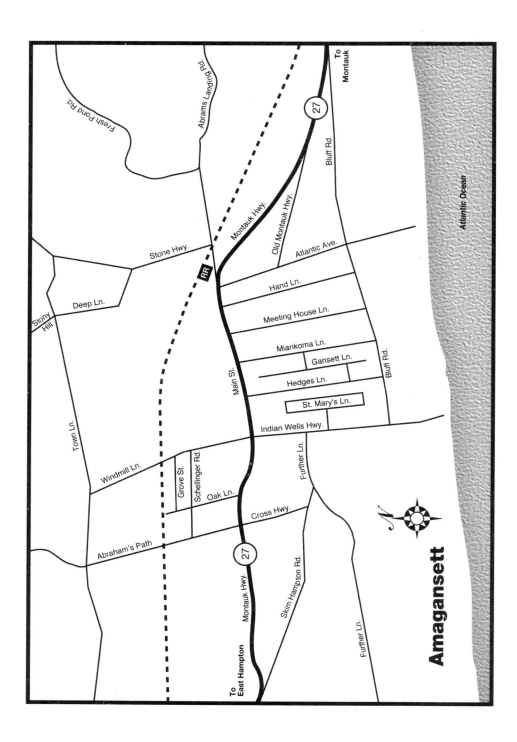

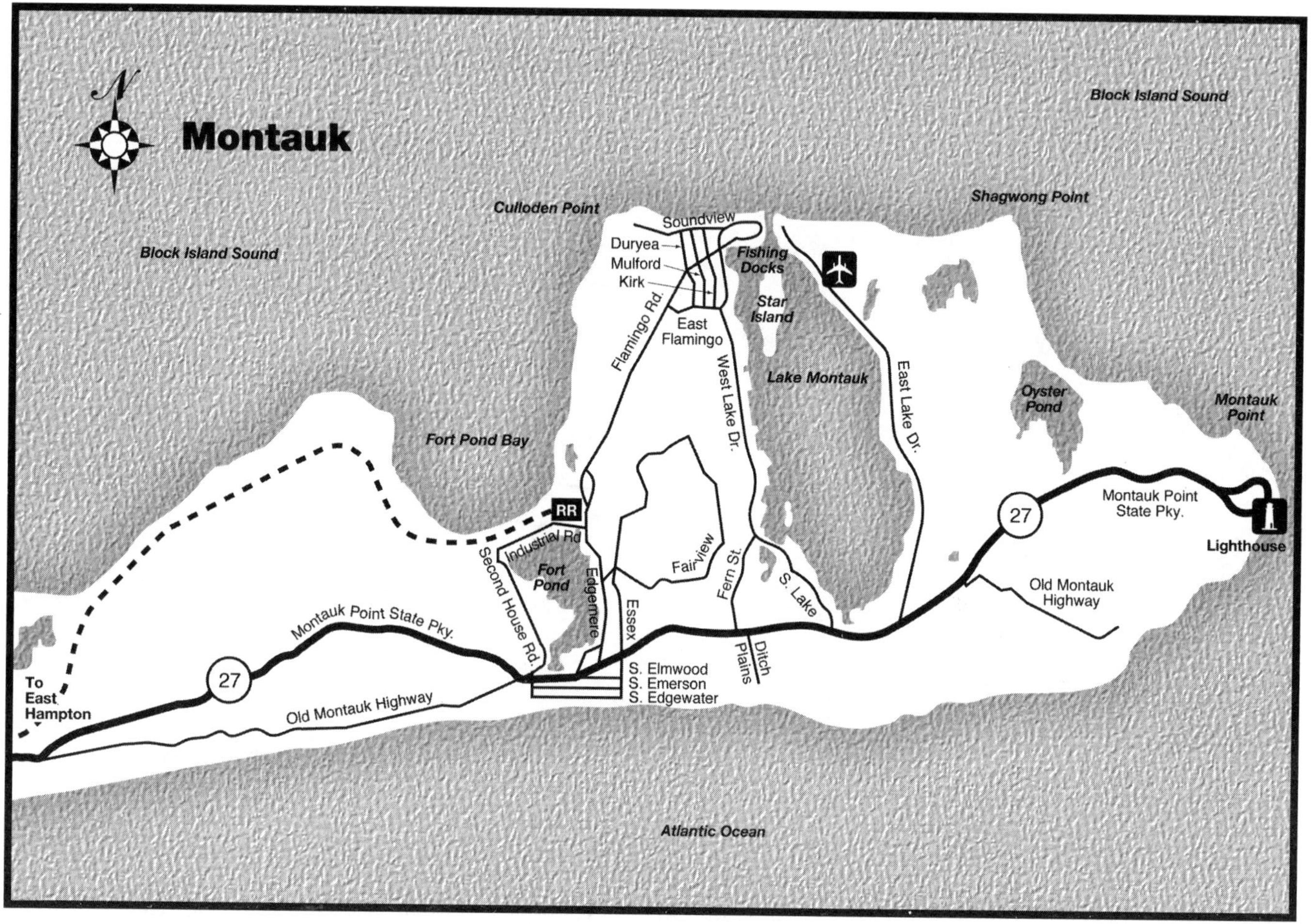

Montauk

Block Island Sound

Block Island Sound

Shagwong Point

Montauk Point

Lighthouse

Montauk Point State Pky.

27

Old Montauk Highway

Oyster Pond

East Lake Dr.

Lake Montauk

S. Lake

Ditch Plains

Fishing Docks

Star Island

West Lake Dr.

Fern St.

Soundview

East Flamingo

Fair View

Essex

Duryea

Mulford

Kirk

Flamingo Rd.

S. Elmwood
S. Emerson
S. Edgewater

Culloden Point

Edgemere

RR

Industrial Rd.

Fort Pond

Fort Pond Bay

Second House Rd.

Montauk Point State Pky.

Old Montauk Highway

27

To East Hampton

Atlantic Ocean

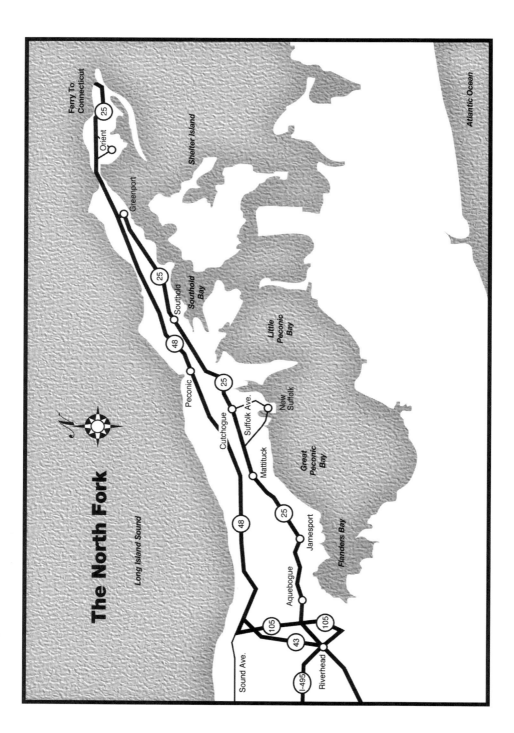

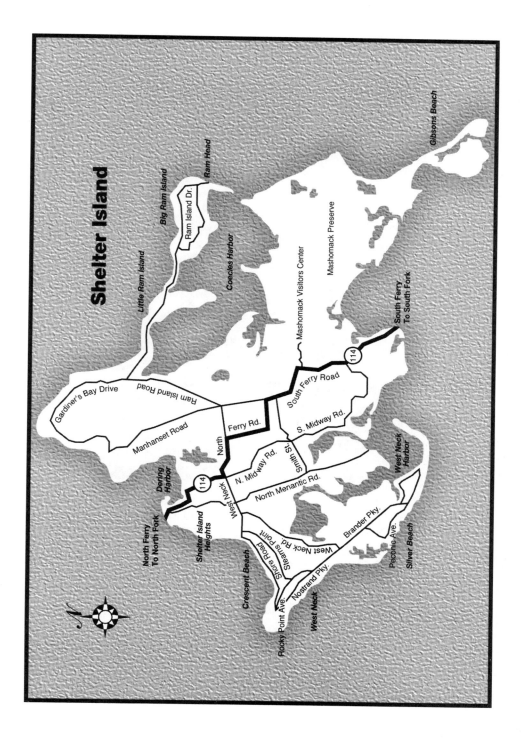

About the Author

Suzi Forbes Chase was raised in Seattle, but now calls the East Coast home. After obtaining BA and JD degrees from the University of Washington, she moved to Manhattan in 1979, where she worked in public relations, while also pursuing her writing career. After frequently traveling to the Hamptons in all seasons and spending summers there, she is now living in the Hamptons and writing full-time. A member of the American Society of Journalists and Authors, she has written fourteen travel books, a cookbook (*The New Red Lion Inn Cookbook*, published by Berkshire House), and numerous magazine and newspaper articles.